A LIFE OF WILLIAM SHAKESPEARE

THE CHANDOS PORTRAIT OF SHAKESPEARE

A Life of
William Shakespeare

BY

JOSEPH QUINCY ADAMS
Professor of English in Cornell University

Library Edition

WITH ILLUSTRATIONS

BOSTON AND NEW YORK
HOUGHTON MIFFLIN COMPANY
The Riverside Press Cambridge

The Riverside Press
CAMBRIDGE · MASSACHUSETTS
PRINTED IN THE U.S.A.

TO MY BROTHER

RICHARD WRIGHT ADAMS

A TRUE SPORTSMAN AND A LOVER OF SHAKESPEARE

I DEDICATE THIS VOLUME

IN MEMORY OF MANY HAPPY DAYS

WITH THE QUAIL IN THE SEDGE-FIELDS

OF SOUTH CAROLINA

PREFACE

THE materials for a life of Shakespeare have been gradually assembled by the industry of hundreds of scholars, extending through more than two centuries; and probably little new matter of importance remains to be discovered, except through a happy, and at present quite unforeseen, accident. The arduous labors of Professor and Mrs. Wallace in the manuscript archives of England, during the course of which they examined over a million documents, recently yielded some fresh information; yet the small number of their "finds" assures us that nearly all that we are likely to know of the personal affairs of the great dramatist has already been made public. This stagnation in discovery is perhaps responsible for the tendency, especially marked in the last decade, for writers to deal in fanciful speculation, evolving from slight evidence, or none worthy of the name, bizarre and often elaborately detailed hypotheses regarding Shakespeare's relations with his contemporaries. But the results of such ingenuity are likely to be as perilous as they are unsubstantial, and for the most part must be ignored by the biographer. On the other hand, some valuable information is now being derived from a study, largely bibliographical, of the origin of the Shakespearean texts, and of their transmission to us through the medium of the playhouse and the press. True, much remains to be done in this field of endeavor before absolutely final conclusions are established, yet the main facts — which alone are needed for a general biography — are already clear.

The labor of assembling the material for a life of the

poet having thus been virtually completed, the task that remains is properly to interpret this material. And such an interpretation, it goes without saying, should be attempted only by one who has made a detailed study of the social, the literary, and, above all, the theatrical history of the Elizabethan age. For many of the incidental and miscellaneous data we possess regarding Shakespeare in themselves carry little significance, yet may at any time become pregnant with meaning when correlated with facts derived from allied sources; other data are quite fragmentary, and have to be pieced out from the fuller records of the actors, the companies, and the playhouses, or from the literary history of the time. When, however, the scattered parts have been truly illuminated, and rightly pieced out, and then assembled — like the members of a jig-saw puzzle — in their proper order, the resultant picture should be clear and, at least in the main, self-evidently correct.

In attempting to present this assembled picture I have chiefly aimed at clarity. Accordingly, I have avoided, in so far as possible, prolonged arguments on points that cannot be settled, preferring rather to give my own interpretation of the facts, with the reasons therefor. And I have purposely omitted æsthetic criticism, since this may be found elsewhere in abundance. Furthermore, I have left detailed discussions of the sources and of the dates of the several plays to the editors of Shakespeare. These topics I have not entirely ignored, for the sources of the plays are always of interest as revealing the nature of the poet's education and the extent of his reading; and the dates of their composition, of course, are of prime importance to the biographer. Some of the plays can be exactly dated, of many the date falls within narrow limits, of a few it remains genuinely doubtful; but opinion as to the order in which the plays were produced is now fairly well crystallized. Although I cannot hope to win unanimous assent to the exact dates I have accepted — some of them are necessarily tentative — I have tried to judge each case in the light of all the available evidence, combined with biographical facts and general laws of probability.

Next to presenting Shakespeare's biography with clarity, I have sought to picture the dramatist against a background of contemporary theatrical life. However much we may think of him as a genius apart, to himself and to his age he appeared primarily as a busy actor associated with the leading stock-company of his time; as a hired playwright — often, indeed, a mere cobbler of old plays — writing that his troupe might successfully compete with rival organizations; and, finally, as a theatrical proprietor, owning shares in two of the most flourishing playhouses in London. Thus his whole life was centred in the stage, and his interests were essentially those of his "friends and fellows," the actors, who affectionately called him "our Shakespeare." To portray the dramatist, therefore, in the atmosphere in which he lived and worked seemed to me the correct procedure.

There remains only the pleasant duty of acknowledging the assistance I have derived from various quarters; and first comes my indebtedness to earlier laborers in the field. I regret that I have not been able in the case of every detail to indicate the scholar to whom the credit of discovery belongs. The store of Shakespearean knowledge has been slowly accumulated by countless investigators, and to assign to each one his particular contribution to the whole would be difficult, if not indeed impossible. Yet in all the more important instances I have, I believe, duly recorded in footnotes my obligation. A few outstanding sources of indebtedness demand further and special mention. Foremost among these I must rank Halliwell-Phillipps' monumental *Outlines of the Life of Shakespeare*, a work printing in convenient form the bulk of the scattered materials upon which every biography of the poet necessarily reposes. Without this indispensable collection, the task of examining at first hand the original documents would be well-nigh impossible. Sir Sidney Lee's encyclopædic *Life of William Shakespeare* has also proved a mine of information; and though I have frequently found myself unable to accept its interpretation of fact, I have invariably accorded to the opinions of its distinguished author the consideration which his great reputation demands. To the labors of Professor Wallace is due, especially in the chapters dealing with theatrical history, more credit than perhaps would seem to be the case from my scanty footnotes; but so well-known are his discoveries that one may now take detailed acknowledgment to be a work of supererogation. The same may be said of the copious industry of Mrs. Charlotte C. Stopes. Finally, to the researches of Mr. Walter Wilson Greg, Mr. Alfred W. Pollard, and Mr. J. Dover Wilson, whose studies have recently illuminated the whole field of Shakespearean bibliography, the last three chapters are almost entirely indebted, as I hope the footnotes will properly indicate.

To various friends I wish to express my gratitude for aid generously rendered: to Professor Lane Cooper for reading my manuscript with the sagacious criticism which those who know him have learned to expect from his good taste and judgment; to Mr. Henry Roenne for the drawings of the Globe, which he executed as a labor of love; to Mr. Beverly Chew, the dean of American book-collectors, for permitting the reproduction of certain engravings in his library; to Mr. William A. White, of Brooklyn, for freely placing at my disposal his priceless collection of Shakespeareana; and to my colleagues,

PREFACE

Professor Lane Cooper, Professor Clark S. Northup, Professor Martin Wright Sampson, and Professor William Strunk, Jr., for help in the task of reading the proofs, and for many wise suggestions.

Finally, to Mr. August Heckscher, of New York City, I wish to record a special obligation. Through his bounty in establishing at Cornell University the Heckscher Foundation for the Advancement of Research I came to be relieved for a time from the routine of class-room instruction in order that I might complete my investigations and prepare my manuscript for the press. But for this welcome relief I should have had to defer publication for some years.

CONTENTS

CONTENTS

A LIFE OF
WILLIAM SHAKESPEARE
.·.

CHAPTER I

ANCESTRY

WHAT'S in a name? petulantly asks Juliet. The answer
is, as every student of the subject knows: In some names,
little or nothing, in others, possibly a great deal. The
latter alternative seems to be the case with the name of our
most distinguished English poet. In the sixteenth and
seventeenth centuries, as to-day, the word "Shakespeare"
unquestionably suggested to the mind of every one what
its two syllabic elements so clearly indicate — military
prowess. But the suggestion was then far more obvious
than now, for the age was nearer to chivalry, and the
phrase "the shaking of the spear" was almost a commonplace as expressing the doughtiness of warriors. Laya-
mon, in his *Brut*, represents the valiant British earls as
leaping upon their horses and thus defying the Roman
hosts:

> Heo scaeken on heore honden speren swithe stronge.

The English rendering of Job, xli, 29, takes the form:
"He laugheth at the shaking of the spear." John Marston,
in *Histriomastix* (1598), writes humorously:

> When he shakes his furious spear,
> The foe in shivering, fearful sort
> May lay him down in death to snort;

and John Davies of Hereford, in *Humour's Heau'n on
Earth* (1609), exclaims:

[1]

> No human power can their force withstand;
> They laugh to scorn the shaking of the spear.

Illustrations might be multiplied, showing that the significance of the poet's name could not have escaped his contemporaries.

It is duly noted by the early etymologists of proper names. Thus Verstegan, writing in 1605 *Of the Surnames of our Ancient Families*, observes that "*Breakspear, Shakspear*, and the like, have been names imposed upon the first bearers of them for *valour and feats of arms*"; [1] and the learned William Camden, who as Clarenceux King of Arms was especially interested in such matters, makes the same statement in his *Remaines* (1605). Thomas Fuller, in his sketch of the poet's life, first of all notes that he was "*Martiall* in the *Warlike* sound of his Sur-name (whence some may conjecture him of a *Military extraction*), *Histri-vibrans* or Shake-speare." Spenser, Jonson, and other poets took occasion to point out that his name did "heroically sound," the Elizabethan printers felt impelled to emphasize its military significance by the use of a hyphen, and the officers of the College of Heralds embodied this significance in a canting design for the Shakespeare coat of arms, with a crest of the warlike falcon shaking a spear in its talons. The poet himself, no doubt, believed that military prowess was the true, as it was the apparent, origin of his patronymic; and possibly in composing his dedicatory letters to the great Earl of Southampton, whose patronage he was seeking, he felt a mild sense of pride as he signed his name in its most suggestive spelling — "Shakespeare."

But whether some early ancestor was really distinguished by military prowess, or whether the designation

[1] Richard Verstegan, *A Restitution of Decayed Intelligence*, 1605, p. 294. See also John Done, *Polydoron*, 1631, cited in *Notes and Queries*, 3d Series, i, 266.

was jocularly foisted upon "the first bearers of the same," we cannot say. Nor can we say whether the name was a straightforward and simple English coinage of the twelfth or thirteenth century when such compounds were being freely created for those who had no patronymic, or whether it was a natural corruption through popular etymology of some earlier and less significant form. That the name originally bore so patent a meaning is open to doubt. Some of the early spellings may be cited as pertinent: "Saxberd," "Shagspere," "Shaxbere," "Shakespur," "Shexper," "Chacsper," "Saxper," "Shaxber," "Shaxberd." And hence some scholars have tried to find the origin of the name in such fanciful sources as "Sigisbert" and "Jacques-Pierre." Mrs. Stopes, in her admirable work, *Shakespeare's Family*, gives up the attempt, simply saying: "The origin of the name 'Shakespeare' is hidden in the mists of antiquity."

Yet it has often been observed that the given names of the family in England suggest a Norman origin. "Whereever Shakespeare families are found," writes one scholar, "they invariably show a very great preponderance of Christian names that are characteristically Norman." And it is quite possible that the Shakespeares came over with the throng that followed in the wake of William the Conqueror.

It may be significant, therefore, that a name like Shakespeare's occurs in the Great Rolls of Normandy for the year 1195. In a list of mainpernors in the Bailiwick of Oximin, situate in the diocese of Bayeux, who were owing money to King Richard, we read:

William Sakeespee reddit computum de ij marcis pro eodem [i.e., pro plegio]. In thesauro v solidos sterlingorum. Et debet i marcam, viij solidos, iiij denarios.[1]

---

[1] *Magni Rotuli Scaccarii Normanniae*, ed. by Thomas Stapleton, 1840–44, i, 242. I have expanded the clerk's crabbed abbreviations in the manu-

Three years later a return from the same bailiwick notes that William Sakeespée had made "no further payment," and was still indebted to the crown for the sum recorded in 1195:

William Sakeespee i marcam, viij solidos, iiij denarios sterlingorum, pro plegio Raḡ Bladarii.[1]

A careful search through the Rolls, which extend to the year 1203, yielded no other allusion to this William Sakeespée; possibly he had already left the diocese. There is, however, a reference to a Roger Sakeespée in a neighboring diocese.

In printing the Norman Rolls, Stapleton points out that their chief value will be "to enable each descendant of a family of Norman origin readily to trace out the locality or epithet from which his surname is derived." Hence the appearance in these Rolls of a William Sakeespée indicates the possibility, if not the probability, that the poet's family, like so many distinguished English families, came from across the Channel during the rule of English Kings over northern France. If this be the case, exactly when the Shakespeares settled in England is not clear. The name, however, does not appear in the *Domesday Book*, 1086, in which William the Conqueror listed the taxable inhabitants of each shire. Indeed, the earliest reference to the family in England which the well-nigh exhaustive search carried on through many years by hundreds of Shakespearean scholars, expert genealogists, and minute archæologists, has yet discovered, bears the date 1248. The form the name takes is "Saksper," the given appellation is "William," and the place is within

script. The entry may be translated as follows: "William Sakeespée renders account for two marks on the same score [i.e., as security for some person]. In the treasury five shillings sterling. And he owes one mark, eight shillings, and fourpence."

[1] *Op. cit.*, ii, 411. "William Sakeespée, one mark, eight shillings, fourpence, as security for Raḡ. Bladarius."

a few miles of Stratford. In 1260 we find a "Simon Shakespeye," who seems to reappear in 1278 as "Simon Sakesper." [1] From this time on the name occurs with great frequency in Warwickshire and the adjacent counties. As we have seen, however, the entries in the Norman Rolls show that about fifty years before the name begins to appear in English records, a "William Sakeespée" was living under English rule in northern France. We find him registered as a debtor to King Richard for a sum which apparently he did not find it easy to pay. We cannot, of course, say that in the reign of this sovereign the Sakeespées migrated to England; but we are reminded of Christopher Sly's humorous boast: "The Slys are no rogues. Look in the chronicles; we came in with Richard Conqueror." And we have positive evidence that the Sakeespées did migrate from Normandy, and ultimately became transformed into an English family. [2] From the year 1260 on the name is not uncommon. For example, in the *Calendar of the Charter Rolls*, 1310, we find records of an English family with the surname variously spelled "Sakespeie," "Sakespey," "Syakespeye," "Saxpey," and "Shakespeie."

Of the early history of the Sakeespée family in Normandy I have been able to discover little. The name apparently was of rare occurrence. It was not unknown, however, in northern France, and the family was not without some distinction, at least at a later date. There is reason for believing that one of these Norman Sakeespées was endowed with "the heavenly gift of poesy." An acrostic at the end of the better of the two extant manuscripts of the important romance *Le Chatelain de Couci*, written in the latter part of the thirteenth

---

[1] See C. C. Stopes, *Shakespeare's Family*, 1901, p. 4.

[2] Ernest Weekley, in his *Surnames*, 1916, observes that the name "Sacquespée" occurs frequently in early English records.

or the early part of the fourteenth century, seems to declare that the author is named "Jakemes Sakesep" (i.e., Jacques Sakeespée).[1] "Jakemes" is a form peculiar to Normandy, and the author of the romance unquestionably spoke the Picard dialect. Again, in the year 1408 a Sakeespée was mayor of a village in the north of France — a man of some means and education. To a document, now preserved in the Bibliothèque Nationale, he signed his name clearly "Jacques Saquespée."

If the name of the English family was originally "Saquespée," or "Sakeespée," it passed through various corruptions, such as were common to English surnames, until it emerged through folk-etymology into the thoroughly anglicized form "Shakespeare."

Probably this evolution was largely determined by the Norman pronunciation of the first syllable of the name, *saque* or *sak*, preserving the hard sound of *k*, which in England would promptly identify it with the English word *sak*, a common form of *shake* (derived from O.E. *scacan*). It was natural that, as the intrusion of the letter *h* grew more and more into usage until *shake* completely replaced the earlier forms, this letter would make its appearance in the first element of the proper name we are considering. It should not be forgotten that the earliest form of the name in England is "Saksper," and that this form long persisted. For example, the poet's uncle was entered in the burial register of Snitterfield in 1596 as "Henry Sakspere," and his wife shortly after as "Margret Sakspere, widow, being tymes the wyff of Henry Shakspere." Since the first element of the name, both in its original form *sak* and in its later form *shake*,[2] suggested

---

[1] A second manuscript makes the acrostic read "Jakemes Makesep." See G. Paris, in *Histoire Littéraire*, xxviii, 353, and Ch.–V. Langlois, *La Société Française au xiii⁰ Siècle*, 1911, pp. 187, 221.

[2] Cf. the English variant of 1260, "Shakespeye," and of 1310, "Shakespeie."

the idea of shaking *something*, the second element *espée* might readily suggest the modification into "Shake-a-speare," [1] or "Shakespeare"; for in the twelfth and thirteenth centuries, under the influence of the allegory and of folk-etymology, such was the general tendency of compound proper names.

Possibly, too, this slight modification in sound in order to make sense was assisted by the meaning of the name in its French form, a meaning more clearly revealed in the spelling "Saquespée." The first element, *saquer*, a Norman variant for *sacher* (derived probably from *sac*), means "to draw out vigorously"; the second element, *espée*, an earlier spelling for *épée*, means "a sword." Hence the name in its French form had a military significance, "to draw out the sword quickly." And that this significance was obvious to contemporaries is shown by the fact that in the Norman Rolls the name is variously written "Sake Espée," "Sake espée," and "Sakeespée." Such an obvious military significance would, in a measure at least, justify the modification, in English terms, to "Shake-speare." [2]

It is further interesting to note the appearance in early English records of the surname "Drawsword," 1273, an exact translation of the French "Sakeespée," and the curious hybrid form "Drawespée." The latter, it would seem, was an attempt in a bilingual age to prevent in the name "Sakeespée" the inevitable confusion of the French word *sak*, "to draw," with the common English word *sak*, "to shake." Still more significant is the appearance of the surname "Drawspere," which may be a corruption

[1] Cf. the early variants "Shakaspeare," "Shakyspeare," "Shakispeare." The Stratford records commonly refer to the poet's father as "John Shakyspeare."

[2] Cf. also the form "Shakeshaft." The poet's grandfather, Richard Shakespeare, is referred to in 1541 as "Richard Shakeschafte"; see C. C. Stopes, *Shakespeare's Environment*, p. 16.

of "Drawespée"; for although one might easily *shake* a spear, it is difficult to understand how one could *draw* a spear.

If Shakespeare was in truth of Norman origin on his father's side, there was, of course, mingled in his veins a steady stream of Saxon blood from the middle shires of England. And thus in him were combined, in what we may suppose were ideal proportions, the two important racial elements that have gone to the making of the greatest Englishmen.[1]

Whatever be the earlier history of the family, in the fourteenth and fifteenth centuries the Shakespeares, though fairly well-distributed throughout England, were especially numerous in Warwickshire and the neighboring counties. The earliest person of the name, of whom a notice has yet been discovered, lived, as has been stated, in the first half of the thirteenth century at Clopton, about seven miles from Stratford-on-Avon, and bore the given appellation "William." He rose to doubtful fame through the commission of a robbery, for which he was duly hanged in 1248. We have no reason, however, to connect him with the antecedents of the poet. Indeed, among the host of Shakespeares that crowd the records of the fifteenth and the earlier half of the sixteenth century we are unable to trace the particular family which was destined to produce England's greatest genius. Yet from a study of the records of these numerous Shakespeares we may feel reasonably sure that the poet's ancestors, for several generations back at least, were plain husbandmen, engaged in tilling the soil.

Our definite knowledge of the dramatist's family begins with his grandfather, Richard Shakespeare, a farmer

[1] Carlyle wrote of Shakespeare: "The finest figure, as I apprehend, that Nature has hitherto seen fit to make of our widely diffused Teutonic clay. Saxon, Norman, Celt, or Sarmat, I find no human soul so beautiful these fifteen hundred years — our supreme modern European man."

living in the small village of Snitterfield, about four miles from Stratford. Richard owned no land himself, but was a tenant on the estate of a wealthy squire, Robert Arden. The farm that he cultivated is thus described by his landlord: "All that messuage, with its appurtenances, in Snitterfield, which are in the tenure of the said Richard Shakespeare; and all those my lands, meadows, pastures, commons, with their appurtenances, in Snitterfield aforesaid, belonging and appertaining to the same messuage, which now are in the tenure of the aforesaid Richard Shakespeare." His dwelling in Snitterfield is described as "lying between the house which was sometime the house of William Palmer on the one side, and a lane called Merrel Lane on the other, and doth abut on High Street."[1] No doubt it was an ordinary thatched farmhouse, not unlike that occupied by the Hathaways at Shottery.

Of such an inconspicuous person the records preserved are naturally accidental, and for the most part trivial; yet even so they are of interest to students of the poet, and deserve at least brief citation here.

In 1528 Richard was presented by John Palmer, tithingman, for owing suit of court.[2] In 1535 he was fined 12*d*. for obstructing with his own stuff the village commons. In 1543 he was the recipient of a generous benefaction from Thomas Atwoode, *alias* Tailor, of Stratford, who mentions him in his will as follows: "Unto Richard Shakespeare, of Snitterfield, my four oxen, which are now in his keeping." In April, 1559, he was associated with the wealthy "Mr. William Botte" in making an inventory of the goods of Roger Lyncecombe. In July, 1550, and again in May, 1560, Robert Arden, in legal documents, makes mention of the farm at Snitterfield as then

---

[1] C. C. Stopes, *Shakespeare's Environment*, pp. 32, 66.
[2] C. C. Stopes, *Shakespeare's Environment*, p. 16. There are frequent subsequent notices of him by Palmer down to 1542.

being "in the tenure of Richard Shakespeare." In October, 1560, his name appears in the proceedings of a View of Frank Pledge. But shortly after this he must have died, for on February 10, 1561, letters of administration of his goods were issued to his son John (the poet's father), who is described as a farmer (*agricola*) of Snitterfield. The formal inventory of his goods reckoned their value at £38 17s.; but such estimates were commonly much below the actual value of an estate; for example, the inventory of the goods of Annes Arden in 1581 appraised "five score pigges" at 13s. 4d. — a trifle over a penny and a half each. Nor was the estimated value of Richard's possessions small for a man in his position. W. Stafford, in *A Compendious or Brief Examination* (1581), writes: "In times past, and within the memory of man, he hath been accounted a rich and wealthy man, and well able to keep house among his neighbours, which, all things discharged, was clearly worth £30 or £40." If this be true, the inventory of Richard's goods, some twenty years earlier, at £38 17s. indicates that he was at least a well-to-do husbandman, occupying a respectable position in the little farming-community of Snitterfield.[1]

Besides his son John, just mentioned, Richard left also a son named Henry, who spent all his life in or near Snitterfield, tilling a farm of considerable importance. To his neighbors he was generally known as "Harry Shakespeare"; and though our records of him are scanty, they are sufficient to show that he had a strongly-marked personality. In 1574 he engaged in a fight with Edward Cornwell (who had married his brother's wife's sister), in which "he drew blood to the injury of the said Edward

[1] Sir Sidney Lee, *Life*, p. 3, states that the estimated value of Richard's estate was £35 17s., and Edgar I. Fripp, Introduction to *Minutes and Accounts of the Corporation of Stratford-upon-Avon*, 1921, p. xlix, gives the estimate as £38 7s. The correct sum, however, is £38 17s.

Cornwell"; and was accordingly fined. In 1581 he resolutely declined to pay tithes on his farm, refused to submit to the decision of the Ecclesiastical Court, and, after being censured, was excommunicated. In 1582 he was fined "for not labouring with teams for the amending of the Queen's highway"; and the following year he was again fined because he refused to wear a cloth cap on Sundays and holidays as required by statute. Clearly he had a mind of his own.

Although he was married (his wife was named Margaret), he seems to have had no children — at least none that lived to maturity. The young William, we may suppose, was a frequent visitor in the home of his "Uncle Harry" and "Aunt Margaret," and on their farm, perhaps, acquired some of his wide knowledge of rustic types and of country life.

In his business undertakings Henry seems to have been consistently unfortunate. In 1586 he was unable to pay a certain debt for which his more prosperous Stratford brother had become surety, and the creditor was forced to bring suit against John Shakespeare for the sum.[1] In 1591 he was imprisoned for debts to Richard Ainge; and in 1596 he was again attached for debts to John Tomlyns. His very death was rendered pathetic by the clamor of creditors. John Blythe, of Allesley, it seems, had sold two oxen to "Henry Shakespeare of Snitterfield" for £6 13s. 4d., which Henry promised to pay on a certain date. He died, however, with the debt unpaid, and Blythe brought suit against one William Meades for recovery of the sum, declaring that "Shakespeare, falling extremely sick about such time as the money was due, died about the time whereon the money ought to have been paid,

---

[1] The documents in this case make the relationship between John, of Stratford, and Henry, of Snitterfield, perfectly clear: "Henricus Shakesper frater dicti Johannes."

having it provided in his house against the day of payment. . . . Now so it is . . . that Shakespeare, living alone, without any company in his house,[1] and dying without either friends or neighbours with him or about him, one William Meades, dwelling near unto him, having understanding of his death, presently entered into the house of the said Shakespeare after that he was dead, and pretending that the said Shakespeare was indebted to him, ransacked his house, broke open his coffers, and took away divers sums of money, and other things," including, we are told, "all the goods and household stuff belonging to the said Shakespeare," a mare out of the stable, and "the corn and hay out of the barn." [2]

The record of his troubled life is closed by a notice of his burial in the Snitterfield churchyard on December 9, 1596. Six weeks later, "Margaret Sakspere, being tymes the wyff of Henry Shakspere," was laid beside him.[3]

[1] William Meades replied that Henry's wife Margaret was in the house; but since Margaret died six weeks later she may at the time referred to have been confined to her bed.

[2] C. C. Stopes, *Shakespeare's Environment*, p. 69. It should be added that William Meades denied that he ransacked the house.

[3] It is barely possible, but I think quite unlikely, that there was a third brother named Thomas. The history of Thomas is so vague, and his connection with the poet's family so doubtful, that other than a footnote reference to him is unjustified. For what is known of him, see Halliwell-Phillipps, *Outlines*, ii, 212.

CHAPTER II

PARENTAGE

THE poet's father, John, doubtless spent his youth on the parental farm at Snitterfield, and by hard labor in the fields, ploughing "with sturdy oxen," earned the designation *agricola*, which, as we have seen, was bestowed on him in the letters of administration of his father's estate. But at some date before 1552, prompted by vaulting ambition, he transferred his activities to the neighboring town of Stratford, a thriving place of some two thousand inhabitants.[1] Here he engaged his energies in various enterprises. In 1556, and again in 1586, he is described in legal documents as a glover, and that seems to have been his chief business throughout life.[2] Yet, like other glovers of the time,[3] he probably did not confine himself to the narrow limits of this trade. In a suit of 1573 he is referred to as a "whyttawer" (white-tawer), a tanner of white leather; and we learn, though on less authoritative evidence,[4] that he was "a considerable dealer in wool." Furthermore, from the nature of the lawsuits in which he became involved, it seems that he dealt also in grain, malt, and other farm-products.[5]

[1] The estimate of Fripp, *op. cit.*, p. xii. Fripp also gives (pp. xxxii–iii) an interesting, but problematical, account of John's apprenticeship to the glover's craft.

[2] It will be remembered that Sir John Mennes describes him in his old age as a glover still to be seen in his shop.

[3] See Halliwell-Phillipps, *Outlines*, ii, 328, note 191.

[4] That of Nicholas Rowe, who gathered his information largely from Betterton. Betterton made a visit to Stratford about 1690 to learn what he could of the poet and his family.

[5] Probably he continued for a time his interest in farming at Snitterfield; as Fripp observes, "many of the Stratford tradesmen were yeomen," and "most tradesmen supplemented their earnings by farming, malting, or victualling."

Our first notice of him in Stratford is in April, 1552, when, along with two other citizens, he was fined 12d. for having allowed a pile of filth (*sterquinarium*) to accumulate before his house in Henley Street — the very house, it appears, in which twelve years later the poet was born. At this early date John was unmarried, and though he probably used the Henley Street house as his bachelor residence, he must have chiefly employed it as his shop, and as a warehouse for such stuff as passed through his hands.

Through industry at his chosen trade of glove-making, and good judgment in his miscellaneous speculations, he early laid the foundation of prosperity. The numerous suits he instituted in the courts against persons who owed him money, as well as the suits brought by others against him, clearly indicate the variety and extent of his activities. On June 28, 1553, Stratford received a charter of incorporation, and John, as one of the rising young business men of the town, was called upon to take a part in the municipal government; the records show that he was frequently required to serve on juries, and otherwise to perform the duties of citizenship.

By October 2, 1556, he had so prospered that he was able to buy two houses in Stratford. One of these, situated in Greenhill Street, with a garden, croft, and appurtenances, including a barn and an outhouse, was purchased, it would seem, as a speculation; no further record of it is to be discovered, and the presumption is that he shortly disposed of the property. The other, situated in Henley Street and adjoining the dwelling he already occupied there on a lease (to-day it constitutes the eastern half of the double house known as "Shakespeare's Home"), was acquired, no doubt, in order to provide increased accommodations for his growing business. Its common designation as the "Wool Shop" would indicate that it was mainly used for the storage of wool, grain, hides, and the like. At an early date the two houses were connected by inside doorways, as they are at present, and thus made into a single building. Together they must have formed one of the most pretentious business establishments in the village.

The rise of John to a place of importance in Stratford was accelerated in the autumn of the following year,

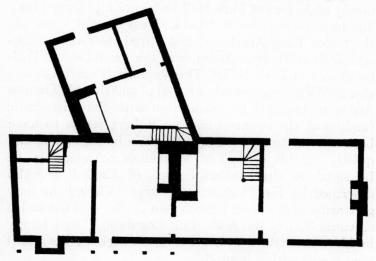

GROUND PLAN OF THE SHAKESPEARE HOUSES IN HENLEY STREET
(The "Wool Shop" at the right, the family residence at the left.)

1557, by his marriage to Mary Arden, daughter and chief heir of Robert Arden, his father's landlord. Robert Arden was a wealthy "gentleman of worship" living at Wilmecote, about three miles from Stratford. He owned two farmhouses at Snitterfield with more than a hundred acres of arable land, which he let to tenants; and at Wilmecote he owned two estates which he himself cultivated, namely, a copyhold estate of unknown extent, where he seems to have resided, and — apparently the richest possession of all — a valuable estate known as Asbies, consisting of a house and approximately sixty acres of land.

But more important to us than the property he possessed was the gentle blood that flowed in his veins. For it is now virtually certain that through a younger branch he was descended, as the poet maintained, from the noble family of Ardens of Park Hall,[1] who proudly traced their line back to the Sheriff Ailwin, Great Guy of Warwick, the Saxon King Athelstan, and Alfred the Great. Robert's father, Thomas Arden, was the second son of Walter Arden of Park Hall.[2] This younger branch was settled at Wilmecote as early as 1501;[3] and though Thomas Arden maintained his connection with the aristocratic families of the county,[4] his son Robert seems to have been content to lead the life of a plain husbandman, and quietly till his estates at Wilmecote. Apparently he belonged to that splendid type of English franklin described by Sir Thomas Overbury: "Though he may give arms with the best gentlemen . . . he says not to his servants 'Go to the field,' but 'Let us go,'" and, happy in his own little world, remains throughout life "lord paramount within himself."

His house in Wilmecote must have been large and well-furnished. It was adorned, we know, with no fewer than

[1] "That most ancient and worthy family," says Dugdale, who connects its name with the great Forest of Arden.

[2] Mrs. Stopes has effectively presented the right of the poet to this pedigree, in her *Shakespeare's Environment*, 1914, and *Shakespeare's Family*, 1901.

[3] Halliwell-Phillipps, in his *Life of Shakespeare*, 1848, p. 8, states in error that the Arden property at Snitterfield was conveyed to Thomas Arden de Wylmecote in 16 Henry VI, i.e., 1438; this would render the above pedigree impossible. He should have said 16 Henry VII, i.e., 1501. The error has created no little confusion among students of the poet's ancestry.

[4] See the documents printed by Mrs. Stopes in *Shakespeare's Family*, pp. 27–28, and *Shakespeare's Environment*, pp. 12–13.

eleven "painted cloths," which in middle-class homes took the place of the more expensive tapestry. There was a "hall" beautified with two of these painted cloths, a great chamber decorated with five, and other rooms of less importance in which the remaining four were distributed. An inventory of his "goods" made after his death shows that on his own farm in Wilmecote he had eight oxen for the plough, four horses, three colts, seven cows, two bulls, four calves, fifty sheep, besides swine, bees, poultry, etc. The inventory, after the usual conservative fashion, reckoned his goods at £77 11s. 10d. — as such estimates then went, a large sum. And this, of course, did not take into consideration his real property, consisting of his lands and houses.

The Shakespeares had long been tenants on one of Robert Arden's farms at Snitterfield; and through this relationship, perhaps, young John had come to know the Arden family, and had met his future wife. Mary, the youngest of eight children [1] (all daughters), was apparently her father's favorite. When Robert Arden late in life took a second wife (by whom he had no children), he made a special settlement of his real property, in order, it may be, to placate certain of his daughters. He had already, it seems, provided for Elizabeth, who had married John Scarlet; and now, by deeds executed in 1550, he divided his Snitterfield estates into six equal parts, giving one part to each of six daughters, subject, however, to the life-interest of his wife. Mary alone is not mentioned in these deeds. Can it be that she had made no objection to his marriage, and thus had won the heart of her father? However that may be, he most bountifully cared for her upon his death in 1556. To her he left by will ten marks

[1] Sir Sidney Lee says that there were only seven children; apparently he forgot Elizabeth who married John Scarlet. Moreover, he expresses some doubt (p. 7) whether Mary was the youngest daughter; she is so described by her father in his will.

as a dowry (the conventional sum), and the freehold of his most valuable possession, the estate of Asbies, with its house, almost sixty acres of land, "and the crop upon the ground, sown and tilled as it is." Mary was thus regarded among the yeomen of Warwickshire as an heiress of importance.

John Shakespeare married her about a year after the death of her father, and brought her to his residence in Stratford. The "Wool Shop," or eastern half of the double house in Henley Street, he continued to use for business purposes; the western half he converted into a home. The bride, having by will received a share of her father's goods,[1] must have brought with her some furniture and household stuff, including we may suppose a few of the painted cloths, so often alluded to by the poet. In the home thus established, William and the other children were born and reared, and here John and Mary lived their entire lives and died. The building, therefore, is most intimately associated with the name of Shakespeare, and is now rightly preserved as a shrine for all lovers of English poetry.[2]

Through the acquisition of his wife's property, added to his own, John became an even more important member of the Stratford community; and this importance quickly revealed itself in various ways. In 1557 he was elected one of the ale-tasters, officers who had supervision of malt liquors and bread;[3] and near the close of the year was chosen a burgess. In 1558 the twelve jurors elected him one of the four constables,[4] an office of no

---

[1] This seems to be the correct interpretation of the clause following the bequest to Alice; but I am not absolutely sure. For the will in full see Halliwell-Phillipps, *Outlines*, ii, 53.

[2] The house remained the residence of John's descendants until 1806.

[3] For a history of this office, and a statement of its precise duties, see C. I. Elton, *William Shakespeare, His Family and Friends*, 1904, p. 78.

[4] The duties of a village constable are humorously described in Shakespeare's sketch of Dogberry. As Fripp, *op. cit.*, p. xlvi, points out, John

little consideration, to which he was reëlected the following year. In 1559 he was appointed an affeeror, a person
who decided the fine or other punishment to be imposed
on those who had been convicted of a fault for which no
express penalty had been prescribed by the statutes. In
1561 he was reappointed affeeror, and also elected one
of the two chamberlains, officers who had charge of the
finances of the municipality. This was a distinct recognition on the part of his fellow-tradesmen of his probity and
business ability. They reëlected him to the position in
1562; and although after serving two terms he retired
from the office, the municipal records show that he continued to help in managing the finances of the town. Not
only did he on several occasions superintend and audit
the accounts of the regular chamberlains, but when the

the marke [on] of mary Shakespeare

the marke [+] of John Shakespeare

necessity arose he actually advanced money to the corporation out of his own pocket. Clearly he was a public-
spirited citizen, deeply interested in the welfare of the
village.[1]

From the fact that he invariably signed documents
with a mark, sometimes a plain cross, sometimes a crude
representation of a pair of dividers used in the trade of
glover, it may be inferred that he could not write his

found the office no sinecure, for cases of assault were numerous. A certain
Welshman had to be fined not only for a fray, but also for "giving opprobri-
ous words" to the constables. For the record of the constables see pp. 88–90,
92–95.

[1] Fripp, *op. cit.*, pp. l–lii (cf. pp. 120–22, 126–30), shows that as Chamberlain John was very energetic in making repairs on town property and in
advancing the condition of the borough; and (pp. liii–v) that several times,
"to his great credit," he undertook the duties of Acting Chamberlain.

name.[1] This, however, carried with it no reproach in Stratford, where most of his fellow-citizens left the mystery of penmanship to learned clerks. "Dost thou use to write thy name?" asks Cade in *II Henry VI*, "or hast thou a mark to thyself, like an honest, plain-dealing man?" Nor does it warrant the charge of "absolute illiteracy" [2] sometimes thoughtlessly brought against him by modern scholars. He may have kept his accounts with the old-fashioned tallies instead of a pen, but his stewardship of the town's finances, and the variety of his business activities, show that by the standards of his community he was far from ignorant.

And he seems to have enjoyed not only the respect of his fellows, but also their sincere liking. We have evidence that he was of a genial disposition, a quality he transmitted to his son of whom Bishop Fuller wrote, "his genius generally was jocular and inclining him to festivity." The only description we have of John dates from a later period in his life, but unquestionably reveals his innate disposition. A contemporary who once saw him "in his shop" reported that he was "a merry-cheekt old man that said, 'Will was a good honest fellow, but he darest have crackt a jest with him at any time.'" This merry disposition, combined with recognized success in business and a genuine interest in the welfare of the borough, would naturally make him popular with the townsmen. We may suppose, too, that he was kindly of heart; his frequent and generous contributions to those in distress

[1] Yet with regard to his using a mark in the various corporation records, Fripp, *op. cit.*, p. 134, after an exhaustive study of the documents, notes that some of John's educated fellow-officers did likewise: "Quyny, we know, could write, and it is likely that others, including John Shakespeare, who used their marks, could also write. It is scarcely possible that a man of his business capacity, for three successive years acting-chamberlain, was illiterate."

[2] The words are those of Halliwell-Phillipps, who, in a desperate effort to avoid anything like hero-worship, goes to the opposite extreme.

indicate as much, and the following incident may be cited as further evidence. On February 1, 1558, he sued one, Matthew Bramley, for debt; but when the case came up again on February 15, he incurred the usual penalty of 2d. for not following his suit. "Apparently," says Fripp, "he declined to prosecute in consequence of the illness of Bramley's wife, who was buried on the 22nd."

On Saturday, April 22, or Sunday, April 23, 1564, an important event took place in the Shakespeare home in Henley Street: a son and heir was born to John and Mary.[1] A few days later, on Wednesday, April 26, he was baptized with the name "William."[2] The entry in the baptismal register reads: "1564, April 26, Gulielmus, filius Johannes Shakspere."

Two earlier children, both girls, had died in infancy, and probably Mary, in her determination not to lose this third child, exercised the utmost care over its health. And she had special need to do so, for early in July, 1564, there broke out in Stratford a severe epidemic of the plague that carried away approximately one out of every seven inhabitants.[3] During these days of terror, when the ominous red cross, with the inscription "Lord have mercy on us," was chalked upon so many doors, John Shakespeare contributed liberally towards the relief of the sufferers — though not the largest, also not the least donations recorded. The largest sum was contributed by

[1] The precise day of his birth cannot be determined; it is even possible that he was born on April 21. But he was baptized on April 26, and it was customary to perform this ceremony three days after birth. The tradition that he died on his birthday, that is April 23, is too late to carry much weight. That day, however — the day of St. George, the patron saint of England — would be especially appropriate.

[2] The ancient font, said to be the one at which he was baptized, is shown at Stratford. One should not forget, however, the possibility that the ceremony was performed in the home.

[3] Malone's reckoning, *Variorum*, ii, 68; Charles Knight says one out of six.

the wealthy owner of the fine mansion called New Place, a "Mr. William Botte, gent.," with whom the glover could hardly be expected to compete. The plague, providentially, we may believe, passed over the home in Henley Street where the "first-born" child of England lay in his cradle, and with the coming of the winter months its ravages were ended.

The following year, 1565, Mr. William Botte, the wealthy gentleman just mentioned as the owner of New Place, was expelled from the Council of Aldermen,[1] and John Shakespeare was promptly elected in his stead. Thus the prosperous glover arrived at that high dignity in the world which, according to his son, justified the wearing of a ponderous thumb ring.[2] In the little village of Stratford the position of alderman was indeed one of great distinction; and soon after this John begins to appear in the town records with the dignified prefix "Master." Of this prefix the Oxford Dictionary says: "Originally used only in speaking of or to a man either of high social rank, or of learning"; and by way of illustration it cites B. *Discolliminium* (1650): "I could wish we might be allow'd to call him *Master* Charles, for most men think he is a gentleman born." Sir Thomas Smith, in his *Commonwealth of England* (1594), writes: "*Master* is the title which men give to esquires and other gentlemen." It is obvious, therefore, that in bestowing on John this title his fellow-townsmen acknowledged his high standing in the business, social, and civic life of Stratford.

In 1568 he received the greatest honor in the gift of the citizens, election to the position of High Bailiff, or as we should now say, Mayor. In this capacity he presided at all meetings of the Town Council, and in his precepts he

---

[1] For the cause, and a general account of Botte, see Fripp, *op. cit.*, pp. lvii–x, 144–46.
[2] See *Romeo and Juliet*, I, iv, 56; *I Henry IV*, II, iv, 364.

styled himself "John Shakespeare, Justice of the Peace, and Bailiff of the Town." The position carried with it unusual dignity: "The Bailiff was waited upon daily by his Sergeant, and once a week by the Town Clerk. On Leet Days, Fair Days, and certain other occasions, Aldermen and Burgesses attended in their gowns at his house to escort him to Church, or through the market, or in perambulation of the Borough boundaries." [1] The silver mace that was borne before John while he was in office is probably among those still preserved at Stratford. [2]

In 1571, his term as High Bailiff having expired, he was elected Chief Alderman. In 1572 the confidence his fellow-citizens had in the value of his judgment is attested by their appointing him to assist the then High Bailiff in the settlement of certain important affairs concerning the municipality. The resolution of the Town Council reads: "At this hall it is agreed by the assent and consent of the Aldermen and Burgesses aforesaid that Mr. Adrian Quiney, now Bailiff, and Mr. John Shakespeare shall at Hillary term next ensuing deal in the affairs concerning the commonwealth of the borough according to their discretions." What these affairs were in which "Master" John Shakespeare was to assist the High Bailiff we do not know; but we learn from the Chamberlain's account that in prosecuting them he and Quiney gave a dinner in Stratford to Sir Thomas Lucy, and that subsequently Quiney was compelled to visit London, probably to seek the aid of men connected with the Court and Parliament.

In the meantime the family in Henley Street was rapidly growing. In 1566 a son, Gilbert, was born; in 1569 a daughter, Joan; in 1571 another daughter, Anne; in 1574 a son, Richard; and in 1580 a son, Edmund.

[1] Fripp, *op. cit.*, p. xxxviii.
[2] For a picture of this mace see G. R. French, *Shakespeareana Genealogica*, 1869, p. 561.

In 1575 John Shakespeare purchased for the sum of £40 the western half [1] of the double house in Henley Street which he had so long occupied. The eastern half, known as the "Wool Shop," he had acquired as early as 1556; the western half, apparently, he had held only on lease. Since the purchase seems to have been unwise (at least it was quickly followed by pecuniary embarrassment), we may suspect that his lease on the house had expired, and he was forced to buy the property in order to preserve his home. But that he was still in relatively easy circumstances is indicated by his contributing the following year, 1576, the generous sum of 12d. towards the salary of the beadle.

Indeed he had now reached the climax of his career. And if we can believe the statement in the two grants of 1596 relating to a Shakespeare coat of arms, he took occasion about this time to apply to the Heralds' College in London for authority to "write himself gentleman." That he was entitled to the dignity of a coat of arms cannot be doubted. Sir John Ferne, in *The Glory of Generositie* (1586), says: "If any person be advanced into an office or dignity of public administration, be it either ecclesiastical, martial, or civil . . . the Herald must not refuse to devise to such a public person, upon his instant request,

[1] The legal description runs: "De duobus mesuagiis, duobus gardinis, et duobus pomariis, et pertinenciis." The exact location of these "two houses" is not stated. The chief house was unquestionably the home adjoining the Wool Shop, for in 1590 John is listed as the owner of both the Wool Shop (which we know he purchased in 1556) and also the adjoining house, and of nothing else. The second house referred to in the deed was doubtless a small tenement attached to the Henley Street home. Too much attention need not be paid to the legal phraseology; in 1579 when John mortgaged Asbies to Lambert, the property was described "de duobus mesuagis, duobus gardinis," whereas in 1589 and subsequently it is described "unum mesuagium sive tenementum" (see Halliwell-Phillipps, *Outlines*, ii, 11). Clearly the "two houses" in the case of Asbies were the main dwelling and some unimportant outhouse; and the same was probably true in the case of the Henley Street property. But the house itself might be described as two houses; see the ground plan, p. 15.

and willingness to bear the same without reproach, a coat of arms, and thenceforth to matriculate him, with his intermarriages and issues descending, in the register of the gentle and noble. . . . In the civil or political state, diverse offices of dignity and worship do merit coats of arms to the possessor of the same offices, as . . . Bailiffs of cities and ancient boroughs or incorporated towns."

Unquestionably, therefore, John had the right to apply for this honor. And there were various reasons why he might desire to do so. A number of his fellow-townsmen not more wealthy, or more prominent in the affairs of the corporation than he, enjoyed heraldic distinction; and he might well feel that he should have the same honor, for he was an ambitious man. Perhaps, too, he secretly cherished the desire to restore to his wife Mary the right to bear the arms of her Arden ancestors, which she had been obliged to forfeit through her marriage to "one who was no gentleman." [1] But his chief reason, we may suspect, was the wish, natural to every English yeoman, to establish a gentle family. Harrison, in his *Description of England* (1577), observes that commonly yeomen, by honest labor and thriftiness, "come to great wealth, insomuch that many of them are able and do buy the lands of unthrifty gentlemen, and often setting their sons to the schools, to the universities, and to the Inns of the Court, or, otherwise, leaving them sufficient lands whereupon they may live without [manual] labour, do make them by these means to become gentlemen." John now possessed two or more houses in Stratford, the important estate of Asbies at Wilmecote, and a share of the Arden farms at Snitterfield. All this would make a creditable endowment for a future gentle family, with his eldest son

[1] The law of heraldry declared that if a woman "marry one who is no gentleman, then she is clearly exempted from" the right to the arms of her ancestors; see *The Calendar of State Papers, Domestic, Elizabeth*, 1562, **xxi**, v31.

and heir, William Shakespeare, at its head. And the dream of establishing such a gentle family may well have come to the prosperous "Bailiff and Justice of the Peace," as it certainly was later the dream of his son William.

That he actually received from the Heralds' Office a tentative sketch of a proposed coat of arms, and that he kept this sketch by him for years, is positively stated in the grant of 1596: "This John hath[1] a pattern thereof under Clarenceux Cooke's hand[2] in paper xx years past. A Justice of Peace, and was[3] Bailiff, Officer, and chief of the town of Stratford upon Avon." It is true that no record has been discovered in the archives of the College regarding John's coat of arms, but since it is not asserted that the attempt went beyond the preliminary stage of Cooke's submitting a tentative sketch, the absence of a formal record need not be regarded as invalidating the statement.

To secure a coat of arms, however, was an expensive undertaking. In *The Cobler's Prophecy* (about 1580), an officer of the Heralds' College is made to say:

> We now are fain to wait who grows to wealth
> And come to bear some office in a town;
> And we, for money, help them unto arms.

Without money, of course, the honor could not be secured; and according to Sogliardo, in *Every Man Out of*

[1] The word is not clear in the manuscript; some scholars read it as "sheweth."

[2] Robert Cook, Clarenceux King of Arms in 1576. It is worth noting that Warwickshire fell in his province, and that he had his visitation commission there in 1568, the year in which John Shakespeare was High Bailiff and Justice of the Peace. It may be, therefore, that this visitation aroused John's ambitions. Cook is said to have granted no fewer than five hundred coats of arms.

[3] Does this mean "had been Bailiff"? John Shakespeare was Bailiff in 1568; the pattern of his coat was said to be "in paper xx years past," i.e., 1576. It may be added that he was Justice of Peace both as High Bailiff and as Chief Alderman.

his Humor, the fees charged amounted to not less than £30. If John actually made the application in 1576, his sudden pecuniary reverses might explain the fact that he failed to carry the project through.

In 1577 he is first recorded as being absent from the meetings of the Town Council. This ominously marks the beginning of his business troubles, which rapidly passed from bad to worse. In January, 1578, at a meeting of the Council (John, as usual, being absent), a levy was made for the purchase of military equipment for the soldiers drawn from Stratford. The order of the Council reads: "At this hall it is agreed that every Alderman, except such under-written excepted, shall pay towards the furniture of three pikemen, two billmen, and one archer, vi*s*. viii*d*." The Aldermen who were excepted were "Mr. Plumley, v*s*., Mr. Shakespeare, iii*s*. iv*d*." This shows that the glover's business troubles were then well known, and that his old friends sympathized with him. At a later meeting of the Council (John again being absent), the following resolution was passed: "Item, it is ordered that every Alderman shall pay weekly towards the relief of the poor iv*d*., saving Mr. John Shakespeare and Mr. Robert Bratt,[1] who shall not be taxed to pay anything."

The ultimate cause for this reverse in fortune may have been the general decline of Stratford as a centre of the woolen trade and allied industries. In 1590 the Bailiff and Burgesses wrote to Lord Burghley, the Lord High Treasurer: "The said town is now fallen much into decay for want of such trade as heretofore they had by clothing and making of yarn, imploying and maintaining a number of poor people by the same, which now live in great penury and misery by reason they are not set at work as before

---

[1] As Halliwell-Phillipps observes, Robert Bratt was one of the poorest members of the Council, "his subscriptions in the plague year of 1564, although he was an Alderman, being, with a single exception, the lowest of all in amount."

they have been." And we have much other evidence to the same effect. John Shakespeare, as a glover, tanner, and "extensive dealer in wool," would thus be directly affected. But doubtless there were more immediate causes for his sudden and we may suppose unexpected difficulties. As early as 1573 Henry Higford, gent., formerly Steward of the Court in Stratford [1] but now resident in Solihull, Warwickshire, instituted suit [2] against him for the sum of £30. If the suit ultimately went against him, the payment of the £30, together with the purchase of the Henley Street house for £40, would furnish us with an explanation of his sudden pecuniary embarrassment.

On November 14, 1578, he mortgaged his wife's valuable estate at Wilmecote, known as Asbies, to his brother-in-law, Edmund Lambert. The mortgage, according to the usage of the time, was drawn up in the form of an absolute sale, with the proviso that if the money were repaid on or before September 29, 1580, the sale would be null and void. Asbies, to be sure, was worth more than £40; but there seemed to be no danger in this transaction, for the Lamberts were near relatives, held in great affection by John and Mary, who named a son, Edmund, and

[1] He appears in this capacity in the Stratford records of 1566, in connection with one of the lawsuits involving Richard Hathaway, for whom John Shakespeare had served as bail and perhaps security; see Halliwell-Phillipps, *Outlines*, ii, 230.

[2] For the details of this suit see C. C. Stopes, *Shakespeare's Environment*, p. 331. The defendant is described as John Shakespeare, of Stratford on Avon, Whyttawer (i.e., tanner of white leather, such as was used in the manufacture of gloves). The only other John Shakespeare of Stratford was the shoemaker, who first arrived in the town "in or very shortly before 1584," that is more than ten years later than this suit. That glovers were often sheep-skin-dressers we know; see Halliwell-Phillipps, *Outlines*, ii, 328, note 191. As Fripp observes, *op. cit.*, pp. xxxii–iii, John Shakespeare, in order to ply his trade, was required to become a member of the Stratford guild of "Glovers, Whittawers, and Collarmakers." It is interesting to note that Thomas Dickson, *alias* Waterman, of Bridge Street, Stratford, is described as a "glover and whittawer."

a daughter Joan, after them; and John, of course, would see to it that before the expiration of the time the redemption-money was duly tendered.

The sum thus raised (was it to pay for the home in Henley Street?) did not furnish the glover relief from his difficulties. This is shown by the facts that during the years 1578 and 1579 he attended no meeting of the Town Council, and that in March of the latter year he is recorded as having failed to pay his military levy [1] which the Aldermen had charitably reduced to iiis. ivd.

On October 15, 1579, he sold his wife's small share in the Snitterfield property for the sum of £4. This had probably come to her on the division of the estate of one of her sisters (Joyce?),[2] and, according to the deed, was then all her holdings in her father's valuable farms there (which, it will be remembered, had been distributed in six equal parts to six of his elder daughters). Shortly after making this sale, however, Mary seems to have received by will from another of her unmarried sisters (Alice?) a full sixth part in the Snitterfield estate. John Shakespeare promptly sold this full "sextam partem" for £40, with the specific object, we may suspect, of redeeming Asbies.[3] Possibly Alice, who was closely associated with Mary as executor of her father's estate, was aware of the

[1] Various others, including Nash and Reynolds, men of means, are also recorded as delinquent. We cannot say that John Shakespeare did not ultimately pay his assessment.

[2] Elizabeth Scarlet came into possession of a small share, probably in the same way, for according to the original settlement she had no portion of the Snitterfield estate.

[3] Halliwell-Phillipps, followed by Lee and others, supposes that Mary received her portions of the Snitterfield estate by some reversion provided for in the early settlement following Arden's second marriage. There is no evidence to support this hypothesis. The above-named scholars accordingly suppose that the two sales of Mary's property, in 1579 for £4, and in 1580 for £40, are in reality identical, and that there is an error in the first of £4 for £40. But this assumption is gratuitous. The documents are carefully drawn up, and would hardly be in error on the most important point of all.

straitened condition of the Shakespeares, and the danger of Mary's losing Asbies, and therefore left her by will the sixth part of the Snitterfield property which she had inherited.

At any rate, on the appointed day, September 29, 1580, John Shakespeare came "to the dwelling house of the said Edmund Lambert," and tendered the £40 due for the redemption of Asbies. But Lambert flatly refused to accept it, "saying that he owed him other money, and unless that he, the said John, would pay him all together, as well the said forty pounds as the other money which he owed him over and above, he would not receive the said forty pounds." Possibly this "other money" was that referred to in a list of debts due to Roger Sadler, appended to Sadler's will (proved on January 17, 1579): "Item, of Edmund Lambert and . . . Cornish, for the debt of Mr. John Shakespeare, *vli.*" Lambert, no doubt, was forced to pay the sum, and hence his angry insistence that his brother-in-law refund that amount before redeeming the Wilmecote property. John, however, was unable to pay both sums demanded; and thus Asbies, as well as the Snitterfield properties, was lost to the Shakespeares for ever.[1]

But the £40 in cash which Lambert refused to accept did not, as we should naturally expect, ease the pecuniary distress of the unfortunate glover. Possibly this was due to his being at once called upon to pay a fine of £40 imposed on him by the court at Westminster.[2] The Coram Rege Roll, Trinity, 22 Elizabeth (i.e., May 22–June 12, 1580), shows that "John Shakespeare, of Strat-

---

[1] From later suits over the property it appears that Lambert orally promised that, after the other moneys owing to him had been paid, he would at any time accept the £40, and restore Asbies to the Shakespeares. Lambert died in 1587, and his son refused to abide by his father's promise.

[2] For the details that have been discovered see C. C. Stopes, *Shakespeare's Environment*, pp. 41–42.

ford-super-Avon, in Co. Warr., yeoman," [1] was fined £20 because he failed to appear before the Queen in her court at Westminster, as summoned, to be bound over to keep the peace; and his two securities, John Awdley, of Nottingham, in the neighboring county of Notts, hat-maker, and Thomas Colley, of Stoke, in the adjacent county of Stafford, were each fined £10. At the same time John was fined an additional £20 because, as one of the sureties for Awdley, he failed to bring that person before the Queen on the day specified. The nature of the indiscretion which warranted a summons to the court at Westminster is not revealed, but the records, brief as they are, suggest an important unwritten chapter in John's life. The payment of the two fines amounting to £40 must have been a serious blow to him in his already straitened circumstances. [2]

We are not surprised to discover that during the next five years, from 1580 to 1585, he was absent from all meetings of the Town Council [3] — with a single exception: in 1582 he attended one meeting, apparently in order to vote for his friend John Sadler, [4] then a candidate for the office of High Bailiff. At last, in 1586, he was dropped from the list of Aldermen, and another person was elected in his place, the reason assigned being: "Mr. Shakespeare doth not come to the halls when they be warned, nor hath not done, of long time." The kindly sympathy of his fellow Aldermen is revealed by their long sufferance in his case, and by the fact that during

---

[1] The shoemaker by the name of John Shakespeare did not come to Strat-ford until four years later; see Halliwell-Phillipps, *Outlines*, ii, 137–40.

[2] Possibly this is why he was not able to accept Lambert's offer for re-deeming Asbies, as explained in note 1, page 30.

[3] So far as the records show, and these are almost complete. Very often John was the only Alderman absent.

[4] The brother of Hamnet Sadler, for whom the poet named his only son. There seems to have existed the warmest friendship between the Sadlers and the Shakespeares.

all these years they had exacted from him no fine for absence.[1]

John had now sunk to the very bottom of his fortunes, and we must next turn our attention to his eldest son, who was destined soon to restore the family prestige, and to make the name "Shakespeare" far more illustrious than the village glover could ever have dreamed in the palmiest days of his success as "Justice of the Peace and Bailiff of the Town" of Stratford.[2]

[1] Halliwell-Phillipps, followed by Lee and others, states that the John Shakespeare harassed in the courts during 1585 and 1586 by John Brown for a certain debt, was the poet's father. There is considerable doubt about this. In 1586, after securing a writ of distraint, Brown made a return that the said John "had nothing whereon to distrain." But the poet's father had not a little property in Stratford. In this year he was accepted in Coventry as sufficient bail for one Pryce indicted for felony; in the following year he offered to redeem Asbies with £40, and in 1590 he is listed as the owner of two houses in Henley Street. Even Halliwell-Phillipps admits that the words "are not to be taken literally." Mrs. Stopes suggests that the person was the John Shakespeare who lived at Clifford Chambers near Stratford. Furthermore the John Shakespeare mentioned in a list of recusants in 1592 as "not coming monthly to church" because of "fear of process of debt," may not be, as some scholars suppose, the poet's father. The records of 1591 and 1592 show him not as hiding from the constable, but as conspicuous in the law courts themselves, and as serving with other well-known citizens in making the *post mortem* inventories of the goods of Ralph Shaw and of Henry Field. Nor is there any definite reason for believing that he had not conformed to the established religion. It was while he was Chamberlain of the town that the images in the Guild Chapel were "defaced"; when he became High Bailiff he took the oath of supremacy; and in 1571, while he was Chief Alderman, the ecclesiastical vestments were ordered to be sold. For further and convincing evidence that John was a Protestant, see Fripp, *op. cit.*, pp. xxxi, xlvii–viii, li, 128. The recusant may have been the shoemaker, John Shakespeare, who had attained some prominence in Stratford, having been elected ale-taster in 1585, and Constable in 1586; and in the year of this return he was serving as Master of the Company of Shoemakers. His disappearance from Stratford shortly after may have been the result of this persecution. Or, as has been suggested by others, the person may have been the John Shakespeare of Clifford Chambers. In view of the doubt attaching to both of these episodes, it seems proper to treat them only in a footnote.

[2] Most of the documents on which this chapter is based will be reproduced in J. O. Halliwell-Phillipps' monumental *Outlines*, ii, 11–17, 173–82, 215–48; and in Richard Savage and Edgar I. Fripp, *Minutes and Accounts of the Corporation of Stratford-upon-Avon*, 1921. Other documents have been referred to in the footnotes.

CHAPTER III

BOYHOOD AND EARLY ENVIRONMENT

FOR two and a half years William was "the only child" of John and Mary. Upon him, therefore, the fond young parents would lavish all their affection. Moreover to him, as their "first-born son and heir," they would tie their heartstrings in a way that probably set him apart from the later children. He was to inherit, so they thought, all the family property — Asbies, the gem of the Arden estate, a portion of the Snitterfield farms once tilled by his grandfather, and the valuable Stratford realties gradually being accumulated by his father. If we may believe that in 1576 the prosperous Alderman made a tentative step towards securing a coat of arms, we catch a glimpse of the secret ambition he cherished for his son. Surely it was in William, rather than in the other children, that John and Mary garnered up their hearts.

It is not difficult for us to picture the boy. We know that he had auburn hair, large hazel eyes, ruddy cheeks, a high forehead, and a gentle disposition. Perhaps this last quality came to him from his mother. "Mary Arden! the name breathes of poetry!" exclaims Knight. May we not safely add that her son's poetry breathes of her? For surely it was at his mother's knee that he acquired his conception of those gentle and noble elements of woman's character which he so effectively embodied in his plays. His father was of a different type, frankly bourgeois, with a cheery disposition and a readiness to "crack a jest" that won him favor with his neighbors. The Plume Manuscript,[1] on the authority of Sir John Mennes, sup-

[1] Anecdotes compiled by Archdeacon Thomas Plume about 1656.

plies us with a vivid description of him, which, though already quoted, will bear repetition:

He (Shakespeare) was a glover's son. Sir John Mennes saw once his old father in his shop — a merry-cheekt old man that said, "Will was a good honest fellow, but he darest have crackt a jest with him at any time." [1]

Brief as this is, it gives us a full-length sketch of the village tradesman. And it reveals to us, too, the genial relations that must have existed between him and his little son, who, we know, inherited much of his temper. Bishop Fuller, writing of the dramatist, tells us that his "genius generally was jocular," and we have evidence of his ability to hold his own with the best wits of the day. When, indeed, we consider the diversified characters of his mother and father we can understand the extraordinary range of his sympathies — from a Desdemona and an Imogen to a Falstaff and a Dogberry — a range unequaled by any other poet.

In the Henley Street home, among reasonably well-to-do circumstances, at least at first, young William grew up as the eldest of six children. Gilbert was two and a half years younger, Joan five years younger, Anne seven and a half years younger, Richard ten years younger, and Edmund, the baby, sixteen years younger. All lived to maturity except Anne, [2] who died at the attractive age of eight. We may suppose that William, as the eldest brother, was required to care for the smaller children; and this, perhaps, constituted his earliest training for his

---

[1] Sir John Mennes could hardly have said that he himself saw John Shakespeare in his shop; but doubtless he was quoting some one who had seen him there. The error is probably due to the writer of the Plume MS.

[2] The affection in which little Anne was held is indicated by the fact that her father, though at this time in very straitened circumstances, ordered at her funeral not only the bell but also the use of the pall, which was commonly dispensed with.

later work as a dramatist, in that it gave him some of his remarkable insight into the elements of human nature.

On special occasions he must have made visits to the home of his Aunt Margaret (*née* Arden), who had married Alexander Webbe, and with six children, his first cousins, was living in his grandfather's old house at Snitterfield. Sometimes, too, he must have visited the home of his Uncle Harry Shakespeare at Snitterfield, and the more pretentious home of his Aunt Joan, who had married Edmund Lambert of Barton-on-the-Heath. But these were mere incidents in the long-drawn-out years of boyhood, and most of his early experiences were associated with the village of his birth.

At this time Stratford was a small and very quiet country town lying open to the fields, without turreted walls, or monasteries, or moated castles. It was peopled not with noble families, but with simple honest folk, who plied their trades, and rarely bothered their heads with matters that lay beyond their horizon. For the most part they were unable to read or write; yet they possessed native shrewdness, and exhibited, no doubt, strongly marked personalities, including such types as Dogberry, Sly, and Bottom the weaver. Butchers, haberdashers, grocers, woolen-drapers, glovers were elected to posts of the highest honor in the civic government, and constituted the aristocracy of the village. The streets were narrow and winding, and, as the records show, often polluted with trash and standing pools of water. The houses were crazy affairs, built of stucco with timber beams showing, and covered with thatched roofs. To us they would seem picturesque, to the Elizabethans they were merely commonplace and unworthy of a second glance. The old Clopton Bridge of solid masonry with its fourteen arches, the handsome village church with its high steeple of wood, and the fine old Guild Chapel with its curious frescoes, were objects of special pride to the citizens. But beyond these features there was nothing to excite the interest of a sixteenth-century traveler [1] — unless he took a second look at the shallow, slow-flowing Avon with its milldam, which added a touch of pastoral beauty to the scene.

In this quiet country town the young William probably led the typical life of a village lad. Through allusions in his plays we catch glimpses of him as he "played at push-pin with the boys," or "ninemen's-morris," or "more sacks to the mill," or "hoodman blind," or led the game of "hide fox and after all," "whipped top" with the most expert, and on occasions more than one "troubled with unruly" pranks the sedate citizens. In "Avon's wind-ing stream" he could find endless sources of pleasure. There, for instance, was the cool swimming-pool, the haunt of all the barefoot lads. We can imagine him as at first venturing on the water timidly, "like little wanton boys that swim on bladders," later, "like an unpractis'd swimmer, plunging still with too much labour," and at last, boldly challenging his comrades, as Cæsar did Cas-sius, to leap in "and swim to yonder point." In the river, too, he could discover innumerable quiet places in which to "betray the tawny-finned fishes." Only one who had learned the sport as a boy, and had actually experienced the joy of a swift strike, could in the turmoil of a busy life in London have written: "The pleasantest angling is to see the fish cut with her golden oars the silver stream and greedily devour the bait." [2]

Furnivall, who is second to none in a sympathetic un-derstanding of the poet, has attempted to characterize the youthful Shakespeare in words that are probably not far

---

[1] See, for example, Leland's *Itinerary*, 1535-43, ed. by L. T. Smith, ii, 48-50.

[2] See H. N. Ellacombe, *Shakespeare as an Angler*, 1883.

from the truth: "Taking the boy to be the father of the man, I see a square-built yet lithe and active fellow, with ruddy cheeks, hazel eyes, a high forehead, and auburn hair, as full of life as an egg is full of meat, impulsive, inquiring, sympathetic; up to any fun and daring; into scrapes, and out of them with a laugh; making love to all the girls; a favorite wherever he goes — even with the prigs and fools he mocks; untroubled as yet with Hamlet doubts, but in many a quiet time communing with the beauty of earth and sky around him."

The regions about Stratford were in truth among the most beautiful in England, with dark primeval forests, "murmuring streams," and "pastures with their green mantles so embroidered with flowers that," to a contemporary observer, "it seemed another Eden." The poet's eye was surely glancing in memory over familiar scenes when in *Lear* he describes a midland section of England —

> With shadowy forests, and with champains rich'd,
> With plenteous rivers, and wide-skirted meads.

And we cannot doubt that the developing boy, endowed with the sensitive nature of the poet, soon learned to find there "tongues in trees" and "books in the running brooks." Michael Drayton, himself a Warwickshire lad born just a year before Shakespeare, grows eloquent when he speaks of the beauty of his native county —

> That shire which we the Heart of England well may call.[1]

First he notes here the presence of the "ancient Forest of Arden," or "what is now the Woodland in Warwickshire"; and at great length he celebrates the "sylvan joys" of its "shady groves":

> With solitude what sorts that here's not wondrous rife!

It is not astonishing that later, in the woodland scenery of *As You Like It* and *A Midsummer Night's Dream,*

[1] This and the quotations that follow are from Drayton's *Poly-Olbion.*

we find the influence of these sylvan joys upon Shakespeare's boyish imagination.

As to Warwickshire's treasury of flowers, Drayton is unable to express his emotions. His list of "unnumb'rd sorts of simples" fairly exhausts his botanical vocabulary —

> Which justly to set down, even Dodon short doth fall,
> Nor skilfull Gerard yet shall ever find them all.

And of "the feath'red sylvans, perched with many a speckled breast upon the highest spray of every mounting pole," he declares that on a summer's day they —

> So strain their warbling notes
> That hills and valleys ring, and even the echoing air
> Seems all composed of sounds about them everywhere.

Among these he singles out for particular mention "the throstell with shrill sharps," the "woosell with golden bill," the merle that plays upon a "dulcet pipe," the nightingale with "lamenting strains," the linnet, "that warbling bird," the wood-lark, the redbreast, the wren, the yellow-pate ("scarce hath any bird a finer pipe than she"), the goldfinch, the tydie, the "laughing hecco," the "counterfeiting jay." These, and many more, "some hid among the leaves, some in the taller trees, some in the lower greaves, thus sing away the morn."

If the boy Drayton found so much to delight him in the natural beauties of his native Warwickshire, we may be sure that the boy Shakespeare found therein quite as much pleasure; and his verse shows that he observed these things with a clearer eye and a more understanding heart. In the noise of London theatres he wrote of blue-veined violets "that strew the green lap of the new-come spring," of "freckled cowslips," "ladies'-smocks all silver white," the "throstle with his note so true," the "lark that tirra-lyra chants," the "wren with little quill"; and often there flashed upon his inward eye pictures of willows growing "aslant a brook," or of orchards when "the moon tips with silver all the fruit-tree tops." For such was the education of Nature by which his growing genius was being molded.

Nor was sensuous beauty all with which his native Warwickshire could endow him. The regions near Stratford were unusually rich in historic traditions and places of romantic association. Within seven miles was the quaint old town of Warwick —

> Brave Warwick, that abroad so long advanced her Bear,
> By her illustrious Earls renownèd everywhere.

Its "magnificent castle" — so Leland describes it — "set upon a high rock of stone" overlooking the river Avon, was one of the most splendid relics of ancient chivalry then in existence, a fortress of great strength and extraordinary delight, with its Cæsar's Tower, supposed to have been erected by Julius Cæsar, and Guy's Tower, bringing to mind the famous deeds of Great Guy of Warwick. As Drayton observed, the hoary old castle was "loaden with antique fables"; and in later times, almost within the memory of men, it had been the centre of the War of the Roses, where Richard Neville, Earl of Warwick, named the King-maker and Last of the Barons, made it his pleasure "to crown and depose kings." [1]

Not far from Warwick was Guy's Cliff, a spot famous in legend, where the popular hero was supposed to have spent his last days in retirement. William Camden, who visited the place in Shakespeare's time, has preserved for us a description which shows how much it could move even an antiquarian: "Hard by the river Avon standeth Guy-Cliff. There have ye a shady little wood, clear and

---

[1] Shakespeare, *III Henry VI*, III, iii, 157, calls him the "setter up and puller down of kings."

crystal springs, mossy bottoms and caves, meadows always fresh and green, the river rumbling here and there among the stones, with his stream making a mild noise and gentle whispering; and besides all this, solitary and still quietness, things most grateful to the Muses."

Within easy reach, too, was Coventry; "one of the bravest cities in England," writes William Smith in 1588; with "strong and high walls" adorned with "many beautiful gates and stately turrets," all "still remaining, and second to none in England." [1] Besides its handsome and wonderfully well-preserved walls, suggesting the days when knighthood was in flower, the city was notable for its fine monastic buildings, its beautiful spires, and its treasury of legend, including the story of Godiva.

But perhaps the place that most stirred the imagination of the youthful Shakespeare was Kenilworth, the home of the Earl of Leicester, the powerful and magnificent favorite of Queen Elizabeth. The castle, originally erected in the eleventh century, was, according to Dugdale, a fortress of "extraordinary strength and largeness," enclosing no fewer than seven acres within its walls, which were so thick, "in many places of fifteen or twenty foot thickness," that "two or three persons together may walk upon most places thereof." [2] It had played a conspicuous part in the history of England, notably when it was held by the Barons against Henry III. Elizabeth had presented it to the Earl of Leicester, who is said to have spent £60,000 (equivalent now to approximately $3,000,000) in enlarging it. "The rooms," says Dugdale, were "of great state . . . all carried upon pillars and architecture of freestone, carved and wrought, as the

---

[1] See Dugdale's description in his *Warwickshire*.
[2] Dugdale saw it, of course, after further improvements had been made; but the passages quoted apply to the castle as it existed in Leicester's time.

like are not within this kingdom"; and "by the walls of the castle" gleamed a fair lake "containing one hundred and eleven acres."

In *Kenilworth*, Sir Walter Scott presents a vivid picture of the castle, with its towers, and courts, and battlements, and gardens, and "immense range of kitchens." He gives, too, a spirited account of the princely festivities with which Leicester there entertained Queen Elizabeth in July, 1575. The celebrations must have created great excitement in Stratford; and it is more than likely that William, then in his twelfth year, stood with the other boys of the town, an admiring spectator of the open-air pageants with which Leicester amused Her Majesty. Could the boys have been kept away when, as we are told, the arrival of the Queen was marked by such salvos of cannon and great display of fireworks that "the noise and flame were heard and seen thirty miles off"? Stratford was only about ten miles distant as the crow flies. At any rate, many scholars have found in one of the Kenilworth pageants the inspiration of Oberon's vision in *A Midsummer Night's Dream*.

Surely all these places with their storied past would make the youthful Shakespeare dream dreams of the glorious days gone by, and with their splendid present fire him with ambition to have a part in the activities of the great world outside of Stratford.

But in the exuberant years of boyhood he was occupied with other things than communing with the beauty of earth and sky, and dreaming dreams of the glorious past. He must have rejoiced in those village amusements common to the Merry England of Queen Bess's time, such as May-poles, bear-baitings, wakes, morris-dances, fairs,[1] and harvest-homes. And into those outdoor pastimes

[1] The name "Bull Ring" shows that there was in Stratford a place for animal baiting; and the village was famous for its fairs.

which are the peculiar heritage of the country-born lad he must have thrown himself with full enthusiasm. It cannot be doubted, for example, that he was devoted to the chase, and had the hunter's love for dogs and horses. The glowing accounts of such sport embedded in his earliest poem, *Venus and Adonis*, show this. Where can one find a more realistic and sympathetic description of the "timorous flying hare" swiftly pursued by "the hot, scent-snuffing hounds"? —

> By this, poor Wat, far off upon a hill,
> Stands on his hinder legs with listening ear.

Or where a more vivid description of a pack of hounds in full cry? —

> Another flap-mouth'd mourner, black and grim,
> Against the welkin volleys out his voice;
> Another, and another, answer him,
> Clapping their proud tails to the ground below,
> Shaking their scratch'd ears, bleeding as they go.

And this keenly sympathetic interest in sport appears in many of his plays; for example, in the description of the chase in *A Midsummer Night's Dream*, where the baying of the hounds leads Hippolyta to exclaim:

> Never did I hear
> Such gallant chiding: for, besides the groves,
> The skies, the fountains, every region near,
> Seem'd all one mutual cry. I never heard
> So musical a discord.

Such discord, it may be observed, would be musical only to the enthusiastic sportsman. And the same is true of the beauty of the dogs described by Theseus:

> My hounds are bred out of the Spartan kind,
> So flew'd, so sanded, and their heads are hung
> With ears that sweep away the morning dew;
> Crook-knee'd, and dew-lapp'd like Thessalian bulls;
> Slow in pursuit, but match'd in mouth like bells
> Each under each. A cry more tuneable
> Was never holla'd to, nor cheer'd with horn.

Any possessor of a hunting-dog — I speak from experience — will bear testimony to the natural and fully justified pride in the good hound Silver of *The Taming of the Shrew:*

> Saw'st thou not, boy, how Silver made it good
> At the hedge-corner in the coldest fault?
> I would not lose the dog for twenty pound.

Possibly Shakespeare was here embalming the memory of a real dog, for Silver appears again in *The Tempest:*

> Hey, Silver! There it goes, Silver!

His love for horses was not less conspicuous, and some of the most beautiful descriptions literature has of that noble animal have come from his enthusiastic pen. I have already spoken of his devotion to the quieter pastime of angling; and many writers have commented on his knowledge of hawking and deer-hunting. Not for a moment can it be doubted that he fully entered into all the outdoor sports that Warwickshire offered him.

Nor, in an age when the drama was the chief form of public amusement, were dramatic entertainments denied him. As has been suggested, he may have witnessed a part of the splendid pageants exhibited at Kenilworth in 1575. We are on surer ground, however, when we assert that he was a witness of the mystery plays annually presented at Coventry by the trade guilds on waggons moving in procession through the streets from station to station. The performance of these plays, ancestors of the modern drama, was a great event in the lives of the common people, and the citizens of the neighboring towns were especially invited to be present. The mysteries at Coventry were among the best in England, so famous indeed that in the seventeenth century mystery plays in general were vulgarly called "Coventry plays." [1]

[1] Hence Richard James, librarian to Sir Robert Cotton, when he received

Dugdale states that "the confluence of people from far and near to see that show was extraordinary great." On more occasions than one, probably, young William, with his father or with the other boys of the town, made his way thither, and stood the better part of the day in the open, watching one waggon after another as it rolled up, presented its story, and rolled away. The play which seems to have made the deepest impression upon him was that acted by the Guild of Shearmen and Taylors, in which Herod of Jewry took the leading rôle. This vain-glorious braggart was costumed in a most astounding fashion, with red gloves and "gorgeous array" —

> Brighter than the sun in the midst of the day.

At one point in the play his ravings became so violent that, according to the stage-direction, he leaped off the pageant-waggon into the crowd of spectators: "Here Herod rages in the pageant, and in the street also." To emphasize his anger he carried a large club stuffed with wool, with which he belabored all who came within range. Possibly on one occasion he bore down with all the terror of this club upon the future dramatist. At any rate Shakespeare never forgot the scene. Among the references to it in his plays we may note the following:

> What a Herod of Jewry is this! (*Merry Wives*, II, i, 20.)
>
> It out-herods Herod! (*Hamlet*, III, ii, 16.)
>
> To whom Herod of Jewry may do homage.
> (*Antony and Cleopatra*, I, ii, 28.)
>
> Herod of Jewry dare not look upon you
> But when you are well pleased. (*Ibid.*, III, iii, 3.)

Another scene in the same play that deeply affected him was the slaughter of the children by Herod's cruel sol-

---

for cataloguing a manuscript of mysteries of unknown origin, wrote on the fly-leaf: "*vulgo dicitur hic liber Ludus Coventriae, sive ludus Corporis Christi.*" Cf. also John Heywood's *Four PP*.

diers, when the women fought valiantly with pot-ladles and other "womanly geare." He refers to it in *Henry V* (III, iii, 41): "As did the wives of Jewry at Herod's bloody-hunting slaughtermen." Most of the Coventry mysteries have been lost, but luckily this particular play has been preserved, and from it we are able to judge how profoundly these crude representations stirred his boyish imagination.

But these amateur folk-performances, already regarded as antique and rapidly falling into decay, were not the only form of histrionic art that came to stimulate his latent dramatic genius; for in Stratford itself he was able on occasion to witness the newer drama as acted by the professional troupes before the Queen and the citizens of London. During his father's term as High Bailiff, in 1568, companies of London actors visited Stratford for the first time, the Queen's Players, the best in the kingdom, and the Earl of Worcester's Players, among the best. Upon their arrival they were offered the hospitality of the town, and allowed to play in the Guildhall. It was then customary to invite the players, thus received, to give their first performance [1] before the High Bailiff, or Mayor, to which all the city officials with their families and guests, and others,[2] were admitted free of charge, in return for which the actors were rewarded by the corporation. The records of Stratford show that by way of this reward John Shakespeare, as High Bailiff, presented the Queen's Players with 9s., and the Earl of Worcester's Players 1s.[3] In 1573 the town was visited by the Earl of Leicester's Players, in 1576 by the Earl of Worcester's

[1] They might give as many subsequent performances as they found profitable.

[2] Sometimes, however, the actors were allowed to take a gathering at the door from the rabble; see J. T. Murray, "English Dramatic Companies in the Towns," *Modern Philology*, ii, 543.

[3] The difference in the amount of the reward is to be accounted for in part by the difference in the rank of the players' patrons.

and the Earl of Warwick's Players, in 1577 by the Earl of Leicester's and the Earl of Worcester's Players, etc. On these notable occasions we may suppose that John Shakespeare, in both his official and private capacities, showed the actors such courtesies as he could, and that he took his little son William to witness their performances.

A person named Willis, born within a year of Shakespeare, has left us an account of "A stage-play which I saw when I was a child," that furnishes us with a good notion both of the type of plays then in vogue and the circumstances under which they were presented before the town officials:

In the city of Gloucester the manner is, as I think it is in other like corporations,[1] that when players of interludes come to town, they first attend the Mayor to inform him what nobleman's servants they are, and so to get license for their public playing. And if the Mayor like the actors, or would show respect to their lord and master, he appoints them to play their first play before himself and the Aldermen and Common Council of the city; and that is called the Mayor's play, where every one that will comes in without money, the Mayor giving the players a reward as he thinks fit to show respect unto them. At such a play my father took me with him, and made me stand between his legs as he sat upon one of the benches, where we saw and heard very well.

The play was called *The Cradle of Security*, wherein was personated a King or some great Prince [named Wicked-of-the-World], with his courtiers of several kinds, amongst which three ladies [Pride, Covetousness, and Luxury] were in special grace with him; and they, keeping him in delights and pleasures, drew him from his graver counsellors, hearing of sermons, and listening to good counsel and admonitions, that in the end they got him to lie down in a cradle upon the stage, where these three ladies joining in a sweet song rocked him asleep, that he snorted again; and in the meantime closely conveyed under the cloths wherewithall he was covered a vizard

---

[1] That Willis is correct in this supposition is beyond doubt; see J. T. Murray, *English Dramatic Companies 1558-1642*, vol. ii, Provincial Companies.

like a swine's snout upon his face, with three wire chains fastened thereunto, the other end whereof being holden severally by those three ladies; who fall to singing again, and then discovered his face that the spectators might see how they had transformed him, going on with their singing.

Whilst all this was acting, there came forth of another door at the farthest end of the stage two old men, the one [End-of-the-World] in blue with a serjeant-at-arms' mace on his shoulder, the other [Last Judgment] in red with a drawn sword in his hand and leaning with the other hand upon the other's shoulder. And so they two went along in a soft pace round about by the skirt of the stage, till at last they came to the cradle when all the court was in greatest jollity; and then the foremost old man [End-of-the-World] with his mace struck a fearful blow upon the cradle, whereat all the courtiers, with the three ladies and the vizard, all vanished; and the desolate Prince, starting up bare-faced, and finding himself thus sent for to judgment, made a lamentable complaint of his miserable case; and so was carried away by wicked spirits. . . .

This sight took such impression in me that when I came towards man's estate it was as fresh in my memory as if I had seen it newly acted.[1]

If this crude play was still so vivid in the mind of Willis at the age of seventy-five, we may infer that the plays acted in Stratford by the best of the London companies exercised a profound influence on the sensitive mind of the youthful Shakespeare. How important this was for his later development as a dramatist can be only a matter of surmise.

[1] R. Willis, *Mount Tabor. Or Private Exercises of a Penitent Sinner . . . Published in the year of his age 75, Anno Dom. 1639*, p. 110.

CHAPTER IV

SCHOOLING

SUCH evidence as we possess indicates that neither John Shakespeare nor Mary his wife was able to write. Yet the new age, under the influence of the Renaissance, was setting a high value on education,[1] and we may be sure that the Chief Alderman of the town saw to it that his son and heir profited by the really excellent opportunity which Stratford afforded its youth of acquiring book-learning. The local free grammar school had been in existence at least as early as 1424; in 1477 its master was able to boast the university degree of Bachelor of Arts; and in 1553, under the royal patronage of Edward VI, it was reorganized as "The King's New School of Stratford-upon-Avon," with an endowment, and a special provision that its master should receive a salary of not less than £20 per annum.[2] This handsome salary (it was double that paid to the Master of Eton[3]) enabled the citizens of Stratford to secure the best teachers, and to build up a school that compared favorably with those of Worcester,[4] Coventry, and even larger towns.

The first Stratford schoolmaster under whose tuition William may have come was Walter Roche, B.A. of Oxford, and Lancashire Fellow. In 1571 Simon Hunt, also B.A. of Oxford, and Fellow, seems to have been appointed to assist him, and probably had charge of the

---

[1] "Every one desireth to have his child learned," writes Dr. Mulcaster, headmaster of the Merchant Taylors' School.

[2] That this sum was regularly paid to the schoolmasters during Shakespeare's boyhood is shown by the Stratford records.

[3] The Master of St. John's College, Cambridge, asserted in 1561 that his university position had an annual value of only £12. See Bass Mullinger, *Cambridge from 1535 to the Accession of Charles*, i, 185.

[4] The schoolmaster at Worcester received a salary of only £10.

beginners. In 1574 Roche was assigned by Elizabeth to the rectory of Clifford Chambers, near Stratford; but he continued to reside in Stratford, and thus added to the scholarly resources of the town. Simon Hunt promptly succeeded Roche as master of the school, and held the position until 1577. It was from Hunt, therefore, that Shakespeare received most of his training. Hunt was followed by Thomas Jenkins, Oxford graduate and Fellow of his college, who failed, however, to give satisfaction, and was supplanted in 1579 by John Cotton, B.A. of Oxford.

The school-building, adjoining the ancient Guild Chapel, is preserved to-day in much the same condition as it was when William sat on its benches and gazed at the dingy beams of the timbered oak roof with carved bosses in the middle where they joined — for the school-rooms were on the second floor, reached by an outside tile-covered stairway of stone, now removed.[1]

A boy's education in the sixteenth century was begun at tender years. Charles Hoole writes: "It is usual in cities and greater towns to put children to school about four or five years of age, and in country villages, because of further distance, not till about six or seven."[2] In all

---

[1] It has been mistakenly assumed that in Shakespeare's day the school was held in the Guild Chapel. During John Shakespeare's term as High Bailiff, 1568, the town records show the expenditure of various sums for "repairing the school," "dressing and sweeping the school-house," "groundselling the old school, and taking down the sollar over the school." Obviously the school-house was then being put in better condition for the use of the students. It seems to have needed repairs again in 1595–6, for on February 14, 1596, the Town Council ordered that "School was not to be kept in the Chapel." The assumption that the school was regularly held in the Chapel is based solely on this last entry.

[2] *A New Discovery of the Old Art of Teaching School, The Petty School*, p. 1; cf. p. 23. This interesting book, though not printed until 1659 (the general title-page bears the date 1660), was written, as the title-page informs us, in 1636. The author was himself a country school-teacher, and describes the rules and the curriculum prevailing in England during the half century before he wrote. That the statements quoted from him apply to Shakespeare's day is abundantly shown by other evidence which cannot be so conveniently cited.

probability, then, at the age of six or seven, William took his place as a *petit* in the beginner's form,[1] and thus started on the weary road to learning.

As to the hours kept [2] and the regulations enforced in the Stratford school we have no definite evidence, but some notion of these may be gained by a study of the customs prevailing in similar schools elsewhere. John Brinsley, in *Ludus Literarius, or The Grammar Schoole* (1612), writes: "The school-time should begin at six"; Peacham, in *The Compleat Gentleman* (1622), notes the time of beginning as commonly "before six in the morning"; and Hoole likewise states: "In many schools I observe six o'clock in the morning to be the hour for children to be fast at their books." The statutes drawn up in 1561 for The Merchant Taylors' School in London, doubtless embodying the rules and regulations current in grammar schools of the day, specify that "the children shall come to the school in the morning at seven of the clock both winter and summer, and tarry there until eleven, and return again at one of the clock, and depart at five." Brinsley, who would begin school at six, tentatively suggests, as an innovation, that the pupils be allowed an intermission at nine o'clock of fifteen minutes, and, "to countervail the time of the intermission," be held until fifteen minutes after eleven. A similar brief intermission, he suggests, might be allowed at three, and the pupils held until five-thirty, "thereby in that half-hour to countervail the time at three." But the dismissal from studies was to be followed by the reading of a chapter from the Bible, the singing of a Psalm, and lastly "a

---

[1] "And in the first form shall be placed the young beginners, commonly called *petits*" — Statutes of the Guisborough Grammar School, Yorkshire, 1561.

[2] In *The Taming of the Shrew* Bianca protests:
I am no breeching scholar in the schools,
I'll not be tied to hours nor 'pointed times.

prayer to be used by the master." The school hours thus devised would extend from 6 A.M. until nearly 6 P.M. Even so, Brinsley feared lest the granting of the two brief intermissions might lead to "the reproach of the school" by parents who would complain that their sons did nothing but play.

The discipline with which these seriously-minded schoolmasters governed their pupils was commonly severe if not harsh. They taught with the book of knowledge open in one hand, and the rod menacingly poised in the other: [1]

> A domineering pedant o'er the boy,
> Than whom no mortal so magnificent.[2]

Roger Ascham, in his *Schoolmaster*, quotes the opinion of Sir William Peter, 1563, "that the rod only was the sword that must keep the school in obedience," to which Master Haddon, we are told, heartily agreed, with the observation that "the best schoolmaster of our time was the greatest beater." Beyond a doubt one of the best schoolmasters of the time was Nicholas Udall, headmaster of Eton and later of Westminster; and his reputation for using the rod was not less great than his fame as a classical scholar. Thomas Tusser records that on one occasion Udall gave him fifty-three strokes:

> For fault but small, or none at all,
> It came to pass that beat I was.

Henry Peacham, in *The Compleat Gentleman* (1622), says "I knew one who in winter would ordinarily on a cold morning whip his boys over, for no other purpose than to get himself a heat"; and he complains of the "immoderation, or rather plain cruelty," commonly used by school-

[1] The master is usually so represented in early woodcuts; see for example, the title-page of *Pedantius*, 1631.
[2] *Love's Labour's Lost*, III, i, 179–80; cf. also *I Henry VI*, I, i, 36; *Two Gentlemen of Verona*, II, i, 22; *Coriolanus*, III, ii, 116.

masters, who believe that "there is no other method of making a scholar than by beating him," with the result, as Peacham observes, that the master's "very name is hateful to the scholar, who trembleth at their coming in," and looks upon them "as his deadly enemies."

Unquestionably Shakespeare was drawing upon the memories of his boyhood when in *As You Like It* he describes —

> The whining schoolboy, with his satchel
> And shining morning face, creeping like snail
> Unwillingly to school.

Nor was he more enthusiastic when in *The Taming of the Shrew* he wrote:

> As willingly as e'er I came from school;

or in *Romeo and Juliet:*

> Love goes toward love as schoolboys from their books,
> But love from love, toward school with heavy looks.

And perhaps he wrote with special relish in *II Henry VI:*

> Thou hast most traitorously corrupted the youth of the realm in erecting a grammar school.

In view of this evidence we can hardly believe that in leaving the school after an arduous day he was careful to observe the instructions of the pious Francis Seager, who in his *Schoole of Virtue and Book of Good Nurture for Chyldren* (1577), urges his model pupil to walk sedately home, soberly, "with countenance grave," taking formal leave of his fellows, and courteously "free of cap" to all the elders he passes —

> Not running on heaps as swarms of bees,
> As at this day every man it now sees;
> Not using, but refusing, such foolish toys
> As commonly are used in these days, of boys,
> As hooping and hallowing as in hunting the fox.

William doubtless whooped and hallooed with the best,

for he was no prig, and his animal spirits were not to be suppressed by stupid rules of conduct drawn up by wrinkled age.

The curriculum through which he was put by his Stratford masters is reasonably well-known to us, for village grammar schools in this respect differed very little.[1] "The usual way to begin with a child," says Hoole, "when he is first brought to school is to teach him to know his letters in the horn-book."[2] This curious implement of education consisted of a single sheet of paper placed on a small wooden board, and protected by a thin sheet of transparent horn. The printed matter usually consisted of the sign of the cross (to promote piety), followed by the alphabet, first in small letters, then in capital letters; next the five vowels; next the simplest syllables; and finally (to end with piety), the Lord's Prayer. There was a handle by which to grasp the "book," often pierced with a hole through which a cord was run, enabling the pupil to hang it about his neck or tie it at his girdle.[3] Shakespeare's acquaintance with the horn-book is well attested in his plays, notably in *Love's Labour's Lost.*

From the mysteries of the horn-book, the scholar proceeded to the *A B C*, with the catechism. "The ordinary way to teach children to read is, after they have got some knowledge of their letters, and a smattering of some syllables and words in the horn-book, to turn them into *A B C*,

[1] On this topic consult Thomas Baynes, *Shakespeare Studies*, 1894; H. R. D. Anders, *Shakespeare's Books*, 1904; Foster Watson, *The Curriculum and Text-books of English Schools*, 1903, and *The English Grammar Schools to 1660*, 1909; Charles Hoole, *A New Discovery*, 1660; John Brinsley, *Ludus Literarius*, 1612.

[2] *Op. cit.*, p. 4. It is not necessary to suppose, as many scholars do, that John and Mary had to employ tutors to teach their son to read before he could be admitted into the school. Of the schoolmaster in *Love's Labour's Lost* it is said "he teaches boys the horn-book." Village schools nearly always provided for the instruction of beginners.

[3] See A. W. Tuer, *History of the Horn-book*, 1896.

or Primer."[1] Shakespeare's familiarity with the contents of the primer is revealed in *King John* (I, i, 195 ff.):

> "I shall beseech you," — that is *Question*, now.
> And then comes *Answer*, like an absey-book:
> "O, sir," says *Answer*, "at your best command;
> At your employment; at your service, sir."

And he may possibly be echoing an actual experience when in *The Two Gentlemen of Verona* (II, i, 23) he describes the forlorn lover as sighing "like a school boy that had lost his *A B C*."

At the same time he was taught to write by the use of a copy-book: "Fair as a text B in a copy-book," exclaims Katherine in *Love's Labour's Lost*. The style of writing employed in the Stratford school was what is now called the old English script, resembling in some respects German script. It differed in many ways from the Italian character which was then being gradually introduced into England, and which has since completely supplanted the older style. It is important to bear this difference in mind, for persons are apt to assume that because the signatures of Shakespeare are hard for them to read he must have written an illiterate hand. Quite the contrary is the case. The distinguished paleographer, Sir Edward Maunde Thompson, declares that Shakespeare wrote "the native English hand with nothing particularly characteristic in it to distinguish it," and he suggests that "Shakespeare had received a more thorough training as a scribe than has been thought probable."[2]

Immediately after acquiring some ability to read and write, the pupils were set to the study of Latin, for all Elizabethan schools, it should be remembered, were primarily schools for teaching Latin. The mastery of this language was accomplished with the aid of William

---

[1] Charles Hoole, *op. cit.*, p. 20.
[2] *Shakespeare's Handwriting*, 1916, pp. 54-55.

Lilly's famous *Grammatica Latina* (with a woodcut on the title-page of a large tree bearing luscious fruit, and small boys climbing up to gather from its branches), a book which for several generations before, and for many generations after, supplied the first classical nourishment to English schoolboys.[1] They were required to commit the whole of it to memory, whether they understood it or not; and as the plays of Shakespeare show, parts of this grammar he never forgot. In *The Merry Wives of Windsor* a country schoolmaster, Evans, quizzes a boy out of Lilly. It is curious, and possibly significant, that the boy bears the name of "William," and if for "Evans" we substitute the name "Hunt" we have the picture complete:

Evans. Come hither, William. Hold up your head; come.

Mrs. Paige. Come on, sirrah. Hold up your head. Answer your master. Be not afraid.

Evans. William, how many numbers is in nouns?

William. Two. . . .

Evans. What is "fair," William?

William. Pulcher. . . .

Evans. What is *lapis*, William?

William. A stone. . . .

Evans. What is he, William, that does lend articles?

William. Articles are borrowed of the pronoun, and be thus declined: *singulariter, nominativo, hic, haec, hoc.* . . .

Evans. What is your genitive case plural, William?

William. Genitive case?

Evans. Ay.

William. Genitive, *horum, harum, horum.*[2]

Along with the *Grammatica Latina* went the equally famous *Sententiæ Pueriles*, a collection of brief Latin sentences, likewise to be committed to "the ventricle of memory." Passages quoted in *Love's Labour's Lost* attest

[1] A reprint of this grammar will be found in the Shakespeare *Jahrbuch*, vols. xliv and xlv. As the authorized grammar its use was required.

[2] For other recollections of Lilly's grammar see *Love's Labour's Lost*, IV, ii, 82; V, i, 10; V, i, 84; *The Taming of the Shrew*, I, i, 167; *I Henry IV*, II, i, 104; *Much Ado*, IV, i, 22; *Twelfth Night*, II, iii, 2; *Titus Andronicus*, IV, ii, 20–23.

the poet's intimacy with the volume.[1] The entire instruction of the pupil, including the formal conversation with the teacher, was now conducted in the Latin tongue.

After acquiring the elements of Latin grammar and some facility in translating, the pupils were set to reading Æsop's Fables and Cato's Maxims, and, when somewhat more advanced, the Eclogues of Mantuanus, an Italian writer of the Renaissance whose Latin poems were greatly admired for their purity of style.[2] Shakespeare, who refers to him as "good old Mantuan," and who quotes from one of his eclogues —

> Fauste precor, gelida quando pecus omne sub umbra
> Ruminat,

seems to have had a genuine affection for him: "Old Mantuan, old Mantuan," he exclaims, "who understandeth thee not loves thee not!"[3] The study of Mantuanus was quickly followed by a reading of Virgil's Eclogues. Here for the first time Shakespeare came into contact with really great poetry, and he must have been deeply stirred by the majesty of the Virgilian verse, as was his contemporary Warwickshire friend and fellow-poet, Michael Drayton. My schoolmaster, writes Drayton, —

> First read to me honest Mantuan;
> Then Virgil's *Eglogues;* being entered thus
> Methought I straight had mounted *Pegasus,*
> And in his full career could make him stop,
> And bound upon Parnassus' by-cleft top.[4]

Of all the Latin authors studied, however, Shakespeare seems to have acquired the deepest affection for Ovid. In

---

[1] Its influence has also been traced in *The Two Gentlemen of Verona,* III, ii, 15, *Coriolanus,* V, iii, 141, and *Cymbeline,* III, v, 37.

[2] Battisto Spagnuoli, of Mantua. His Eclogues have been edited by W. P. Mustard, 1911, and well repay study.

[3] So likewise Drayton, in *The Owl:*

> O moral Mantuan! live thy verses long!
> Honour attend thee and thy reverend song!

[4] *To my most dearly-loved friend Henry Reynolds, Esquire,* ll. 36–40.

later years he was able to go back to him with pleasure, and to read him both in Latin and in Golding's excellent translation. He refers to Ovid more often than to any other ancient writer, and on the title-page of "the first heir" of his invention, *Venus and Adonis* (itself based on the *Metamorphoses*), he placed a graceful couplet chosen from this his favorite author.[1]

Nor were the Roman playwrights neglected. Terence, who, as Hoole observes, "of all the school authors we read doth deservedly challenge the first place," he could not well have omitted. And he seems to have read also Seneca and Plautus: "Seneca cannot be too heavy, nor Plautus too light," exclaims Polonius. The former probably did not much appeal to him, although Senecan influence is clearly marked in his tragedies.[2] Plautus must have delighted him more; the Plautine comedies gave him some of his early inspiration, and supplied him with the plot of his *Comedy of Errors*. Perhaps his familiarity with these authors went beyond a mere reading, for we know that in many schools the performance of a scene from Terence or Plautus was a weekly exercise.[3]

---

[1] There is preserved in the Bodleian Library at Oxford a copy of the 1502 Aldine edition of Ovid's *Metamorphoses* in Latin, bearing on the title-page just above the Aldine anchor the abbreviated signature "Wm Shre." Facing this title-page is the manuscript note: "This little Booke of Ovid was given to me by W. Hall, who sayd it was once Will. Shakesperes. T.N. 1682." This identity of "T.N." is unknown; the "W. Hall" may be the William Hall, an admirer of the poet, who visited Stratford in 1694, and wrote to a friend: "Dear Neddy, I very greedily embrace this occasion of acquainting you with something which I found at Stratford upon Avon. That place I came unto on Thursday night, and ye next day went to visit ye ashes of the Great Shakspear." The authenticity of the signature on the title-page cannot be asserted, yet various circumstances tend to indicate that it may be genuine. And in this connection we are reminded of a line in *Titus Andronicus*, IV, i, 42: "'T is Ovid's *Metamorphoses*; my mother gave it me."

[2] The influence of Seneca's philosophical works on Shakespeare has also been demonstrated.

[3] See W. H. Woodward in *The Cambridge History of English Literature*, iii, 429–30, and Foster Watson, *The English Grammar Schools*, pp. 319–24.

Other Latin works which he was made to read — if we may judge by the curriculum of similar schools — were the poems of Horace, the letters of Cicero (upon which he was required to mold an epistolary style), the colloquies of Erasmus, and possibly Sallust.

But quite as important as the curriculum in the sixteenth-century schools was the method of study. Fortunately for us Hoole has preserved a detailed account of exactly how village schoolmasters taught their pupils; and this account relates to the generation preceding his (i.e., to the days of Shakespeare), for he gathered his information, he tells us, by careful inquiry from various men taught by his predecessors in the profession. The passages that are quoted below may be a little tiresome in reading, but will abundantly repay any one who is interested in the subject of Shakespeare's education. Of the grammar school students of the late sixteenth century Hoole writes:

These were first put to read the Accidents [in Lilly's *Grammatica Latina*], and afterwards made to commit it to memory; which when they had done they were exercised in construing and parsing the examples in the English rules; and this was called the first form. . . .

The second form was to repeat the Accidents for Parts; to say forenoon's lessons in *Propria quæ maribus*, *Quæ genus*, and *As in præsenti*, which they repeated memoriter, construed, and parsed; to say an afternoon's lesson in *Sententiæ Pueriles*, which they repeated by heart, and construed, and parsed; they repeated their tasks every Friday memoriter, and parsed their Sentences out of English.

The third form was enjoyned first to repeat two parts together every morning, one out of the Accidents and the other out of that forementioned part of the Grammar; and together with their parts, each one was made to form one person of a verb Active in any of the four conjugations. Their forenoon's lessons were in Syntaxis, which they used to say memoriter; then to construe it, and parse only the words which contain the force of the rule. Their forenoon lessons were two days in Æsop's Fables and other two days in Cato; both which they construed and parsed, and said Cato memoriter: these lessons they translated into English, and repeated all on Fridays construing out of the translations into Latin.

The fourth form having ended Syntaxis, first repeated it and *Propria quæ maribus*, etc., together for parts, and formed a person of a verb Passive, as they did the Active before. For lessons they proceeded to the by-rules, and to Figura and Prosodia; for afternoon lessons they read Terence two days and Mantuan two days, which they translated into English, and repeated on Fridays as before [i.e., construing their English translations back into Latin].

The fifth form said one part in the Latin, and another in the Greek Grammar together. Their forenoon's lessons were in Butler's Rhetoric, which they said memoriter and then construed and applied the example to the definition. Their afternoon's lessons were two days in Ovid's Metamorphosis and two days in Tully's Offices, both which they translated into English. They learned to scan and prove verse in *Flores Poetarum;* and repeated their week's work on Fridays as before.

So Hoole proceeds to the sixth, seventh, eighth, and ninth forms. Whether in the fifth form Shakespeare acquired the little Greek of which Jonson speaks, we cannot say. His teachers, graduates of Oxford and Fellows of their colleges, were certainly able to give instruction in the language.

Although the curriculum was mainly concerned with the classics, pupils were commonly required to become familiar with the Bible [1] (in the Geneva version, which is very close to the King James's version). The young Shakespeare seems to have read with avidity the stirring histories contained within its pages, and he shows an intimate knowledge of both the Old and the New Testament. Probably more than any other single book it helped to mold his English style, and to supply him with the noble vocabulary he was later to use with such effectiveness.

[1] See Foster Watson, *The English Grammar Schools*, pp. 50–62.

How many books he had access to outside the school we do not know. Doubtless not many in his own home,[1] or in the home of his father's most intimate friends. On the other hand, from his schoolmasters, from his vicar, and from the homes of the better educated,[2] he could, were he so disposed, have borrowed books on various subjects, particularly chronicles, the Latin classics, a few romances, and innumerable theological treatises; and that he borrowed some we must believe, for in general unless the habit of reading is formed before the age of twelve it is not easily acquired in later life. We have no evidence, however, that at this early date he was a voluminous reader. Probably he found his chief pleasure in outdoor sports, and in "nature's infinite book," which in the regions about Stratford lay wide open before him in unusual attractiveness.

[1] That John Shakespeare on one occasion, at least, bought a book is shown by Mrs. Stopes, *Shakespeare's Environment*, p. 61.

[2] Mrs. Stopes, *Shakespeare's Environment*, p. 57, has shown that Stratford was by no means a bookless place.

CHAPTER V

APPRENTICESHIP AND MARRIAGE

WITH the passing of the years and the coming of his father's pecuniary troubles, the more serious problems of life began to close in upon the growing boy. It is generally asserted that he was taken from the Stratford free school "at an unusually early age," but of this there is no proof.[1] Master John Shakespeare was at no expense in keeping his son in the school, nor were his difficulties at first so distressing — the earliest indication of them appears in 1577 when William was beginning his fourteenth year — that he would have to sacrifice the education of his first-born. The likelihood is that William remained in the Stratford school until he completed, or nearly completed, the courses of study there provided. This would be at about the age of fourteen, when he began to "speak between the change of man and boy with a reed voice."

Upon finishing his schooling he was probably set to learn a trade,[2] for such was the common practice even among the better classes. Sir Thomas Elyot, in *The Governour* (Book i, Chapter xv), writes: "The aptest and most proper scholars, after they be well instructed in speaking Latin and understanding some poets, being taken from their school by their parents, and either be brought to the Court and made lackies or pages, or else

---

[1] Rowe clearly speaks without definite information on the subject. William's younger brother Gilbert was apparently well educated, for his signature to a conveyance in 1610 is an admirable specimen of handwriting; and Edmund, sixteen years younger, became a successful actor in London, showing that at least he could read.

[2] The customary age was fifteen. Cf. the case of the other Stratford boy, Richard Field, who after proper schooling, was apprenticed at the age of fifteen to a London printer, and later became eminent in his trade.

are bounden prentises." In the case of Shakespeare the latter course doubtless was followed.

Beyond this it is hardly safe to conjecture, although we must take cognizance of the several traditions, late and more or less untrustworthy, which have come down to us.

Rowe, who in writing his biography of the poet, 1709, gathered most of his information from the great actor Betterton [1] ("his veneration for the memory of Shakespeare having engag'd him to make a journey [about the year 1690] into Warwickshire on purpose to gather up what remains he could"), states that the poet's father took him into "his own employment." The same assertion is made by Aubrey, who likewise visited Stratford, about 1662, and interviewed some of Shakespeare's neighbors (so he is pleased to call them): "I have been told heretofore by some of the neighbours that when he was a boy he exercised his father's trade." We may suppose, then, that he entered his father's shop in Henley Street, and assisted in the manufacture and sale of gloves, and perhaps also in handling wool, yarn, and malt. This would seem the most natural course for him to pursue, for, as Halliwell-Phillipps observes, the eldest son "had a kind of prescriptive right to be brought up to his father's occupation."

But there was also a tradition in Stratford that he had been bound apprentice to a butcher. Dowdall, who made a journey into Warwickshire in 1693, and took occasion to write a long description of Shakespeare's monument in the Stratford church, added at the close of his description: "The clarke that shew'd me this church is above 80 years old; he says that this Shakespeare was formerly in this towne bound apprentice to a bucher." [2]

---

[1] "I must own," says he, "a particular obligation to him for the most considerable part of the passages relating to his life which I have here transmitted to the public."

[2] *Traditionary Anecdotes of Shakespeare*, 1838. The parish clerk at this

Aubrey on his earlier visit had also heard the same story, and secured two amusing, though far from convincing, anecdotes relating thereto: "When he killed a calf, he would do it in high style, and make a speech"; and "There was at that time another butcher's son in this town that was held not at all inferior to him for a natural wit, his acquaintance and coetanean, but died young." Thus, unless Aubrey interviewed the same loquacious "clarke" who showed Dowdall the church,[1] it seems that by the end of the century the tradition was fairly well-established in Stratford that as a boy Shakespeare had been apprenticed to the butcher's trade.

Aubrey, however, is absolutely alone in stating that Shakespeare's father was the butcher to whom William was apprenticed. The way in which he puts it suggests the possibility of his having drawn the inference himself by combining the two current traditions, first that William had entered his father's employment, and secondly that he had been apprenticed to a butcher. In order to reconcile these two stories, Aubrey, in his ignorance of John's real occupation, would necessarily draw the conclusion that the poet's father was the butcher referred to. That such was really the case, however, seems altogether unlikely. In the remarkably full records of Stratford, John Shakespeare is referred to many times, but in none

time, William Castle, was only sixty-five or sixty-six years old. It is hard to understand how Dowdall could have been so mistaken as to his age. Possibly some assistant to Castle, or some native guide, showed Dowdall over the church. Gray, in *Shakespeare's Marriage*, pp. 250–51, points out the possibility that J. P. Collier may have forged the letter. The manuscript, however, passed into the possession of Halliwell-Phillipps, who printed a facsimile of it, and never questioned its authenticity; see, for example, his *Outlines*, i, x–xi. And Castle may have seemed older to Dowdall than he actually was; in the Vestry Minute Book, under the date March 11, 1697, we read: "William Castle declared that hee was willing to resigne upp his sexton's place."

[1] Or, one might add, unless Collier forged the Dowdall letter, and drew the statement from Aubrey. But I see no good reason for questioning the authenticity of the Dowdall letter.

of the records is there the slightest indication to suggest that he was ever in any way connected with the butcher's trade.[1] In legal documents, too, both in Warwickshire and without, he is often alluded to, most commonly as a yeoman, sometimes as a glover, once as a whittawer, but never as a butcher. Furthermore, as Elton points out,[2] the trade of butcher was stringently regulated by statute, and John Shakespeare would not have been permitted lightly to enter upon the sale of raw meat; nor, if he were a tanner of leather, as is indicated in the legal document of 1573, and as would be quite natural in view of his occupation of glove-making, could he have been also a butcher, for the well-known Tanners' Act forbade all tanners of leather to have anything to do with the sale of meat.[3] Apparently, therefore, we are fully warranted in rejecting Aubrey's unsupported statement that John Shakespeare was a butcher.

But whether we can so confidently reject the tradition that William had been at some time "bound apprentice to a butcher" is doubtful; for it is quite possible that upon first leaving school he was taken by his father into the paternal glove-making establishment, and that later, as a result of the father's declining fortunes in that trade, his services were no longer needed, and he was set to the task of learning a more profitable trade.

If this interpretation of the two traditions be accepted, we may venture to go a step further and hazard the guess that John apprenticed his son to William Tyler, a butcher in Sheep Street. Tyler had prospered in his trade, and contemporaneously with John Shakespeare had succes-

---

[1] As Halliwell-Phillipps, well-qualified to speak with authority, observes: "If that had been the case, there would assuredly have been some allusion to the fact in the local records." (*Outlines*, ii, p. 329.)

[2] *William Shakespeare, His Family and Friends*, 1904, p. 350.

[3] Glovers and whittawers in Stratford were not even allowed to purchase skins before removal from the beasts. See Fripp, *op. cit.*, pp. xxxiii, xli.

sively held the offices of constable, affeeror, chamberlain, burgess, and alderman. John Shakespeare in his long association with Tyler in the management of the town's affairs (twice he assisted him in making out his report as Chamberlain) may have won the butcher's friendship, and have induced him to take William into his shop to learn the "mystery" of slaughtering calves. This may explain the poet's entry in the first draft of his will: "Item, I give and bequeath to Mr. Richard Tyler the elder xxvi*s*. viii*d*. to buy him a ring." Richard was the son of William Tyler, the butcher, and being approximately of the same age as the poet, may have been associated with him as a fellow apprentice. If so, we have here evidence of cordial relations existing between the youthful Shakespeare and his master's family.

But we should bear in mind that this is mere speculation, itself based on a late and untrustworthy tradition. It is safe only to say that after William was taken from school he was set to learn some occupation by which, now that he had lost his valuable Arden inheritances of Asbies and the Snitterfield farms, he could earn his future livelihood as a tradesman. Whether this occupation was that of glover, or butcher, is a detail of less importance.

We may, however, imagine Shakespeare during the next few years as an apprentice, busy all day at his trade, assisting his master in various tasks, and crying "What do you lack?" to the customers. Yet after folding away his apron he found time for courtship. And if his sympathetic understanding of love as revealed in his earliest plays, and his complete knowledge of lovers' ways, were derived from personal experience, we may suppose that his courtship was not without the glamour of romance. In the evenings and on Sundays he would stroll across the fields to a little group of houses called Shottery, lying about a mile from his home. and there meet Anne Hathaway. With an intellect far in advance of his years it is not strange that he should be attracted by a young lady who was seven or eight years his senior. Nor is it at all strange that after having won her heart, and perhaps plighted troth with her, he should delay marriage, for his position as an apprentice (if he were formally bound) did not allow him to take a wife, and his poverty would hardly justify so serious a step.

The young lady of his choice was the daughter of a well-to-do farmer, Richard Hathaway, of Shottery. That Richard was a substantial husbandman is clearly shown by his will which bequeathed in cash the unusual sum of £43 6s. 8d., and in addition left his farm, of about seventy-five acres, his house, and his "goods, movable and unmovable," to his wife, with the express provision that she allow his eldest son Bartholomew "the use, commodity, and profit of one-half yard land," or else pay him in cash £40. All this indicates that he was a person of means. And as bearing on his social standing it is worth notice that in his will he bequeathed his "body to be buried in the church, or church-yard" of Stratford. Burial within the church, it should be observed, was a distinction allowed only to the more important persons of the parish. His farmhouse, now popularly known as "Anne Hathaway's Cottage," is still to be seen at Shottery. During the centuries that have elapsed it has naturally undergone numerous alterations, yet it remains an excellent specimen of the farmhouses of the day, such as were occupied by the poet's grandfather at Snitterfield, and by his Uncle Harry.[1]

Doubtless the Shakespeare and Hathaway families,

[1] The house, which, with its accompanying land had long been in the possession of the Hathaways, remained in the possession of the family until 1838. It is now the property of the Birthplace Trustees, and has been restored to something like its original state for the benefit of the thousands of tourists who annually make their way to Stratford.

living close together in a small community, were intimately acquainted with each other; the senior members may have been on friendly terms — at least we find John Shakespeare in 1561 acting as bail, and also it seems as security, for a Richard Hathaway in two separate suits brought against him in the Stratford courts; and the probability should not be ignored that William had known Anne all his life. Her father died in 1582,[1] leaving her [2] the conventional dowry of ten marks, the same sum that Robert Arden bestowed on his daughter Mary. A few months later she became the wife of William Shakespeare, then in his nineteenth year.

The circumstances under which the marriage was contracted were somewhat unusual, and have given rise to much curious speculation. Briefly stated, the facts are that Shakespeare and Anne were married, not with the conventional thrice-asking of the banns, but, through a special license from the Bishop of Worcester, after only one asking of the banns; and that a child was born to them six months later. Some scholars, unfamiliar with the usages of the time, have presented the case in a very unfavorable light, representing the young William as sowing his wild oats, and Anne as a woman of easy morals; and they have inferred, without properly considering the evidence, that the friends of the Hathaway family applied for the license on their own initiative, and forced William to marry the woman he had compromised.

Such an interpretation of the case obviously stains the reputation of both William and Anne. But "good name in man and woman," as the poet warns us, "is the immediate jewel of their soul," and we should not attempt to

---

[1] His will was proved on July 9, 1582.

[2] In his will he calls her "Agnes," a variant of "Anne," and the variant that Richard Hathaway himself used, for he so designates the daughter of his brother Thomas, who was baptized with the name "Anne" (see the Stratford register of baptisms).

filch this without the most careful examination of the evidence. Fortunately an English scholar, Mr. J. W. Gray, well qualified for the task, has made an exhaustive study of all the facts involved, and in his book entitled *Shakespeare's Marriage* (1905), has completely freed the poet from many false surmises injurious to his reputation. It remains for the biographer only to summarize the results which Mr. Gray has presented with admirable clearness, and substantiated with abundant documentary evidence.

In order to approach the matter fairly, it is necessary first to realize that in the days of Elizabeth marriages were often effected in a way now unfamiliar to us. A contract of marriage could then be entered into with little formality, and no official record; all that was required was the verbally expressed agreement of the two parties in the presence of witnesses. This simple procedure constituted a formal betrothal, and such a betrothal was for ever binding. It gave each party a legal claim to the completion of the ceremony before the ecclesiastical authorities, and rendered invalid the marriage of either to another person.[1] Accordingly, a formal troth-plight was often supposed to carry with it the full privilege of marriage, a privilege which, if used, constituted what Bishop Cranmer called "perfect matrimony before

[1] The plays of the day give abundant evidence of the moral and legal validity of the betrothal; on this point one could not do better than read *The Miseries of Enforced Marriage* (1607), written by George Wilkins, and acted by Shakespeare's troupe at the Globe. The key-passage to the whole plot may here be quoted. The hero, having made a troth-plight with Clare by saying, "This hand thus takes thee as my loving wife," and acknowledging the fact to a third person who subsequently entered, declares (Act I, Scene i):

> Such power hath faith and troth 'twixt couples young,
> Death only cuts that knot tied with the tongue. . . .
> I have done so much that, if I wed not her,
> My marriage makes me an adulterer,
> In which black sheets I wallow all my life,
> My babes being bastards, and a whore my wife.

God." The law itself recognized this privilege by declaring legitimate the offspring of such a contract, even though no further ceremony were performed. In many cases — the records of them are abundant — the final sanction of the Church was not sought until the contracting parties were ready to live before the world as husband and wife, or until the imminent birth of a child [1] rendered the ecclesiastical ceremony desirable.

In the case of Shakespeare and Anne Hathaway it is only fair for us to assume the possibility of their having entered into a troth-plight. Evidence, to be sure, we have none; and we could expect none, for such contracts were never made a matter of record. Yet the forming of such contracts being a wide-spread custom, we should grant the possibility, if not the probability, that the youthful apprentice, realizing his temporary inability to support a wife, entered into a troth-plight with Anne, with the sincere intention — later carried out — of securing in due time the sanction of the Church. If he took advantage of the privileges such a contract was supposed to give, it could not have offended the moral sensibilities of the Stratford folk; [2] as Halliwell-Phillipps puts it: "No question of morals would in those days have arisen, or could have been entertained." Such a procedure, in harmony with the usage of the day, explains simply and naturally all that follows.

Exactly when the betrothal was entered into — assuming that a betrothal existed — it is impossible to say, for, as just stated, betrothals were not a matter of record. But near the close of November, 1582, Anne revealed to William the fact that the Church ceremony, completing the marriage, should be performed without delay. This,

---

[1] The registers of the marriages and births at Stratford are eloquent on this point.

[2] How common the practice was in Stratford may be discovered by examining the marriage and birth registers of the village.

as it chanced, presented a difficulty — a difficulty, however, that could be surmounted with slight effort and a trifling expense. Normally the ecclesiastical ceremony would be performed after three askings of the banns on three separate Sundays or holy-days. But a special law of the Church forbade the asking of banns, or the performance of the marriage ceremony, during the period falling between Advent Sunday and the Octave of Epiphany. In 1582 this period of prohibition began on December 1 and ended on January 13, 1583, in effect making it impossible for William and Anne to celebrate their marriage after the usual manner without the lapse of over two months. For obvious reasons Anne did not care to wait so long.

The Church, however, made a special provision by which marriages might be accelerated. In return for a small clerk's fee, 3*s.* 8*d.*, the Bishop of the diocese could issue a license permitting the ceremony to be performed after only one asking of the banns. The granting of such licenses was by no means uncommon; in the year that Shakespeare made his application, the register of the diocese records no fewer than ninety-eight, and the register, it has been shown, is often far from complete.[1]

The Bishop, however, had to be shown a satisfactory reason for granting the license, and he had to be duly protected from any abuse of the privilege. At this time the Bishop of Worcester, in whose diocese William and Anne lived, was no other person than John Whitgift, famous for rigorous discipline, the suppression of abuses, and the introduction of reforms. Before granting a license he probably required, as Gray shows from an examination of many records, first, an "allegation," sworn to by the applicant, stating that the parents or guardians of both contracting parties gave their consent to the marriage,

---

[1] For example, in 1573 forty-five bonds were filed, but only two licenses were recorded in the registers.

and clearly setting forth the reason why the customary triple publication of the banns was to be dispensed with; secondly, a "bond" to guarantee the accuracy of the allegation, and indemnify the Bishop in case of any suit or difficulty arising out of the grant of the license; thirdly, a "letter" from some person of standing, known to the Bishop or to his officials, vouching for the contracting parties, and certifying to the fact that no impediment to the marriage existed. Upon the satisfactory presentation of these documents, and the payment of the required clerk's fee, a license would readily be issued, addressed to the clergyman of the church in which the ceremony was to be performed.

From the foregoing evidence it is apparent that William could not have secured the license without the express consent of his father. Such consent, writes Gray, "was regarded as one of the most important of the precautions then taken against carelessness, collusion, or fraud"; and in this particular case it was doubly necessary, for William, not being of age, was in the eyes of the law an infant. Gray's summary is emphatic: "It is almost certain, in view of the reasons already stated, that the license could not have been obtained without it, unless John Shakespeare were mentally incapacitated," a supposition which, as Gray observes, "is absolutely untenable." Moreover, besides giving evidence of the consent of his father, William would be required clearly to set forth the reason why a license was sought, and such, declares Gray, "would be subjected to full investigation, and the control being in such firm hands [as Whitgift's], evasion or fraud would have but little chance of remaining undetected." Finally, he would have to deposit with the Bishop a bond for the sum of £40, signed by men whose pecuniary resources made them acceptable to the Church officials.

With this general explanation of the machinery by which Bishop Whitgift was accustomed to grant licenses, we are prepared to turn to an examination of Shakespeare's case.

Desiring to marry Anne before the imminent Period of Prohibition would delay them unduly, he followed the well-accepted custom of the day, and applied to the proper ecclesiastical officers of his diocese for a license to marry after only one publication of the banns. His application being satisfactorily supported with the necessary documents, the license was promptly issued without objection.

Of the various documents involved in this rather commonplace transaction most have quite naturally been lost. We should be glad to have the formal "allegation" and the "letter," but it was not the custom at Worcester to give permanent housing to these documents, which having already served their purpose had no further value. The clerk merely made a record of the granting of the license, and carefully filed away in safe-keeping the bond which protected the Bishop in case of any suits at law. And both of these have come down to us.

The bond was not signed by William's father, probably for the simple reason that at this time he was known to be in pecuniary straits, and his name would not, perhaps, be regarded by the officers of the Church as satisfactory for so large a sum.[1] Instead, two friends of Anne Hathaway affixed their signatures, Fulk Sandells and John Richardson. The former had been named one of the supervisors of the will of Richard Hathaway, who described him as "my trusty friend and neighbor"; the latter served as one of the witnesses of the will, and was likewise a neighbor

---

[1] The very sum, it will be observed, which he was unable to pay for the redemption of Asbies.

and friend.[1] The bond, dated November 28, 1582, runs in part as follows:

The condition of this obligation is such that if hereafter there shall not appear any lawful let or impediment by reason of any precontract, consanguinity, affinity, or by any other lawful means whatsoever, but that William Shakespeare on the one party and Anne Hathaway of Stratford, in the diocese of Worcester, maiden, may lawfully solemnize matrimony together, and in the same afterwards remain and continue like man and wife, according unto the laws in that behalf provided; and, moreover, if there be not at this present time any action, suit, quarrel, or demand, moved or depending before any judge ecclesiastical or temporal, for and concerning any such lawful let or impediment; and moreover, if the said William Shakespeare do not proceed to solemnization of marriage with the said Anne Hathaway without the consent of her friends; and, also, if the said William do upon his own proper costs and expenses defend and save harmless the right reverend Father in God, Lord John, Bishop of Worcester, and his officers, for licensing them, the said William and Anne, to be married together with once asking of the banns of matrimony between them, and for all other causes which may ensue by reason or occasion thereof, that then the said obligation to be void and of none effect, or else to stand and abide in full force and vertue.[2]

As Gray shows, there is nothing unusual about this document, which throughout is couched in the terms conventional with the Worcester bonds. Nor is the absence of any reference to the consent of John Shakespeare significant, for a study of the records proves that at this time "no special condition providing for the consent [of the parents or guardians] in the case of either of the parties

[1] Could it be that they were the witnesses before whom the betrothal had been made? That would explain their present interest, and would justify them in signing the bond.

[2] Detractors of Shakespeare have tried to make much of the fact that the seal to this bond bore the initials "R. H.," presumably from the seal ring of Richard Hathaway. Gray, however, shows that the initials are really "R. K." and that "the seal was in common use at the Registry for several years."

was inserted in the Worcester bonds"; it was not until seven years later that the consent of the parents or guardians of the bridegroom was first included. Hence those biographers who draw the inference that the marriage was arranged without the knowledge or consent of Shakespeare's father err in ignorance of the usage at Worcester.

The signing of the bond was followed by the delivery of the license addressed to the particular clergyman who had been selected to perform the ceremony. This license, which had to be retained by the clergyman, has not, of course, been preserved. But the Bishop's clerk entered in the Registers a brief record of the issuance of the license at Worcester. These entries, it seems, were made "from a temporary memorandum, or from the allegation" which had been submitted by the applicant, and therefore in the hands of the careless clerk were subject to frequent errors of a minor sort. The clerk's record of Shakespeare's license, entered under the date of November 27, 1582, runs as follows:

Item, eodem die similis emanavit licencia inter W^m. Shaxpere et Annam Whateley de Temple Grafton.

The fact that the clerk dates the issuance of the license November 27, whereas the bond bears the date of November 28, presents no difficulty, "for on comparing the two series of documents [the bonds, and the clerk's entries in the register] for the years 1582 and 1583, it is found that out of 166 bonds executed during that period, 45 are dated after the register entry." If in the case of Shakespeare the clerk was basing his entry on the allegation, we may suppose that the allegation had been drawn up in Stratford on the day before the parties came to Worcester for the license, and therefore bore the date of November 27. The bond itself, however, was executed in Worcester, and thus is to be considered the more authoritative evidence as to the date when the license was actually granted.

The appearance of the name "Anne Whateley" for "Anne Hathwey" presents a more serious difficulty, yet lends itself to explanation. It has been shown that the clerk, writing in Latin, often made errors in proper names; for example, "Baker" for "Barbar," "Darby" for "Bradley," "Edgcock" for "Elcock." In this particular case his error may have been the result of a simple *lapsus mentis*, for throughout 1582 and 1583 he was much occupied with the name "Whatley," and on November 27 the Consistory Court dealt with the suit of a William Whatley against Arnold Leight.[1] The confusion in the clerk's mind might have been occasioned by the writing of the name "William" Shakespeare, subconsciously suggesting the name "William" Whateley; or the confusion may have come through the similarity in sound between "Whatley" and "Hathwey";[2] or it may have been caused by the resemblance between the two names as closely written, "Annam hathwey" readily appearing to the careless and hurried eye as "Anna whatley"[3] through the similarity of "m h" and "wh." However the mistake originated, there can be little doubt that the register entry refers to the license issued to Shakespeare. There is no other record of the issuance of the license to William and Anne; there is no bond for a license to an Anne Whateley; and it is hardly probable that at the same time a second William Shakespeare applied to the same clerk for a license to marry a woman with the same name, Anne.

[1] The records of which he was probably writing up at the same time he was recording the Shakespeare license.

[2] If, as Gray suspects, the clerk transcribed the entry from a rough memorandum jotted down from a verbal statement of the names, the mistake is naturally explained.

[3] In the Worcester record the entry appears "Annā Whateley."

The third and last difficulty which scholars have found in the register entry is the mention of Temple Grafton, a small village four or five miles from Stratford. Yet this difficulty too finds a plausible explanation. As is well-known, Shakespeare's marriage to Anne did not take place in the Stratford parish, the registers of which have been carefully preserved. Yet the canon law required that a marriage under the authority of a license should be celebrated "in the parish church or chapel where one of them dwelleth, and in no other place." In the great majority of the licenses granted at Worcester the ceremony was designated to take place in the parish in which the bride was living; and this was the proper procedure. John Johnson, in *The Clergyman's Vade-Mecum* (1709), writes: "'Twas an ancient custom, and a very good one, that a marriage should be performed in no other church but that to which the woman belonged as a parishioner; and therefore to this day the Ecclesiastical Law allows a fee due to the curate of that church whether she be married there or not." And Gray has discovered from his exhaustive study of the Worcester records "that the terminal place-name in the list of marriage licenses was in all cases intended as the residence of the bride." Thus we can hardly escape the inference that Temple Grafton was then the residence of Anne, that the license was addressed to the curate of that church, and that the marriage ceremony was there performed.

We may suppose that after the death of her father, Anne, not caring to live with her stepmother (the phraseology of Richard Hathaway's will clearly suggests a coldness between the children of his first wife and their stepmother), went to reside with relatives or friends at Temple Grafton.[1] This would explain why the clerk issued the license to the curate there, why the ceremony was not

---

[1] Possibly Anne's mother had come from Temple Grafton.

performed in Stratford, and, since the marriage registers of the Temple Grafton church have been lost, why no record of the marriage has ever been discovered in the various other parishes of the diocese. It is true that Sandells and Richardson in their bond referred to Anne as of the parish of Stratford, but they would naturally think of Shottery as her home.

Presumably, therefore, on November 30 — Saint Andrew's Day — the banns were proclaimed at the door of the Temple Grafton church, and immediately afterwards the ecclesiastical ceremony was performed.

Thus there is no reason to suppose that the marriage was not one of true love; nor are there any grounds for the theory, largely based on a misinterpretation of the marriage license, that Anne failed to make a good wife to her actor-husband under conditions not of the best. [1] Contrary to the general belief, he seems to have had her with him in London until he was able to provide for her and himself a fine home in Stratford; and at an early date he withdrew from the pleasures of a brilliant career in the city to spend his time quietly with his family. Moreover, Mrs. Shakespeare seems to have been an affectionate mother, deeply loved by her children. The inscription placed by them over her body breathes the utmost tenderness. And if we may accept the adage of "like mother, like daughter," we find some evidence of her character in the epitaph inscribed to Susanna, whose rearing was almost wholly in her hands:

> Then, passenger, ha'st ne're a tear
> To weep with her that wept with all?
> That wept, yet set herself to cheer
> Them up with comfort's cordiall.

---

[1] Any attempt to prove that Shakespeare's marriage was unhappy by quoting passages from his plays is exceedingly perilous; for, as Sir Philip Sidney warns us, "the poet nothing affirmeth."

> Her love shall live, her mercy spread,
> When thou hast ne're a tear to shed.

All the definite evidence we have, slight though it be, points to that harmony of married life so eloquently expressed by the poet in his *Sonnets*,[1] and generally represented in his plays.

[1] Note especially Sonnet 8.

CHAPTER VI

DEPARTURE FROM STRATFORD

AFTER his marriage to Anne Hathaway, William, then in his nineteenth year, brought his bride, who was twenty-six, to the crowded little home in Henley Street. And there, six months later, in May, 1583, a daughter was born to them, who was baptized in the Stratford church with the name Susanna. A year and nine months later Mrs. Shakespeare presented her youthful husband with twins, a boy and a girl. Shakespeare took them to the Stratford church, and christened them Hamnet and Judith, after his friend Hamnet Sadler and Hamnet's wife Judith. Thus he had ceased to be what Bagehot characterizes as "an amateur in life," and was called upon to assume the vexing problems and responsibilities of the paterfamilias.

But how was he to provide for his wife and children? We may suppose that for a time he continued to work as an apprentice on small wages or none. Yet the pecuniary embarrassment of John Shakespeare could hardly have been helped by the coming of a second family to his home; nor could William expect to remain indefinitely in the crowded little Henley Street house, now taxed beyond its capacity by his father, his mother, his brothers, and his sister, besides himself, his wife, and his three children. The fact must have been painfully obvious to him as he approached his majority that, having given hostages to fortune, he was under the necessity of finding some employment which would enable him to support his present station in life. It is not strange, therefore, that when he was about twenty-one years of age he left the shelter of the parental roof. The record of the baptism of his twins in 1585 is the last trace we find of him or of his wife and children in Stratford until years later, when he had become one of the most successful authors in the metropolis, and was able to return to his native town and purchase as his residence its finest mansion.

The circumstances of his departure from Stratford, beyond what has just been said, are unknown to us. Yet tradition, quite naturally, has sought to embellish with interesting anecdotes this most critical step in his career, leading, as it did, to subsequent wealth and fame. Two stories have been told, both of late origin, the one contradicting the other, and neither worthy of acceptance.

The earlier story is attributed to the gossipy Stratford "clarke" who showed Dowdall about the church in 1693: "He says that this Shakespeare was formerly in this town bound apprentice to a butcher, but that he run from his master to London, and there was received into the playhouse as a serviture." There is nothing to support this naïve and commonplace anecdote of the "runaway apprentice." In 1585 Shakespeare had attained his majority; and if he had been formally bound apprentice at the age of fourteen, his seven years' term of service had expired. Nor is it likely that after he was the head of a family he "ran away from his master," schoolboy fashion; or that he so lightly abandoned his wife and three children, a point quite ignored by the clerk. The story bears every evidence of having been the product of a guide's obliging, but not very fertile, imagination.

The second story relates that Shakespeare was caught poaching for deer on the estate of Sir Thomas Lucy, and was driven from Stratford by the harsh persecutions of that irate gentleman. The anecdote has taken a strong hold upon the imagination of the public, probably because it represents the youthful Shakespeare as a victim of rancor, torn from his family, driven out of his native town, and, like the hero in popular juvenile stories, ultimately rising thereby from an obscure career as a butcher in Stratford to a brilliant career as a man of letters in London. It is a pity to dispel this pretty romance, yet the evidence does not justify us in accepting it.

We need not, be it said at the outset, seek to discredit the story through any sentimental desire to protect the reputation of the poet. In the sixteenth century, as every one knows who is familiar with the literature of the age, no odium attached to deer-stealing. It was, indeed, as the author of the play *The Wizard* called it, a "gentleman-like" sport; even the high-minded Sir Philip Sidney characterized it as "a pretty service." John Davies of Hereford expresses the general opinion in the following terms:

> Some colts (wild youngsters), that ne'er broken were,
> Hold it a *doughty deed* to steal a deer.
> If cleanly they come off, they *feast* anon,
> And say their prey is good fat venison;
> If otherwise, by them it doth appear
> That that which they have stolen then is dear.[1]

The more spirited students at the not distant University of Oxford were especially fond of the sport; many a distinguished clergyman, we are told, looked back with keen relish upon the poaching escapades of his student-days; and one contemporary records that he regretted all his life having been denied such a desirable part of a youth's education. Shakespeare himself exclaims in *Titus Andronicus*: "What! hast not thou full often struck a doe, and borne her cleanly by the keeper's nose?" The most abject apologists, therefore, might readily grant that in his youth William, with the other colts of the village, sometimes engaged in this laudable pastime.

It is on other grounds that we must reject the story.

[1] *Wit's Bedlam*, 1617, Epigram 93.

One objection is the lateness of the tradition. Nothing is heard of it in the early records of Stratford gossip. It was apparently unknown to the old Elizabethan theatrical manager Beeston, who gave an entirely different account of the poet's doings before coming to London. It was unknown to those "neighbors" at Stratford to whom Aubrey, about 1662, applied for just such information. It was unknown to the gossipy literary circles in London which Aubrey haunted for many years in search of biographical anecdotes. It was unknown to the garrulous clerk who showed Dowdall about the church in 1693 and explained the poet's departure from Stratford on an altogether contradictory score. It was unknown to the Reverend William Fulman, who died in 1688 leaving an important manuscript containing jottings on the life of Shakespeare. The story, indeed, makes its appearance about the beginning of the eighteenth century, long after Shakespeare, and Sir Thomas Lucy, and all who might supposedly be informed on the matter, had passed away.

The first record of it came about in the following manner. When the Reverend William Fulman died in 1688, his manuscript, containing brief notes on the lives of various poets, including Shakespeare, came into the hands of the Reverend Richard Davies, vicar of Sapperton, in Gloucestershire. Davies, at some date before 1708, made various additions of a trivial and usually inaccurate sort to the notes left by Fulman. To the account of Shakespeare he added: "Much given to all unluckinesse in stealing venison and rabbits, particularly from Sir . . . Lucy, who had him oft whipt, and sometimes imprisoned, and at last made him fly his native country, to his great advancement; but his revenge was so great that he is his Justice Clodpate [Davies means Justice Shallow], and calls him a great man, and that, in allusion to his name, bore three lowses rampant for his arms."

It is not difficult, I think, to discover how this story came into existence a hundred years after the play was written, and at a time when Shakespeare's comedies were being widely read. Justice Shallow had been created in *II Henry IV* to serve as a whetstone for Falstaff's wit, and to fill out the humorous sub-plot now that Prince Hal was dedicated to more serious purposes. As a satire on country justices the stupid "starveling" won unbounded applause, even rivaling the fat Falstaff in popular favor, and becoming almost at once proverbial. When Queen Elizabeth ordered Shakespeare to continue the comic vein of *Henry IV* in another play, and represent Falstaff as falling in love, he produced *The Merry Wives of Windsor* to please Her Majesty. According to a well-founded tradition he wrote in great haste, completing the comedy in fourteen days so that the Queen might have it acted at Windsor before the end of the Christmas holidays. Naturally he made use of the character of Justice Shallow, which, having already achieved great popularity, stood ready to his hand; and in the first scene of the play he laughs at Shallow's ancient coat of arms by punning on the similarity in the pronunciation of the word "luce," a fish of the pike family frequently used in heraldry,[1] and the word "louse," the body-pest which furnished Elizabethan playwrights with innumerable jests. The passage appears in the opening lines of the play, where its vulgar and obvious humor would serve the necessary purpose of catching the attention of the groundlings:[2]

Slender. All his successors gone before him hath done't; and all his ancestors that come after him may. They may give the dozen white luces in their coat.
Shallow. It is an old coat.

---

[1] For example, in the arms of the Way and Geddes family, and the arms of the Company of Stockfishmongers.
[2] Such was Shakespeare's use; cf. the opening lines of *Romeo and Juliet.*

Evans. The dozen white louses do become an old coat well; it agrees well, passant. It is a familiar beast to man, and signifies love.[1]

Now it happens that the coat of arms of Sir Thomas Lucy, in canting fashion, showed three luces. Possibly in Warwickshire, where the Lucys were unpopular with certain classes, the country-people were accustomed to jest about the "louses" on the coat of Sir Thomas. Shakespeare may have remembered this jest, and have made use of it in the opening catch-attention lines of *The Merry Wives* — but with the "patible difference" of twelve for three, and without any thought that his London audiences would connect the jest with the provincial Lucy family in Warwickshire. Indeed, if the London and Court audiences (for by tradition the play was originally composed for the Court) were tempted to identify the "twelve white luces" with any real coat of arms, they would more naturally do so with the well-known coat, quarterly of four grand quarters, of the Earl of Northampton, which displayed twelve "lucies hauriant argent." But Shakespeare could have had no such fear, for by no stretch of the imagination could the portrait of Justice Shallow be taken as a satirical portrait of Northampton.

Nor by any stretch of the imagination could it be regarded as a satirical portrait of Sir Thomas Lucy. There is not the slightest similarity between the stupid country justice pictured with full details in *II Henry IV* and in *The Merry Wives* — a penurious bachelor, without title or influential friends, a toady seeking an introduction through Falstaff to Court and government circles — and the aristocratic master of Charlecote — a married man, a Knight (and, it may be added, with a son who enjoyed the like title), Sheriff of Warwickshire and Worcester-

---

[1] The jest is very common; see *Dr. Faustus*, I, iv: "They are too familiar with me already."

shire, and an energetic member of Parliament on terms of familiarity with many distinguished noblemen. If Shakespeare cherished a grudge against Sir Thomas deep enough to have rankled so long, and desired at last to square accounts, surely he would have introduced some points of resemblance, or at least would not have rendered his portrait of Justice Shallow so different in essential details as to make the identification well-nigh impossible. One example must suffice to illustrate. The chief physical characteristic of Shallow is his astonishing thinness of body — a "starveling," "the very genius of famine," so lank that "his dimensions to any thick sight were invincible," he beat John a Gaunt's own name, "for you might have thrust him, and all his apparel, into an eelskin." [1] Yet the effigy of Sir Thomas Lucy in the Charlecote Church shows that he was, if not stout, at least of goodly proportions. Indeed, it may be said that Justice Shallow is no more like Sir Thomas Lucy than — to complete the comparison imposed by the tradition — Sir John Falstaff is like Shakespeare.

Moreover, if Shakespeare felt a strong personal resentment at Sir Thomas, he would naturally, we may think, have taken his revenge earlier. *I Henry VI*, revised in 1594–95 and again in 1598–99, gave him a pat opportunity, for among the *dramatis personæ* is Sir William Lucy, an ancestor of the Lucys of Charlecote; yet he treats this representative of the family with great respect. It is hard to believe that the mature Shakespeare, in the midst of his greatest successes in London, would have attacked an old man then living far away in retirement, and within a few months of his death. It is equally hard to believe that he would allow private animosities to stalk unblushingly

---

[1] Does not this clearly reveal Shakespeare's purpose to make Shallow serve as an effective dramatic foil to the corpulent Falstaff, rather than to serve his own ends in personal invective?

through two of his most genial plays, for it was his custom to avoid the popular hatreds of the day which so often sully the work of contemporary dramatists. Sir Sidney Lee, who would have us believe that the poet is here attacking Sir Thomas, is careful to point out that in *I Henry VI* not Shakespeare but George Peele, the original author, is to be held responsible for the vilifying of Joan of Arc under the sway of Anti-Romanism, and that in revising *King John*, Shakespeare took pains to eliminate "the narrow polemical and malignant censure of Rome and Spain which disfigures the earlier play." Shakespeare was too great an artist to admit into his canvases ungracious attacks upon nations or creeds, and, we may suppose, upon private individuals or personal enemies. But, even granting that at this late date he was bent on revenge, and that to get it he was willing to sacrifice his well-established artistic principles, it is hard to see how he could hope for much satisfaction through *The Merry Wives*, for he was not writing for publication, the London audiences could not be expected to understand the allusion, and there was small, or no, likelihood that the play would be performed in Stratford.

Yet some scholars have asserted that Justice Shallow, in both *II Henry IV* and *The Merry Wives*, is "beyond doubt" a satirical attack on the owner of Charlecote. The ablest champion of this opinion, Sir Sidney Lee, presents the following as his most effective argument: "A 'luce' was a full-grown pike, and the meaning of the word fully explains Falstaff's contemptuous mention of the garrulous country justice as 'the old *pike*.'" The passage referred to (*II Henry IV*, III, ii, 323–25) was spoken in soliloquy by Falstaff when making up his mind to victimize the stupid justice in order to reline his purse: "If the young dace be a bait for the old pike, I see no reason in the law of nature but I may snap at him." It is clear that

Falstaff here likens *himself* to the voracious (not garrulous) pike, and resolves to snap up the foolish country justice who offers such a tempting bait; as he adds, "Let time shape." To establish the identification in *The Merry Wives*, Sir Sidney says: "The temptation punningly to confuse 'luce' and 'louse' was irresistible, and the dramatist's prolonged reference in *The Merry Wives* to the 'dozen white luces' on Justice Shallow's 'old coat' fully establishes Shallow's identity with Sir Thomas Lucy of Charlecote."

It is true that the temptation punningly to confuse "luce" and "louse" was irresistible; and here perhaps we have the explanation of how the theory that in Justice Shallow Shakespeare was lampooning Sir Thomas Lucy, first related by Davies about the beginning of the eighteenth century, originated. For as long as the pronunciation of the two words "luce" and "louse" remained similar, the Lucy family, we can hardly doubt, would be subject to this rustic pleasantry. The survival in Warwickshire of the old jest about the "louses" on the Lucy coat of arms into the period when Shakespeare's plays were being widely read furnishes a plausible starting-point for the late tradition. At last some one familiar with the popular jest at the expense of the Lucys discovered the jest in *The Merry Wives*, and promptly jumped to the conclusion that Shakespeare may have been satirizing Sir Thomas in the character of Justice Shallow. To such a person, however, the question would at once present itself, Why should Shakespeare make so bitter an attack upon his near neighbor, the leading gentleman of Warwickshire? The answer, of course, would be sought in the play. The only complaint that Justice Shallow makes in this scene of *The Merry Wives* concerns the stealing of deer. The Lucy family in these latter days possessed an excellent deer-preserve, "a fayre park called Fulbrooke."

Hence the ready imagination suggested the possibility of Shakespeare's having stolen a deer from the famous Lucy preserve. This explanation, at first tentatively suggested as a possibility, would of course soon take the form of a probability, and finally be quoted as a fact. In due course the story came to the dignity of being recorded, and was gradually adorned with suitable details.

It was first put into print in 1709 by Nicholas Rowe, who in his life of the poet writes:

> He had by misfortune common enough to young fellows, fallen into ill company; and amongst them, some that made a frequent practice of deer-stealing engag'd him with them more than once in robbing a park that belong'd to Sir Thomas Lucy of Cherlcote, near Stratford. For this he was prosecuted by that gentleman, as he thought, somewhat too severely; and in order to revenge that ill usage, he made a ballad upon him. And tho' this, probably the first essay of his poetry, be lost, yet it is said to have been so very bitter that it redoubled the prosecution against him to that degree, that he was oblig'd to leave his business and family in Warwickshire for some time, and shelter himself in London.

Rowe also, of course, duly records the theory that in the Justice Shallow of *The Merry Wives* Shakespeare had taken bitter revenge on his persecutor.

Again, according to Capell (who died in 1781), a certain Mr. Thomas Wilkes had heard his father quote his father [1] to the effect that a certain —

> Mr. Thomas Jones, who dwelt at Turbich, a village in Worcestershire a few miles from Stratford upon Avon, and died in the year 1703, aged upwards of ninety, remembered to have heard from several old people at Stratford the story of Shakespeare's robbing Sir Thomas Lucy's park, and their account of it agreed with Mr. Rowe's, with this addition, — that the ballad written against Sir Thomas by Shakespeare was stuck upon his park-gate, which exasperated the Knight to apply to a lawyer at

---

[1] See Malone in Boswell's *Variorum*, ii, 140; and cf. *Notes and Queries*, 1861, p. 183.

Warwick to proceed against him. Mr. Jones had put down in writing the first stanza of this ballad, which was all he remembered of it, and Mr. Thomas Wilkes (my grandfather) transmitted it to my father by memory.

The stanza recorded is as follows:

> A parliemente member, a justice of peace
> At home a poor scare-crowe, at London an asse,
>   If *lowsie* is Lucy, as some volke miscalle it,
>   Then *Lucy* is *lowsie*, whatever befall it.
> He thinks himself greate, yet an asse in his state
> We allowe by his ears but with asses to mate.
>   If *Lucy* is *lowsie*, as some volke miscalle it,
>   Sing lowsie Lucy, whatever befall it.[1]

Sir Sidney Lee, who accepts the deer-stealing episode, confesses that "no authenticity can be allowed the worthless stanza." Even if it be as old as 1703, which is open to grave doubt, it merely shows that the Lucy family was still the victim of the luce-louse jest, and has in it nothing to suggest a poaching episode.

All the significant evidence on the deer-stealing tradition is now before the reader, who can judge for himself as to its credibility. It seems hardly necessary to add that Sir Thomas Lucy had no deer-park, no lodge, no lodge-gate, no keeper (and therefore no keeper's daughter), or to point out that the deer-stealing episode in *The Merry Wives* is far more discreditable to the poachers (who broke Slender's head and then robbed him) than to Justice Shallow, who has a perfect case in law and in common equity against them.

Yet on the basis of these two doubtful traditions biographers have commonly represented Shakespeare as suddenly abandoning his wife and children, and running

---

[1] The stanza was later increased by the addition of six others, and the "whole ballad" was published by Malone in 1790. The additional stanzas are quite obviously based in phraseology and thought on the Justice Shallow scene in *The Merry Wives*. There can be no doubt that it is an eighteenth-century fabrication.

away to London to start life anew. That he deserted his wife and children is surely not in keeping with that gentleness of disposition to which his friends so often testify, or that sensitiveness to domestic virtue which all his plays show was an essential element of his character. Nor is it likely that at his age, and with his training, he rashly fled to London to accept a position in a playhouse as a common servant. The period we are dealing with falls between the ages of twenty-one and twenty-eight, the period when men are at their prime. Shakespeare had an excellent schooling, and was gifted with an unusual mind. During these important years he must have been doing something in harmony with his training, and worthy of his intellect. When we next catch sight of him, he is a man of letters in London, giving every indication of book-culture, and exhibiting a sure literary sense.

Nor is it at all necessary to suppose that on leaving the parental roof he went at once to London. And there is no evidence that when he left Stratford he failed to take his wife and children with him. The pecuniary troubles of his father, now at their height, as well as the crowded condition of the Henley Street house, would certainly suggest to him the propriety of removing his growing family to some other place, and securing some employment that would enable him to support them.

What then did William, now of full age, a dignified head of a family, master of some Latin and less Greek, do to support his wife and three small children? Have we any evidence, more credible than these very improbable traditions, to show how he spent the years immediately preceding his appearance in London as a gifted poet?

William Beeston, the eminent Elizabethan theatrical manager, made a positive statement regarding Shakespeare's career before his coming to London, a statement that is far more deserving of credence than the two late traditions just examined. The author of this statement was the son of Christopher Beeston, who, as a member of the London troupe which Shakespeare joined, was on intimate terms with the poet during his earliest days in London. He could hardly have been ignorant of Shakespeare's career before joining the actors' profession. Christopher was not only a distinguished performer, but throughout his entire life was most closely associated with the theatrical fraternity. In 1612 he became the manager of the Queen's Company, and in 1617 he built the Cockpit Playhouse in Drury Lane. His son William grew up as his assistant, and upon the death of the father in 1639 assumed full control of the Cockpit and its company of players. In his capacity as theatrical manager he too was on terms of familiarity with actors and playwrights, and he seems to have taken a deep interest in poets and poetry; for example, as a friend of Thomas Heywood he contributed one of the beautiful copperplate illustrations to *The Hierarchy of the Blessed Angels* (1635). Francis Kirkman addressed to him the following dedicatory epistle:

Diverse times in my hearing, to the admiration of all the company, you have most judiciously discoursed of Poesie, which is the cause I presume to choose you for my patron and protector, who are the happiest interpreter and judge of our English stage-plays this nation ever produced; which the poets and actors of these times cannot (without ingratitude) deny; for I have heard the chief and most ingenious acknowledge their fames and profits essentially sprung from your instruction, judgment, and fancy.[1]

Beeston lived into the Restoration, and by his intimate knowledge of the older actors and playwrights won from Dryden the designation "the chronicle of the stage." It was therefore natural that Aubrey, when he began to

[1] Prefixed to *The Loves and Adventures of Clerico and Lozia.*

collect material for his *Lives*, should seek from him information about Shakespeare. In his manuscript we find the jotting: "W. Shakespeare — quære Mr. Beeston, who knows most of him." The last clause was doubtless true; Beeston must have known much about the most distinguished playwright of his day; he surely knew more than the authors of the two late traditions we have just considered. In a second jotting Aubrey writes: "Did I tell you that I have met with old Mr. [Beeston], who knew all the old English poets, whose lives I am taking from him?" And this is what Aubrey took from Beeston: "Though, as Ben Jonson says of him, that he had but little Latin and less Greek, he understood Latin pretty well, for he had been in his younger years a schoolmaster in the country." To make sure of his authority for this statement, so contradictory of the current belief that Shakespeare's classical attainments were limited, Aubrey jotted down in the margin opposite it: "from Mr. Beeston."

Far too little attention has been paid to this assertion of Beeston's, mainly because persons have been attracted by the more romantic deer-stealing tradition of a later date. Yet the statement, based upon early and apparently authentic information, deserves our careful consideration. There is nothing unlikely about the assertion that Shakespeare secured a country school, probably not far from Stratford, and that for a few years he taught Lilly's *Grammatica Latina*, the *Sententiæ Pueriles*, Ovid, Terence, Plautus, and such other books as he had studied under his Stratford schoolmasters. It is quite possible that he had gained some experience in teaching while a pupil in the grammar school, for, as we know, the elementary instruction was often assigned to the more advanced students. The statutes of the Guisborough Grammar School, 1561, provide that in the first form "shall be placed the young beginners, commonly called *Petits*, whom the Master himself shall not be bound to teach so long as they continue there, but only assign so many of his scholars in the third and fourth forms as may suffice to instruct them." And at Bungay the statutes required that "some of the highest form shall weekly, by course, instruct the first form, both in their accidence, and also in giving them copies to write." The custom seems to have been general, and may have supplied Shakespeare with the experience that suggested to him his first humble effort to provide support for himself and his family.

For the position of country school-teacher his preparation was adequate. The King's New School of Stratford-upon-Avon, with its royal endowment and a master who was an Oxford graduate and Fellow of his college, would have been regarded in Warwickshire as among the best institutions of its kind. Shakespeare had thus been educated in a first-class school, under the tuition of one of the most thoroughly trained teachers that could be had. With a mind far superior to that of the average student, he must have acquired an easy mastery of the conventional grammar-school curriculum. This was all that he needed for the position he is said to have assumed, for a university training was not demanded of teachers in the rural schools. As Donald Lupton states, so late as 1632: "There are many set in authority to teach youth which never had much learning themselves," though he acknowledges that "there are some who deserve the place" through having stayed at "the university until learning, discretion, and judgment had ripened them." And Thomas Fuller bitterly complains that many "before they have taken any degree in the university commence schoolmaster in the country, as if nothing else were required to set up this profession but only a rod and a ferula. Others, who are able, use it only as a passage to better preferment, to patch rents in their present fortune till they can provide a new one, and betake themselves to a more gainful calling." [1] It may well be, therefore, that Shakespeare made the profession of school-teaching his temporary resource.

There are many reasons that should lead us to accept this account of the poet's career before coming to London. First, it is significant that Beeston's main concern was to deny the then current notion that Shakespeare's classical training was limited, a notion due largely to Jonson's famous dictum of "small Latin and less Greek." He was well aware of Jonson's statement, for he quotes it; yet in spite of the authority of the great literary dictator, whose word at this time carried the weight of oracular truth, he dared assert in contradiction that Shakespeare "understood Latin pretty well," and cited the specific reason for his belief. He would have taken issue with the mighty Jonson only if he thought he had trustworthy evidence for a contrary opinion.

Secondly, as late as 1587, two years after Shakespeare left Stratford, he seems to have been still within reach of his native town, for certain legal negotiations regarding his mother's estate of Asbies furnish, as Halliwell-Phillipps puts it, "a substantial reason" [2] for believing that he was personally in conference with the various parties interested, and gave his formal consent to the proposed settlement of a lawsuit which involved his private interests.

Thirdly, Beeston's statement would free us from the necessity of supposing that Shakespeare abandoned his wife and children; for as a country school-teacher he could provide them with a home while himself waiting the opportunity for further advancement.

---

[1] *Holy and Profane State.* Dr. Mulcaster, too, protests at "the school being used but for a shift afterwards to pass thence to the other professions."

[2] *Outlines,* i, 91.

Fourthly, his two earliest original plays, *The Comedy of Errors* and *Love's Labour's Lost*, contain not only amusing sketches of school-teachers, but also, embedded in the speeches of other personages, tags from school-books, and intimate echoes of the pedagogue's life. How much technical knowledge of school-books is to be found in *Love's Labour's Lost* will be realized only after reading Baynes' essay on the topic.[1] It should not be forgotten that a young playwright at the outset of his career naturally draws material from his recent and most vivid experiences. Nor should it be overlooked that his first play, *The Comedy of Errors*, was directly based on two plays of Plautus which had not as yet been translated into English. As a schoolmaster he would have been called upon to teach Plautus, and it may be that his familiarity with the plays gained in this fashion enabled him to dramatize them for the public stage.

Lastly, not to exhaust the reasons that might be cited, a career as school-teacher would splendidly equip the non-university trained Shakespeare for his subsequent career as a man of letters. As every one knows, the best way to acquire a thorough education in books is to teach. If we can imagine Shakespeare as spending a few years with books in the school-room, we can better understand the correct and forcible use of language, and the sure literary sense, which mark his first attempts at composition. On the other hand, if we are forced to think of him as early snatched from school, working all day in a butcher's shop, growing up in a home devoid of books and of a literary atmosphere, and finally driven from his native town through a wild escapade with village lads, we find it hard to understand how he suddenly blossomed out as one of England's greatest men of letters with every mark of literary culture.

[1] In his *Shakespearean Studies*, 1894, pp. 147–249.

The transformation of a school-teacher into a man of letters is common in the history of literature. Samuel Johnson, it will be recalled, left a country school with three acts of a play in his pocket, and came to London with the youthful Garrick who was ambitious of finding employment at the theatres. Possibly Shakespeare in like fashion brought with him to the metropolis a draft of his earliest play with which to recommend himself to the attention of the actors.

We have every reason, therefore, to accept Beeston's statement, made with conviction, and based on what he obviously regarded as trustworthy information; and accepting it, we may imagine Shakespeare as for some five years teaching a country school, and thus mastering the elements of grammar and composition, acquiring a thorough grounding in the best of Latin culture — Ovid, Cicero, Horace, Virgil, Terence, Plautus, Seneca — and by these means securing the training that was necessary to prepare him for his sudden emergence as the chief poet of the English Renaissance.

CHAPTER VII

THE RISE OF PROFESSIONALISM IN THE DRAMA

LET us leave Shakespeare teaching classical literature in his country school, and glance at the rise of the new professions of acting and of playwriting which were shortly to tempt him to the great city of London.

The earliest forms of dramatic entertainment in England, offshoots from the liturgy of the Church, were acted by clerics as a part of the religious service. After these simple representations had grown into long and complicated plays, they were taken out of the church buildings, in the twelfth or thirteenth century, and turned over to the laity for more elaborate performance. With the establishment of the Corpus Christi Festival in 1311, the various Biblical episodes of the Old and New Testament were made into separate plays, and each was intrusted to one or more of the trade guilds, which were required to assume full responsibility for its staging, and to supply from their own members suitable actors. And as the drama became generally recognized as an effective and entertaining means of religious instruction, churches, villages, schools, and miscellaneous organizations began to devise short plays dealing with the lives and miracles of their patron saints, or teaching in allegorical form the plan of salvation. Finally local history, and even secular stories, were put on the stage for the edification and amusement of audiences. But the acting of all these plays was in the hands of amateurs, and such a thing as the commercialization of the drama was virtually unknown.

Not infrequently, however, these amateur actors took

their plays to neighboring towns in order to give others the benefit of their labors, in return for which, of course, they expected to be suitably rewarded. And with the rapid increase in the popularity of the drama as a form of entertainment, there arose, especially in the larger cities, groups of men, tradesfolk for the most part, who devoted their idle time to presenting religious or semi-religious stage-performances. Finding this profitable, they more firmly organized themselves, and at last began to travel, even to considerable distances, and thus to make for themselves a fair living.

In their attempts to supply the growing demand for dramatic exhibitions they were almost at once joined by another class of actors, more definitely committed to the business of entertaining the public. Throughout the Middle Ages minstrels, jugglers, tumblers, rope-walkers, sleight-of-hand artists, animal leaders, and such like strollers visited the towns and villages several times a year to amuse the citizens and take a hat-collection. As a rule they went about in small groups for comradeship or mutual protection, often sharing with one another their precarious earnings. Their reputation with the officers of the law was deservedly bad, for they were given to pilfering from the farmers, picking the purses of their spectators, and even on occasion, we are told, stealing horses, which they disposed of at the next town or fair. In the first half of the fifteenth century, as nearly as we can now determine, some of these itinerant entertainers, finding the public to be passionately fond of dramatic shows, hit upon the notion of acting a play in addition to, or it may be instead of, their stale tricks; and discovering this innovation to be more lucrative than their old trade, they banded themselves together into small troupes, and began systematically to tour the country. They performed wherever they could find accommodation, sometimes on barrel-heads at a street-corner, sometimes in barns, but most often in the yards of public inns. A platform temporarily erected in the centre of the yard supplied the needs of the actors, the rabble stood in a circle about the stage, and the gentlefolk who might desire to see the performance occupied the galleries.

Thus acting as a profession came into being.

The plays these early troupes rendered were at first the then popular moralities, such, for example, as *The Cradle of Security*, the plot of which has been summarized.[1] But the actors, especially those recruited from the strollers, being naturally more anxious to entertain the audience than to inculcate wholesome ethical doctrines, introduced into their performances much broad comedy and a liberal amount of gross obscenity. The text of *Mankind* well illustrates this. Though the play was originally designed to show how the efforts of the World, the Flesh, and the Devil to ensnare the soul of Mankind could be defeated by Mercy and divine love, as corrupted in the hands of the traveling troupe which acted it in inn-yards it may aptly be called an "immoral morality." And such plays as these professionals might themselves originate through ready extemporization were even more disreputable. Many complaints were made that the performances of the strollers were detrimental to the welfare of the public; and as the troupes rapidly increased in number, vigorous efforts were made to suppress them.

About the same time there arose a superior type of professional actor to furnish entertainment for the upper classes of society. Most of the greater noblemen of the realm maintained a host of retainers, among whom were usually four or five minstrels whose duty it was to amuse their lord and master on festive occasions with songs of knightly deeds, and with feats of activity and jugglery.

[1] See above, p. 46.

In the summer these minstrels were accustomed to travel, visiting the palaces of other noblemen and the homes of the rural gentry. When the drama became the predominant form of diversion in England, they began to act short plays instead of relating their familiar stories of chivalric adventure, a change that rendered their entertainment more modern, more lively, and in general more acceptable. Following their old custom, they traveled in the summer, turning an honest penny by presenting their plays before fresh audiences. Wearing their master's livery, and having his good name in their keeping, they did not, as a rule, act on the public street-corners or in the vulgar inn-yards; instead they gave their performances in the homes of the wealthy, and before the better class of citizens in town-halls, schools, or churches. Their plays, too, were free from the coarse vulgarity and the open obscenity which usually characterized the efforts of the common strollers.

Thus by the end of the fifteenth century we find two well-marked types of professional actors, the one made up of unattached strollers who catered chiefly to the rabble, the other, of noblemen's servants who catered to their masters, his friends, the country gentry, and the more respectable citizens.[1] But the unattached strollers far outnumbered the noblemen's servants, and by the coarseness of their plays, and the disorders that frequently attended their performances in inn-yards, brought reproach upon the new profession, and upon the secular drama it was developing. At last they became so numerous, and made so much trouble for the officers of the law, that the governors of the land began to devise regulations to control them. In various towns and cities stringent ordinances were passed, either forbidding plays

[1] There were also town companies, about which we know very little. For our purposes they may be ignored.

entirely, or so restricting dramatic performances by inflicting onerous conditions on acting, that the troupes found it exceedingly difficult to maintain their existence.

But these laws, passed by local authorities, could not be enforced upon actors who belonged to a nobleman's household. Through feudal rights, such household servants were responsible only to their master, and were free from molestation by petty officers. Thus they had a distinct advantage over the unattached strollers, whom any Dogberry might order to be flogged in public, or set in the stocks.

The outcome of this situation was that a troupe of professional players, in order to exist with any degree of safety and comfort, had to secure the protection of some nobleman, who would grant them the privileges of wearing his livery and of traveling under his name. As a rule noblemen were not unwilling — indeed many seem to have been eager — to patronize dramatic companies. Possibly they felt that it gave them standing among their fellow-noblemen; and they were, of course, glad to have a troupe at their command when they desired entertainment for themselves or their guests. Thus the better companies of actors had little difficulty in securing the patronage now quite essential to their welfare. But the privilege carried with it certain responsibilities: a troupe wearing the livery and bearing the name of a nobleman would have to safeguard the dignity of its master both with respectable plays and with honest behavior while traveling. This obligation naturally had a wholesome effect on the profession of acting, and on the drama itself; for disreputable persons were for the most part driven into other courses of livelihood, and the standard of plays was lifted in cleanliness and in excellence. As a result we find that throughout the sixteenth century, with a few exceptions, the patronized troupes were heartily welcomed by town officials and citizens alike, and were treated with respect and often with generous hospitality.[1]

To insure this welcome their master commonly furnished them with a license certifying that they were his servants, and authorizing them to play in his name. In addition he would sometimes supply them with letters of recommendation to other noblemen, as may be illustrated by the following letter from the hand of the Earl of Leicester:

To the right honourable, and my very good Lord, the Earl of Shrewsbury.
My good Lord:

Where my servants, bringers hereof unto you, be such as are players of interludes, and for the same have the license of diverse of my lords here, under their seals and hands, to play in diverse shires within the realm under their authorities, as may amply appear unto your Lordship by the same license, I have thought, among the rest, by my letters to beseech your good Lordship's conformity to them likewise, that they may have your hand and seal to their license for the like liberty in Yorkshire; being honest men, and such as shall play none other matters (I trust) but tolerable and convenient, whereof some of them have been heard here already before diverse of my lords: for whom I shall have good cause to thank your Lordship, and to remain your Lordship's to the best that shall lie in my little power. And thus I take my leave of your good Lordship. From Westminster, the . . . of June, 1559.

Your good Lordship's assured,

R. DUDLEY.

When such patronized actors, displaying embroidered on their sleeves their master's coat of arms, visited a town, they at once presented their credentials to the mayor. If this official did not treat them well they would

---

[1] Sometimes the town officials sent the players presents of wine; sometimes the mayor gave them a dinner; when a company of English players visited Aberdeen in 1601 its leading actor, Fletcher, received the freedom of the city.

inform their master of the fact, and the corporation was likely to suffer when next it sought a favor at Court. Accordingly, it was the custom for the mayor to receive the players with courtesy, in order, as Willis puts it, to "show respect to their Lord and Master." He would grant them permission to use the town-hall or some other suitable place, and have them present their first play before the officers of the town with a suitable reward as a gift from the corporation. The amount of this reward varied with the dignity of the actors' patron, with the size and excellence of the troupe, or with the anxiety of the mayor to please the particular nobleman represented. Even if the town officials happened to be opposed to plays for puritanical or other reasons, they hardly dared offend a patronized company. Hence when a nobleman's troupe came to present its license, they gave the actors the usual reward, and sent them on their way without allowing any performance at all — an arrangement which seems to have been satisfactory to all concerned.

With the development of the drama as the most popular form of social diversion among the aristocracy and common people alike, the Court would naturally keep pace. Attached to the royal palace were eight "players of interludes," who corresponded to the players attached to the households of the noblemen. In their dramatic activities they differed in no essential way from other patronized troupes. Through several reigns they performed plays at Court for the amusement of their sovereign, and during the summer toured the provinces; and in the days of Elizabeth, as the Queen's Men, they occupied a regular theatre, and figured conspicuously among the rival companies that supplied London with entertainment.

But at the Court there was developed also a special group of actors destined to exert a refining influence upon the nascent public drama. During the reign of Henry

VIII the members of the Chapel Royal (an organization consisting of a Master, twenty-four singing-men, and eight boy-choristers) were engaged in presenting before His Majesty pageants and masques of great beauty, enriched with songs, instrumental music, and gorgeous stage-effects. Out of such performances gradually came plays, usually of a spectacular nature, and equipped with expensive costumes and properties. Composed by the Master, or his assistants, and acted by the singing-men with the aid of the boys, they were especially designed to please courtly audiences. With the coming of Elizabeth, however, this Court drama underwent a change. The new ruler's taste was not so much for spectacular pageantry as for legitimate plays, and she frankly preferred the acting of the little boy-choristers to that of the adult singing-men. Under her influence, "the children," as they were called (now increased in number), developed into what was virtually a troupe of well-trained actors, who were expected annually to amuse the Queen with delicate comedies, romances, tragedies, or histories, adorned with beautiful costumes and equipped with painted stage-settings. One of the chief functions of the Master of the Chapel now was the preparation of such plays for the delectation of the Queen. Richard Edwards, appointed to the position by Elizabeth in 1561, won great fame through the composition for the children of such pieces as *Damon and Pithias* and *Palemon and Arcite*. With its superior refinement of plot and language, and its more elaborate stage-effects, this Court-drama exercised upon the noblemen's troupes an elevating influence. But, of course, the main stream of the English drama continued to flow in the plays written for the professional companies, and acted before the general public.

As might be expected, there ultimately arose in London certain troupes of unusual size and excellence, which catered to the city's population, and seldom found it necessary to travel in the provinces. They maintained the higher standard of performance demanded by metropolitan audiences, and reaped a much richer harvest than did the humbler traveling troupes. Since they could not make use of school-houses, or churches, or town-halls, they were forced to employ almost entirely the yards of public inns. After securing permission to use an inn for a given afternoon, they would erect their temporary stage in the yard, and by a street procession with flags and drums summon their audience to the play.

But this scheme had many unsatisfactory features. The actors could not always be sure of an inn-yard; they were forced to put up with temporary stages; and they had to call together their audience on each occasion. Such a makeshift arrangement could not last indefinitely, for the troupes were yearly growing in dignity and wealth, and the audiences were increasing in size and importance. About the year 1560 — or shortly before the birth of Shakespeare — certain men were shrewd enough to see that it would pay to devote an inn solely to plays. Accordingly, a few large inns were fitted up for the special use of the actors. Permanent stages were erected in the yards, fully equipped to meet the demands of dramatic representation, and wooden benches were built in the galleries to accommodate the gentlemen and ladies who did not care to stand in the yard below. Then these made-over inns were let to the actors on an agreement by which the proprietors shared in the takings at the door. Five "great inns" of London were thus converted into playing-places regularly devoted to afternoon dramatic performances, namely the Bell and the Cross Keys, both in Gracechurch Street, the Bull in Bishopsgate Street, the Bell Savage on Ludgate Hill, and the Boar's Head in Whitechapel Street just outside Aldgate. The troupes seem to have been quite content with these inns, which indeed were not ill-suited to their purpose.

Trouble, however, was brewing for the metropolitan actors. As the companies increased in number, and as the Londoners flocked in ever larger crowds to witness plays, the animosity of two forces was aroused — Puritanism and the city government. The Puritans attacked the drama as contrary to Holy Writ, destructive of church-going and piety, and subversive of public morality. In pulpit and in pamphlet they waged an unceasing war on the theatre, charging actors with "abuses" of all kinds, and characterizing dramatic performances as lewd, ungodly, and even idolatrous. The extravagance of their language and the zeal with which they urged their attacks were altogether fanatical. "What is there," demands the author of *A Second and Third Blast of Retreat from Plaies and Theatres*, "which is not abused thereby? Our hearts with idle cogitations; our eyes with vain aspects, gestures, and toys; our ears with filthy speech, unhonest mirth, and ribaldry; our whole bodies to uncleanness; our bodies and minds to the service of the Devil; our holy days with profaneness; our time with idleness; all our blessings, health, wealth, and prosperity to the increase of Satan's Kingdom are there abused: that not unfitly they are termed, as of late, 'The School of Abuse' by one; 'The School of Bawdry' by another; 'The Nest of the Devil' and 'Sink of All Sin' by a third; so, long ago, 'The Chair of Pestilence' by Clement Alexandrius; by Cyril and Salvianus 'The Pomp of the Devil'; 'The Sovereign Place of Satan' by Tertullian." Perhaps the very intemperance of these attacks kept the Puritans from doing more serious damage to the drama in this its most important stage of development.

The officials of the city were opposed to the players on other and more practical grounds. In the first place, they knew that the great "throng and press" of people to see shows tended to spread the plague. The dreaded "sickness" made its appearance almost every summer — the time when plays were at their height — and threatened at any moment to develop into a calamitous epidemic. In the face of such a real danger it was quite natural for the authorities to regard the inn-yard theatres with disfavor. In the second place, they were seriously annoyed by the disorders that all too frequently attended dramatic performances. One mayor declared that "plays and players" gave the authorities more trouble than anything else in the entire administration of municipal affairs. Sometimes, as we know, turbulent apprentices and factions met by appointment at plays for the sole purpose of starting riots or jail-deliveries. And often there arose frays, ending in bloodshed, among "such as frequent the said plays, being the ordinary places of meeting for all vagrant persons and masterless men that hang about the city." [1] The danger of civil disturbance was increased by the fact that the proprietors of the inns made a large profit from the wine, beer, ale, and other drinks dispensed to the crowds before, after, and even during the performance. "Upon Whitsunday," writes the City Recorder to Lord Burghley, "by reason no plays were the same day, all the city was quiet." [2] One of the Lord Mayors exclaims in despair: "The Politique State and Government of this City . . . by no one thing is so greatly annoyed and disquieted as by players and plays and the disorders which follow thereupon." [3]

These annoyances, which the city authorities felt so keenly, were aggravated by the fact that the troupes enjoyed the patronage of great noblemen — one enjoyed

---

[1] So they are described by the Lord Mayor; see The Malone Society's *Collections*, i, 75.
[2] *Ibid.*, i, 164.   [3] *Ibid.*, i, 69.

the patronage of the Queen herself — and the attempts on the part of the Lord Mayor and the Aldermen to regulate the players were often interfered with by other and higher authority. Sometimes a particular nobleman, whose request was not to be ignored, intervened in behalf of his troupe; most often, however, it was the Privy Council, representing the Queen and the nobility, which championed the cause of the actors and countermanded the decrees of the Mayor and the Aldermen. The players, aware of the power of their patrons, could afford to treat the officers of the city with disdain. Thus the Recorder, upon the occasion of a riot, summoned James Burbage to come before him, with this result: "He sent me word he was my Lord of Hunsdon's man, and that he would not come at me; but he would in the morning ride to my lord." Clearly it was impossible to have an efficient city government when there were two authorities with conflicting interests.

The situation reached a crisis about 1573 — shortly after Shakespeare began his labors in the grammar school at Stratford — when Puritans succeeded in electing a Lord Mayor, and secured control of the Board of Aldermen and of the Common Council. Thus to the natural desire of the civic authorities to safeguard public health and maintain order was added a fanatical hatred of all dramatic performances in themselves. At first the Mayor and the Aldermen attempted to keep acting permanently inhibited on the old excuse that plays spread the infection of the plague. The troupes appealed to their patrons, who brought the matter before the Privy Council, and the Privy Council immediately ordered the lifting of the ban. The Mayor and Aldermen being thus foiled, called a meeting of the Common Council, which on December 6, 1574, passed a special ordinance placing such severe restrictions on the performing of plays as to render the existence of acting if not impossible at least exceedingly difficult. The long preamble of the ordinance clearly shows the puritanical bias of the Council:

Whereas heretofore sundry great disorders and inconveniences have been found to ensue to this city by the inordinate haunting of great multitudes of people, specially youths, to plays, interludes, and shows: namely, occasion of frays and quarrels; evil practises of incontinency in great inns having chambers and secret places adjoing to their open stages and galleries; inveighling and alluring of maids, specially orphans and good citizens' children under age, to privy and unmeet contracts; the publishing of unchaste, uncomly, and unshamefaced speeches and doings; withdrawing of the Queen's Majesty's subjects from divine service on Sundays and holy days, at which times such plays were chiefly used; unthrifty waste of the money of the poor and fond persons, sundry robberies by picking and cutting of purses; uttering of popular, busy, and seditious matters; and many other corruptions of youth; and other enormities; besides that also sundry slaughters and maimings of the Queen's subjects have happened by ruins of scaffolds, frames, and stages, and by engines, weapons, and powder used in plays. And whereas in time of God's visitation by the plague such assemblies of the people in throng and press have been very dangerous for spreading of infection. . . . And for that the Lord Mayor, and his brethren the Aldermen, together with the grave and discreet citizens in the Common Council assembled, do doubt and fear lest upon God's merciful withdrawing his hand of sickness from us (which God grant) the people, specially the meaner and most unruly sort, should with sudden forgetting of His visitation, without fear of God's wrath; and without due respect of the good and politique means that He hath ordained for the preservation of common weals and peoples in health and good order, return to the undue use of such enormities, to the great offense of God. . . . Be it enacted by the authority of this Common Council that from henceforth . . .

The chief restrictions imposed on playing by the ordinance may be briefly summarized:

1. Before being acted all plays must be "first perused

and allowed, in such order and form, and by such persons, as by the Lord Mayor and Court of Aldermen for the time being shall be appointed."

2. Inns, or other buildings, used for acting, and their proprietors also, must be licensed by the Lord Mayor and the Aldermen.

3. The proprietors thus licensed must, in addition, be "bound to the Chamberlain of London" by a sufficient bond to guarantee "the keeping of good order, and avoiding of" the various abuses cited in the Preamble.

4. No play must be acted during the time of "the sickness," or during any inhibition ordered at any time by the Lord Mayor.

5. No plays must be acted during "any usual time of divine service," and no persons must be admitted into playing-places until after divine services were over.

6. The proprietors of all playing-places must pay towards the support of the poor a sum to be fixed by the city authorities.

The restrictions thus placed on dramatic performances, and the increasing hostility of the city authorities, of which this ordinance was an ominous sign, led to the construction of buildings called "playhouses," specially designed to accommodate actors, devoted solely to the drama, and situated outside the city, beyond the jurisdiction of the Common Council. As the Reverend John Stockwood indignantly exclaims in a sermon preached in 1578. "Have we not houses of purpose, built with great charges, for the maintenance of plays, and that without the liberties, as who should say, 'There! let them say what they will say, we will play!'"

Undoubtedly it was the hostility of the city authorities that immediately led to the erection of playhouses; yet two other causes combined with this to make the step sooner or later inevitable. The first was the inadequacy of the old inn-yards, and the real need of special buildings designed for dramatic performances, a need that was yearly growing more pronounced as plays developed in complexity, and as audiences increased in size and in dignity. The second cause was the pecuniary gain that could be derived from such buildings.

The man who first realized that profit could be made from a playhouse, and had the courage to put his savings into the venture, was James Burbage. Originally a poor carpenter, he gave over that trade for the more lucrative profession of actor. So successful was he in his new calling that by the year 1572 we find him at the head of Leicester's excellent troupe, and serving as its manager. His difficulties with the ordinances of the city, his experience with the unsatisfactory arrangements in the inn-yards, but above all his dream of the "continual great profit" to be had from a building devoted solely to the drama, led him in 1575 to resolve upon erecting a playhouse. He did not take his troupe into his confidence, but ventured on the undertaking as a private business speculation.

The first problem that faced him was the selection of a suitable location. Two conditions narrowed his choice: first, the site had to lie outside the jurisdiction of the city authorities; secondly, it had to be as near as possible to the centre of London's population. He was able to meet both conditions through the existence in and about the city of certain territories, called "liberties," which were free from the ordinances of the Common Council. These liberties had come about in an interesting way. During the Middle Ages there were in or near London various religious establishments, such as the Monastery of Blackfriars, the Monastery of Whitefriars, the Priory of Holywell, each with its buildings, cloisters, and gardens walled in for privacy. By law these enclosed precincts were free from all local ordinances, free from molestation by the sheriff and his officers, and subject only to the ruling sovereign. When Henry VIII abolished religious houses, and seized their buildings and land, these liberties came into the possession of the Crown. Henry soon gave away the property, and it was quickly divided up and sold to various individuals; but the old law was not changed, so that the regions continued to be free from the local government.

The chief of these liberties were Blackfriars in the city, Whitefriars close by, the Clink on the Bankside, and Holywell to the north. In any one of these the actors could find a grateful escape from the annoying interference of the Common Council. Which was Burbage to select? Possibly he considered them all. Blackfriars and the adjacent Whitefriars were ideal so far as situation was concerned; but their land was occupied either with the dwellings of noblemen and other aristocratic persons, or with closely-built shops. Moreover, a site here, even if found, would be far too expensive for his lean purse. The Liberty of the Clink on the Bankside was not subject to these particular objections, and had much to recommend it. It was near; it could be easily reached by boat, or on foot over the London Bridge; and it was already established as London's place of amusement, for here were the bull- and bear-baiting rings, to which thousands of pleasure-seekers daily flocked, and hard by were the fields for archery, football, and other outdoor sports. Burbage, however, rejected this site, possibly because the presence on the Bank of the licensed houses of ill fame gave it a bad reputation, and he did not wish to place the first home of the drama in a locality which would supply the Puritans with fresh ammunition for attack. All things considered, the Liberty of Holywell seemed best to suit his purpose. It was reasonably near, though not so near as the other liberties; it was largely undeveloped, so that a site there could be secured cheaply; and being adjacent to Finsbury Field (a large open tract which since 1315 had been in the possession of the city as a public playground, where families could picnic, archers could exercise their sport, and the militia could drill), it was definitely associated with the idea of entertainment.

From a gentleman named Giles Alleyn he obtained a small tract of land in this liberty, having a frontage on Finsbury Field, and separated from that municipal playground only by a brick wall. He did not purchase the land — either he was too poor, or Alleyn was unwilling to sell — but leased it for a term of twenty-one years, with a promise, under certain conditions, of a renewal for ten years longer.

Having thus secured a site, Burbage had next to draw the plans of his playhouse. He had no model to follow, for this was the first structure of its kind in England, or for that matter in Europe. Yet for the task he was admirably qualified. In the first place, he was by training and early practice a carpenter and builder; in the second place, he was an actor of experience; and, in the third place, he was the manager of one of the most important troupes in London. In other words, he had an exact knowledge of what was needed, and the practical skill to meet those needs.

The building he designed was unique in the history of architecture; a German traveler applied to it the adjective "sonderbar." It was circular or polygonal in shape, with the centre open to the sky, and the frame, consisting of galleries three in number, covered with thatch. The unroofed pit, or "yard" as the Elizabethans called it, was for the accommodation of those who were willing to pay only a penny for admission, and were content to stand during the entire performance. The galleries, provided with benches rising one above the other, were for the better class of spectators who could afford to pay for the convenience of seats and some protection from the weather. The stage was a simple platform projecting into the yard with dressing-rooms at the rear. Above the dressing rooms was a balcony used by the actors for representing scenes that took place "aloft." And extending partly over the stage was a "shade" to protect the actors in case of inclement weather. High above all was a flagstaff for the purpose of informing the Londoners when a play was to be presented.

Having secured his site, and drawn up his plans, Burbage faced the more difficult problem of financing the erection of the building. To him the problem was a serious one, for he was not a rich man, and the undertaking called for a large outlay of money. He started out bravely and alone; but after a short time, when he had spent all he possessed, and the building was far from complete, he realized that he should have to admit a partner to share with him the great profits which he confidently expected. Luckily he had a wealthy brother-in-law, a grocer in the city, named Braynes, whom he was able to interest in the project. Braynes was so impressed with the possibilities of making a fortune out of the venture that he promptly sold his grocery-store, and then his home, and even pawned his wife's clothes, putting all into the new playhouse. By the autumn of 1576 the two partners had the building completed at a total cost of about £700. And to it they gave the name "The Theatre."

The structure was of wood on a brick foundation, with the exterior of plaster ornamented with boards in the familiar Tudor style. The interior, as in the case of modern playhouses, was unusually ornate. Thus T[homas] W[hite], in *A Sermon Preached at Pawles Crosse, on Sunday the Thirde of November, 1577*, exclaims: "Behold the sumptuous Theatre houses, a continual monument of London's prodigality"; John Stockwood, in *A Sermon Preached at Paules Cross, 1578*, refers to it as "the gorgeous playing-place erected in the Fields"; and Gabriel Harvey could think of no more fitting epithet for it than "painted."

Though as to the size of the building we can only guess, we may feel sure that it was large. The cost of its erection indicates as much. The Fortune, one of the largest and handsomest of the later playhouses, cost only £520, and the Hope, also very large, cost £360; the Theatre, therefore, built at a cost of approximately £700, could not have been small. It is commonly referred to, even so late as 1601, as "the great house, called the Theatre," and the author of *Skialetheia* (1598) applies to its interior the adjective "vast." Burbage, no doubt, had learned from his experience as the manager of a successful troupe the desirability of having an auditorium large enough to accommodate all who might come. Exactly how many people the building would hold we cannot say. The Reverend John Stockwood, in 1578, exclaimed bitterly: "Will not a filthy play, with the blast of a trumpet, sooner call thither a thousand, than an hour's tolling of the bell bring to the sermon a hundred?" And Fleetwood, the City Recorder, in describing a quarrel which took place in 1584 "at Theatre door," states that when the altercation began, "near a thousand people" quickly assembled. Probably the building would accommodate not far from 1500 spectators.[1]

To provide for these spectators ready access to the playhouse, Burbage opened a gate through the brick wall

---

[1] Fynes Moryson (*Itinerary*, ed. by Hughes, p. 476) states that in London there were "four or five companies of players, with their peculiar theatres capable of many thousands." The old Bear Garden, which collapsed in 1583, was said to hold "above a thousand people," and it was probably not so large as the Theatre.

which separated the old Priory from Finsbury Field. Thus he made the city's playground serve as an avenue of approach to dramatic performances, a bit of humor that was doubtless not lost on the authorities. The author of *Tarlton's Newes out of Purgatory* (*c.* 1589) speaks of the great "concourse of people through the fields" to see plays, indicating that it was a notable sight.

The opening of the first playhouse to the public was indeed a sensation in London, and marked an important step in the history of the English drama. At this time Shakespeare, in his thirteenth year, was probably applying himself to his books — including Terence, Plautus, and Seneca — in the Stratford grammar school, and thus preparing himself for his later triumphs in this very building, where his plays, acted by James Burbage's young son Richard, were to throng the yard and galleries with applauding audiences.

Upon its completion the Theatre was occupied by Leicester's Men, with whom Burbage was affiliated. The possession of a handsome playhouse, with unexampled accommodations for both actors and audiences, naturally gave Leicester's company a distinct advantage over the other troupes that had to put up with the much smaller inn-yards and submit to the restricting ordinances of the city authorities. This promptly led to the erection in the following year, 1577, of a second playhouse, called "The Curtain." It stood just a stone's throw to the south of the Theatre, and in all details was an imitation of Burbage's structure, except that it was considerably smaller.

To these two playhouses the people, so the Lord Mayor tells us, flocked in "great multitudes," and the actors reaped a rich harvest from the takings at the door. This, it may be, set those who had control of the child-actors at Court to thinking. They observed that their charges as a rule had more excellent plays than the professional troupes, and were better furnished with costumes and stage-equipment; and since they, as managers, were called upon to expend a great deal of effort in devising plays and training the children for the single presentation before Her Majesty, they felt that they should be allowed to present these plays before the public in order to remunerate themselves suitably for their pains. This they proposed to do under the excuse of giving private performances before select audiences for the sake of practising the boys. Accordingly, Richard Farrant, Master of the Windsor Chapel, no doubt with the tacit consent of the Queen, secured in the district of Blackfriars a small upstairs hall, approximately forty-six feet in length and twenty-five feet in breadth, which he fitted up for the use of the boy-choristers of Windsor and of the Royal Chapel. Here early in 1577 the children began to present plays before the public, charging high prices of admission.

The operation of the Blackfriars hall as a "private playhouse" (so it was called) did not seriously compete with the great open-air playhouses and the far more important professional troupes. But the polished plays of the children, designed for courtly audiences, and the more beautiful stage-effects made possible through the resources of the Queen's purse, set before the London public a new standard of dramatic entertainment, and indirectly exercised upon the professional actors and playwrights a refining influence. This influence was shortly increased by the coming of John Lyly to write for the boys. Having already attained fame as a literary craftsman through the publication of his novel *Euphues*, he was suddenly, in 1583, put in charge of Blackfriars, and his energies directed towards dramatic composition. His first plays, *Campaspe* and *Sapho and Phao*, won unbounded applause at Court, and charmed London with their sparkling wit, graceful songs, and altogether delightful plots. Early in 1584, however, the owner of the Blackfriars building, disturbed by the success of the plays there, drove the children out, and converted the hall into private residences. The Queen, unwilling to lose the services of so excellent a playwright as Lyly, appointed him vice-master of the boy-choristers of St. Paul's, and made it possible for him to transfer his efforts to the small singing-school attached to the cathedral. Here the children of Paul's for a number of years entertained the public with "Court comedies," which for polite audiences had a charm not possessed by the farcical comedies and bloody tragedies of the professional actors. Naturally the writers for the professional troupes began to imitate the plays of the children, and to reproduce on the public stages the courtly atmosphere, the fanciful plots, and the brilliant repartee which characterized the performances of the private stage and reflected the taste of the upper classes. Shakespeare himself found much inspiration in Lyly; his *Love's Labour's Lost* reproduces the courtly atmosphere, his Mercutio and Benedick the sparkling repartee, and his *Midsummer Night's Dream* the fanciful plots, that had so long delighted the Queen and the aristocratic audiences of Blackfriars Hall and Paul's Singing-School. But beyond this influence, these first private playhouses have no special significance for the history of the national drama, which was developed by the professional actors and their writers under the tuition of the great London public gathered in the open-air playhouses.

The Theatre and the Curtain, standing side by side, competed with each other in keen rivalry for the patronage of the audiences that came flocking over Finsbury Field. In 1585, however, — the year in which Shakespeare probably began his labors as a country schoolteacher — Burbage secured the management of the Curtain, and thus established a monopoly of playhouses.[1] This could hardly have been welcome to the actors; and in 1587 a wealthy and shrewd business man, named Philip Henslowe, broke the monopoly by setting up on the Bankside, where he owned much property, a new playhouse, called the Rose. From his *Diary* we learn that the building was of timber, the exterior of lath and plaster, and the galleries covered with thatch, and that there were an unroofed yard, a stage, and a flagpole, as in the playhouses to the north of the city. In other words, the Rose differed in no essential way from the Theatre and the Curtain, after which it was closely modeled.

Thus by the year 1587, or shortly before Shakespeare came to the city, there were in London three large and "sumptuous" playhouses, erected at great cost, and specially designed to accommodate both the actors and the public. And there were excellent troupes of well-trained actors who were growing rich out of the throngs that daily came to see plays. But one thing was lacking — a body of professional authors who could keep these troupes supplied with plays, especially such plays as were demanded by the growing intelligence of the public.

Fortunately just at this time there was arising in London a group of professional authors, young men of education, most of them university graduates, who were seeking to make their living in the great city by the use of their pens. The chief members of this group were Thomas Kyd, the son of a London scrivener, Christopher Marlowe, the son of a shoemaker in Canterbury, Robert Greene, the son of a saddler in Norwich, George Peele, the son of a charity-school clerk in London, Thomas Lodge, the son of a grocer in London, and Thomas Nashe,

---

[1] The reason assigned was that Burbage regarded the Curtain as an "esore" [i.e., eyesore] to the Theatre — presumably through competition.

the son of a poor stipendiary curate in Lowestoft, Suffolk. These young men had received a thorough classical training, all of them, save Kyd, at the university. Equipped with an excellent education, they did not care to enter a trade. They had no desire to devote their lives to the Church, nor with their lack of high family connections could they successfully enter politics. They had been prepared only to live by their wits; so in the great city, where the new trade of printing and publishing was beginning to flourish, they sought to earn their bread by writing for the press.

The first of this school of professional authors to compose plays for the actors seems to have been Thomas Kyd. He had not, to be sure, enjoyed the advantages of the university, but he had received a good grammar school education at the Merchant Taylors' School in London under the instruction of the famous Dr. Mulcaster. For a while he possibly assisted his father as a scrivener, but his interests lying in the direction of letters, he became a translator and hack-writer for the press. In or before 1587 he composed for the actors a play entitled *Hieronimo*, or, as it is now called, *The Spanish Tragedy*, full of sensational murders, and developing for the first time the motive of revenge with a ghost. Upon its presentation at the Theatre, it was received with wild enthusiasm, and young Edward Alleyn, through his effective assumption of the leading rôle, attained undying fame. A second play, possibly also by Kyd, quickly followed, entitled *Hamlet*, like its predecessor full of murder and revenge, with a ghost as the inciting force. This play, too, won the enthusiastic approval of theatre-goers, and as later rewritten by Shakespeare, still maintains its original popularity. Kyd wrote other plays, now lost or surviving only in revampings. But we have enough of his work to discover that his success lay chiefly in his ability to astound London with sensational plots. His importance in the history of the drama is twofold: first, he showed the professional actors what a trained man of letters could do if he turned his hand to the drama; secondly, he showed the professional authors that they could win both money and fame by dramatic composition.

When Kyd thus opened up to men of letters this new and profitable field of endeavor, they quickly bent their energies towards the making of plays. Christopher Marlowe almost at once achieved a tremendous success with *Tamburlaine the Great*, a success which called for a sequel within a few months. *Tamburlaine* was followed by *Dr. Faustus*, *The Jew of Malta*, *Edward II*, and other plays, which easily lifted their author into the position of the leading dramatist of his time. He possessed, indeed, a remarkable dramatic genius. Kyd had shown how to create thrilling scenes that startled the audience; but his plays lacked the touch of great poetry. Marlowe, too, could astound his audiences with effective situations; and, in addition, he was able to add the charm of wonderful verse. His "mighty line," and the rich poetic glamour with which he clothed all his scenes, constitute the chief glory of his plays. Henceforth the public expected from a playwright both the thrill of tense situations, and the glow of beautiful poetry. He contributed other things, also, to the national drama. He showed playwrights the value of blank verse, and taught them how to use this most effective vehicle of dramatic expression; he concentrated attention upon character, and revealed that this could have an appeal as well as the plot; and he created the one-man type of play, in which a single hero dominates for the time being the whole world. On the other hand he was deficient in certain respects, notably in a sense of humor, and in the ability to portray romantic love.

Robert Greene, who had hitherto spent his energies in composing love-romances, quickly followed the lead of Marlowe, and began to write plays for the public actors. In imitation of *Tamburlaine* he produced *Alphonsus*, and in imitation of *Dr. Faustus* the more genial *Friar Bacon.* In a short time he became, if we may use his own language, "famous for an arch-playmaking poet." But he was not successful in imitating the high-buskined style of Marlowe. His real ability lay in telling a pretty, idyllic romance, and his contributions to the development of the Elizabethan drama were made in the field of comedy rather than tragedy, in the treatment of love, and in the conception of that ideal type of heroine which Shakespeare copied in Rosalind, Juliet, Desdemona, and Miranda.

George Perle, completing a triumvirate, likewise devoted his energies to the composition of plays, rivaling Marlowe and Greene with his tragedies, comedies, and histories, no less deserving than the other two, in some things rarer. Possessed of a delicate fancy and a graceful style, he is one of the most attractive of Shakespeare's predecessors. Lodge and Nashe, both experienced literary craftsmen, also wrote plays, and apparently were successful, though few of their dramatic works are now extant. And other young men with education and ambition in letters were drifting to London to try their hands at "the swelling bombast of a bragging blank verse" in imitation of Marlowe, or at light romantic comedy in imitation of Greene.

At last the crowd was augmented by the arrival of William Shakespeare, son of a glover in Stratford, without a university education — an "upstart crow," who immediately began to plume up his feathers by close imitation of the "university wits."

CHAPTER VIII

ARRIVAL IN LONDON, AND LABORS FOR THE PEMBROKE'S COMPANY

THE circumstances under which Shakespeare came to London are obscure. It is often said by his biographers that he probably joined a troupe of London actors traveling through Warwickshire, and accompanied them back to the city. But this is unlikely. When a company of city players took the road, it reduced its personnel to a minimum; and even so the large London companies barely made their expenses on a tour. For example, in 1592 the Lord Strange's Men, forced out of the city by the plague, attempted a tour of the provinces; but in a short time, discovering that they could not pay their expenses, they returned to London, and petitioned the Privy Council for special permission to reopen their playhouse, complaining that "our company is great, and thereby our charge intollerable in traveling the country"; and in 1593 the Pembroke's Men were actually wrecked, "for they cannot save their charges with travel." About the last thing that a London troupe of players would do while on a tour would be to add to its number, especially an untrained and inexperienced person.[1]

It seems far more likely that Shakespeare left his country school and came directly to London, with the distinct intention of throwing in his lot with the rising drama both as an actor and as a writer of plays. His first biographer, Aubrey, who, it should not be forgotten, de-

[1] An Elizabethan actor had not only to understand the peculiar psychology of the boisterous inn-yard audiences, but also on occasion to be skilful at extemporizing his parts.

[123]

rived much of his information from the "neighbors" at Stratford and from the old Elizabethan theatrical manager Beeston, wrote: "This William, being inclined naturally to poetry and acting, came to London." A more plausible explanation could hardly be asked for such a step on the part of an ambitious country school-teacher, who realized that he had brains, and who felt stirring within him a natural inclination to literary composition.

We may suppose that his desire to better his pecuniary state led him to combine the uncertain profession of letters with the more surely remunerative profession of acting; for at this time acting was reputed to be "the most excellent vocation in the world for money." As Dekker wrote in his *News from Hell:* "Marrie, players swarm there [in Hell], as they do here, whose occupation being smelt out by the Cacodemon, or head-officer of that country, to be lucrative, he purposes to make up a company, and be chief sharer himself." The rapidity with which actors rose from poverty to wealth is satirized in the university play *The Return from Parnassus:*

> England affords those glorious vagabonds,
> That carried erst their fardels on their backs,
> Coursers to ride on through the gazing streets,
> Sooping it in their glaring satin suits,
> And pages to attend their masterships.

Every one believed with Henry Cross that "these copperlace gentlemen grow rich," and with Henry Parrot that acting brought "damnable excessive gains." Shakespeare, therefore, could not fail to understand that this new profession offered him the surest and quickest means to recuperate the family fortunes. Nor could he fail to realize that his skill in poetic composition might enable him, upon more familiarity with the stage, to become a successful dramatist, the goal that men of letters — Marlowe, Greene, Peele, and the rest — were now eagerly striving for. Moreover, the combination of the two careers of actor and writer was common among young men of scholarly training. It was, indeed, the very course recommended to Cambridge students in the university play *The Return from Parnassus* as the easiest way to opulence. Thomas Heywood, a Fellow of Peterhouse, Cambridge, came to London about the time Shakespeare did, joined a company of players, and quickly attained success, both in acting and in writing plays. Ben Jonson, also without a university degree, but with an excellent grammar-school training, and with pronounced literary tastes, at this same time combined acting and play-making. So, we have some reason to believe, did Robert Greene and George Peele, as unquestionably did Anthony Munday, Samuel Rowley, Robert Wilson, William Birde, Richard Brome, Nathaniel Field, Robert Armin, Richard Gunnell, William Rowley, Charles Massye, and others. Whatever purpose Shakespeare had in mind in coming to London, he arrived there in or shortly before 1590, and promptly entered the dual profession of actor and playwright.

The city which he found was not the vast metropolis we are accustomed to think of to-day. Within its limits proper there were only about 100,000 inhabitants; and with the outlying suburbs and the adjacent town of Westminster, the total population was not much more than 200,000. Thus, relatively speaking, it was a small place. Nor did it differ in material respects from the towns of Worcester and Coventry with which he was already familiar, except, of course, in its larger area.

Upon his arrival in the city he doubtless could count on the friendly aid of at least one person, Richard Field, the son of the Stratford tanner, Henry Field. The Shakespeares and Fields lived as near neighbors in Stratford, and the relationship of the tanning to the glove-making industry must have thrown the senior members of the families into close business association. When Henry Field died, John Shakespeare was called upon to take an inventory of his property. The two boys, William and Richard, were of about the same age, attended the Stratford grammar school together, and as near neighbors must have joined in common sports. In all probability, therefore, they were intimate friends. At the age of fifteen, Richard had gone in 1579 to London to be apprenticed to the famous printer Thomas Vautrollier, a Huguenot refugee who had presses both in London and in Edinburgh. "As a printer," writes McKerrow, "Thomas Vautrollier ranks above most of his contemporaries, both for the beauty of his types and the excellence of his presswork." Richard Field prospered in London. In February, 1587, he was admitted a freeman of the Company of Stationers, and later in the same year, upon the death of his master, married the widow, and thus came into possession of one of the best printing establishments in England. It seems only natural that Shakespeare upon his arrival in the city should renew his acquaintance with the friend of his boyhood; and evidence that he did reëstablish this friendship is to be found in the fact that in 1593 Field printed his *Venus and Adonis*, and a year later his *Lucrece*.

Exactly how soon Shakespeare sought out his old acquaintance, however, and to what extent Field was able to assist him in getting a start in London we do not know. Some scholars have hazarded the guess that for a time Shakespeare may have worked in Field's printing-office as a proof-reader, or even as a typesetter; but all the evidence points to the contrary. From the very outset he seems to have been associated with the drama, and to have established himself among the actors.

At the playhouses there were, besides the musicians,

three classes of persons — sharers, hirelings, and servants. The "sharers" were the most important actors, who formally constituted the "company," and who divided among themselves the daily "takings at the door." According to their merits they enjoyed either half-shares or whole-shares, as indicated by Hamlet:

> *Hamlet.* Would not this, sir, and a forest of feathers (if the rest of my fortunes turn Turk with me), with two Provincial roses on my razed shoes, get me a fellowship in a cry of players, sir?
> *Horatio.* Half a share.
> *Hamlet.* A whole one, I.

Below the sharers in rank were the "hirelings," who did not profit by the large takings of the theatre, but were engaged by the "company" on a fixed and usually small weekly stipend. Gosson, in *The School of Abuse* (1579), writes of "the very hirelings of some of our players, which stand at the reversion of vis. by the week"; somewhat later, in 1597, Henslowe engaged William Kendall as a hireling at ten shillings "for his said service every week of his playing." The hirelings, especially the younger ones, may be regarded as apprentices; at least they were hopeful of being sooner or later admitted into the "company" as half-sharers or full-sharers. Dekker represents a hireling as "swearing tragical and buskined oaths" that he would "be a half-sharer at least," or else join some traveling company and "strowle." The third class were the servants, men employed by the "company" as prompters, stage-hands, property-keepers, money-gatherers, and caretakers of the building. Shakespeare must have begun his career in one of these latter two classes, but the facts in the case are unknown to us.

Curiosity, of course, has bred some late traditions, which, though they may not convince us, at least deserve our consideration. A certain J. M. Smith, according to a communication to *The Monthly Magazine*, February,

1818, is quoted as having said that he often heard his mother, who was a lineal descendant of Shakespeare's sister Joan Hart, state that "Shakespeare owed his rise in life and his introduction to the theatre to his accidentally holding the horse of a gentleman at the door of the theatre on his first arriving in London; his appearance led to inquiry and subsequent patronage." If we could trust this statement, not printed until 1818, we might suspect that it recorded a story handed down in the Hart family from the sixteenth century. But even so it would not help us to understand how Shakespeare secured employment within the theatre, or in what capacity. I fear that it is merely a weak echo on the part of this estimable lady of a more detailed story already well-known in print. The earliest version of it appears in a manuscript note written about 1748, and now preserved in the University Library, Edinburgh.[1] It was first awarded the dignity of print in 1753, in *The Lives of the Poets*, a poor compilation by Dr. Samuel Johnson's assistant, Robert Shields. Shields introduces the story to the reader with the following doubtful pedigree:

Sir William Davenant told Mr. Betterton, who communicated it to Mr. Rowe [yet Rowe does not mention it in his life of the poet]; Rowe told it to Mr. Pope [yet Pope fails to mention it in his life of the poet]; and Mr. Pope told it to Dr. Newton, the late editor of Milton; and from a gentleman who heard it from him, 'tis here related.[2]

The story, however, is best told by Dr. Samuel Johnson, who, while keeping to the main facts, has added some flourishes from his own imagination — for so a tradition grows. I quote his account below for what it may be worth:

[1] For this version see Halliwell-Phillipps, *Outlines*, ii, 286.
[2] Vol. i, p. 130. The *Lives* were published as by Theophilus Cibber; but Shields seems to have been chiefly responsible for the hack-work.

His first expedient was to wait at the door of the playhouse and hold the horses of those that had no servants, that they might be ready again after the performance; — in this office he became so conspicuous for his care and readiness that in a short time every man as he alighted called for Will Shakespeare, and scarcely any other waiter was trusted with a horse while Will Shakespeare could be had; — this was the first dawn of better fortune: — Shakespeare finding more horses put into his hand than he could hold, hired boys to wait under his inspection, who, when Will Shakespeare was summoned, were immediately to present themselves, "I am Shakespeare's boy, sir"; — in time Shakespeare found higher employment, but as long as the practice of riding to the playhouse continued, the waiters that held the horses retained the appellation of "Shakespeare's boys."

It is true that gallants were accustomed to ride to the playhouses, both to those in the fields and to those on the Bankside, and the custom persisted into the seventeenth century; but the story as narrated above is too fanciful, and its pedigree far too doubtful, to warrant more than passing notice.

Another tradition is recorded by Dowdall, who visited Stratford in 1693. He quotes the garrulous "clarke" who showed him over the church to the effect that Shakespeare was at first "received into the playhouse as a serviture," that is, as a common servant. Rowe, in 1709, contents himself with the cautious statement that "he was received into the company [of players] then in being at first in a very mean rank"; and Malone, in 1780, speaks of "a stage-tradition that his first office in the theatre was that of prompter's attendant."

These late traditions can be accepted only as presenting the obvious fact that Shakespeare must have begun his new career in some fairly humble capacity. But in view of his age (he was no mere "boy") and of his excellent schooling, it seems more plausible to suppose that he was first taken on as a hireling and set to performing unimportant parts until he acquired greater skill. This, we know, was the case with the actor-playwrights Thomas Heywood and Samuel Rowley. And in *The Return from Parnassus*, Burbage is represented as eager to engage inexperienced young scholars as hirelings, "at a low rate," for, although they may be poor actors, "a little teaching will mend these faults, and it may be besides they will be able to pen a part."

In whatever capacity Shakespeare began his career at the theatre, whether as "serviture" or "hireling," he rapidly rose in the profession, for by 1594 we discover him as one of the full-sharers in his company. And an important factor in this rapid rise was unquestionably his ability "to pen a part." [1]

It has been generally assumed that from the outset he was associated with the Lord Strange's Company, the troupe with which he is first known to have been connected in 1594. This, however, is altogether unlikely. We have remarkably full records of the Strange's Men, both as to their personnel and their repertoire of plays. His name does not appear in the list of actors affixed to the stage "plot" of *The Seven Deadly Sins*, 1592, nor in the company's traveling license of 1593. Moreover, in the detailed records of the company kept by the industrious Henslowe or embodied in the Alleyn papers, extending from the spring of 1592 to the summer of 1594, there is no mention of him. If Shakespeare belonged to this troupe, naturally he wrote for it his early plays. Now to this period of his career Sir Sidney Lee assigns *Love's Labour's Lost*, *The Two Gentlemen of Verona*, *The Comedy of Errors*, *Romeo and Juliet*, *I Henry VI*, *II Henry VI*, *III Henry VI*, *Richard II*, *Richard III*, and

---

[1] Thomas Heywood and Samuel Rowley, who, as noted above, began their careers as hirelings, became sharers within four years; and they, too, had the ability to "pen a part."

Titus Andronicus. Yet not a single one of these plays,[1] which doubtless took London by storm, appears in the list of plays acted by Strange's Men at the Rose, or at Newington Butts. Why in 1594 he should have associated himself with the Strange's Company will be later explained.

It seems far more likely, if not indeed almost certain, that when Shakespeare came to London he joined the Earl of Pembroke's Men. This excellent company, whose chief actor was the famous Gabriel Spencer, was of great size and importance, performing entirely in London. Henslowe, writing of them in 1593, says that they "are all at home [i.e., in London], and have been these five or six weeks, for they cannot save their charges with travel." Very little is known of their history. But they probably were organized [2] about 1590, and at once assumed a conspicuous place among the London troupes. They secured as their chief playwright Christopher Marlowe, the most popular dramatist of the day. Marlowe had written *Tamburlaine,* Part I (1587), *Tamburlaine,* Part II (1587–88), *Doctor Faustus* (1588–89), and *The Jew of Malta* (1589–90), all for the Admiral's Men; but in 1590 he transferred his allegiance to the newly-organized Pembroke's Company. His services were probably secured for these players by no less a person than the Earl of Pembroke himself, who at the same time seems to have taken Kyd also under his patronage. Kyd declares in 1593: "My first acquaintance with this Marlowe rose upon his bearing name to serve my Lord,[3] although his Lordship never

[1] For a discussion of the *Henry VI* of Henslowe's *Diary* see pp. 136–39, 214.

[2] Or, it may be, reorganized, for there was a provincial troupe travelling under Pembroke's name in 1575–76. But we hear nothing else of this early troupe, and the likelihood is that a new company was organized in 1590.

[3] Kyd does not name this lord, but the evidence, it seems to me, points unmistakably to Pembroke.

[131]

knew his service but in writing for his players"; and in the same letter he speaks of having served His Lordship "almost these three years." This carries us back to 1590 as the date of Kyd's becoming a member of His Lord ship's household. He speaks further of "some occasion of our writing in one chamber two years since," that is, in 1591. The natural inference is that the Earl of Pembroke, taking a deep interest in the new company organized under his patronage, attempted to provide it, at some expense to himself, with the best playwrights to be had. For the Pembroke's Men Marlowe wrote *Edward II*, *The True Tragedy*, *The Contention*, and possibly other plays. If, therefore, Shakespeare joined this troupe, he acquired his first training in dramatic literature through acting in the plays of Marlowe; and we find the influence of Marlowe clearly revealed in his early style. Possibly his allusion to Marlowe as the "dead shepherd" in *As You Like It*, the only time he refers to a contemporary writer, may indicate the existence of friendly if not affectionate relations between them. But the company secured plays from other dramatists, too. In their repertoire were the famous stage-favorites *Titus Andronicus*, *The Taming of the Shrew*, and *Hamlet*, with all of which Shakespeare's name is now associated.

Possibly, as has already been hinted, Shakespeare introduced himself to the favorable notice of this new company by submitting to it the manuscript of an early play written in the country. "Will not this, sir," exclaims Hamlet waving the manuscript of his *Mouse-Trap*, "get me a fellowship in a cry of players?" The play that Shakespeare may have used to get himself a fellowship in the Pembroke's Company, I venture to suggest, was *The Comedy of Errors*. The form in which we now have *The Comedy* shows in parts drastic revision, made, presumably, on the occasion of its presentation before Gray's Inn in 1594; but the parts that remain untouched or slightly altered clearly show by the verbal jests, the elaborate rhyme, the painful balancing of speeches, and the patches of doggerel verse that this was one of his earliest efforts at dramatic composition, if not indeed his very earliest. It is mainly based on the *Menaechmi* of Plautus with certain additions from the *Amphitruo*, neither of which appeared in English translation until 1595;[1] and it may well have been the product of his days as a "schoolmaster in the country."

If he was able to submit this play to the actors upon his arrival, he probably could not at once devote much time to further composition. He would be too busy learning the profession of acting, memorizing his parts, and familiarizing himself with the life of the city. But the Pembroke's Men were soon to need his facile pen, for in 1592, it seems, they lost the services of their chief playwright, Marlowe. Apparently we have a clue to the cause in a letter written by Kyd after his arrest in May, 1593, on the charge of being the author of an atheistical pamphlet found in his study. After attributing the pamphlet to Marlowe, he says: "Never could my Lord endure his name or sight, when he had heard of his conditions," i.e., his atheistical inclinations. That Marlowe had left the employ of the Earl of Pembroke long before Kyd's arrest is shown by a second letter from Kyd: "It was his custom, when I knew him first, and as I hear say he continued it, in table-talk and otherwise to jest at divine scriptures"; and "I left and did refrain his company," he says, "by my Lord's commandment."[2] That Marlowe had

[1] It has been suggested, but unconvincingly, that the obscure young actor may have had the privilege of seeing the manuscript of Warner's translation before it was printed. As P. J. Enk, in *Neophilologus*, 1920, pp. 359–65, shows, Shakespeare took over proper names from the original that do not appear in the translation at all.

[2] This letter, recently discovered, may be found in the *Literary Supplement* of the London *Times*, June 2, 1921.

ceased to write for the Pembroke's Men in 1592 is further indicated by the fact that in January, 1593, the Lord Strange's Men brought out his *Massacre at Paris* as a new play. In May, 1593, when Kyd was arrested, Marlowe's residence is said to have been in "the house of Mr. T. Walsingham, in Kent."

The loss of Marlowe would naturally throw some of the burden of dramatic revision and composition upon the shoulders of the new arrival, who had already, we may suppose, demonstrated his ability to pen a part. And at once we find Shakespeare exercising his skill in touching up several of the old stock pieces belonging to the company, plays, no doubt, in which he himself had been called upon to act. Perhaps one of these was *Titus Andronicus*,[1] mainly, if not entirely, by George Peele,[2] a crude tragedy which through its sensationalism and bloody horrors was popular with theatre-goers. The success of the somewhat similar play, *The Spanish Tragedy*, bears eloquent testimony to the murderous tastes of the early audiences. At the end of the performance, after giving a detailed catalogue of all the ingeniously devised deaths, nine in number, which had been presented for the delectation of the spectators, Andrea exclaims:

Aye, these were spectacles to please my soul!

And in the remarkably bloody play of *Selimus* (about 1590), the author says to his audience:

[1] That Shakespeare was not responsible for the whole play is, I think, obvious. Edward Ravenscroft, who wrote a new version of it in 1678, states: "I have been told by some anciently conversant with the stage that it was not originally his, but brought by a private author to be acted, and he only gave it some master touches to one or two of the principal parts or characters."

[2] Mr. H. Dugdale Sykes, who has made an exhaustive study of Peele's style, confidently declares (*Sidelights on Shakespeare*, 1919, p. 125), that "almost every page" of *Titus Andronicus* "exhibits traces of Peele's vocabulary and phrasing."

> If this First Part, gentles, do like you well,
> The Second Part shall greater murders tell.

Shakespeare could hardly have had a genuine artistic interest in the bloody *Titus*, but his business shrewdness showed him the opportunity of turning it into a great money-maker for his company. In this he was more than successful. Nearly a quarter of a century later Ben Jonson declared:[1] "He that will swear *Jeronimo* [i.e., *The Spanish Tragedy*] or *Andronicus* are the best plays yet, shall pass unexcepted at here as a man whose judgment shows it is constant and hath stood still these five-and-twenty or thirty years."[2] That the play as thus revised by Shakespeare was acted by the Pembroke's Company is clearly stated on the title-page of the first edition, issued in February, 1593–94.

But our first definite reference to the success of Shakespeare in this kind of revision appears in the summer of 1592. The Pembroke Company's chief rival, the Lord Strange's Company, then newly established at the Rose,

---

[1] In his Induction to *Bartholomew Fair*, 1614. With reference to the date of *The Spanish Tragedy* and *Titus Andronicus* Jonson, of course, is speaking in round numbers and from general recollection.

[2] Tne later history of the play is not without interest. In 1593, when Pembroke's Company was disbanded, the Lord Strange's Men bought a number of its best plays, including *Titus*. This they acted in the country as Derby's Men. On January 23, 1594, the Sussex' Men acted the play at Henslowe's Rose while the Strange-Derby company was absent. Either they purchased a second copy from some member of Pembroke's Company, or, as seems more likely, Henslowe, in his desire to make money in a lean year, lent them the copy he had purchased as manager for the Strange-Derby troupe. In his record of the performance he marks it "ne." or new, meaning, I presume, that it had not before been acted at his theatre (cf. his entry of *Edward I*), or possibly not acted by this company. The Pembroke's Company seems also to have parted with a copy to a publisher, who entered it in the Stationers' Registers on February 6, 1593–94, and published it shortly after. Until recently the existence of this edition was doubted; but in 1905 a copy turned up in Sweden, and was purchased by an American collector for £2000. The title-page states that the play had been acted by "the Earle of Derbie, Earl of Pembroke, and Earle of Sussex their Servants," which agrees with the history of the play as sketched above.

brought out early in 1592 a play by George Peele,[1] possibly assisted by Robert Greene, entitled *Henry VI*. Henslowe, business-manager for the Strange's Men, notes its first performance on March 3, marking it "ne.," that is, a new play. It proved to be the chief sensation of the year, and Henslowe records no fewer than fifteen performances of it between March 3 and June 22, when the playhouses were closed by order of the Privy Council. Peele's friend, Thomas Nashe, writing in July, 1592, exclaims: "How would it have joyed brave Talbot (the terror of the French) to think that after he had lain two hundred years in his tomb he should triumph again on the stage, and have his bones new embalmed with the tears of ten thousand spectators at least (at several times), who in the tragedian that represents his person imagine they behold him fresh bleeding." [2]

The astonishing popularity of this Lord Strange's play led the Pembroke's Men to seek a rival attraction, for such was the custom among theatrical troupes. In order to enable his company to compete with Peele's great success, Shakespeare, it would seem, hurriedly revised Marlowe's [3] twin plays, *The Contention betwixt the Two Famous Houses of York and Lancaster*, and *The True Tragedy of Richard Duke of York*, both, as it happened, dealing with the reign of Henry VI. Since the manuscripts belonged to the Pembroke's Men, Marlowe could

---

[1] For the authorship and history of the play see C. F. Tucker Brooke's edition of *I Henry VI* in The Yale Shakespeare Series. I may add that before the appearance of this volume my own study of the authorship of the play led me to the same conclusion.

[2] *Pierce Penniless*, entered in the Stationers' Registers on August 8, 1592.

[3] See C. F. Tucker Brooke, *The Authorship of the Second and Third Parts of "King Henry VI,"* 1912. There is no ground for the supposition that Greene had a share in these plays; see J. C. Collins, *The Plays and Poems of Robert Greene*, i, 68–69. On the other hand, it seems quite possible that George Peele was associated with Marlowe in their composition: see H. Dugdale Sykes, *Sidelights on Shakespeare*, pp. 108 ff.

raise no objection to any changes the owners might see fit to make in them. And the plays, of course, were widely advertised by the actors in bills posted all over the city as "newly revised, with additions by William Shakespeare," and as presenting "the history of King Henry VI." [1]

The connection of these two revisions with Pembroke's troupe is clearly revealed by the publication of *The First Part of the Contention* in 1594 (entered in the Stationers' Registers, March 12, 1593–94), and the Second Part, *The True Tragedy*, in the following year, both by the same publisher, and with the statement on the title-page of the Second Part: "as it was sundrie times acted by the Right Honourable the Earl of Pembroke his servants." The plays show unmistakable signs of Shakespeare's workmanship. As still further revised by the master, they were included in the First Folio, 1623, with the titles *II Henry VI* and *III Henry VI*. The Folio editors made use of the ancient playhouse manuscripts secured from the archives of Shakespeare's company; and in some of the old prompter's stage-directions reproduced by the printers we discover embedded the names of three actors, Gabriel Spencer, John Sinklow, and Humphrey Jeffes, two of whom were certainly Pembroke's Men, and the third may have been. [2]

These two plays, after Shakespeare's hurried but effective revision, met with unusual success. Naturally this success, built directly on the labors of Marlowe and competing with George Peele's popular *Henry VI*, would lead to resentment among the University Wits, — "those that lived by their wits, and such as were of the livery of

---

[1] "I refer you to the Players' bill, that is styled *Newly revised, with Additions*." — Thomas Campion, *Fourth Book of Airs*, To the Reader.

[2] For an interesting discussion of these plays see A. W. Pollard, "The York and Lancaster Plays in the Folio," *The Times Literary Supplement*, 1918, pp. 438, 452.

learning," [1] — who would regard the new arrival from Stratford as an "upstart" beautifying himself with stolen feathers. Robert Greene, dying in poverty and neglected by the actors — possibly the Pembroke's Men [2] — who had formerly employed him as their dramatist, wrote a bitter attack upon the "upstart," in which he urged his fellow University Wits to quit the trade of play-making. This attack, in the form of an open letter, was embodied in his *Groat's-worth of Wit*, the manuscript of which he sold to a publisher at some time before his death on September 3, 1592. The manuscript being illegible, for at best Greene wrote a crabbed hand, Henry Chettle attempted to prepare it for the press. It was entered in the Stationers' Registers on September 20, 1592, by the bookseller, William Wright, and doubtless appeared shortly after that date.

Greene's remarks, primarily directed to the three most famous University Wits, Christopher Marlowe, George Peele, and Thomas Nashe, begin thus: "To those gentlemen, his quondam acquaintance, that spend their wits in making plays, R. G. wisheth a better exercise, and wisdom to prevent his extremities." First he addresses Marlowe, with a glance at Marlowe's well-known atheistical tendency: "Wonder not, for with thee will I first begin, thou famous gracer of tragedians, that Greene, who hath said with thee, like the fool in his heart, there is no God, should now give glory unto His greatness; for penetrating is His power; His hand lies heavy upon me; He hath spoken unto me with a voice of thunder; and I have felt; He is a God that can punish enemies." Next he addresses

---

[1] Thomas Dekker, *Knight's Conjuring.*

[2] Greene's editor, J. Churton Collins, says: "Greene, as we know from Nashe, wrote, and wrote much, for the Lord Pembroke's Men." Mr. W. W. Greg seems to be inclined to the same opinion. Greene's attack upon Shakespeare indicates that this was likely, but I have not been able to discover any unmistakable evidence of Greene's having written for Pembroke's Company.

young Thomas Nashe, known as the sharpest satirist of the day: "With thee I join young Juvenal, that biting satirist, that lastly with me together writ a comedy." Finally he addresses George Peele, with an obvious allusion to his name: "And thou, no less deserving than the other two, in some things rarer, in nothing inferior, driven (as myself) to extreme shifts,[1] a little have I to say to thee; and were it not an idolatrous oath I would swear by sweet S[aint] George thou art unworthy better hap, since thou dependest on so mean a stay," i.e., as actors. Then follows his attack upon the players, who, deserting the older writers, now look to the upstart Shakespeare for their success:

Base-minded men all three of you, if by my misery ye be not warned; for unto none of you, like me, sought those burres [i.e., the actors] to cleave,[2] those puppits, I mean, that speak from our mouths, those anticks garnisht in our colours. Is it not strange that I, to whom they all have been beholding, is it not like that you, to whom they all have been beholding, shall, were ye in that case that I am now [i.e., in dire need], be both at once of them forsaken? Yes, trust them not; for there is an upstart crow[3] [i.e., Shakespeare] beautified with our feathers,[4] that with his *Tyger's heart wrapt in a Player's hide* [quoted, with alteration, from *III Henry VI*: "Tiger's heart wrapt in a woman's hide"] supposes he is as well able to bumbast out a blank

---

[1] The "extreme shifts" to which Peele was driven are well illustrated in *The Jests of George Peele*, published after his death.

[2] Thomas Nashe wrote of Greene: "He was chief agent for the company, for he writ more than four other." This, however, does not necessarily refer to plays, as Fleay and Collins suppose.

[3] Marlowe wrote his first play in 1587 or 1588, probably in the latter year; Greene began his career as a playwright later in imitation of Marlowe, probably in 1589; Nashe, presumably, later still. They could hardly regard Shakespeare as an "upstart" if, as some critics suppose, Shakespeare began to compose plays as early as 1587 or 1588. The likelihood is that Shakespeare was an "upstart" in the summer of 1592, when Greene was writing.

[4] The author of *Greene's Funerals* (1594) writes:

> Nay more, the men that so eclipst his fame
> Purloyned his *plumes;* can they deny the same?

verse as the best of you; and being an absolute *Johannes Facto-tum* [i.e., Jack-of-all-work — actor, revamper of old manuscripts, and writer of plays], is, in his own conceit, the only Shake-scene in a country.

Both Marlowe [1] and Shakespeare resented the publication of this ill-natured attack, though for different reasons. At first a rumor was circulated that in reality Thomas Nashe was the author of the pamphlet, or in some way responsible for the offensive parts of the letter. Nashe thereupon made haste to issue a public denial. In a formal Epistle prefixed to the second edition of his *Pierce Penniless*, printed about October 15, 1592, [2] he writes:

Other news I am advertised of, that a scald, trivial, lying pamphlet called *Greene's Groat's-worth of Wit* is given out to be of my doing. God never have care of my soul, but utterly renounce me, if the least word or syllable in it proceeded from my pen, or if I were any way privy to the writing, or printing, of it.

Nashe's vehemence indicates considerable anxiety to be freed from any responsibility for Greene's attack. Finally the blame was placed, where it should with more justice rest, on the head of Chettle, who had prepared the manuscript for publication. Chettle at once made a frank and full apology to Shakespeare, though stoutly refusing to do the same to Marlowe. This he published in an address "To the Gentlemen Readers," prefixed to his *Kind-Heart's Dream*, entered in the Stationers' Registers on December 8, 1592. First he explained to the public his slight share in the issuing of Greene's pamphlet: "About three months since died M. Robert Greene, leaving many papers in sundry booksellers' hands, among others his *Groat's-worth of Wit*, in which a letter, written to diverse

[1] Marlowe and Greene seem never to have been on good terms with each other. Greene was jealous of Marlowe's greater success as a playwright, just as later he became jealous of the upstart Shakespeare.

[2] See McKerrow, *Nashe*, iv, 78–79.

playmakers, is offensively by one or two of them taken; and because on the dead they cannot be avenged, they wilfully forge in their conceits a living author; and after tossing it to and fro, no remedy but it must light on me. . . . I had only in the copy this share: — it was ill writ ten, as sometimes Greene's hand was none of the best; licensed it must be ere it could be printed, which could never be if it might not be read. To be brief, I writ it over, and as near as I could followed the copy; only, in that letter I put something out, but in the whole book not a word in; for I protest it was all Greene's, not mine, nor Master Nashe's as some unjustly have affirmed." [1] Chettle further states: "With neither of them that take offence was I acquainted, and with one of them I care not if I never be." The last clause doubtless refers to Marlowe, who had been directly accused by Greene of atheism, and who was then under grave suspicion by others. Then follows the apology to Shakespeare, indicating, it will be observed, that possibly Chettle of his own initiative had "put something out" of Greene's letter in order to mitigate the attack on the new poet:

The other, whom at that time I did not so much spare as since I wish I had, for that as I have moderated the heat of living writers, and might have used my own discretion, — especially in such a case the author being dead, — that I did not, I am as sorry as if the original fault had been my fault; because myself have seen his demeanor no less civil than he excellent in the quality he professes [i.e., acting [2]]; — besides, diverse of worship have reported his uprightness of dealing,

---

[1] Chettle is doubtless telling the truth. The publisher, Wright, entered the book in the Stationers' Registers with the special protecting clause "upon the perill of Henry Chettle."

[2] The word "quality" is often applied to acting. So Shakespeare uses it in *Hamlet* of the child-actors: "Will they pursue the quality no longer than they can sing?" Cf. Thomas Middleton's elegy entitled "On the death of that great Master in his art and quality, painting and playing, R. Burbage."

which argues his honesty, and his facetious grace in writing, that approves his art.[1]

These constitute our first references to Shakespeare in his new career in London. Greene was jealous of the success of the "upstart." Chettle, a man of letters, had made inquiries about him, had actually met him, and was deeply impressed by his courteous demeanor, which he declared in public print to be not less excellent than his recognized skill as an actor. Moreover, "diverse of worship" — who could not have been players — had vouched for his "uprightness of dealing," and had favorably commented on his "facetious grace in writing." Clearly he had made a fair beginning both as actor and author, and had already established that reputation for gentle behavior which attended him through life.

But the career of Pembroke's Company, with which Shakespeare had thrown in his fortunes, was soon to be interrupted. On June 11, 1592, a riot broke out in Southwark, which started with certain apprentices under "pretence of their meeting at a play." The Privy Council thereupon ordered the closing of all playhouses for three months and a half. Before the expiration of this time, the appearance of the plague in London led to a second inhibition of acting, which extended to the last week in December. Thus for more than six months the city companies were forced to be idle.

During this period of freedom from the onerous duties of acting, Shakespeare, in all probability, devoted his energies to composing *Love's Labour's Lost*. It has recently been shown that 1592 is the earliest date that can possibly be assigned to the play, and that it is "probable

[1] The fact that Chettle, himself a playwright, apparently did not know Shakespeare before, even by reputation, but learned of him upon inquiry, tends to invalidate the common assumption that Shakespeare had begun his dramatic career as early as 1587, and had by this time produced some of his masterpieces.

that the latter part of that year was the actual time of composition." [1] If so, it came at a happy moment, for the company at once had occasion to use it. The plague, though it kept the actors from performing before the public, did not interfere with their annual performances before the Court; [2] and the Pembroke's Men were summoned to give a play before the Queen on December 27, 1592, and again on January 6, 1593. On one of these dates, we may suppose, they acted Shakespeare's new comedy, which obviously had been composed with the audience at Court in mind. It was closely modeled on the style of John Lyly, whose plays were then in high favor with the Queen.

On December 29, the deaths from the plague having fallen below fifty (the number fixed by law for automatically preventing the assembly of people), the inhibition of playing was raised, and the actors promptly resumed their performances before the public. But their respite was short. The plague soon broke out with renewed fury, and about February 1 acting was again prohibited. The year rapidly developed into one of the worst plague years in history; between ten and fifteen thousand persons died. Realizing that an early reopening of the playhouses was unlikely, the Pembroke's Men, reducing their personnel, [3] began to travel in the provinces. Shakespeare, it seems, either because he was one of the less necessary actors, or because he preferred to stay behind and devote his energies to composition, did not accompany them on their arduous tour. He could not foresee that his enforced leisure would be unduly protracted;

[1] See the able study of the evidence by H. B. Charlton in *The Modern Language Review*, July, 1918. The biographical evidence both supports and is supported by this convincing article.

[2] During the winter of 1592–93 the Lord Strange's Men gave three performances at Court.

[3] This was customary. The license of the Strange's Men in 1593 contains the names of only six players, though this was probably not complete.

doubtless like the other actors he expected the plague to subside within a short time. From month to month, however, the plague increased in violence, and even with the coming of winter it gave no signs of abating. The inhibition of the playhouses, in reality, was to last for two years.

Thus ends the first chapter of Shakespeare's dramatic career; and for a while his energies, no longer needed for plays, had to be directed into other channels.

CHAPTER IX

PERIOD OF NON-DRAMATIC COMPOSITION

DURING the long months of leisure enforced by the plague, Shakespeare was able to accomplish much in the way of quiet study and wide reading to make up for the deficiencies of his rather narrow education and provincial sympathies. Fate, indeed, under the guise of misfortune, had thrown before him, in the prime of his young manhood, and at the very outset of his literary career, a golden opportunity. That he took advantage of this opportunity we may be sure. It is significant that his taste led him not only to popular contemporary writers, such as Spenser, Daniel, Lodge, and Drayton, but also to "old father Chaucer," whose antique pen and aged accents exercised over him a special charm. Moreover, we have evidence that he read extensively in the modern writers of France and Italy. That he should acquire a reading knowledge of French and Italian, living as he did in an atmosphere surcharged with the Renaissance literature of the Continent, may be regarded as inevitable. With his mastery of Latin, and his retentive memory, the acquisition of these languages would be to him an easy matter; and there are unmistakable indications that he acquired some facility in both.

How much this study of native and foreign literature contributed to his rapidly developing genius cannot well be estimated; but its influence is quickly apparent, for almost at once he turned his pen to imitation, and produced works that placed his name in the front rank of contemporary artists. Marlowe, whom in all probability he numbered among his close acquaintances, was engaged on an amorous poem, *Hero and Leander;* Lodge had recently published a similar poem, *Glaucus and Scilla;* Daniel had won great fame in 1592 by his amorous *Complaint of Rosamond;* Nashe was privately circulating a superlatively erotic poem, *The Choice of Valentines;*[1] Drayton was shortly to publish *Endimion and Phœbe.* Thus amorous poems in a richly jeweled style were now distinctly the fashion. With these examples before him Shakespeare selected an amorous theme from his favorite author Ovid (Books iv, viii, and x of the *Metamorphoses*), and working under the inspiration of the Renaissance literature he had been studying, produced the ornate and voluptuous poem to which he gave the title *Venus and Adonis.* The six-line stanza he employed had recently become popular in England, where it had been effectively used by Spenser in his elegy on the death of Sir Philip Sidney, and by Lodge in his *Glaucus and Scilla.* Shakespeare's handling of the stanza clearly shows the influence of both these masters, but particularly of Lodge, whose poem he had frankly chosen as his model.[2] The following passage from Lodge will enable the reader to observe the similarity in spirit, and also the superiority in craftsmanship exhibited by the upstart from Stratford:

> Glaucus, my love (quoth she), look on thy lover,
> Smile, gentle Glaucus, on the nimph that likes thee.
> But stark as stone sat he, and list not prove her. . . .

[1] Writing at some date before July, 1593, Gabriel Harvey refers to this poem as then well known. It was too erotic to be printed, but was being widely circulated in manuscript.

[2] It may be significant that Lodge in *Glaucus and Scilla* described the death of Adonis and the grief of Venus, and that he drew his plot and inspiration from Ovid. For a general discussion of the influence of Lodge on Shakespeare see J. P. Reardon, "Shakespeare's *Venus and Adonis* and Lodge's *Scilla's Metamorphosis*" in The Shakespeare Society's Papers, 1847, iii, 143, and Sir Sidney Lee's introduction to his facsimile reprint of *Venus and Adonis,* 1905. Marlowe, too, in *Hero and Leander,* alludes to a grove —

> Where Venus in her naked glory strove
> To please the careless and disdainful eyes
> Of proud Adonis that before her lies.

> Lord, how her lips do dwell upon his cheeks,
> And how she looks for babies in his eyes,
> And how she sighes, and swears she loves and leeks. . . .
>
> How oft with blushes would she plead for grace,
> How oft with whisperings would she tempt his ears,
> How oft with cristal did she wet his face,
> How oft she wipt them with her amber hairs.
>
> But Glaucus scorns the nimph that waits relief,
> And more she loves, the more the sea-god hated.

It has commonly been suggested by scholars that Shakespeare wrote *Venus and Adonis* while still at Stratford; yet a close examination of all the facts renders the supposition unlikely. Three reasons have been advanced to support a Stratford date of composition. In the first place, it is said, the ornate style and the voluptuous nature of the poem suggest adolescence. But these qualities are inherent in the type of literature to which the poem conforms. The same qualities are found in *Hero and Leander*, *Glaucus and Scilla*, *Endimion and Phœbe*, and the other amorous poems written by the most popular authors of the day; and, as already indicated, the selection of the theme and the style of verse were both dictated by a prevailing fashion. In the second place, it is said, Shakespeare's description of *Venus and Adonis* as "the first heir of my invention" proves it his earliest composition. But the poem is indeed the first product of Shakespeare's pen intended for the press, which is all that the statement necessarily implies. Plays were not designed for publication; moreover, in view of the general opprobrium attaching to dramatic composition, he may have regarded this as his first essay in the realm of pure literature. Nor should one forget that it was a conventional form of flattery with young authors to inform a dedicatee that he was the first choice of their Muse. Thus it is dangerous to interpret the phrase too literally, or to see in it more than the simple fact that *Venus and Adonis* was the first work published as from Shakespeare's pen. In the third place, it is said, the imagery of the poem is mainly drawn from the country, and concerns flowers and spring and "the changing aspects of the sky." Scholars who write thus forget that the rural setting of the poem renders such imagery as inevitable as it is appropriate, that Venus is commonly associated with flowers and the spring, and that Adonis is always pictured in outdoor country life. Furthermore they overlook certain other imagery that quite as clearly points to the London experiences of the poet; for example the theatrical note in the lines —

> And all this *dumb play* had his *acts* made plain
> With tears which *chorus-like* her eyes did rain.

Or the reference to the plague raging in 1592–93:

> To drive infection from the dangerous year
> That the star-gazers, having writ on death,
> May say, the plague is banish'd by thy breath.

Or the essentially London echoes in such lines as —

> Like shrill-tongu'd tapsters answering every call.

Worse still, they overlook the numerous similarities in thought, diction, and metre between the poem and works of Shakespeare that are known to have been produced about this time. In *Love's Labour's Lost*, written in the latter half of 1592, we find him tentatively experimenting with the six-line stanza that he adopted for *Venus and Adonis*. In *Romeo and Juliet* we discover a reference to the earthquake noted in lines 1046–48 of the poem; and the simile of the bird "tam'd with too much handling" appears in both. And in the *Sonnets* we discover innumerable similarities of a most striking nature, both of concept and diction.

But this is not the place for an extended discussion of the date of composition of *Venus and Adonis*. No good reason has been advanced to show that the poem was produced during Shakespeare's Stratford period, and internal evidence as well as biographical probability is against the theory. Even if we grant the possibility that it was first drafted in Stratford, we can affirm with confidence that it was subjected to a thorough revision in London during the winter and early spring of 1592–93.

In turning from the writing of plays for the professional actors to the composition of poems for the reading public, Shakespeare had two readily discoverable motives. In the first place, he desired to win recognition in the literary circles of London. Not a line of his had yet appeared in print. His plays were not designed for the critical reader, were not intended for publication, and, so far as the author and his fellow-actors could prevent it, would not be allowed to fall into the hands of the printers. Even if his plays were surreptitiously issued, they would not admit him into the society of the best men of letters, or enroll him in the category of such poets as Spenser, Daniel, Sidney, Ralegh, Barnfield, and Drayton. Plays were regarded as ephemeral products intended only for the mouths of actors; and, as mercenary works, they did not confer literary distinction on the author. As Daniel exclaims: "God forbid I should my papers blot with mercenary lines. . . . No, no; my verse respects not Thames nor Theatres." Such notoriety, therefore, as Shakespeare enjoyed was limited to the applause of vulgar London playgoers in the scorned "public theatres." Henry Chettle, it will be remembered, who was something of a man of letters, knew nothing about him in the summer of 1592. It was thus but natural that Shakespeare should desire to introduce himself into the politer circles of literary London.

In the second place, now that the plague had robbed him of his former means of livelihood, he found it necessary, if he followed the career of letters, to secure a patron. Possibly he contemplated abandoning the "mercenary stage" and henceforth devoting his poetic gifts to the higher, and, as it was thought, nobler, forms of literature. He had just read in *Glaucus and Scilla* how Lodge had vowed —

> To write no more of that whence shame doth grow,
> Or tie my pen to penny-knaves' delight,
> But live with fame, and so for fame to write;

a thought which he shortly echoed in a sonnet addressed to his friend:

> My name be buried where my body is,
> And live no more to shame nor me nor you;
> For I am shamed by that which I bring forth.

But Shakespeare could not thus dedicate himself to Fame and to the free service of the Muses without the aid of a Mæcenas. It was customary for poets to present their work to some nobleman, who in return for the honor would bestow on them a pecuniary reward, and who might, if greatly pleased and generously disposed, become a permanent patron. Spenser's career had been made possible largely through the patronage of Sir Philip Sidney and the coterie that met at the home of the Earl of Leicester. Daniel had just found a munificent patron in the Countess of Pembroke, whom he thus apostrophizes:

> Great Patroness of these my humble rhymes,
> Which thou from out thy greatness dost inspire!
> Sith only thou hast deign'd to raise them higher,
> Vouchsafe now to accept them as thine owne.

And he promises: "If my times, hereafter better laboured, shall purchase grace in the world, they must remain the monuments of your honourable favour." Drayton, about the same time, secured generous patrons in the Earl and Countess of Bedford. Shakespeare now sought the patronage of the youthful Earl of Southampton, who had recently come into control of his fortune, and was just beginning a career of extravagance. Moreover, he was known to be ambitious of being recognized as a patron of letters. Nashe, in dedicating *The Unfortunate Traveller* [1] to him, writes: "A dear lover, and cherisher, you are, as well of the lovers of Poets as of Poets themselves." We may suspect that in choosing so young, extravagant, and ambitious a patron Shakespeare was exercising the shrewdness that characterized all his business enterprises.

The dedicatory epistle prefixed to *Venus and Adonis* implies that he had not secured in advance the permission of the Earl to issue the volume under his patronage. I quote the letter in full as an interesting specimen of Shakespeare's epistolary style at this early date, and as giving us a glimpse of his elusive personality: [2]

To the Right Honourable Henry Wriothesley, Earl of Southampton and Baron of Tichfield.
Right Honourable:

I know not how I shall offend in dedicating my unpolished lines to your lordship, nor how the world will censure me for choosing so strong a prop to support so weak a burthen. Only, if your honour seem but pleased, I account myself highly praised, and vow to take advantage of all idle hours, till I have honoured you with some graver labour. But if the first heir of my invention prove deformed, I shall be sorry it had so noble a godfather, and never after ear [plough] so barren a land, for fear it yield me still so bad a harvest. I leave it to your honourable survey, and your honour to your heart's content — which I wish may always answer your own wish, and the world's hopeful expectation.

Your honour's in all duty,
WILLIAM SHAKESPEARE.

---

[1] Entered in the Stationers' Registers on September 17, 1593.

[2] Halliwell-Phillipps, *Outlines*, i, 119, observes that this letter, and the one prefixed to *Lucrece*, "are perfect examples of the judicious fusion of independence with courtesy."

Shakespeare's friend, Richard Field, undertook the printing of the volume, which he executed in his usual beautiful style. On the title-page the poet set a graceful Latin motto from Ovid:

> Vilia miretur vulgus; mihi flavus Apollo
> Pocula Castalia plena ministret aqua.[1]

And in all probability he corrected the proof himself [2] with all the meticulous care a young author is apt to bestow on the first heir of his invention. The slender but handsome volume was sold by the distinguished publisher John Harrison [3] at his shop, the White Greyhound, in Paul's Churchyard. Since it had been entered in the Stationers' Registers on April 18, 1593, it must have been offered to the public shortly after; we have record of the purchase of a copy as early as June, 1593.[4]

In this fashion Shakespeare made his formal bow to the literary world. Now for the first time readers were able to judge the worth of the new poet who had already attracted some notoriety in theatrical circles. The public received the volume with unbounded enthusiasm, calling for no fewer than seven editions within less than ten years. Men of letters were charmed by the "mellifluous" verse, and critics promptly bestowed on the author the epithet "honey-tongued." At once he was set in the front rank of

---

[1] Thus translated by Marlowe:

> Let base conceited wits admire vile things,
> Fair Phœbus lead me to the Muses' springs!

Does the choice of this motto indicate that Shakespeare, like Lodge, then contemplated abandoning the drama?

[2] For evidence that the author was expected to proof-read his work see Phœbe Sheavyn, *The Literary Profession in the Elizabethan Age*, 1909, p. 82. Writers often complain of errors due to their absence at the time their books were printed.

[3] He was three times Warden of the Stationers' Company, and three times its Master.

[4] Malone, *Inquiry*, 1796, p. 67. The price, apparently, was 6d. In 1919 a copy of the fourth edition, 1599, sold in London for £15,000.

contemporary poets, a position he was to hold throughout the rest of his life. Thomas Edwards, in *Cephalus and
Procris*, printed in 1595, includes him among the best
poets of the day, such as Spenser, Daniel, and Marlowe,
on the score of —

> Adon deafly masking thro
> Stately troupes rich conceited.[1]

As might naturally be expected, the poem had an immense popularity with "the younger sort," who, we are
assured, took "much delight" in the voluptuous appeal of
the theme, and in the ornate beauty of the verse. The
author of the university play *The Return from Parnassus*
makes one of the Cambridge students exclaim: "Let this
duncified world esteem of Spenser and Chaucer; I'll worship sweet Master Shakespeare, and to honor him will
lay his *Venus and Adonis* under my pillow."

It pleased, also, the young Earl of Southampton, whose
fondness for erotic literature seems to have been well-
known. The most lascivious poem in Elizabethan, possibly in all English literature, had recently been dedicated
to him — "Thus hath my pen presum'd to please my
friend" — by Thomas Nashe,[2] who presented it in manuscript form, for it was too sensual for publication. We
may well believe that *Venus and Adonis* exactly suited
the tastes of the young nobleman whose name graced the
dedication. Moreover, he must have been pleased with

[1] See *L'Envoy to Narcissus*. An amorous poem, written "in direct imitation of Shakespeare's *Venus and Adonis*, and in the same metre," *The
Scourge of Venus, or the Wanton Lady. With the Rare Birth of Adonis*, has
been incorrectly attributed to Thomas Heywood. See A. M. Clark, *The
Library*, Series 4, vol. iii, p. 210.

[2] This is the commonly accepted interpretation of the dedicatory title "To
the Right honorable the Lord S." The following year Nashe dedicated to
Lord Southampton his *Jack Wilton*, thus apparently fulfilling his promise:
"better lines ere long shall honor thee." McKerrow suggests, however, the
possibility that Lord Strange may be the "Lord S" to whom the work is
dedicated.

the unusual fame the poem achieved, and the honor thereby reflected upon him. He promptly took the poet into his patronage, and — we have Shakespeare's own word for it — gave him full "warrant" of his bounty and "honorable disposition." Rowe quotes on the authority of Sir William Davenant, who as Shakespeare's godson "was probably very well-acquainted with his affairs," the story that Southampton "at one time gave him a thousand pounds." Though this doubtless is an exaggeration, we may readily believe that the young Earl rewarded the author with a gift of money large enough to enable him to continue his career as a poet, so promisingly begun.

While Shakespeare was thus writing non-dramatic verse, and winning the applause of the literary world, his old friends and fellow-actors, the Pembroke's Men, were having trouble in their attempted tour of the provinces. On September 28, 1593, Henslowe, business-manager of the rival Lord Strange's Men, wrote to Edward Alleyn, who was leading that company on its tour: "As for my Lord of Pembroke's [Men], which you desire to know where they be, they are all at home, and have been these five or six weeks, for they cannot save their charges with travel, as I hear, and were fain to pawn their apparel." [1] Presumably, not being able to make their expenses in the country, they had to dispose of their costumes to secure money with which to return to London. The plague, still raging with unbated fury, offered them no chance to recuperate their fortunes in the city; and soon after they sold their stock of plays, and permanently disbanded. [2] This marks the end of the great troupe

---

[1] W. W. Greg, *Henslowe Papers*, p. 40.

[2] When a company sold its stock of plays, it formally "gave up the ghost." Henslowe was able to purchase a number of these plays for the Strange's Men. The publishers also secured some, including *Titus Andronicus* (entered in the Stationers' Registers on February 6, 1593–94) and *The Taming of*

with which Shakespeare had originally thrown in his lot.[1]

Seeing his company first go bankrupt, and then permanently dissolve, and seeing the plague still raging unabated,[2] Shakespeare must have even more seriously contemplated abandoning the theatre and devoting himself to a purely literary career. The change now seemed feasible to him, since he had acquired a generous patron. At any rate, he had thrust upon him more "idle hours" which would enable him to produce that "graver labor" he had promised Southampton; and he at once set himself to the task.

Some of the "wiser sort" of critics had objected, with good reason, that *Venus and Adonis* was too lascivious[3] to deserve unqualified praise. The opinion is perhaps best expressed by John Davies of Hereford in his *Paper's Complaint:*

> Another (ah Lord help me) vilifies
> With Art of Love, and how to subtilize,
> Making lewd *Venus* with eternal lines
> To tie *Adonis* to her love's designs.
> Fine wit is shew'n therein; but finer 'twere
> If not attirèd in such bawdy geare.

Accordingly, Shakespeare determined next to treat the theme of chastity. From his beloved author, Ovid, he se-

---

the Shrew (entered May 2, 1594), both of which seem also to have been sold to the Strange's Men.

[1] In 1597 a new company was organized under Pembroke's patronage to occupy the Swan playhouse. The two companies must not be confused. See my *Shakespearean Playhouses*, p. 168.

[2] Cf. Henslowe's letters to Alleyn, in W. W. Greg, *Henslowe Papers*, pp. 37, 39, 40.

[3] It was commonly placed in the category of erotic literature. Middleton, in *A Mad World* (1608), writes: "I have conveyed away all her wanton pamphlets, as *Hero and Leander, Venus and Adonis*"; in *The Dumb Knight* (1608), it is called "Maid's Philosophy"; Cranley, in *Amanda* (1635), lists it with *Hero and Leander* as usually in a courtesan's library. Robert Southwell in *Saint Peter's Complaint* (1595), writes:

> Still finest wits are stilling Venus Rose,
> In paynim toyes the sweetest vaines are spent.

lected the story of Lucrece,[1] and supplementing Ovid's narrative, it seems, with a reading of the story as related by Livy, and by Chaucer in his *Legend of Good Women*, produced the beautiful poem *Lucrece*. For his model this time he used Daniel's exceedingly popular *Complaint of Rosamond*.[2] First printed in 1592, this had been generally acclaimed as a noble lesson in morality most delightfully taught. For example, Nashe, in the Preface to *Pierce Penniless* (1592), says to the Puritan clergy of England: "You shall find there goes more exquisite pains and purity of wit to the writing of one such rare poem as *Rosamond* than to a hundred of your dunsticall sermons." [3] The metre Shakespeare adopted for *Lucrece*, the seven-line stanza, was doubtless taken over directly from Daniel's poem; but it had been used by other writers, and Shakespeare was familiar with it as employed by Chaucer, and by Spenser in *The Ruins of Time*.

Upon completing the poem he dedicated it to his patron, the Earl of Southampton, knowing this time that it was "assured of acceptance"; and again he entrusted the press-work to his friend Richard Field. The volume was entered in the Stationers' Registers in May, 1594, and shortly after was being sold on the stalls of John Harrison's shop, the White Greyhound, in Paul's Churchyard. Beautifully printed, it made, like its predecessor, *Venus and Adonis*, though a slender yet a handsome quarto.

The dedicatory epistle, showing the development of a warm friendship with the young Earl, runs as follows:

---

[1] From the *Fasti*, which had not as yet been translated into English.

[2] The title, *The Ravishment of Lucrece*, under which Shakespeare's poem was entered in the Stationers' Registers, and which may have been the title he first gave it, suggests Daniel's title.

[3] Cf. also John Marston's *Satires*, 1598, iv, 81. The same sentiment is also expressed by Thomas Churchyard in the Dedication of his *Shore's Wife*, 1593, written in imitation, but "not in any kind of emulation," of *Rosamond*, "so excellently set forth."

*To the Right Honourable Henry Wriothesley, Earl of Southamp-
ton, and Baron of Tichfield.*

The love I dedicate to your lordship is without end; whereof
this pamphlet, without beginning, is but a superfluous moiety.
The warrant I have of your honourable disposition, not the
worth of my untutored lines, makes it assured of acceptance.
What I have done is yours; what I have to do is yours; being
part in all I have, devoted yours. Were my worth greater, my
duty would show greater; meantime, as it is, it is bound to your
lordship, to whom I wish long life, still lengthened with happiness.

Your lordship's in all duty,
WILLIAM SHAKESPEARE.

The success of *Lucrece* was equal to that of *Venus and
Adonis*. The charge of "wantonness" which had been
made against the earlier poem could not be raised against
this second effort. As Thomas Freeman, in *Rubbe and a
Great Cast*, wrote:

Who loves chaste life, there's *Lucrece* for a teacher,
Who list read lust, there's *Venus and Adonis*.

The great scholar at Cambridge University, Gabriel Harvey, wrote: "The younger sort take much delight in
Shakespeare's *Venus and Adonis*, but his *Lucrece*," he
adds, has in it "to please the wiser sort." The poem, indeed, was viewed as a beautiful exposition of womanly
chastity, and was universally commended for its moral
values.

From all sides rose a chorus of praise. A few of the
printed contemporary notices may here be inserted to indicate its popularity. Sir William Harbert, in an Elegy on
Lady Helen Branch (1594), placing Shakespeare among
the greater poets, addresses him as —

You that have writ of chaste Lucretia,
Whose death was witness of her spotless life.

The poet Drayton, in his *Legend of Matilda* (1594), writes
of —

Lucrece, of whom proud Rome hath boasted long,
Lately reviv'd to live another age.

William Covell, fellow of Cambridge University, in his *Polimanteia* (1595), declares that "*Lucretia*" by "sweet Shakespeare" is "all-praise-worthy." The satirist, John Weever, felt called upon (in 1597?) to celebrate the popular enthusiasm for Shakespeare's works in an epigram:

Ad Gulielmum Shakespeare

Hony-tongu'd *Shakespeare*, when I saw thine issue,
I swore *Apollo* got them and none other;
Their rosy-tinted features, cloth'd in tissue,
Some heaven-born goddess said to be their mother.
Rose-cheekt *Adonis* with his amber tresses,
Fair fire-hot *Venus* charming him to love her,
Chaste *Lucretia* virgin-like her dresses,
Proud lust-stung *Tarquin* seeking still to prove her.

The author of the Cambridge play, *The Return from Parnassus*, makes Judicio, representing the best critical judgment of the university world, exclaim:

Who loves not *Adon's* love, or *Lucrece* rape!

And Richard Carew, in a formal essay on "The Excellencie of the English Tongue" (1595–96), inserted in William Camden's second edition of *Remaines Concerning Britaine*, writes:

Add hereunto that whatsoever grace any other language carrieth, in verse or prose, in tropes or metaphors, in echoes and agnominations, they may be lively and exactly represented in ours. Will you have Plato's vein? read Sir Thomas Smith; the *Ionic?* Sir Thomas More; *Cicero's?* Ascham; *Varro's?* Chaucer; *Demosthenes'?* Sir John Cheeke (who in his treatise to the Rebels hath comprised all the figures of rhetoric). Will you read *Virgil?* take the Earl of Surrey; *Catullus?* Shakespeare, and Marlowe's fragment; *Ovid?* Daniel; *Lucan?* Spenser.

It will be observed that Shakespeare's name is here ranked with the greatest names then known in English literature — Chaucer, Sir Thomas More, Ascham, the

Earl of Surrey, Marlowe, and Spenser. It may be significant that he is the first, and Spenser the last, living writer to be mentioned.

Perhaps, however, the sincerest testimonial to the popularity of *Lucrece* was the publication in the same year of *Willobie his Avisa*, a long poem celebrating female chastity, and avowedly inspired by Shakespeare's work. The fictitious editor (who is doubtless the author, Henry Willoughby [1]), after speaking of the excellent way in which "Shakespeare paints poor Lucrece' rape," proposes in *Avisa* to celebrate "a Britain Lucretia." This notion of an English rival to Lucrece, especially emphasized by the author, serves to explain the whole poem. Thus, in the commendatory verse, probably written by the author himself, we read: "As great a faith in English ground"; "this Britain bird out-flies them all"; "this English

[1] There is no ground for foisting this amateurish production on the famous poet Mathew Royden. Its avowed author, Henry Willoughby, was an Oxford student, referred to in *Polimanteia* (1595) as one of the Oxford men "able to sing sweetly." In 1596, upon the issue of the second edition, his brother, Thomas Willoughby, prefixed a poem in which he refers to his brother as "nuper defunctus." (For the life of Henry Willoughby and his brother Thomas see the *Dictionary of National Biography*.) The use of the fictitious "Hadrian Dorrell" to give the manuscript to the public press in the absence of the author, his friend, was a common device among young men of social standing who desired to publish. So Gascoigne had proceeded in issuing his *Posies*, and Petty in issuing his *Petite Palace*. A close parallel may be found in the case of Barnaby Googe's *Eglogs and Epytaphes*, which, so the preliminary pages inform us, was sent to the press by the author's friend, one named Blundestone, during the author's absence in Spain. Blundestone, like "Dorrell," explains at length, both in prose and verse, that he acted on his own initiative, without his friend's knowledge. Cf. also the address To the Reader, prefixed to Percy's *Sonnets to the Fairest Cælia*. Robert Greene smiles at the well-known convention in his address To the Reader prefixed to *Euphues His Censure to Philautus*. Possibly all this goes back to the publication of Tottel's collection of *Songs and Sonnets*. The disinclination of men of social standing to publish their own verse is shown by John Donne, who writes: "The fault that I acknowledge in myself is to have descended to print anything in verse, which though it have excuse even in our time by men who profess and practice much gravity, yet I confess I wonder how I declined to it, and do not pardon myself." (Gosse, *Life and Letters of John Donne*, i, 303–04.)

eagle soars alone, and far surmounts all others' fame." [1]
The purpose of the poem, we are told, is "to insinuate
how honest maids and women, in such temptations,
should stand upon their guard, considering the glory and
praise that commends a spotless life." [2] Thus *Avisa* is
merely by imitation a compliment to the popularity of
Shakespeare's poem. Further evidence of the same kind
is to be found in the recently discovered continuation of
Lucrece, by Thomas Middleton, 1600, written in the same
stanza, and entitled *The Ghost of Lucrece*.[3]

The success of *Venus and Adonis* and *Lucrece*, with
both the general reading-public and the best literary critics of the day, must have gratified Shakespeare, and
have convinced him that he could win for himself a distinguished place among English poets. Indeed Barnfield
assured him that he had already attained high rank:

> And Shakespeare, thou whose honey-flowing vein
> (Pleasing the world) thy praises doth obtain,
> Whose *Venus* and whose *Lucrece* (sweet and chaste)
> Thy name in Fame's immortal book have plac't.

He did not, however, stop with the writing of these two
amorous poems in the ornate style. He was already at
work on a cycle of sonnets. In this we find him again

---

[1] At the end is a poem entitled "The Victory of English Chastity," beginning:

> Can Britain breed no Phoenix bird
> No constant sense in English field,
> To Greece, to Rome, is there no third?
> Hath Albion none that will not yield?

and ending:

> Our *English* earth such angels breed,
> And can disdain all *foreign* praise.

[2] I have commented somewhat at length on this poem because some persons have attempted to connect it with the personal loves of Shakespeare,
the Earl of Southampton, and Mrs. Jane Davenant, and thereby to explain
Shakespeare's *Sonnets*. This attempt hardly deserves good-natured mention.

[3] The discovery of this hitherto unknown poem was announced in 1920.
The volume was purchased by Mr. H. C. Folger, of New York City, and is
now in his library.

bowing to the literary fashions of the day; for in 1592 there began in England a veritable rage for the composition of sonnet-cycles. Every poet of any pretentions tried his hand at this newly-popularized verse form, and many were attaining fame by the ingenuity and grace with which they devised beautiful sequences addressed to some real or fictitious person.

The sonnet had been introduced into England during the reign of Henry VIII by the young noblemen who went to Italy to learn the fashions of courtly life there; and, under the leadership of Wyatt and Surrey, they cultivated this artificial verse form as a social accomplishment. But Wyatt and Surrey and their imitators wrote merely single sonnets, unrelated to one another, or at least not built up into a unified series presenting something like a story. The composition of formal sequences of sonnets — that is, many sonnets related in theme and unified by a single passion — was mainly due to Sir Philip Sidney. In something over one hundred sonnets he dealt with the romance of his unfortunate love for Penelope Devereux, the beautiful and vivacious daughter of the Earl of Essex. This remarkable cycle was published in 1591 under the title *Astrophel and Stella*. The lyric beauty of the verse fairly swept men of letters off their feet, and started a vogue of sonneteering that is one of the nine wonders of English literary history. Such a wholesale production of sonnets has never been seen in England, or in any other country. With poets of every rank and station in life the composition of ingenious cycles became for a time nothing less than a mania.

In spite of the supposedly private nature of the sequences, and the well-recognized propriety of confining their circulation to manuscript copies, there were printed within a few years numerous collections. In 1592 appeared Daniel's *Delia* and Constable's *Diana;* in 1593

Barnes' *Parthenophil and Parthenope*, Lodge's *Phillis*, Fletcher's *Licia*, Watson's *Tears of Fancie*, and Locke's *Hundred Sonnets* (entered for publication, though its issue was prevented by the author); in 1594, Percy's *Cælia*, Drayton's *Idea*, and the anonymous *Zepheria*, besides enlarged editions of *Delia* and *Diana;* in 1595, Spenser's *Amoretti*, Barnes' *Divine Century*, Barnfield's *Sonnets*, and E. C.'s *Emaricdulfe;* in 1596, Griffin's *Fidessa*, Linche's *Diella*, Smith's *Chloris;* and in 1597, as the vogue was passing, Tofte's *Laura*. To this or the preceding year may be assigned Davies' *Gulling Sonnets* ridiculing the type; and it is significant that with the *Laura* cycle the publication of amorous sequences came to an end. Sir Sidney Lee, who made an attempt to count the sonnets actually printed — not composed — during these few years, informs us that "the aggregate far exceeds two thousand." How many actually were written and never came to press it is impossible to estimate.

In the aristocratic circles of literary men in London, the composition of graceful sonnets was regarded as the test of poetic ability. The greatest poets of the day, Watson, Sidney, Daniel, Spenser, Drayton, were widely acclaimed for their ingenious cycles, and a host of lesser versifiers were winning a ready fame by demonstrating their facility in handling this new musical instrument. As Drayton, in his *Idea*, puts it:

> Many there be excelling in this kind,
> Whose well-trick't rimes with all inventions swell.

And the author of *Zepheria*, addressing English poets in general, exclaims:

> Report throughout our Western Isle doth ring
> The sweet-tuned accents of your Delian sonnetry.

Such being the vogue that was dominating English literary fashions in 1592–94, the years of "idle hours" for

Shakespeare's Muse, it is not strange that, in his ambition to be recognized as a poet among poets, he should join the swelling choir of Elizabethan sonneteers.

That he began to write his sequence in 1592–94 seems beyond reasonable doubt. At this date everything would tempt him to set his pen to the fashionable metrical exercise then at the zenith of its popularity. We may apply to him the words of a fellow sonneteer: "Men may wonder," says Fletcher, "how I come by so much leisure"; and "for this kind of poetry," he flippantly adds, "I did it only to try my humour." Shakespeare, having unexpectedly come by much leisure, may well have liked to try his hand in friendly rivalry with the best poets of the day at "this kind" of verse. *Love's Labour's Lost*, composed in 1592, clearly reveals a lively interest in the sonnet, including as it does seven quatorzains — some woven into the texture of the play, some quoted as fanciful love-offerings, one written experimentally in Alexandrines, — and numerous quatrains combined with each other and with couplets in such a way as to suggest exercises in sonnet construction. Moreover, the many striking parallels in thought, imagery, and phraseology between his *Sonnets* and his early work, most conspicuous by far in *Love's Labour's Lost* and the poems, and gradually disappearing after we pass the year 1594, make the date of the inception of the cycle virtually certain.[1] Nor is external evidence altogether lacking. The anonymous author [2] of

---

[1] I have collected most of these parallels. The way in which they become increasingly rarer and less significant as the plays advance in date is very impressive. That the style of the *Sonnets* is chaster and the thought more compact than in the case of *Venus and Adonis* and *Lucrece* may be attributed in a measure to the different literary types to which they respectively belong, to the restricting influence of the sonnet as a verse form, and to later revision.

[2] Some have actually attributed the play to Shakespeare, but the best critics have no hesitation in denying this attribution. The author may be George Peele.

the play, *Edward III*, entered for publication in 1595, not only echoes the phraseology of several of the sonnets (for example, "scarlet ornaments" of Sonnet 142, "sun flatter our earth" of Sonnet 33), but actually quotes a full line from one of them (Sonnet 94):

> Lillies that fester smell far worse than weeds.

It seems likely that this unknown writer was familiar with Shakespeare's cycle in a manuscript copy; and we are informed in 1598 that such a manuscript copy was well-known among the poet's friends. By 1597 the vogue was passing; and it is hardly possible to think of Shakespeare, the busy actor and playwright, who now had definitely abandoned non-dramatic composition, as setting himself at a later period to a literary type then the object of general ridicule.[1]

That he did not at once give his *Sonnets* to the press, as he did *Venus and Adonis* and *Lucrece*, was quite natural, for amorous sequences, supposedly celebrating a passion for a real person, were regarded as too private for publication. Sidney's sonnets reached the press against his wish, and in spite of the best efforts of his family to prevent their issue. Daniel, when his *Delia* collection was

---

[1] Sonnet 107, with the allusion to the "mortal moon" enduring an eclipse, has sometimes been cited as evidence that a portion of the *Sonnets* was composed after the death of Elizabeth in 1603. But it is not at all clear that the allusion is to the death of the Queen (neither "endure" nor "eclipse" seems appropriate), rather than to some actual eclipse of the moon. The adjective "mortal" may well be applied to the moon, which is nearly always personified by Shakespeare, and which in passing through the shadow calls to mind the Biblical imagery of death, the theme of the Sonnet as a whole. Even if the allusion be to an actual person, it need not be to Elizabeth. Mrs. Stopes, *Southampton*, p. 94, quotes a passage from a curious letter written by Sir Thomas Cecil to Sir Robert Cecil, July 9, 1595: "I left the moon in the wane at my last being at the Court; I hear now it is a half-moon again, yet I think it will never be at the full, though I hope it will never be eclipsed. You know whom I mean." It was customary at this time to allude thus cryptically to distinguished persons, the allusion being generally intelligible in Court circles.

printed contrary to his will, writes: "I rather desired to keep in private passions of my youth from the multitude, as things uttered to myself." Percy, in a similar situation, declares: "I was fully determined to have concealed my sonnets as things privy to myself"; and Smith complains:

> Longer I cannot them in silence keep;
> They will be gadding, sore against my will.

This was the regular attitude of the sonneteer. But manuscript copies were allowed to circulate freely, and sometimes transcripts of these might be made by friends, with the tacit understanding that the wish of the author to prevent publication should be respected. In this manner the cycles received a wide publicity among those who were genuinely interested in poetry. Shakespeare availed himself of the dignity which the observance of this custom would give him; in *Palladis Tamia*, 1598, we read: "As the soul of Euphorbus was thought to live in Pythagoras, so the sweet wittie soul of Ovid lives in mellifluous and hony-tongued Shakespeare; witness his *Venus and Adonis*, his *Lucrece*, his sugred *Sonnets* among his private friends." Doubtless, too, he took advantage of the opportunity which the custom allowed, as did other poets, to revise and improve his sonnets from time to time. This may partly account for their exquisite choice of words, their compact energy of thought, and that enchanting melody of diction which is their crowning grace. Of such revision we have, I think, unmistakable evidence. The two sonnets printed by Jaggard in 1599 show variations from the final text of 1609 which cannot be explained as errors in transcript; the imperfect form of Sonnet 99, with seven superfluous words, indicates an unsuccessful or unfinished effort to hammer the thought into the requisite fourteen lines; Sonnets 36 and 96 awkwardly have the same concluding couplet; and the two final sonnets are merely variants of the same theme. Perhaps the poet was especially applying himself to a revision of the cycle in 1597–98. This might explain the fact that he composed two sonnets as choruses for *Romeo and Juliet*, which he put on the stage late in 1596 or early in 1597,[1] and one as an epilogue for *Henry V*, written early in 1598. It would explain, too, the few but very striking echoes in phraseology between the *Sonnets* and some of the later plays, most notably *I* and *II Henry IV*, 1597. And, of course he might, if so disposed, add an occasional new sonnet.

Shakespeare was able to keep his *Sonnets* in this plastic state for many years, though their widespread fame must have rendered them desirable objects in the eyes of what Daniel called "the greedy printers." In 1599 William Jaggard managed to secure two of them, Sonnets 138 and 144, which, with an appendage of various other poems derived from miscellaneous sources, he promptly issued under the fanciful title *The Passionate Pilgrim*, by W. Shakespeare. His intention obviously was to deceive the unwary purchasers into supposing that here at last they had the opportunity to buy Master Shakespeare's "sugred sonnets." On January 3, 1600, another publisher entered in the Stationers' Register "A book called *Amours* by J. D., with certain other *Sonnets* by W. S." The sonnets thus entered, however, were not published. It has been customary for scholars to assume that the entry referred to a hypothetical cycle by William Smith, whose collection entitled *Chloris* had been issued in 1596. But there is no evidence that Smith composed a second cycle, and no reason why the entry may not refer to Shakespeare's *Sonnets*. If the entry really concerned Shakespeare's collection, as seems at least possible, it is signifi-

---

[1] Since, however, the first draft was probably written in 1593–94, the two sonnets may have been then composed.

cant that the publisher did not proceed with his under-taking. In 1609, however, the fate overtook Shake-speare's manuscript which had long before overtaken the manuscripts of Sidney, Watson, Daniel, Constable, Fletcher, and other poets. A stationer of small repute, Thomas Thorpe, managed to secure a transcript, which he promptly issued as *Shake-speare's Sonnets*, significantly placing the author's name at the head of the title-page, and in unusually large type. Thus at last the cycle, long confidentially circulated among private friends, was is-sued to "the multitude," and preserved for that critical study to which we must now turn.

When in 1592–94 Shakespeare set his pen to a trial of skill with his fellow-poets in sonneteering, he found him-self face to face with certain conventions which, as a loyal artist, he would observe, at least so far as his better judg-ment might allow; for in theme and in treatment the am-orous sequence was as artificial as the pastoral poem, and in some respects more restricted. The sonneteer was expected to celebrate in a series of "conceitful quator-zains" a deep and usually hopeless passion for some "fair cruel one." This passion, which in expression was essen-tially poetical, might shadow a real experience in the life of the writer. So it did in the case of Petrarch, of Sidney, of Spenser, and probably of Drayton. But in the case of certain other poets we know that it was purely fictitious. As Fletcher reminds us in a prefatory letter to his *Licia* cycle: "A man may write of love and not be in love, as well as of husbandry and not go to the plough." The literary artist always has the right to use his imagination; and we do not need a Touchstone to tell us that often "the truest poetry is the most feigning." All that was required of the sonneteer was that he make his passion seem real.

And since the passion was real — or presumably so —

the identity of the person celebrated was carefully hidden under a fanciful name, such as Laura, Stella, Diana, Licia, or Delia; and the autobiographical element, in so far as it was allowed to appear, was rendered shadowy and tenuous, and kept in the background. The foreground was solely occupied with elaborate conceits, designed for the twofold purpose of displaying the wit of the writer, and of furnishing a series of handsome compliments to the person celebrated.

Furthermore, in devising these compliments, the sonneteer was expected to employ certain well-worn stock themes, most of which went back to Petrarch; as, for example, the superlative beauty of the beloved, the transitoriness of that beauty, promises of immortality in verse, the pretended old age of the poet, the pangs of absence, the cruelty (or the graciousness) of the beloved, the apostrophizing of Cupid, and the relief to be found in sleep. In handling such threadbare topics the poet was expressly called upon to demonstrate his skill in presenting them in fresh and beautiful patterns. Thomas Nashe, in his satirical way, describes the sonneteer as "more in love with his own curious forming fancy than her face; and truth it is, many become passionate lovers only to win praise to their wits." [1] One should never forget that the Elizabethan cycle was mainly a *tour de force* in ingenuity, designed to reveal the wit of the author, and his skill in metrical artifice. [2]

In composing his cycle, Shakespeare drew inspiration chiefly from the *Delia* collection by Samuel Daniel, which was published in 1592 along with *The Complaint of Rosamond*, the poem which served as the model for *Lucrece*. Daniel's sonnets had been received by the literary world

---

[1] *Jack Wilton*, ed. by Gosse, p. 104.
[2] See R. M. Alden, "The Lyrical Conceit of the Elizabethans," *Studies in Philology*, (1917), xiv, 130.

with unusual favor. Spenser, whose visits to London kept him in touch with poetic affairs, wrote:

> And there is a new shepherd late up sprong,
> The which doth all afore him far surpasse,
> Appearing well in that well-tunèd song
> Which late he sung unto a scornful lasse.

Drayton, though a rival, graciously refers to him as "excelling in this kind," and the anonymous author of *Zepheria*, as we have seen, characterized all amorous sequences as "Delian sonnetry." [1] Thus in choosing his model Shakespeare, as was usual with him, reflected contemporary taste. From Daniel's sonnets he took his form, acquired much of his sugared style, [2] borrowed not a little imagery and thought, echoed occasional phrases, and learned the trick of nicely linking his poems together. But Daniel, like most of the followers of Sidney, produced merely a disconnected series of sonnets, miscellaneous verse-offerings celebrating in pretty conceits the beauty and unyielding cruelty of a "marble-hearted" mistress. Shakespeare chose to give a firmer unity to his cycle by employing the device, exemplified in Petrarch and Sidney, of stringing his sonnets together in episodes reflecting an autobiographical story; and his genius being essentially dramatic, he rendered this story-element more pronounced than did any of his contempo-

[1] The word "Delian" became recognized as an anagram for Daniel. Weever writes in *Epigrams*, p. 11:

> I cannot reach up to a Delian's straine,
> Whose songs deserve for ever your attention.

As a descriptive adjective applied to sonnet sequences "Delian" could hardly be used without allusion to Daniel's famous *Delia* collection, though in the passage quoted from the author of *Zepheria* there may be also an allusion to the quinquennial festival of Apollo at Delos, noted for its musical contests.

[2] Sweet honey-dropping Daniel doth wage
> War with the proudest big Italian,
> That melts his heart in sugred sonneting.
> — *II Return from Parnassus*, I, ii, 241–43.

raries, even Sidney. Thus his cycle came to differ from its model in a way that has led scholars to underestimate his really important indebtedness to the *Delia* sequence.

Since Shakespeare's *Sonnets* so obviously followed a vogue, and were so patently inspired by a collection which was regarded as the exemplar of English sonnetry — described by one as "Delian sonnetry" — we find, as we might expect, that he observed many of the conventions of the type. There are the familiar themes of the superlative beauty of the beloved, of the transitoriness of that beauty, of immortality in verse, of pretended old age, of the pangs of absence, of death, of the comfort or restlessness of sleep, and such like, though not so many as characterize the work of certain other sonneteers. There, too, is the tireless ingenuity which almost at times tempts us to believe that his verses are merely, as Gabriel Harvey would put it, "dainties of a pleasurable wit."

But in the general theme of his cycle we discover an originality worthy of the master. He refused to celebrate, as did his Italian, French, and English predecessors, a poetical passion for some beautiful and coldly-chaste woman, set high aloft on a pedestal of absolute perfection for saint-worship. Possibly he felt a reaction against the extravagant artificiality in the contemporary imitators of Petrarch. His early plays give evidence of this. In *The Two Gentlemen of Verona* he speaks slightingly of "wailful sonnets." In *Romeo and Juliet* Mercutio jestingly comments: "Now is he for the numbers that Petrarch flowed in : Laura, to his lady, was but a kitchen wench ; marry, she had a better love to berhyme her." The same note of ridicule appears in Sonnet 21:

> So is it not with me as with that Muse
> Stirr'd by a painted beauty to his verse,
> Who heaven itself for ornament doth use,
> And every fair with his fair doth rehearse.

And in Sonnet 130 he laughs at the style of the conventional sonneteer:

> My mistress' eyes are nothing like the sun;
> Coral is far more red than her lips' red:
> If snow be white, why then her breasts are dun;
> If hairs be wires, black wires grow on her head.
> I have seen roses damask'd red and white,
> But no such roses see I in her cheeks.

That he should feel this revolt at the absurd artificiality of the Petrarchists was only natural; Harvey, Chapman, Davies, and others felt it strongly;[1] it occasioned the ridicule so effectively heaped on sonneteering in general, and led to the early downfall of the amorous sequence.

Whatever the reason, Shakespeare selected a new theme for his sonneteering effort, the friendship of man for man. And in developing this theme he wove in the idea — a favorite one in the Renaissance — that the friendship of a man for a man is superior to the love of a man for a woman. The idea doubtless came to the Renaissance from the classics,[2] from such stories as Pylades and Orestes, Theseus and Pirithous, Lælius and Scipio, Damon and Pithias, Achilles and Patroclus, Harmodius and Aristogiton; it was popular in Italian literature, for example in the stories of Palæmon and Arcyte, and Titus and Gisippus; in Spanish literature, for example in the *Diana* of Montemayor; and it was exceedingly common in English literature, especially with courtly writers.

---

[1] It is well-expressed in the play, *Lingua* (about 1603), II, ii: "But these puling lovers, I cannot but laugh at them, and their encomiums of their mistress. They make, forsooth, her hair of gold, her eyes of diamond, her cheeks of roses, her lips of rubies, her teeth of pearl, and her whole body of ivory; and when they have thus idoled her like Pygmalion, they fall down and worship her!"

[2] One should not overlook the Biblical story of David and Jonathan. Cf. especially David's lament over his friend, II Samuel, i, 26: .

> Very pleasant hast thou been unto me:
> Thy love to me was wonderful,
> Passing the love of women.

Richard Edwards had won his greatest fame by his *Palæmon and Arcyte* and his *Damon and Pithias;* and John Lyly effectively celebrated the theme in his novel *Euphues* and in his play *Endimion*. Shakespeare himself used it in *The Two Gentlemen of Verona*. The general conception is perhaps best expressed by Lyly in his *Endimion*, which was published in 1591 and served Shakespeare as a model for *Love's Labour's Lost:*

Shall the enticing beauty of a most disdainful lady be of more force than the rare fidelity of a tried friend? The love of men to women is a thing common and of course; the friendship of man to man infinite and immortal. . . . Love is but an eye-worm, which only tickleth the head with hopes and wishes; friendship the image of eternity, in which there is nothing movable, nothing mischievous. As much difference as there is between beauty and virtue, bodies and shadows, colours and life, so great odds is there between love and friendship. . . . Friendship standeth stiffly in storms. Time draweth wrinkles in a fair face, but addeth fresh colours to a fast friend, which neither heat, nor cold, nor misery, nor place, nor destiny can alter or diminish.

Shakespeare has put this same thought far more beautifully in one of the finest sonnets addressed to his friend, beginning "Let me not to the marriage of true minds admit impediments":

> Love is not love
> Which alters when it alteration finds,
> Or bends with the remover to remove:
> O, no! it is an ever-fixèd mark,
> That looks on tempests and is never shaken. . . .
> Love's not Time's fool, though rosy lips and cheeks
> Within his bending sickle's compass come;
> Love alters not with his brief hours and weeks,
> But bears it out even to the edge of doom.

Perhaps as a foil to this superior affection existing between him and his friend, as well as a laughing satire on the amorous cycles of the day, Shakespeare created the figure of the Dark Lady, who has neither the unalterable loyalty of a genuine friend, nor the marvelous beauty and chastity of the conventional sonnet mistress.

When we come to examine the *Sonnets* as a formal sequence, we discover several well-marked groups.[1] The first group, Sonnets 1–99, are addressed to a young man, and all written soon after first meeting him. The second group, Sonnets 100–125, are addressed to the same young man, but after a lapse of nearly three years, during which the friendship had been allowed to grow cold. The poem numbered 126 is not a sonnet at all, but the envoy, formally marking the close of the cycle. Then follows an appendix, Sonnets 127–152, mainly dealing with the Dark Lady whose shadow was thrown over the cycle addressed to the man. In themselves these do not constitute a cycle, or even a fragment of a cycle, but must be regarded as miscellaneous sonnets, allied in theme to the formal cycle of 125 sonnets already discussed. Finally, attached at the end, are two sonnets, 153 and 154, celebrating the town of Bath and its hot springs famous for their curative powers. These two poems are really different versions of the same theme, and it may be supposed that Thorpe appended them for the sake of completeness, or merely because he found them in the manuscript.[2]

I have already said all that need be said about the artificiality of the *Sonnets*. They are throughout character-

---

[1] The order in which Thorpe's transcript gives the sonnets seems to be in the main, if not completely, that in which Shakespeare arranged them. Where links are discoverable, and they are numerous, the order is demonstrably correct; moreover, in many cases where there is no formal link but a continuity in thought, the order is again correct.

[2] Professor Mackail suspects that this appendix contains miscellaneous sonnets by various writers, some by Shakespeare, and some "pretty certainly not by Shakespeare." He would reject Sonnets 153 and 154 certainly, and 128 and 145 probably, while against Sonnets 135, 136, and 143 he thinks "a plausible case can be made out." (*Essays and Studies by Members of the English Association*, 1912, vol. iii.) I see no reason for rejecting any of these sonnets.

ized by an ingenuity that suggests pride in wit rather than deep emotion. Yet, when full allowance is made for this, the careful and sympathetic student of the *Sonnets* finds in them a residuum that can be explained only by the poet's having embodied in the artificial and ingenious cycle form a real friendship. It may be admitted that much is fiction for the sake of artistic effect; the whole figure of the Dark Lady, "a woman coloured ill," seems to me to be an admirable stroke on the part of the dramatist, serving, as has been said, not only as a satire on the beauty and chastity of the conventional sonnet mistress, but also as a splendid foil to the superiority of friendship over love. By creating, too, an effective triangular situation, the poet was able to heighten the interest in the story-element, an interest which probably constitutes for many readers the chief fascination of the cycle. Thus the Dark Lady can be fully justified on literary grounds. But we must not exclude the possibility that she may have had a real existence in some form. On this point I may quote the remarks of Hadrian Dorrell, about the portrait of the woman in *Willobie his Avisa*:

Whether it be altogether feigned, or in some part true, or altogether true, and yet in most part poetically shadowed, you must give me leave to speak by conjecture and not by knowledge. My conjecture is doubtful, and therefore I make you the judges.

As to the man celebrated, however, we can hardly doubt that he was of flesh and blood, and that Shakespeare entertained for him a high regard. Allowing for the inevitable exaggeration of the sonnet convention, we can picture him with some accuracy, and trace, though not so surely, the episodes in the friendship. He was, when the poet first met him, in the prime of young manhood, with all the beauty of youth. In appearance he was notable for his bright eyes, rosy cheeks, and auburn hair; and he was gifted with a kind disposition and a charming gentleness of spirit. He seems to have been of high birth, but without a great title of nobility, possibly without any title at all — the younger son, we may suppose, of a distinguished house, living in one of the Inns of Court, and devoting his time, as did so many young gallants, to the theatres and men of letters. He had wit, we are told, and learning — at least a university training. He was also possessed of wealth, and was generous to his friends. But the chief distinctions he enjoyed were his beauty of face and his engaging disposition. For a time Shakespeare alone was aware of his superlative excellence, and alone celebrated him in verse.

The *Sonnets* open (1–14) by the poet urging this young man to marry, and thus seek immortality in posterity. Soon dropping this theme, however, the poet promises him immortality in verse (15–19), and proceeds to celebrate his beauty and kindness (20–25). Certain episodes to constitute a story, some quite conventional, some startlingly unconventional, follow. The poet, separated by travel, dispatches three sonnets (26–28) written in absence. Next he addresses to his friend three sonnets (29–31) written in a mood of depression. A single sonnet (32) comments on the progress of English poetry. Then comes the unusual episode (33–35) of the wrong to friendship committed by the young man. He had met the poet's mistress, the Dark Lady, and, tempted by her, had yielded at a moment when loyalty to friendship failed. But he repented with tears, and was forgiven. In the next group (36–39), Shakespeare, painfully conscious of his low rank as an actor and a writer of plays, confesses that he is unworthy of associating intimately in public with his friend. Then (40–42) the friend repeats the original wrong:

> That thou hast her, it is not all my grief,
> And yet it may be said I lov'd her dearly;
> That she hath thee, is of my wailing chief,
> A loss in love that touches me more nearly.

And again the poet, his love for his friend surmounting all else in the world, forgives him. In the following group (43–52), another separation through travel induces thoughts in absence, sonnets marked by ingenuity rather than deep feeling. In the following group (53–55), the constancy of the friend is immortalized in verse. As if by contrast, the next group (56–61) [1] reproaches the friend for wilfully absenting himself in waning love. The poet then (62–65) takes advantage of the time-worn tradition of his assumed old age, and the general decay of all things, to immortalize his friend's beauty. The next group (66–68), written in a mood of cynicism, discusses the vileness of the world, in which his friend alone is good. Another strikingly original theme appears in Sonnets 69–70. The friend has become the victim of public slander, but is comforted by the poet with the assurance that slander usually attacks the innocent and pure. In a very beautiful group (71–74) the poet writes of his own death, and makes a plea to be forgotten. This is followed by a celebration of delight in the friend's love (75–76), and an ingenious sonnet (77) to accompany the gift of a blank table-book.

How long the friendship had lasted we cannot say, but now comes another poet, usually called the Rival Poet, who begins to celebrate Shakespeare's friend, hitherto wholly unnoticed by any writer of verse. He is a younger man than Shakespeare, of great learning, and with a highly ornate style. By his polished rhetoric and his use of gross and fulsome flattery he steals away the love of

---

[1] Sonnets 59 and 60, however, are digressions on the beauty of the friend and the immortality of that beauty in the poet's verse. Such digressions are not uncommon in sonnet cycles.

the friend. That the Rival Poet was a real person seems obvious from the nature of the sonnets (78–86) dealing with this episode. Many details, circumstantial and personal, yet obscure, are without the slightest artistic merit, and wholly without significance unless understood as allusions to a specific individual. Note, for example, the following lines:

> Was it his spirit, by spirits taught to write
> Above a mortal pitch, that struck me dead?
> No, neither he, nor his compeers by night
> Giving him aid, my verse astonishèd;
> He, nor that affable familiar ghost
> Which nightly gulls him with intelligence. . .

If we knew whom Shakespeare had in mind, or what he is referring to in these curious lines, the sonnet might be effective; as matters stand, however, it is quite meaningless, and as literature of little worth.

In the next group (87–93), Shakespeare contemplates the possibility of desertion by his friend, and its probable effects. Then follows (94–96) another most unusual theme: the friend has fallen into a life of gross sensuality, and the poet finds it necessary to rebuke him in the strongest language:

> But if that flower with base infection meet,
> The basest weed outbraves his dignity:
> For sweetest things turn sourest by their deeds;
> Lillies that fester smell far worse than weeds.

The remainder of this first section (97–99) deals in an artificial way with the idea that the changing seasons and the flowers merely serve to remind the poet of his friend.

At this point the composition of the *Sonnets* was interrupted. But after a lapse of two or possibly three years (see Sonnets 100, 102, 104, 108, 115), the poet, like the Prodigal Son, returns to his friend, and after a prologue of apology (100–103), begins again the familiar old themes, celebrating his friend's beauty and constancy, and promising for these immortality in verse (104–108). Again (109–110) he reproaches himself for his long absence and silence. And again (111–112) he laments his low social standing and the brand the world stamps upon his name as an actor. After celebrating his friend's love (113–116), he returns to further apologies for his absence and neglect (117–120), exclaiming, "That you were once unkind befriends me now." The remaining sonnets (121–125) deal with miscellaneous themes, and the cycle is closed by an envoy of ten lines in couplets.

Who this young man was we do not know. The publisher of the manuscript, Thomas Thorpe, knew, or thought he knew; and he dedicated the *Sonnets* in beautiful monumental style to him as their sole inspirer.

It is hardly possible to interpret this dedication, as certain scholars attempt to do, as merely an acknowledgment on Thorpe's part of his indebtedness to some inferior hanger-on of the publishing trade who procured ("begot") the manuscript for him. The word "begetter," especially with the significant modifier "only," would spontaneously suggest to all readers, perhaps then even more strongly than now, the idea of paternity, so familiar in the current renderings of the Bible. Moreover, it was a commonplace for Elizabethan poets thus to describe the inspirer of their verse. Daniel, in dedicating his *Delia* sonnets to the Countess of Pembroke, refers to them as "begotten by thy hand." Donne writes of "her who begot this love in me"; and in dedicating his *Divine Poems* to the Earl of Dorset says:

> See, sir, how the sun's hot masculine flame
> Begets strange creatures on Nile's dirty slime,
> In me your fatherly yet lusty rhyme
> — For these songs are their fruit — have wrought the same.

Thomas Randolph wrote to Ben Jonson:

> And to say truth that which is best in me
> May call you father; 'twas begot by thee.

One need not multiply instances, for the thought is clearly enough expressed by Shakespeare himself in the *Sonnets:*

> Yet be most proud of that which I compile,
> Whose influence is thine, and born of thee.

> How can my Muse want subject to invent,
> While thou dost breathe, that pour'st into my verse
> Thine own sweet argument?

> For who's so dumb that cannot write to thee
> When thou thyself dost give invention light?

> Where art thou, Muse, that thou forget'st so long
> To speak of that which gives thee all thy might.

> Sing to the ear that doth thy lays esteem,
> And gives thy pen both skill and argument.

> For to no other pass my verses tend
> Than of your graces and your gifts to tell.

In coining the phrase "onlie begetter" Thorpe shows that he had read the *Sonnets* to good advantage. And it will be observed that he attributed this parental inspiration merely to "the insuing sonnets," apparently excepting the long poem, *A Lover's Complaint*, which follows, and which likewise he assigns to Shakespeare's pen. Moreover, he specifically wishes for "the onlie begetter" of the *Sonnets* "that eternitie promised by our ever-living poet." Here again he shows that he had read the *Sonnets* with clear understanding, for the poet is constantly promising eternity to the inspirer of his verse, and asserting that his lines are ever-living:

> My love shall in my verse ever live young.

So long as men can breathe, or eyes can see,
So long lives this, and this gives life to thee.

The phrase "the well-wishing adventurer in setting forth" (i.e., meaning well in putting the sonnets into print), is an apology for giving publicity to a manuscript which the author obviously desired to keep private. Such an apology was conventional with piratical "adventurers" from the days of Tottel's Miscellany. Tottel, who had secured his manuscript in the same way Thorpe had procured the *Sonnets*, says in an epistle To the Reader: "It resteth now, gentle reader, that thou think it not evil done to publish, to the honour of the English tongue and for the profit of the studious of English eloquence, those works which the ungentle hoarders up of such treasure have heretofore envied thee." [1] And Thorpe merely means to assure "the onlie begetter," as well as the reading public, that his intentions are good. "Setting forth" was a common technical phrase for "publishing"; note the address to the publisher of Randolph's *Hey for Honesty:* "To his worthy friend, F. J., on the setting forth of this excellent comedy"; or that to the publisher of Richard Brome's *Five New Plays:* "Upon his setting forth Mr. Rich. Brome's playes."

Thus the Dedication is couched in language that is simple, compact, and clear. On its face, it seems to be addressed to the inspirer of the *Sonnets;* and this natural inference is supported by the internal evidence of the poems. From the well-known "Will Sonnets" we are led to believe that the given name of the friend was William.

---

[1] Compare the prefaces to Gascoigne's *Posies*, Pettie's *Petite Palace of Pleasure*, Greene's *Euphues His Censure to Philautus*, Breton's *Bower of Delights*, Jones' edition of *The Court of Civil Courtesy*. We find here the conventional apology to readers in various forms: "accept my good will"; "take them as a token of good will"; "make some favourable conjecture of my good meaning"; "as a testimony of my serviceable heart and good meaning to you."

But this does not help to lift the anonymity of Thorpe's "Mr. W. H." Perhaps, since the *Sonnets* were designed by the poet primarily as literature, it is just as well that we do not know more. Fletcher, in an address prefixed to his *Licia* cycle, after refusing to disclose whom he is celebrating, says to the reader: "If thou like it, take it." And Shakespeare may well say the same thing to us.[1]

The *Sonnets* ended with the usual "Finis"; but to the collection Thorpe appended another work, a poem of 329 lines, entitled *A Lover's Complaint*, which he stated to be also "by William Shakespeare." It is in the same stanzaic form used in *Lucrece*, but is more far-fetched in its conceits, and more labored in its imagery and style than any work positively known to be from Shakespeare's hand; and whether we are justified in accepting Thorpe's attribution is a matter of grave doubt. Scholars, indeed, are not yet agreed what to think of the poem. Dowden declares: "There appears to be no good reason to question the correctness of this ascription"; Mr. Masefield holds that "It is a work of Shakespeare's youth, fresh and felicitous as youth's work often is, and very nearly as empty"; Swinburne seems to be seriously in doubt, referring to it as an "actual or possible work" of Shakespeare, though calling attention to some "superbly Shakespearean" lines in it; Professor J. W. Mackail, who alone has subjected the poem to a careful analysis, concludes positively that it could not have been written by the dramatist.[2] In the 329 lines of the poem he finds twenty-three words that do not elsewhere occur in Shakespeare, seven words that may fairly be regarded as non-Shakespearean, sixteen words that are used in a sense not employed by Shakespeare, and twelve words that are found only in the

[1] For a summary of the many theories advanced by scholars, and a complete bibliography, see the excellent variorum edition of the *Sonnets* by R. M. Alden.

[2] *Essays and Studies by Members of the English Association*, 1912, iii, 51.

master's maturer work; and in addition he notices the writer's special fondness for Latinisms. Under the head of "Syntax," he calls attention to three peculiarities (ellipsis of subject, ellipsis of verb, and asyndeton) which are alien to Shakespeare's ordinary usage. Finally, he points out that by the tests of "phrasing and style" the poem is generally unlike Shakespeare's recognized work.

The evidence which Professor Mackail thus presents seems to carry weight. Yet he admits: "On the other hand, there are more than a few passages in the poem which are like Shakespeare at his best, and of which one would say at first sight that no one but Shakespeare could have written them, so wonderfully do they combine his effortless power and his incomparable sweetness."

As to questioning the accuracy of Thorpe's attribution we need have little hesitancy, for we know how stolen verse-manuscripts were constituted, and what slight effort the publishers often made to discover the real author of the poems contained therein. A study of Jaggard's issue of *The Passionate Pilgrim* will furnish a good illustration, and Elizabethan literature supplies numerous other examples. Possibly Thorpe had secured the common-place-book of some gallant, containing chiefly the *Sonnets* of Shakespeare, but also other poems, some no doubt attributed to their authors, others without signature. And finding there *A Lover's Complaint*, Thorpe might, either in ignorance or with the easy conscience of his kind, print the poem as by Shakespeare in order to increase the size and heighten the importance of his volume.

Our chief difficulty in rejecting Thorpe's ascription lies in the fact that it is hard to discover any one besides Shakespeare to whom we may assign the poem, which despite its many absurd faults has at times a beauty that reflects the art of the great master. Professor Mackail, recognizing this difficulty, would attribute the poem to the mysterious Rival Poet, whom Shakespeare himself had confessed to be gifted with a "golden quill, and precious phrase by all the Muses filed." On this hint Mr. J. M. Robertson would go a step further, and assuming it as proved that the Rival Poet was George Chapman, give the poem to that writer.[1] Both hypotheses seem fanciful and unlikely. Any one who has read Chapman's minor poems could hardly agree that the author of *The Shadow of Night* and *A Coronet* was also the author of *A Lover's Complaint*.

It is safe only to conclude that Thorpe's attribution carries little authority, and that the poem may have been an inferior (it seems to be an incomplete) product of Shakespeare's pen, or an unusually excellent imitation of Shakespeare's popular style, in which the unknown author occasionally, as Professor Mackail observes, "writes like Shakespeare at his best."

[1] *Shakespeare and Chapman*, 1917.

CHAPTER X

WITH THE LORD CHAMBERLAIN'S COMPANY

DURING his two years of freedom from acting and play-making Shakespeare had succeeded in establishing himself as one of England's leading poets. His *Venus and Adonis*, his *Lucrece*, and his *Sonnets* had won him the unstinted praise of literary critics, and had carried his fame even to the cloistered halls of Oxford and Cambridge. From Ireland Edmund Spenser wrote to acknowledge his power, including him, "though last, not least," in his famous list of eminent poets who glorified the Court of Elizabeth:

> A gentler shepheard may nowhere be found,
> Whose Muse, full of high thoughts' invention,
> Doth like himself heroically sound.[1]

Shakespeare's name was indeed sounding wherever men came together to discuss the poetry of the day.

In view of his rapid rise to fame in the courtly circle of writers, he may, as has already been suggested, have contemplated abandoning the actor's profession and dramatic composition, with the purpose of henceforth devoting his energy to the production of works in the realm of pure literature. If so, Fate was soon to determine otherwise. Whether he lost the patronage of the Earl of Southampton, or whether the actors were able to offer him pecuniary inducements that he could not resist, we are unable to say. All that we positively know is that before the end of 1594 he is back again at the "common theatres," as an

[1] *Colin Clout's Come Home Again*, probably written in 1594, published in 1595. It is not certain that Spenser is referring to Shakespeare, but the passage seems to fit no one else so well, and most scholars assume that it alludes to the dramatist. Did Spenser first write "Doth like his name," and subsequently change "his name" to "himself" for the sake of alliteration?

actor treading the rush-strewn stage before the "penny-knaves" of London, and as a literary artist devoting his splendid powers to refurbishing old plays and composing new ones.

He could not, of course, rejoin the Pembroke's Men, for they had ceased to exist. Instead he became affiliated with the Lord Chamberlain's Company, which, having survived the lean years of the plague, was just entering upon a new and brilliant career. Since he was destined to remain with this notable company throughout the rest of his life, and produce for it the plays which render him immortal, we must hurriedly glance at its previous history, and observe the course of circumstances which led it in 1594 to engage the services of England's most promising young poet.

The company was originally known as Lord Strange's Men. It seems to have been constituted a metropolitan troupe in the autumn of 1588, though our first notice of it bears the date of November 6, 1589:[1] the Lord Mayor had peremptorily forbidden the Admiral's and the Strange's Men to perform in the city; the Admiral's Men obeyed, but the Strange's Men, so the Lord Mayor complained, "in a very contemptuous manner departing from me, went to the Cross Keys [Inn], and played that afternoon." Obviously the company was already numbered among the important London troupes; and this importance was augmented in the winter of 1591–92. The Admiral's Company, of which the famous Edward Alleyn was the most conspicuous figure, was temporarily dissolved in 1591 in order to allow some of its chief players to undertake a prolonged tour of the Continent, a custom then popular with English actors. But Alleyn, who at this time was in

[1] There was an earlier troupe enjoying the patronage of Lord Strange, which appears in the provinces from 1576 to 1588, but never in London or at Court. It does not concern us here.

his twenty-fifth year, and at the height of his great fame, declined to accompany them. Instead, with a few other members of the Admiral's organization who failed to go on the tour, he affiliated himself with the Strange's Men, and at once became their leading actor.

Thus enlarged and strengthened, the Strange's Men entered into an agreement with Philip Henslowe by which he was to furnish them the Rose playhouse, and serve as their business-manager. From his *Diary* we learn that he spent a large sum of money in altering, improving, and beautifying his theatre for their occupancy. And on February 19, 1592, they opened that handsome building with a performance of Robert Greene's *Friar Bacon and Friar Bungay.*

Our knowledge of the personnel of the troupe is unusually complete. From the stage "plot" of *The Seven Deadly Sins*, belonging to the year 1592, we derive the names of the following members:

Richard Burbage
Augustine Phillips
Thomas Pope
George Bryan
Henry Condell
William Slye
Richard Cowley
John Duke
John Sinkler
John Holland
Thomas Godall
Christopher Beeston
T. Bell ⎫
Sander Cooke ⎪
Nicholas Tooley ⎪
Robert Gough ⎬ Boys
Robert Pallant ⎪
Ned ⎪
Will ⎭

This list, however, is incomplete, and from the traveling-license we are able to add the names of Edward Alleyn (who still describes himself as "servant to the right-honorable the Lord High Admiral"), William Kempe, and John Heminges. Shakespeare's name, of course, is nowhere mentioned in connection with the troupe, for the simple reason that he was then, as I have attempted to show, connected with the Pembroke's Men.)

This splendid Strange organization, with such expert actors as Alleyn, Burbage, and Kempe, performed at the Rose until June 22, 1592, when, it will be recalled, theatres were closed by order of the Privy Council. On December 29, the plague having subsided, they reopened the Rose, and continued to act there until February, 1593. Henslowe recorded in his *Diary* each day the play that the company presented, and duly noted the appearance of new or revised plays; the long list, however, contains not a single piece that can be identified as Shakespeare's.[1]

The plague breaking out with renewed violence in February, 1593, theatres were again closed; and it becoming evident that the inhibition would last a long time, the Strange's Company, under Alleyn's leadership, began an extensive tour of the provinces, as did also the rival Pembroke's Company. After some months, however, the Pembroke's Company, not being able to make expenses in the country, returned to London, went into bankruptcy, and sold its stock of plays. Henslowe bought a number of its manuscripts for the use of the Strange's Men, including *Hamlet, Titus Andronicus,* and *The Taming of the Shrew.* Whether he also bought some of Shakespeare's earliest plays, as *The Comedy of Errors* and *Love's Labour's Lost,* we do not know, but they were not disposed of to publishers, and Henslowe's judgment would hardly allow good manuscripts like these to slip through his fingers.

[1] The Strange's play of *Henry VI*, as already observed, was by George Peele.

In the course of time Edward Alleyn, who had married Henslowe's only daughter, became weary of traveling, left the Strange's Men, and returned to London. Thereupon Richard Burbage, it seems, took the position as leader of the troupe on its tour, for he was rapidly developing into an actor of the first rank, vying even with Alleyn himself. The Strange's Men, however, could hardly have made much more than expenses, and were merely struggling to maintain their existence as a company.

When on September 25, 1593, their patron succeeded to the Earldom of Derby, they assumed the name of Derby's Men, a title they were to hold less than six months, for Derby died on April 16, 1594. His players, thus left without a patron (for a short time they called themselves the Countess of Derby's Servants), were forced to seek the protection of another nobleman. By good fortune they secured the patronage of Lord Hunsdon, the Lord High Chamberlain; and from this time on they bore the designation The Lord Chamberlain's Men.[1]

Early in the summer of 1594, the plague having at last spent its fury, the actors were gradually reassembling in the city. Naturally, as a result of the long inhibition of the theatres lasting nearly two years, there was disorganization in the big London troupes, and much confusion among the players. The great Pembroke's Company had ceased to exist, other companies had been sadly reduced in size, and there was a general shifting about of actors. The situation was further complicated by the return of certain of the Admiral's Men from their foreign tour.

[1] Except between July 23, 1596, and March 17, 1597. Henry Carey, the Lord Chamberlain, died on July 23, 1596, and the company passed under the protection of his son, George Carey, Lord Hunsdon. On March 17, 1597, however, George Carey, Lord Hunsdon, was appointed Lord Chamberlain, and his players resumed their former title, the Lord Chamberlain's Men.

The old Admiral's players, who had been only temporarily dispersed in 1591, were now reorganized under their former patron; and Edward Alleyn, who had been their leader, and who, even after he became associated with the Strange's Men, continued to describe himself as "servant to the right honorable the Lord High Admiral," rejoined them. Moreover, he persuaded his father-in-law, Henslowe, to become their business-manager, and to allow them the use of the Rose playhouse. Thus reëstablished as a first-class city troupe, they began to act at the Rose while the Lord Chamberlain's Men were still traveling in the country.

On, or shortly before, June 3, 1594, the Chamberlain's Men arrived in London, and reported to their former manager Henslowe. They found — to their dismay no doubt — that Alleyn and Henslowe had deserted them, and that a new and formidable rival company was occupying their playhouse. For a time they seem to have been uncertain what steps to take. Henslowe possibly desired to amalgamate them with the Admiral's Company, in order both to strengthen that organization and to suppress competition. At any rate, the Rose being then closed for painting and repairs, he sent them, along with the Admiral's Men, to act temporarily at the old Newington Butts house; whether they acted in conjunction with the Admiral's Men, or on alternate days, is not clear. But twelve days later, on June 15, the Rose being now ready for occupancy, the Admiral's Company returned to take permanent possession of that excellent playhouse.

Thereupon the Chamberlain's Men broke off their alliance with Henslowe, and undertook to build themselves into a first-class city company to compete on even terms with the Admiral's Men. Doubtless a partial reorganization, with increased personnel, was necessary; for not only had they lost some of their members through their long period of traveling, but presumably, others, like Alleyn, had rejoined their old companions under the Lord Admiral. Moreover, a full-sized city troupe had to have an adequate supply of hirelings and boys, as well as sharers — and, above all, had to have playwrights.

In this reorganization Richard Burbage, whose fame as an actor made him the natural rival to Alleyn, must have taken a prominent part. By virtue of his wonderful power in the presentation of heroic character he became the leading actor for the company. William Kempe, generally conceded to be the ablest clown since Tarlton, became their chief comedian. And, of course, the other sharers of the older organization — experienced actors, and most of them eminent in their profession — were included. But best of all, William Shakespeare, who in his former association with the Pembroke's Men had demonstrated his ability to write plays, and who more recently had attained great fame as a man of letters, was induced to join the company. The players offered him a position as an actor with the rank of full-sharer, and in addition agreed to pay him generously for such plays as he might produce.

Finally, their patron, the Lord Chamberlain, secured for them the immediate use of the Cross Keys Inn, in Gracious Street. On October 8, 1594, he wrote to the Lord Mayor:

After my hearty commendations. Where my now company of players have been accustomed for the better exercise of their quality, and for the service of Her Majesty if need so require, to play this winter time within the city at the Cross Keys in Gracious Street, these are to require and pray your Lordship (the time being such as, thanks be to God, there is now no danger of the sickness) to permit and suffer them so to do.[1]

---

[1] *The Remembrancia*, The Malone Society's *Collections*, i, 73. The earlier editor of the *Remembrancia* reads "my new company" instead of "my now company."

And Richard Burbage secured for them the permanent use of his father's large and splendid playhouse, the Theatre, in Finsbury Field. Possibly during the company's stay at the Cross Keys the Theatre was repaired, improved, and repainted for their future occupancy.

The chief members of the company as now constituted were:

> Richard Burbage
> William Shakespeare
> William Kempe
> John Heminges
> Thomas Pope
> Henry Condell
> Augustine Phillips
> Christopher Beeston
> William Slye
> Richard Cowley
> George Bryan
> John Duke

In addition there was the usual supply of hirelings and boys. Most of these men remained with the organization throughout the rest of their lives, and the first six, as we shall see, became Shakespeare's intimate and trusted friends. For histrionic skill the most distinguished member of the company was Richard Burbage; but one should not forget the presence in the troupe of William Kempe, whose reputation as early as 1589 extended beyond the shores of England. Thomas Nashe, in dedicating *An Almond for a Parrat* (1590) to "That most comicall and conceited cavaleire, Monsieur du Kempe, Jestmonger and Vice-gerent generall to the Ghost of Dicke Tarlton," writes:

For comming from Venice the last summer, and taking Bergamo in my waye homeward to England, it was my happe, sojourning there some foure or five dayes, to light in felowship with that famous Francatrip Harlicken, who perceiving me to bee an English man by my habit and speech, asked me many particulars of the order and manner of our playes, which he termed by the name of representations: amongst other talke he enquired of me if I knew any such Parabolano here in London as Signior Chiarlatano Kempino. Very well (quoth I,) and have beene oft in his company. He, hearing me say so, began to embrace me anew, and offered me all the courtesie he colde for his sake, saying, although he knew him not, yet for the report he had hard of his pleasance, hee colde not but bee in love with his perfections being absent.

And we have much other testimony to the same effect. The combination of Burbage and Kempe, with Shakespeare as playwright, made the Chamberlain's Company the most excellent troupe in England, surpassing even the Admiral's Men under Alleyn's brilliant leadership and Henslowe's experienced management.

Having become a full-sharing actor and dramatist for this great company, Shakespeare henceforth had few "idle hours" at his disposal. Elizabethan troupes, it should be remembered, not only performed as a rule every week day, and often on Sundays, but also changed their plays from day to day in a most astonishing fashion. The following list from Henslowe's record of performances at the Rose in 1594 will illustrate how taxing this must have been on the memory of the actors:

Friday, September 2, *The Jew of Malta*
Saturday, September 3, *Tasso*
Sunday, September 4, *Phillipo and Hippolito*
Monday, September 5, *The Venetian Comedy*
Tuesday, September 6, *Cutlack*
Wednesday, September 7, *Massacre of France*
Thursday, September 8, *Godfrey of Bulloigne*
Friday, September 9, *Mahomet*
Saturday, September 10, *Galiaso*
Sunday, September 11, *Bellendon*
Monday, September 12, *Tamburlaine*

To care for such an elaborate repertoire, the forenoons of the actors were commonly spent in rehearsals, absence or even tardiness being heavily fined.[1] The afternoons, of course, were occupied with performances before the public, lasting from two or three o'clock until five or six. As to the evenings, not a small share of the time, surely, had to be devoted to learning new, or refreshing the memory on old, plays. In all this busy stir of rehearsing and performing plays Shakespeare, as a full-sharing actor, would be called upon to take his part. In addition he was expected to provide new manuscripts for the company, and often to revamp old ones.[2] If his fellows made his duties as an actor less burdensome in order that he might create plays for them,[3] his responsibility was none the lighter, and the time they placed at his disposal was not his own.

Thus it is obvious that he could not now find that leisure to produce poems for the literary public, or devote himself to those "graver labours" he once had in mind. Henceforth all his energies were to be spent in aiding his troupe at the Theatre to compete with the Henslowe-Alleyn troupe at the Rose. The whole theatrical history of London throughout the remainder of the century resolved itself into a keen rivalry between the Chamberlain's and the Admiral's Men. The great fame of Alleyn's acting was able for a time to fill the yard and galleries of the Rose; but the matchless genius of Shakespeare soon lifted the Chamberlain's Company to a position of easy superiority that could not be challenged. Young Richard Burbage, or "Dick" as he was affectionately known to the public, quickly rose, through his excellent rendition

---

[1] See *Henslowe Papers*, ed. by W. W. Greg, p. 124.

[2] Of Thomas Heywood, who like Shakespeare was a full-sharing actor and playwright for the Queen's Men, Francis Kirkman writes: "As I have been informed, he was very laborious, for he not only acted every day, but also obliged himself to write a sheet every day." (Address to the reader affixed to *A True, Perfect, and Exact Catalogue*, 1671.)

[3] "There's better law amongst the players yet, for a fellow shall have his share though he do not play that day." (*A Cure for a Cuckold*, II, iii.)

of the heroic rôles specially created for him, to the pinnacle of histrionic fame. And within a few years the sharers in the Company — including Shakespeare — had acquired such affluence as to draw down upon them the abuse of many satirists.

The Elizabethan playwright, Thomas Randolph, in discussing the power of money, exclaimed: "Did not . . . Shakespeare therefore write his comedy?" [1] And many years later Alexander Pope cynically declared:

> Shakespeare (whom you, and every playhouse bill,
> Style the divine, the matchless, what you will)
> For gain, not glory, wing'd his roving flight,
> And grew immortal in his own despight. [2]

In this statement, no doubt, there is a grain of truth; but it would be fairer to say that Shakespeare labored for gain *and* glory, with the added comment that in pursuing both he lifted his plays from the level of the mercenary and ephemeral to the heights of enduring art. And surely we, who are the heirs of his "glory," have no right to begrudge him the relatively small "gain" to which he was justly entitled.

Yet perhaps he himself at times regretted his inability to devote his genius to what were regarded as nobler forms of literature — to the making, let us say, of some great epic like the *Faerie Queene*. In one of his Sonnets he exclaims:

> O, for my sake do you with Fortune chide,
> The guilty goddess of my harmful deeds,
> That did not better for my life provide
> Than public means.

And he may occasionally have felt that his nature was "subdued to what it works in." If, however, he had such

---

[1] *Plutophthalmia Plutogamia, or Hey for Honesty*, I, ii. The play was written after Shakespeare's death.

[2] *The First Epistle of the Second Book of Horace.*

moments of regret, they must have been fleeting, for his whole life, with all of its interests, was now centred in the theatre; and we cannot doubt that he was happy in the companionship of his "friends and fellows," who seem to have loved him only "this side idolatry," and that he rejoiced in the success his company was able to attain under his rapidly developing powers as a dramatist. Nor could he have been unmoved by the applause of the public in the "throngèd theatres," thus described by his contemporary playwright Drayton:

In pride of wit, when high desire of fame
Gave life and courage to my lab'ring pen,
And first the sound and virtue of my name
Won grace and credit in the ears of men,
With those the throngèd theatres that press,
I in the circuit for the laurel strove,
Where the full praise, I freely must confess,
In heat of blood a modest mind might move;
With shouts and claps at every little pause,
When the proud round on every side hath rung.[1]

Such applause, we know, Shakespeare gained in abundant measure. As Leonard Digges exclaimed:

Oh how the audience
Were ravish'd! With what wonder they went thence!

And it was no mean thing for him to ravish the audiences then, and since, as no one else has been able to do. We might like to have from his pen a great epic like the *Faerie Queene*, dealing, let us say, with the Trojan War, a theme which always fascinated him; on the other hand, we should not be willing to pay the price by giving up *Hamlet, Othello, Lear, Macbeth, Cymbeline*, and *The Tempest*, which he could have produced only as a result of years of painstaking effort in dramatic composition. After all, is it not enough that he has won from the

[1] *Idea* (1605), Sonnet 47.

world such praise as is thus expressed by Browning? —

> "Shakespeare"! — to such name's sounding, what succeeds
> Fitly as silence? Falter forth the spell, —
> Act follows word, the speaker knows full well,
> Nor tampers with its magic more than needs.
> Two names there are: That which the Hebrew reads
> With his soul only: if from lips it fell,
> Echo, back thundered by earth, heaven, and hell,
> Would own, "Thou didst create us!" Naught impedes
> We voice the other name, man's most of might,
> Awesomely, lovingly: let awe and love
> Mutely await their working, leave to sight
> All of the issue as — below — above —
> Shakespeare's creation rises: one remove
> Though dread — this finite from that infinite.

CHAPTER XI

LONDON RESIDENCES AND ACTOR FRIENDS

Now that Shakespeare, after some uncertainty, had found his permanent place in the world, and had settled down into the regular existence he was thenceforth to lead, we may turn to consider his more personal affairs.

His first residence in London, so far as our knowledge goes, was in the Parish of St. Helen's, Bishopsgate, near the Theatre where his company was acting, and close by the homes of his friends the Burbages. From the Subsidy Rolls we learn that in 1595–96 (how much earlier is not indicated) he was a householder in this parish, and that upon his goods the tax collectors had set the very respectable assessment of £5. In the same Rolls, Richard Burbage, who had inherited property from his father in addition to what he had accumulated as a successful actor, was assessed only £3; and his brother Cuthbert, the owner of the Theatre, and a prosperous man of affairs, who with his family was occupying the dwelling his father had erected in Holywell, was assessed only £4. That Shakespeare as a householder was assessed more than either of these men indicates that he was living in better circumstances than they, and suggests that he had with him in London his wife, Anne, and his three children, Susanna, Judith, and Hamnet.

But his home in St. Helen's was soon to be broken up, as is shown by the following facts. In 1593 Parliament had voted to Queen Elizabeth three subsidies,[1] each of 2s. 8d. in the pound on personal assessment. The third subsidy (for the year 1595) was divided into two install-

[1] For a reprint of these records see *The Athenæum*, March 26, 1904.

ments, the first, of 1s. 8d. in the pound, due on or before February 1, 1596, the second, of 1s. in the pound, due on or before February 1, 1597. In preparing to collect this second installment the officers of St. Helen's, in October 1596, made up their usual list of subsidy-payers, and set Shakespeare down as owing 5s. on his original assessment of £5. But when they came to collect the sum early in 1597, they did not find him at his former address; and in their report, dated November, 1597, they entered his name among the defaulters: "William Shakespeare, vli. — vs." The inference is that he had moved away from the Parish of St. Helen's at some date between February, 1596, when the previous installment had been paid, and February, 1597, when the second installment was due. And this inference is verified by Malone, who had in his possession a document showing that at some date in 1596 Shakespeare was a resident of the Bankside in Southwark: "From a paper now before me, which formerly belonged to Edward Alleyn, the player, our poet appears to have lived in Southwark, near the Bear Garden, in 1596."[1]

Presumably, if he had his family with him, he broke up housekeeping, probably early in the summer of 1596, and sent his wife and children to live in Stratford. For this there may have been good reasons. The crowded housing conditions of London, as well as the unwholesome marshes of Moorfields close by, might have rendered it desirable for him to rear his children in the fresh air and open life of Warwickshire. In this connection, too, it may be significant that in August, 1596, his only son, Hamnet, aged eleven and a half, died in Stratford. As a twin-child he was possibly not strong physically; and his declining

---

[1] *Inquiry into the Authenticity of the Shakespeare Papers*, 1796. The document, like many others once belonging to Alleyn, is now lost, but the integrity of Malone is above suspicion, and we may safely accept the authenticity of the document in his hands, especially in view of the evidence to follow.

health would furnish an adequate motive for the poet's sending his family back to the country.

Shakespeare's grief at the loss of his only son must have been poignant, yet in none of his plays does he allow an echo of this sorrow to obtrude itself upon his audiences, nor did he write an elegy on the boy, for by nature he was too shrinking to give utterance to his private emotions. His fellow playwright, Ben Jonson, who was less reserved in such matters, some time afterwards lost his little son, and published a tender elegy celebrating his grief, the opening and closing lines of which may supply for us the lack of one from Shakespeare:

> Farewell, thou child of my right hand, and joy.
> My sin was too much hope of thee, loved boy. . . .
> Rest in soft peace; and asked, say: "Here doth lie
> Ben Jonson his best piece of poetry."

The removal of his family to Stratford may have caused the dramatist to purchase there in May, 1597, the fine estate of New Place, one of the handsomest houses in the village, as a home for his wife and his two little girls. In their native town, amid numerous relatives and friends, and surrounded by the beautiful Warwickshire country, they could be happier than in the crowded city. Moreover the children would be subject to more wholesome influences than those that attended the lives of actor-folk, or that crept into the parish of St. Helen's from the neighboring regions of Shoreditch.[1]

But let us return to the records of the poet himself in London. In 1597 Parliament granted the Queen three further subsidies at the old rates. The collectors of St. Helen's, still supposing that Shakespeare was a householder in that parish, or, what is more likely, working

---

[1] Here were many of the city's houses of ill fame. Beeston said of Shakespeare: "lived in Shoreditch, would not be debauched." It was probably the most disreputable section of London.

with the old tax-lists, set him down as due 13s. 4d. on his original assessment of £5. But when early in 1598 they called at his former address to collect the subsidy, they were again unable to find him, and learning upon inquiry that he had moved away from the parish, inserted his name among those who "have no goods or chattels, lands or tenements, within the limits" of their jurisdiction. So large was the deficit of the returns from this particular parish, that the officers were required to seek out the defaulters, and collect the taxes due the Queen. Accordingly, they traced the dramatist — it must have been an easy task — to his new residence in Southwark. In the Rolls for 1598 we find the entry: "William Shakespeare, in the Parish of St. Helen's, in Bishopsgate Ward, owes 13s. 4d. of the subsidy; and he answers in the following Roll in Residuum Sussex." The "following Roll," to which we are thus referred, deals with the residents of both Sussex and Surrey, over which there was a single sheriff. Upon examining this Roll, we find Shakespeare's name, and the old debt, duly recorded. In the margin is written "Episcopo Wintonensi," meaning that since Shakespeare was a resident of the Bankside in the Liberty of the Clink, a district under the jurisdiction not of the sheriff but of the Bishop of Winchester, the matter had to be referred to the ecclesiastical authorities. It may gratify the reader to learn that the officers subsequently marked the debt as paid in full.

The precise location of Shakespeare's new residence has not been discovered; it could not have been far, however, from the Rose, and from the homes of Alleyn and Henslowe — hence, possibly, the allusion to him in one of Alleyn's papers of 1596, as noted by Malone. That he should have moved to the Bankside was natural, for this was the centre of the theatrical fraternity. Several of the leading members of the Chamberlain's Company resided there, and it is quite possible that he secured lodgings with one of them — with Pope, or with Phillips, both men of wealth, living no doubt in excellent houses.

This suggests, what we might otherwise suspect, that the poet's life was now largely bound up with the lives of the actors, and that his most intimate friends and comrades were the "fellows" of his own troupe — Burbage, Kempe, Heminges, Condell, Phillips, Pope, Slye, and the rest. We have abundant evidence of their affection for him, and it may be noted that to all who were surviving at the time of his death he left memorial rings as tokens of his love.

What sort of folk were these actors? Perhaps a close view of the Burbage family will give a partial answer, for they were the leading spirits in the Chamberlain organization: James Burbage was the owner and manager of the Theatre; his elder son, Cuthbert, was later proprietor of the Theatre, and largely responsible for the erection of the Globe; his younger son, Richard, was the chief actor for whom Shakespeare wrote, was associated with the building of the Globe, and was proprietor of the Blackfriars Playhouse. Shakespeare must often have been in their home, and throughout his life was on terms of the closest intimacy with them. The following episode, selected from many, dealing with their ownership of the Theatre, will serve to reveal something of their personality.[1]

James Burbage, it will be remembered, at first owned merely a half-interest in the Theatre; his brother-in-law, John Braynes, who bore most of the expense of erecting the building, owned the other half. After some years the two partners found it necessary to mortgage the playhouse to a money-lender named Hide, giving him as security the title to the building. Braynes died with the

[1] For this and other episodes, see my *Shakespearean Playhouses*, 1917.

mortgage unpaid; whereupon his widow, we are told, visited the money-lender with an offer to settle the debt in full if he would make over the deed entirely to her, and Burbage made the same unfair proposal. Hide apparently was too upright to yield to their solicitations; but at last, the mortgage remaining long unpaid, he lost patience, and declared that whoever first brought him the money might have the deed to the Theatre. Cuthbert Burbage, acting for his father, promptly paid the mortgage, came into full possession of the deed, and at once excluded the widow from any share in the revenues of the building.

In her distress the widow appealed to a friend, Robert Miles, who brought suit, and secured a written order from the Court of Chancery in her favor. Armed with this order, he came to the Burbages' dwelling near the playhouse, called to the door Cuthbert Burbage, and demanded one-half the profits of the Theatre for the plaintiff. James Burbage, "being within the house, hearing a noise at the door, went to the door, and there found his son, the said Cuthbert, and the said Miles, speaking loud together." The father joined in the talk, and being "dared by the said Miles, with great threats that he would do this and could do that," lost his temper, and offered to beat Miles off the grounds. This promptly ended the interview, and Miles took the order of the Court and went away.

Next day the widow herself, attended by Miles and other men, visited the Burbage home, "to require them to perform the said award" of the Court of Chancery. They were met at the door by James Burbage's wife, who "charged them to go out of her grounds, or else she would make her son break their knaves' heads." Aroused by these words, "James Burbage, her husband, looking out a window [above] upon them, called the complainant [Mrs.

Braynes] a murdering whore, and the others villains, rascals, and knaves." When the widow held up to him the order of the Court, "he cryed unto her, 'Go! Go! A cart, a cart for you! I will obey no such order, nor I care not for any such orders, and therefore it were best for you and your companions to be packing betimes, for if my son Cuthbert come home he will thump you hence.'" Just then Cuthbert did "come home, and in very hot sort bid them get hence, or else he would set them forward, saying 'I care for no such order. The Chancery shall not give away what I have paid for.'" And so, after "great and horrible oaths" by James Burbage and his son, the widow and her friends "went their ways," taking with them again the order of the Court of Chancery.

Foiled in this second attempt, the widow, with her faithful attendant Robert Miles, and a friend named Bishop, went "to the Theatre, upon a play-day, to stand at the door . . . to take and receive for the widow half the money that should be given to come in." When they entered the empty Theatre they were met by young Richard Burbage, then nineteen years old, and his mother, who seem to have been engaged in sweeping the building. Richard promptly "fell upon the said Robert Miles, and beat him with a broom-staff, calling him murdering knave." When Bishop dared to protest at this, and spoke of the contemptuous treatment given the order of the Court of Chancery, "the said Richard Burbage," so Bishop deposed, "scornfully and disdainfully playing with this deponent's nose, said that if he mixed in the matter he would beat him also, and did challenge the field of him at that time." One of the actors, John Alleyn (brother of Edward Alleyn), hearing all this noise, came out of the dressing-room, and "found the foresaid Richard Burbage, the youngest son of the said James Burbage, there with a broom-staff in his hand; of whom, when this deponent, Alleyn, asked what stir was there, he answered in laughing phrase, how they came for a moiety [i.e., a half-interest], 'but,' quoth he, holding up the said broom-staff, 'I have, I think, delivered him a moiety with this, and sent them all packing.'" Miles and the others had indeed fled from the broom-staff wielded by young Richard with histrionic fervor. Then the father, James Burbage, came bustling into the Theatre. The actor, Alleyn, felt called upon to warn the Burbages that Miles could bring an action for assault and battery against them. "Tush!" exclaimed the father. "No! I warrant you! But where my son hath now beat him hence, my sons, if they will be ruled by me, shall, at their next coming, provide charged pistols, with powder and hempseed, to shoot them in the legs."

Such were the Burbages. But this picture, drawn from a rather sordid episode, reveals only one side of their character. Richard Burbage, at least, was a man of wide intellectual interests, an excellent painter as well as a distinguished actor, and gifted with a personality that endeared him to his friends. Upon his death many touching elegies were written on him. One that deals with him as a man may here be cited. The Earl of Pembroke, writing to the Ambassador to Germany, gives the Court news about the mighty ones of the kingdom: "My Lord of Lenox made a great supper to the French Ambassador this night here, and even now all the company are at a play; which I, being tender-hearted, could not endure to see so soon after the loss of my old acquaintance Burbage."

The other sharers of the company were likewise men of note in their profession, whose acquaintance was prized by those interested in the drama and literature. I have already cited testimony to the amiability of William Kempe as a companion; Nashe declares that he was "oft in his company." The poet, John Davies of Hereford, addressing actors in general, and singling out two members of the Chamberlain's Company in particular, exclaims: "Players, I love yee"; and as a class they must have been very interesting men. They did not possess a university training, yet they all had a general education, were well-versed in the world, and were endowed with a natural wit that made them kings of good fellows. Young noblemen and gallants sought their society, and often entertained them at expensive suppers in the taverns.[1] Perhaps in their intellectual alertness, their lively personalities, and their genial spirits they differed in no essential way from the better grade of actors to-day.

Moreover — and this fact has not been properly stressed — the leading members of the Chamberlain's Company were distinguished by a probity of character that impresses the close student of their lives. John Heminges was universally admired for his integrity, and, as we know, generously gave of his time and energy to helping his fellows. Both he and Condell were churchwardens of St. Mary, Aldermanbury, where they resided most of their lives. The moral earnestness of Phillips is clearly revealed in his will, a document that makes us feel that we should be proud to have such a man as our friend. Thomas Pope, who lived as a bachelor on the Bankside, left by testament "unto Susan Gasquine, whom I have brought up ever since she was born, the sum of one hundred pounds . . . and all my household stuff," with "all that house or tenement wherein I now dwell, in the parish of St. Saviour's"; to a certain young Thomas Bromley he left "the sum of fifty pounds . . . in regard the use thereof may bring up the boy"; and to his mother, his brothers, and to various friends he gave benefactions

---

[1] See Dekker, *The Gul's Horn-book;* and Jonson, *Every Man in His Humor*, Character of the Persons; *Poetaster*, III, i; *Bartholomew Fair*, V, iii.

in words that express great affection and kindness **of** heart.[1]

These were the people with whom Shakespeare was henceforth to live on terms of close familiarity. We may well believe that he found their companionship to his liking. And so thoroughly did he make himself one of them, that Heminges and Condell call him not only "friend and fellow" but, speaking for the whole company, "*our* Shakespeare."

[1] For the wills of these actors, and other materials relating to them, see J. P. Collier, *Memoirs of the Principal Actors in the Plays of Shakespeare,* 1846.

CHAPTER XII

LABORS FOR THE CHAMBERLAIN'S MEN, 1594–1598

SHAKESPEARE'S task now was to provide the Chamberlain's Company with an adequate supply of plays, both through frequent revision of old manuscripts, and through the annual composition of two or more original pieces. Upon joining the troupe he was probably able to furnish the actors at once with a new comedy, *The Two Gentlemen of Verona*, on which, it seems, he had been working during his long period of enforced leisure. The play, with its Italian setting, gives unmistakable evidence of that wide reading in the Renaissance literature of the Continent which occupied much of his time from 1592 to 1594. Not only are various elements of the plot to be found in French and Italian story-tellers, but the main theme, of Proteus and Julia, was derived from the popular Spanish romance of *Diana*, by Montemayor. Since there was no printed English translation of this voluminous romance, the natural inference is that Shakespeare read it in the original, or in the French translation of 1578.[1] The influence of Lyly's *Euphues*, too, popular in fashionable circles, and of his "Court comedies," well-approved by the Queen, is unmistakable. Indeed, the play seems to have been devised with a courtly audience distinctly in mind. This may explain why in style and in spirit it is closely akin to *Love's Labour's Lost*, written late

---

[1] Shakespeare's ability to read French cannot be questioned, and we have evidence, though less certain, that he had some command of Spanish. The English translation by Young was not printed until 1598, and then privately. There is, of course, a possibility that Shakespeare had the privilege of reading Young's manuscript; but the bulkiness of the work would prevent many transcripts, and the chance of his seeing a copy was not great.

in 1592 when the plague made the Christmas performance before Elizabeth the chief concern of the actors. Although there is no positive evidence to fix the exact time of its composition, we may feel sure that *The Two Gentlemen* was produced after *Love's Labour's Lost;* and scholars are generally agreed that the date 1593–94 cannot be far astray.

If, as seems virtually certain, the play was ready for the actors in the autumn or early winter of 1594, it came at a most opportune moment; for the Chamberlain's Men were summoned to give two performances before Her Majesty during the Christmas festivities that followed.

And now for the first time, we discover Shakespeare's name associated with the Chamberlain organization. The record of the Treasurer reads:

To William Kempe, William Shakespeare, and Richard Burbage, servants to the Lord Chamberlain, upon the Council's warrant, dated at Whitehall xvto Marcii 1594 [i.e., 1595], for two several comedies or interludes showed by them before Her Majesty in Christmas time last past, viz., upon St. Stephen's Day [December 26, 1594] and Innocents' Day [an error [1] for St. John's Day, December 27, 1594], xiii*li*. vi*s*. viii*d*., and by way of Her Majesty's reward, xi*li*. xiii*s*. iv*d*.; in all, xx*li*.

The linking of Shakespeare's name with those of Kempe and Burbage in order clearly to identify the troupe,[2]

---

[1] The treasurer's account elsewhere shows that on Innocents' Day, December 28, the Admiral's Men played before Her Majesty; and we know that on that day the Chamberlain's Men played before the members of Gray's Inn. It was the Queen's custom to have a play on December 27. The truth seems to be that the Chamberlain's Company performed before the Queen at Greenwich on December 26 and 27, and returned to London for their performance at Gray's Inn on December 28, and that, as the record shows, the Admiral's Men entertained the Queen on the latter date. Thus we must assume an error in the scribe's record, unless we resort to several unlikely suppositions.

[2] I do not understand how Sir Sidney Lee supposes that, not the troupe as a whole, but these three actors alone were summoned, presented not complete plays, but selected scenes ("all the scenes came from Shakespeare's repertory"), and shared the reward among themselves. See his *Shake-*

gives unmistakable testimony to the commanding position which at this early date he enjoyed in London theatrical circles, and is in striking contrast with the total
absence of any allusion to him, or to his plays, in the
Henslowe-Alleyn documents relating to the same troupe
before June, 1594. This is merely one of many bits of
evidence indicating that he was not connected with the
Chamberlain's Company until its reorganization after
the plague.

The brief record of the treasurer does not supply us
with the titles of the "two several comedies" acted by
the Chamberlain's Men at Greenwich. One of them, as
has been suggested, may well have been *The Two Gentlemen of Verona*, the courtly style of which would render it
highly suitable for performance before Her Majesty. The
other, we may guess, was *The Comedy of Errors*, just rewritten by Shakespeare for a great Christmas celebration
to be held by the members of Gray's Inn. Through our
good luck in having a detailed account of this celebration,
we are able to visualize an interesting episode in the early
career of the dramatist.

The Inns of Court, four in number — the Inner Temple, the Middle Temple, Gray's Inn, and Lincoln's Inn —
were societies which gave instruction in the law, and exercised the exclusive right of admitting persons to practice
at the bar. By ancient custom the members, consisting
of benchers, barristers, and students, frequently devised
plays, masques, and other entertainments for the amusement of themselves and invited guests. Following this
custom, in December, 1594, the members of Gray's Inn
held "a grand revel" — a veritable Feast of Fools — in
which they elected one of their members, Henry Helmes,
Lord of Misrule. Bestowing on him the title "Prince of

speare and the Modern Stage, 1907, pp. 33–35, and *A Life of William Shakespeare*, 1916, pp. 55, 87, 153.

Purpoole," they celebrated his reign of folly, which lasted throughout the Christmas holidays, with hilarious merriment. The title-page of the printed account of these revels, with its allusions to nearly all the famous places of ill-repute about London, gives a fair notion of the spirit with which the young lawyers threw themselves into their fun-making: "Gesta Grayorum: or, The History of the High and Mighty Prince, Henry, Prince of Purpoole, Arch-Duke of Stapulia and Bernardia, Duke of High and Nether Holborn, Marquis of St. Giles and Tottenham, Count Palatine of Bloomsbury and Clerkenwell, Great Lord of the Cantons of Islington, Kentish-Town, Paddington and Knights-bridge, Knight of the Most Heroical Order of the Helmet, and Sovereign of the Same; Who Reigned, and died, A.D. 1594." [1]

On the twentieth of December the Prince was formally inducted into office. Attended by all his train, he "marched from his lodging to the great Hall, and there took his place in his throne, under a rich cloth of state; his counsellors and great lords were placed about him." The elaborate ceremonies of coronation were followed by wittily obscene speeches and high-sounding proclamations by various members of the society, lasting several hours. But the climax of the revels was arranged for the evening of December 28, when hundreds of outside guests were to be present. For this occasion the Chamberlain's Men were engaged to present a play. It is worth noting that the young Earl of Southampton was a member of Gray's Inn, and he may have had something to do with the choice of Shakespeare's company; such an assumption, however, is by no means necessary, for Shakespeare's reputation was in itself sufficient to explain why the lawyers should desire a play from his pen.

[1] This was first printed from the manuscript in 1688. There is an excellent reprint by W. W. Greg in *The Malone Society Reprints*, 1914.

As befitting the reign of a Lord of Misrule Shakespeare selected for presentation before the Prince and his guests *The Comedy of Errors*. But for so important an occasion he would naturally revise the play, rewriting such portions as most needed it, or as the limited time at his disposal allowed. The text of the comedy as it has come down to us distinctly shows the marks of this hurried revision. Much of the original doggerel verse and rhyme, the wooden balancing of speeches, and the absurd plays on words, remain; yet in the more pivotal scenes the revising hand of the maturer artist is plainly discernible. The text, indeed, presents a curious mixture of Shakespeare's earliest and worst style, with his later and more masterly style.

To be the special guests of honor at this grand climax of their revels, the members of Gray's Inn sent a formal invitation to the members of the rival Inner Temple, with the request that the latter bring with them an Ambassador properly accredited to the High and Mighty Prince of Purpoole. The Templars accepted the invitation, appointed an Ambassador Extraordinary, and prepared to attend in full force. Unluckily the individual members of Gray's Inn made the mistake of sending out too many invitations to their private friends, so that the Hall could not nearly accommodate all who came.

For what happened on the night of December 28 I may summarize the published account. "There was a great presence of lords, ladies, and worshipful personages that did expect some notable performance"; but the numbers were "so exceeding great, that thereby there was no convenient room." At nine o'clock, the Templars arrived, with their Ambassador "very gallantly appointed, and attended by a great number of brave gentlemen." In spite of the throngs that interfered with the proposed ceremonies, the Ambassador was received with a set speech of mock solemnity, and seated in a place of honor on the stage itself. But, "when the Ambassador was placed, as aforesaid, and that there was something to be performed for the delight of the beholders, there arose such a disordered tumult and crowd upon the stage, that there was no opportunity to effect that which was intended, there came so great a number of worshipful personages upon the stage that might not be displaced, and gentlewomen whose sex did privilege them from violence." The upshot of this embarrassing state of affairs was that at last the members of the Inner Temple, presumably the special guests of honor, became "discontented and displeased," and in unmistakable anger left the Hall. "After their departure the throngs and tumults did somewhat cease, although so much of them continued as was able to disorder and confound any good inventions whatsoever." Finally, at midnight, the turmoil was quieted, and the stage sufficiently cleared to enable Shakespeare and his fellows to begin their performance: "a *Comedy of Errors* (like to Plautus his *Menechmus*)." When the title was announced it must have provoked among the audience considerable laughter by its appropriateness to the occasion; at any rate the point was not lost on the members of Gray's Inn: "So that night was begun, and continued to the end, in nothing but confusion and Errors; whereupon it was ever afterwards called 'The Night of Errors.'" [1]

[1] The following night the students held a mock-trial to inquire into the "great disorders," which were humorously attributed to witchcraft. Among the charges brought against the "Sorcerer or Cunjurer that was supposed to be the cause of that confused inconvenience" was mentioned, in the spirit of fun that characterized the whole proceedings, his fetching in a Play of Errors: "And, lastly, that he had foisted a company of base and common fellows to make up our disorders with a Play of Errors and Confusions." Scholars, forgetting that this was a mock-trial conducted in farcical language, have misinterpreted the passage quoted above. Even Mrs. Stopes, in her recent *Southampton* (1922), pp. 71 ff., says: "The play was considered the crowning disgrace of the evening"; and she advances the theory that the masque

But such things as an appearance at Court, or the revamping of an old comedy for the members of Gray's Inn, were mere episodes in Shakespeare's busy career as an actor and a playwright. We should like to know something of the rôles he assumed before the public, and something of the success he achieved in histrionic art. Chettle, it will be recalled, declared as early as 1592 that he was "excellent in the quality" he professed; and Heminges and Condell, in publishing his comedies, histories, and tragedies, placed his name at the head of the list "of the principal actors in all these plays." But the parts that an actor assumed not being a matter of record, it is only accident when we can say that a given player assumed a given rôle. In the case of Shakespeare, as with most of his fellows, accident has not favored us.[1]

Moreover, not a little of his labor as a dramatist escapes us, for doubtless he was often employed in revamping old plays. When he joined the Chamberlain's Company he found its stock of manuscripts large; as a troupe it had long been in existence, and recently it had acquired by purchase a number of old pieces from the disrupted Pembroke's Company. Many of these would need touching up, and not a few even drastic revision in order to make them effective; for, it should be remembered, the standards of dramatic entertainment were from year to year

presented on January 3 was for the purpose of blotting out the disgrace of a vulgar play. But the passage she cites by way of proof indicates no such thing: "The performance of which night [i.e., the performance on January 3], being carefully and orderly handled, did so delight and please . . . that thereby Gray's Inn did not only recover their lost credit, and quite take away all the disgrace that the former Night of Errors had incurred," but made friends again with the Templars. Clearly the emphasis is on the fact that "the performance" was "carefully and orderly handled," and that, as a result of this orderly handling, the Templars who, it should be remembered, left the hall before the play began) were appeased. The "disgrace" was due to the "Night of Errors" not to the "Play of Errors"; as one of the members of Gray's Inn put it: "That Night had gained to us Discredit, and itself a nickname of Errors."

[1] For a discussion of the rôles he is supposed to have assumed, see pp. 424–27.

being steadily raised. The work of Shakespeare in these revisions cannot now be traced with certainty. Many of the manuscripts he possibly furbished never came into print, and so perished; some were later subjected to further revision, either by Shakespeare or by other playwrights; [1] and a few, perhaps, are extant to-day with hasty lines from his pen that cannot easily be recognized. [2] It is only of the plays that constitute the canon as fixed by Heminges and Condell that we can speak with anything like confidence.

Of these the first that probably received his attention was George Peele's *Henry VI*. By a curious turn of Fortune's wheel, the Chamberlain's Company, which in 1592 scored a remarkable success with this play, had come into possession (through purchase from the bankrupt Pembroke's Company) of *The Contention* and its sequel, *The True Tragedy*, the old chronicles Shakespeare had reworked as a competing attraction. All three plays had met with such hearty approval from theatre-goers that it would be a mistake to suppress any one of them. Shakespeare therefore combined them into a Henry VI trilogy by using Peele's play as an introduction or prologue to the two Marlowe plays — a feat he was able to accomplish with very little manipulation. No doubt the three histories, acted in sequence, continued, as they had done before the inhibition of 1592, to attract great crowds.

The extraordinary success the Henry VI plays had attained with the public was the main reason, we may suppose, that led Shakespeare to continue the historical vein. But there were other reasons also. The patriotic fervor arising from the defeat of the Spanish Armada, and the consequent spirit of national unity, had produced among

---

[1] For example *Hamlet*, which Shakespeare is thought to have touched up long before his final and triumphant revision.

[2] *Sir Thomas More* is a possible example.

Englishmen an intense interest in the history of their country, and had created an unprecedented demand for the "chronicle," a distinctively native type of dramatic entertainment. Moreover, at a time when the Puritans were bitter in their attacks upon the theatre, the actors gained no little credit from the educational value of such studies. As Heywood boasted in his *Apology for Actors:* "Plays have made the ignorant more apprehensive, taught the unlearned the knowledge of many famous histories, instructed such as cannot read in the discovery of all our English chronicles; and what man have you now of that weak capacity that cannot discourse of any notable thing recorded even from William the Conqueror, nay from the landing of Brute, until this day?" Since the vogue of the historical drama was now at its height, it was quite natural for Shakespeare to provide his troupe with plays of this type.

Accordingly, turning to Holinshed's *Chronicle* he took up English history at the precise point where *III Henry VI* left off, namely at the death of the King, and, beginning with the funeral obsequies of that sovereign, created *Richard III*.[1] Although external proof is lacking, internal evidence makes it reasonably certain that the play was being presented on the stage of the Theatre early in 1595. Its style reveals the profound influence which Marlowe's genius exercised upon the youthful Shakespeare, and the text in many ways indicates an intimate association with the three Henry VI plays. But the new play surpassed its prototypes by giving to the episodic chronicle something of artistic unity and tragic effectiveness through the dominating figure of Richard, whose rise and fall constitute the proper movement of the plot, and whose character

---

[1] The theory has been advanced that *Richard III* is a revision by Shakespeare of an older play written as a sequel to *The True Tragedy;* see the *London Times Literary Supplement*, September 20 and 27, 1918, pp. 438 and 452.

forms the central interest. Its immediate success with the public was astounding. Even from men of letters it won high praise; for example, the author of the poem entitled *The Ghost of Richard the Third* (1614), makes the spirit of Richard say:

> To him that impt my fame with Clio's quill,
> Whose magic rais'd me from oblivion's den,
> That writ my story on the Muses' hill,
> And with my action dignifi'd his pen;
> He that from Helicon sends many a rill,
> Whose nectared veins are drunk by thirsty men,
>   Crown'd be his style with fame, his head with bays,
>   And none detract, but gratulate his praise.

Nor was Shakespeare the only one for whom the play won fame; young Burbage attained instant renown by his impassioned utterance of the line —

> A horse! a horse! my Kingdom for a horse!

Such a deep impression did this line as shouted in the Theatre by Burbage make upon the public that for many years after it was a stock expression for quotation and parody. Bishop Corbet, about 1618, relates an interesting anecdote of an old "host," whom he describes as "full of ale and history." On one occasion this merry soul, while acting as a guide to visitors on the battlefield of Bosworth, and eloquently describing the death of Richard — "Why, he could tell the inch where Richmond stood, where Richard fell" — in his fervor of utterance "mistook a player for a king," —

> For when he would have said "King Richard died
> And called 'A horse! a horse!' " he "Burbage" cried.[1]

The success of *Richard III* naturally inspired Shakespeare to attempt other historical plays. Again turning to Holinshed's *Chronicle* he selected the story of King Richard II, dramatizing it apparently with such speed as to be

---

[1] *Iter Boreale*, pp. 193–94.

able to deliver the manuscript to the actors by the summer or early autumn of 1595. Although it failed to achieve the sensational popularity of *Richard III*, it was for many years a favorite with London audiences. Queen Elizabeth, who did not relish its deposition scene, had occasion to complain at the frequency with which it was acted in London; and even so late as 1631 Sir Henry Herbert, Master of the Revels, thought it still popular enough to warrant his choosing it for his benefit performance.

Richard II was promptly followed by another historical play, *King John*, in all probability acted by the Chamberlain's Men before the close of 1595. In its composition Shakespeare made free use of an old two-part chronicle, *The Troublesome Raigne of John, King of England*,[1] long known on the stage, and printed in 1591. But his skilful condensation of the plot, and vivid portrayal of the characters, make this revamping one of the most effective of his historical studies. Its continued favor with London audiences is indicated by the issue of the old source-play in 1611 with the statement on the title-page "written by W. Sh.," and again in 1622 with the bolder statement "written by W. Shakespeare."

Through the production of these six chronicle-plays Shakespeare had established himself as the most famous interpreter of English history to the common people; and the esteem in which his efforts were long held by the public is echoed in Jonson's *The Devil is an Ass*, 1616:

> *Fitz.* I know not that, sir. But Thomas of Woodstock,
> I 'm sure was duke, and he was made away
> At Calice, as Duke Humphrey was at Bury:
> And Richard the Third, you know what end he came to.
> *Meer.* By my faith you are cunning in the chronicle, sir.

---

[1] Almost certainly the work of George Peele; see H. Dugdale Sykes, *Sidelights on Shakespeare*, 1919, pp. 99 ff.

Fitz. No, I confess I have it from the playbooks,
And think they are more authentic.
   Eng. That is sure, sir.

After completing this notable series of historical plays, Shakespeare turned back to the composition of light courtly comedy, which he had begun in *Love's Labour's Lost* and further developed in *The Two Gentlemen of Verona*, and by the spring of 1596 had delivered to his company *A Midsummer Night's Dream.* He drew the Hippolyta-Theseus story from North's translation of Plutarch's *Lives* — our first indication of his acquaintance with this work which was later to supply him with so many excellent plots. A new edition had just been issued from the press of Richard Field in 1595.[1] One would like to believe that Field presented his friend with a copy of this edition, and that *A Midsummer Night's Dream*, giving evidence of a prompt reading of the volume, shows the dramatist's appreciation of the gift.

The epithalamic ending of the play has led scholars to suspect that it was originally composed for performance at the marriage of some great nobleman, and that the complimentary allusion to the "fair vestal throned by the west" indicates the presence on this occasion of Queen Elizabeth. It seems impossible, however, to determine which of the several noteworthy marriages that took place about this time Shakespeare may have been called upon to celebrate.[2] The play, of course, was also presented, perhaps with slight modification, on the public stage;[3] and as one of the airiest products of the poet's

[1] For an excellent reprint of the portions used by Shakespeare, see C. F. Tucker Brooke, *Shakespeare's Plutarch*, 1909.

[2] See E. K. Chambers, "The Occasion of *A Midsummer Night's Dream*," in *A Book of Homage to Shakespeare*, 1916, pp. 154–60.

[3] W. J. Lawrence, "A Plummet for Bottom's Dream," *Fortnightly Review*, May, 1922, ingeniously argues that the play was originally composed for presentation before the public, and was revised for a special performance at Lady Russell's house on her daughter's wedding night.

fancy it won instant favor. The character of Bottom the weaver became then, as it has remained since, a classic in the humor of simplicity. Designed especially for William Kempe, the rôle must have been acted by that great comedian with rare effectiveness.

A second comedy that may be tentatively assigned to the year 1596 is *Love's Labour's Won*, mentioned by Meres in 1598 as among the dramatist's best work. It no longer survives, however, under this title. Probably it is to be identified with *All's Well that Ends Well*, which obviously is a reworking of an early comedy of about this date. It was customary for the actors to give a new title to a revised play in order to enhance its drawing power; "new titles," exclaims Shakespeare's troupe in one of its prologues, "warrant not plays for new." We have no reason to suppose that *Love's Labour's Won* has perished; and *All's Well* can better be identified with Meres' title than any other of the extant plays.

To the latter half of 1596 may also be assigned the appearance on the stage of Shakespeare's first venture in tragedy, *Romeo and Juliet*. Parts of the play he had certainly written as early as 1593 or 1594, while he was engaged in the composition of *Venus and Adonis*, *Lucrece*, and the *Sonnets*. But for some reason, it seems, he had laid the manuscript aside unfinished, and did not give it the final touches and offer it to the public until 1596. There are no references to the play that can safely be dated earlier than 1597; and the great stir it then made precludes the likelihood that it had been on the stage for years. Not only do the numerous allusions to its popularity at this time indicate that it was new to London audiences, but its phenomenal success led to the theft of the text, and the issue in 1597 of a corrupt pirated edition.

The fame of *Romeo and Juliet*, indeed, surpassed that

of any of the dramatist's previous efforts, even *Richard III;* [1] and its appearance must be set down by the historian of the stage as one of the most notable theatrical events in the closing decade of the century. John Marston, in *The Scourge of Villainy*, published in 1598, thus addresses the stage-haunting gallant, Luscus:

> Luscus, what's play'd to-day? Faith, now I know
> I set thy lips abroach, from whence doth flow
> Naught but pure *Juliet and Romeo*.

The play won equal fame at the universities. In the Cambridge *Pilgrimage to Parnassus* (1598) we find several quotations from it; and in the sequel, *The Return from Parnassus* (1600), Ingenioso thus comments on the language of one of the students: "We shall have nothing but pure Shakespeare . . . Mark *Romeo and Juliet!* O monstrous theft!" At Oxford the estimation in which the play was held is shown by evidence of a different kind and of a later date, but not the less conclusive. In the recently discovered original Bodleian copy of the First Folio, which was chained to shelves where it could be read by the students, the wear on the leaves shows that of all the plays of Shakespeare the one which most pleased the young men of the university was *Romeo and Juliet*, and "the page most worn of all is the one which faced a well-known Balcony Scene introduced by the stage direction 'Enter Romeo and Juliet aloft,'" the paper here being "worn completely through, not torn." [2]

In the title-rôle of Romeo young Burbage rose to new heights of popular favor. Marston, in *The Scourge of Villainy* (1598), after mentioning the play in the passage just quoted, asks the gallant, Luscus, a question intended to

[1] John Weever, in an epigram *Ad Gulielmum Shakespeare*, published in 1599 but said to have been written earlier, links the play with *Richard III* in popular favor.

[2] See *The Original Bodleian Copy of the First Folio of Shakespeare*, 1905.

set his tongue going, one that presumably was often discussed among gentlemen fond of the theatre:

> Say, who acts best, *Drusus* or *Roscio*?

The allusion is to Alleyn and Burbage, and to the keen
rivalry between them for first place in the esteem of the
public. Incidentally it suggests also the rivalry between
the Admiral's Men at the Rose and the Chamberlain's
Men at the Theatre, the two great competing troupes
that virtually monopolized the drama in London. The
clownish Peter, we know, was acted by William Kempe,
doubtless with his usual success. Even more successful,
however, seems to have been the comedian (William
Slye?) who assumed the part of the Nurse, if imitation be good evidence; for in the comedy *Wily Beguiled*,
almost certainly revised by Marston and Dekker for the
Paul's Boys in 1598, there is a frank and highly amusing
copy of the rôle in the "old Nurse" attending the heroine Lelia.

In this, Shakespeare's first tragedy, the influence of
Marlowe is again apparent, especially in the rhetorical
passages; but the sympathetic portrayal of romantic love,
which constitutes the chief glory of the play, was quite
beyond Marlowe's power; nor could Marlowe have created the keen wit of Mercutio, or the realistic humor of
the garrulous old Nurse. In these things Shakespeare
was beginning to discover the riches of his own genius,
and from now on he rapidly freed himself from the influence of his early master.

It is worth noting, too, that he seems to have been much
irritated by the corrupt edition of 1597, which gave the
reading public a mangled text of his play. *Love's Labour's
Lost* also had just been piratically issued in a debased
text.[1] Being still sensitive about his reputation with men

---

[1] No copy of this pirated edition of *Love's Labour's Lost* has survived. For
a fuller discussion see pp. 516–17.

of letters, he secured the permission of his company to print both these plays in correct form. The publication was entrusted to Cuthbert Burby, and the actors' own prompt-copies were delivered to the printer for the use of the type-setters, as evinced by the stage-directions; for instance, in one place instead of "Enter Peter" we have the prompter's note, "Enter Kempe." Later Shakespeare became less easily disturbed about his fame as a literary craftsman, but at this early stage of his career he seems to have been eager to maintain his good standing in the poetic circles of London.

In the following year, 1597, he produced *The Merchant of Venice*, or as it often was called, and perhaps originally, *The Jew of Venice*.[1] The main plot he derived from a novella in the *Pecorone* of Ser Giovanni Fiorentino, reading the story in the original Italian, for there was no translation available in English, or for that matter in any other language. For his portrait of the Jew he drew heavily upon Marlowe's successful play, *The Jew of Malta*, as the title *The Jew of Venice* would suggest. Shylock and his daughter Jessica are obvious imitations of Barabas and Abigail. Abigail, like Jessica, loves a young Christian, and deserts her father. Barabas, like Shylock, is cruel and revengeful. There are even numerous echoes of Marlowe's phraseology, although *The Jew of Malta* had not as yet been printed (it was not allowed to come to press until 1633). For example, Barabas exclaims:

> O my girl!
> My gold! my fortune! my felicity! . . .
> O girl! O gold! O beauty! O my bliss!

---

[1] The exact date of composition is a matter of conjecture; but on July 27, 1598, the Chamberlain's Company had their printer friend, Roberts, enter the play in the Stationers' Registers in order to secure the copyright and thus prevent piracy. Roberts, of course, was acting in behalf of the players, and had no intention of printing the play. The license he secured reads: "provided it be not printed without license first had from the Lord Chamberlain," i.e., the patron of the troupe.

Shakespeare, from recollection of the play on the stage, represents Shylock as exclaiming:

> My daughter! O my ducats! O my daughter!
> Fled with a Christian! O my Christian ducats!
> Justice! the law! my ducats! and my daughter!

Again, in Marlowe s play the Jew, Barabas, says:

> I am not of the tribe of Levi, I,
> That can so soon forget an injury. . . .
> I learned in Florence how to kiss my hand,
> Heave up my shoulders when they call me dog.

And Shylock, in ironic vein, echoes this:

> Still have I borne it with a patient shrug. . . .
> Hath a dog money? Is it possible
> A cur can lend three thousand ducats? Or
> Shall I bend low, and in a bondsman's key,
> With bated breath, and whispering humbleness,
> Say this? —
> "Fair sir, you spet on me on Wednesday last;
> You spurn'd me such a day; another time
> You call'd me dog."

Very familiar, too, is Barabas' demand of the Governor, "Let me have law," and the Governor's grim reply, "You shall have law!"

But the superiority of Shakespeare's characterization of the Jew over Marlowe's clearly shows how far he had now advanced in his art: Barabas is a caricature, Shylock is poignantly human. And it is significant that here we have the last trace of the influence of Marlowe on the rapidly developing young dramatist. From this time on, confident in his own powers, he marches forward from play to play without once glancing back at the "famous gracer of tragedians."

A second comedy that Shakespeare provided for his company in 1597 was a revision entitled *The Taming of the Shrew.* The Chamberlain's Men had secured the original play from the disrupted Pembroke's Company, and had presented it at Newington Butts during their temporary stay at that house in June, 1594. Apparently some member of the Pembroke's Company had disposed of a transcript to the printers, for it was entered in the Stationers' Registers on May 2, 1594, and published before the end of the year with the title: *A Pleasant Conceited Historie called The Taming of a Shrew. As it was sundry times acted by the Right Honorable the Earle of Pembrook his Servants*. Many scholars think that before Shakespeare put his hand to it, it had been revised for the Chamberlain's Men by an inferior playwright, who added the Bianca sub-plot.[1] If so, in 1597 Shakespeare undertook a further revision of the play. He retained the main outlines of the old story, and spent his energies chiefly on the Petruchio-Katharina theme. He also touched up with wonderful effectiveness the Christopher Sly Induction by which the play proper is set in a frame. The allusions to Burton Heath (i.e., Barton on the Heath), the home of his uncle Edmund Lambert, and to Wincot, a town near Stratford noted for its good ale, reflect the poet's early associations. It is curious, however, that, having spent so much care in presenting the drunken Sly to the audience, and placing him gloriously in bed to witness the shrew-taming play acted by the traveling troupe, Shakespeare fails to mention him after the first scene, and makes no provision at all for ultimately removing him from his exalted position to his original place in front of the alehouse. No doubt Shakespeare was working in great haste; yet his failure to complete so important a part of the text as the frame in which the whole drama is set, cannot be explained as an oversight. Probably the rôle of Christopher Sly was put into the hands of William Kempe, or William Slye, and Shakespeare, after outlining the comic

---

[1] Its latest editor, Mr. F. S. Boas, stoutly denies this; see his edition in The Shakespeare Classics, 1908, p. xxxix.

setting of the plot, left the working out of the later details to the improvisation of the sharp-witted actor, for the skill of the Elizabethan comedians at extemporization was proverbial. If this explanation be accepted, we must note that the dramatist's well-known advice to the players in *Hamlet*, "Let those that play your clowns speak no more than is set down for them," would not be applicable to his hasty revision of *The Taming of the Shrew*.

It is true that Shakespeare worked hurriedly on the old play, and at times sketchily; yet he succeeded in making it one of the best-liked comedies in the repertory of the Chamberlain's Men. The humor of the drunken Sly, and the almost universal appeal of the wife-taming theme, rendered it for many years a favorite on the stage. Fletcher paid it the compliment of frank imitation by writing *The Tamer Tamed*, 1606, in which the tables were turned on Petruchio, who is reduced to complete submission by his second wife. Even so late as 1633 Herbert notes its performance at Court before King Charles, adding to his brief record the significant — and still pertinent — comment, "likt."

In this same year, 1597, Shakespeare turned again to history, and picking up the thread where he left it at the end of *Richard II*, produced *I Henry IV*. For his material he went to his thumb-worn copy of Holinshed, and at the same time, it seems, read Samuel Daniel's poetic rendering of the events in his fourth book of *The Civil Wars*, 1595. He also availed himself of an old play entitled *The Famous Victories of Henry V*, containing the mad pranks of Prince Hal with his disreputable companions in Eastcheap.[1] This ancient chronicle had been entered for publication in 1594, and may then have been printed,

[1] See J. Monaghan, "Falstaff and his Forebears," *Studies in Philology*, 1921, xviii, 353.

although our earliest extant copy bears the date 1598. It had originally been performed by the Queen's Men before the death of Tarlton in 1588, as we learn from the following jest recorded of that famous clown:

At the Bull at Bishopsgate was a play of *Henry the Fifth*, wherein the judge was to take a box on the ear; and because he was absent that should take the blow, Tarlton himself, ever forward to please, took upon him to play the same judge, beside his own part of the clown: and Knel, then playing Henry the Fifth, hit Tarlton a sound box indeed, which made the people laugh the more because it was he; but anon the judge goes in, and immediately Tarlton in his clown's cloaths comes out, and asks the actors "What news?" "O," saith one, "hadst thou been here, thou shouldst have seen Prince Henry hit the judge a terrible box on the ear." "What, man!" said Tarlton, "strike a judge?" "It is true, yfaith," said the other. "No other like," said Tarlton; "and it could not be but terrible to the judge, when the report so terrifies me that methinks the blow remains still on my cheek that it burns again." The people laughed at this mightily.[1]

Shakespeare studied *The Famous Victories* in connection with the more serious narratives in Holinshed's *Chronicle* and Daniel's *Civil Wars*, and, drawing upon them all for material or inspiration, produced *Henry IV*.

The play, we know, was put on the stage of the Theatre in the latter half of 1597. Immediately Falstaff captured the hearts of all London, and scored for the author the greatest popular triumph in comedy he perhaps ever achieved. The unbounded enthusiasm with which fat Sir John was received then, and later, is indicated by Leonard Digges in thus comparing *Henry IV* with Jonson's most successful plays:

> And though the *Fox* and subtle *Alchemist*
> Long intermitted, could not quite be mist,
> Though these have sham'd all the ancients, and might raise
> Their authour's merit with a crowl : of bayes,

---

[1] *Tarlton's Jests*, ed. by J. O. Halliwell, 1844, p. 24.

> Yet these sometimes, even at a friend's desire
> Acted, have scarce defrai'd the sea-coale fire [1]
> And doore-keepers: when, let but Falstaffe come,
> Hal, Poines, the rest — you scarce shall have a roome,
> All is so pester'd.[2]

But perhaps the most convincing evidence of the success of Falstaff is to be found in the two lines to be quoted below. One should remember that throughout the performance of a play the Elizabethan spectators were continuously eating nuts in the theatre, the noise of the cracking shells being, according to no less an authority than Ben Jonson, "most damnable." Yet the entrance of Falstaff on the stage, we are told, produced in the theatre a sudden stillness as each eager listener held the inevitable nut poised half-way in its progress to the mouth:

> I could praise Heywood now; or tell how long
> Falstaff from cracking nuts hath kept the throng.[3]

The remarkable success of the play would naturally lead the public and the actors alike to demand a sequel; and within a few months Shakespeare had placed on the stage the second part of *Henry IV*, with the further exploits of Sir John, Poins, Pistol, Peto, and Bardolph.[4] To these characters he added the immortal Justice Shallow, who seems to have attained a popularity second only to that of Falstaff. At once he became proverbial. Sir Charles Percy in a letter to Carleton, 1600, writes: "I think you will find me so dull that I shall be taken for

[1] The reference is to the Blackfriars playhouse, which was heated in the winter.

[2] Prefixed to Shakespeare's *Poems*, 1640; the lines, however, were written about 1623.

[3] Verses by Sir Thomas Palmer, prefixed to the First Folio of Beaumont and Fletcher, 1647.

[4] Shakespeare was at work on the play in the autumn of 1597, before he had changed the name of Oldcastle to Falstaff; this is indicated by the catchname "Old." for "Fal." in I, ii, 114, and by the description of Falstaff, in III, ii, 27, as having been a "page to Thomas Mowbray, Duke of Norfolk," which was true of Sir John Oldcastle.

Justice Silence, or Justice Shallow"; and again: "Exempt me from the opinion of Justice Shallow." Jonson, in *Every Man Out of his Humor*, 1600, exclaims: "This is a kinsman of Justice Shallow"; Dekker, in *Satiromastix*, 1602, speaks of "These true heirs of Mr. Justice Shallow"; and Woodhouse, in *The Flea*, 1605, writes: "When thou sittest, to consult about any weighty matter, let either Justice Shallow or his cousin Mr. Weathercock be foreman of the jury."

Shakespeare's gratification at the success of *I and II Henry IV*, however, was marred by an unlucky accident. The name he originally gave to Falstaff was Sir John Oldcastle, taken over directly from *The Famous Victories*. There it had provoked no comment. But the extraordinary notoriety of the character as portrayed by Shakespeare seems to have led to resentment [1] on the part of Henry Brooke, Lord Cobham, a lineal descendant of Sir John Oldcastle. Lord Cobham, we may suppose, made complaint, probably to the Master of the Revels, who was responsible for licensed plays; or, possibly, to his near neighbor the Lord Chamberlain, who had general oversight of dramatic affairs, and who was the patron of the company acting the offending plays; and, in view of this altogether unexpected complaint, Shakespeare agreed to change the name of his comic hero. Casting about in his mind for a new name, he stumbled upon Sir John Fastolfe, who figured as a coward in *I Henry VI*, a play he was then engaged in refurbishing:

> Here had the conquest fully been seal'd up
> If Sir John Fastolfe had not play'd the coward.
> He, being in the vaward, — placed behind
> With purpose to relieve and follow them, —
> Cowardly fled, not having struck one stroke.

[1] Especially occasioned, perhaps, by the performance of the two plays at Court during the Christmas of 1597–98?

Altering the name slightly, Shakespeare rechristened the cowardly Sir John Oldcastle with the new designation Sir John Falstaff. Probably the change made it necessary to delete a few passages, yet one was overlooked; in Act I, Scene ii, of Part I, Hal, addressing Falstaff, exclaims: "As the honey of Hybla, my *old* lad of the *Castle*," a pun which, of course, had now entirely lost its force.[1]

Shakespeare had done what he could to right a wholly unintentional wrong against the Cobham family. Yet so indelibly had the "old lad of the castle" stamped his name upon the minds of the public during the short interval preceding the birth of "Falstaff," that it could not be so easily effaced. For many years afterwards writers of the best intelligence allude to Falstaff as Sir John Oldcastle; and the general public, doubtless, was even slower to accept the change of name in their hero. Shakespeare felt called upon to remind the London audiences in an Epilogue attached to the second part of *Henry IV*, that "Oldcastle died a martyr, and this is not the man." He went even farther. Early in 1598 (the play was entered in the Stationers' Registers on February 25) he gave *I Henry IV* to the press in order to show, in black and white, as it were, that the fat Knight of Eastcheap was called "Sir John Falstaff." But all in vain. The name "Oldcastle" could not be expunged from the minds of the public.

Thereupon, it would seem, Lord Cobham, or his friends, in order to repair the injury done, induced the Admiral's Company to produce a long two-part play [2] narrating to the people the "true life" and martyrdom of the real Sir John Oldcastle. The task of composing the work was put into the hands of some of the best and most

---

[1] In the second part of *Henry IV* the catch-name "Old." appears in one place for "Fal."

[2] Only the first part is extant.

experienced dramatists then writing for the stage, Michael Drayton, Anthony Munday, Robert Wilson, and Richard Hathaway, who produced a tiresome, but presumably veracious, history of the old Lollard martyr, under the title *The True and Honorable Historie of the Life of Sir John Oldcastle, the Good Lord Cobham*. In a Prologue the authors say to the public:

> It is no pamperd glutton we present,
> Nor aged Councellor to youthfull sinne,
> But one, whose vertue shone above the rest,
> A valiant Martyr, and a vertuous peere,
> In whose true faith, and loyaltie exprest
> Unto his sovereigne, and his countries weale,
> We strive to pay that tribute of our Love,
> Your favours merite: let faire Truth be grac'te,
> Since forg'de invention former time defac'te.

The play was acted by the Admiral's Men at the Rose in the autumn of 1599, possibly with Lord Cobham and his friends loudly applauding. And shortly afterwards, in order to give it wider publicity, it was printed and offered to the public from the bookstalls. In 1601, as a still further counterblast to Shakespeare's misrepresentation of the ancestor of the Cobham family, John Weever issued a narrative poem entitled *The Mirror of Martyrs, or The Life and Death of That Thrice Valiant Captain and Most Godly Martyr, Sir John Oldcastle, Lord Cobham*.[1]

But Lord Cobham and his friends, and even Shakespeare himself, were laboring against the stream. In spite of all their efforts the name "Oldcastle" for "Falstaff" simply would not down. For instance, when on March 6, 1600, Shakespeare's company presented *Henry IV* at the Lord Chamberlain's house before Vereiken and the other ambassadors from the Spanish Low Countries,

[1] In the Dedication Weever states that the work "some two years ago 'was made fit for the print."

Rowland Whyte wrote in a gossipy letter to Sir Robert Sidney: "Thursday my Lord Chamberlain feasted him [Vereiken], and made him a very great and a delicate dinner; and there in the afternoon his players acted before Vereiken Sir John Oldcastle, to his great contentment." And even so well-informed a man as Nathaniel Field, actor and playwright, in his *Amends for Ladies*, 1618, writes:

> Did you never see
> The play where the fat Knight, hight Oldcastle,
> Did tell you truly what this "honor" was?

Shakespeare was not altogether happy in the choice of the second name, for some people connected Sir John Falstaff with a certain Sir John Fastolfe, an historical personage of good repute. Later Dr. Richard James, Bishop Fuller, and George Daniel all made protests. But these protests went for naught, so that Sir Paunch still bears the name with which Shakespeare rechristened him.

The dramatist probably was growing tired of Falstaff. At the end of *II Henry IV* he represents him as having deteriorated in character, and as being rejected by Hal, now crowned King of England.[1] When Sir John thrusts himself forward, confident of being received by the new sovereign with open arms, the King frowns upon him, and says:

> I know thee not, old man. Fall to thy prayers.
> How ill white hairs become a fool and jester!

And a few moments later we see him, thus humiliated, carried off to prison. But if Shakespeare hoped to get rid of him so easily, he reckoned without the public, and without Queen Elizabeth. Yielding to the popular demand, he made the following promise in a late Epilogue to *II Henry IV*: "Our humble author will continue the

[1] See A. C. Bradley, *Oxford Lectures on Poetry*, 1909, "The Rejection of Falstaff."

story with Sir John in it, and make you merry with fair Katharine of France; where, for anything I know, Falstaff shall die of a sweat." From this announcement we may infer that the dramatist intended to amuse the public with one more — and the last — representation of Falstaff in his humors; and, in order to get rid of him for ever, planned to end his life in the sweat of some arduous exploit in France.

But before he could carry out this promise, his intentions were interfered with by no less a person than Queen Elizabeth. As was her custom, she summoned the Lord Chamberlain's Men in the Christmas season of 1597–98 to amuse Her Majesty at Windsor with their latest plays. Naturally the actors would present before her the two parts of *Henry IV*, then new, and the chief sensation of London. According to a well-founded tradition, she was so much delighted with Falstaff that she called for the author, and requested him to write specially for her a play in which Falstaff should be made to fall in love.[1] A request from the Queen could not be ignored; and Shakespeare was forced to lay aside his proposed *Henry V*, with his already announced purpose of putting Sir John to death, and at once set to work on a comedy representing the hero in an amorous escapade.[2] Tradition states that he completed the comedy within two weeks, for the

[1] See John Dennis, *The Comical Gallant* (1702), Nicholas Rowe, *Life of Shakespeare* (1709), and Charles Gildon, *Remarks on the Plays of Shakespeare* (1710). These men record the story as an old and trustworthy tradition; Gildon states that he is "very well assured of it"; Malone observes that Dennis probably got his information "from Dryden, who, from his intimacy with Sir William Davenant, had an opportunity of learning many particulars concerning our author." The Queen's interest in love is well known; and the story is borne out by both internal and external evidence.

[2] It has been pointed out by various scholars that in the play Falstaff was originally called Oldcastle. I suspect that Lord Cobham took offense at the time the two *Henry IV* plays were acted at Court, and that shortly after Shakespeare was required to change the name of the comic hero — possibly, though we cannot be sure, before *The Merry Wives* was presented before the Queen.

Queen "was so eager to see it that she commanded it to be finished in fourteen days" — possibly in order to have it acted before the end of the Christmas festivities then in progress at Windsor. It is likely that he merely reworked an old manuscript, entitled *The Jealous Comedy*, which had been in the possession of his troupe since 1593.

In this fashion, we may believe, came into existence *The Merry Wives of Windsor*. The haste in composition will explain the play's lack of that merit both in substance and style which otherwise we might expect from Shakespeare at this period of his development, and also the numerous discrepancies to be observed in the plot. Possibly, too, it explains why the story is placed at Windsor, for Elizabeth's residence there would render this setting highly pleasing to her and her ladies; as Gildon notes: "The fairies in the fifth act make a handsome compliment to the Queen and her palace at Windsor." The title-page expressly states that the play had been presented "before Her Majesty," and tradition adds that she was "very well pleased at the representation." It was also, of course, acted before the public during the winter and spring of 1598. The form in which it was advertised in the players' bills posted throughout the city is possibly indicated by the title-page of the pirated edition which shortly appeared: "A Most pleasant and excellent conceited Comedie, of Syr John Falstaffe, and the merrie Wives of Windsor. Entermixed with sundrie variable and pleasing humors, of Syr Hugh, the Welch Knight, Justice Shallow, and his wise Cousin M. Slender. With the swaggering vaine of Auncient Pistoll and Corporall Nym. By William Shakespeare." A playbill promising so many attractive features as this would surely fill the Theatre to its capacity.

After completing *The Merry Wives* for the Queen,

[233]

Shakespeare turned his attention to *Henry V*, already announced as in contemplation. But he did not carry out his promise of representing Falstaff once more in action. Indeed the Knight gets no nearer the stage than an adjoining room, where, we are told, he lies "shaked of a burning quotidian tertian, that it is most lamentable to behold." And from a comic he has been changed into an almost tragic figure; for his illness was due to the King's harsh renunciation of him — "his heart is fracted." With this slight preparation we are suddenly informed in the next scene that he is dead and gone to "Arthur's bosom." The hostess with language at once amusing and pathetic says: "After I saw him fumble with the sheets, and play with flowers, and smile upon his fingers' ends, I knew there was but one way; for his nose was as sharp as a pen, and 'a babbled of green fields." So the greatest comic creation of the drama "went away an it had been any christom child."

Henry V, carrying the life of Prince Hal to its logical triumph, and burying Falstaff under the green fields of which he babbled, was placed upon the stage in the earlier half of 1598.[1] It marks the end not only of Sir John, but also of Shakespeare's great series of historical studies.[2] In this matchless series, which the editors of the First Folio arranged in chronological order — *King John*, *Richard II*, *I Henry IV*, *II Henry IV*, *Henry V*, *I Henry VI*, *II Henry VI*, *III Henry VI*, and *Richard III* — Shakespeare doubtless felt a justifiable pride. Perhaps this pride is indicated by his refurbishing *I Henry*

---

[1] Scholars have almost unanimously dated the play 1599, on the strength of an allusion to the Essex expedition, March, 1599, contained in a chorus prefixed to Act V. But we may easily regard the allusion as a six-line insertion designed to take advantage of the popular excitement attending Essex' departure for Ireland (see p. 315). The history of Falstaff as sketched above would make the date 1598 more or less inevitable.

[2] With, of course, the exception of *Henry VIII*, mainly the product of Fletcher, and composed at the end of Shakespeare's dramatic career.

VI, in 1598–99, so as to make it more worthy of its place in the sequence.[1]

After *Henry V*, as though weary of Falstaff and the disreputable crew that had grown up about him, Shakespeare turned to tragedy, with the hope, we may suppose, of repeating the success of *Romeo and Juliet*. In North's translation of Plutarch, whence he had recently drawn material for *A Midsummer Night's Dream*, he found the story of Brutus, Cæsar, and Antony told in a beautiful and effective way; and this story he worked into the first of his Roman plays. That *Julius Cæsar* was composed in the later half of 1598 or the earlier half of 1599 is shown by several bits of evidence. John Weever's *Mirror of Martyrs*, written in 1599 [2] as a counterblast to the defamation of Oldcastle in *I* and *II Henry IV*, contains an unmistakable allusion to the famous orations of Brutus and Antony:

> The many-headed multitude were drawn
> By Brutus' speech that Cæsar was ambitious;
> When eloquent Mark Antony had shown
> His virtues, who but Brutus then was vicious?
> > Man's memory with new forgets the old;
> > One tale is good until another's told.

Ben Jonson, who was notoriously slow at composition, in *Every Man out of his Humor*, produced at or soon after the opening of the Globe Playhouse in the summer of 1599, makes Buffone exclaim "*Et tu Brute!*" and has Clove utter this fustian: "Then coming to the pretty animals — as Reason long since is fled to animals, you know." Obviously Jonson was making capital of a play well known to the London public. Finally, we have an actual record of a performance of *Julius Cæsar* at the

[1] See C. F. Tucker Brooke's edition of the play in *The Yale Shakespeare Series*, 1918, pp. 124–25, 136.

[2] Though not published until 1601, the author states in the Dedication that the poem was made ready for the press "some two years ago."

Globe in September, 1599. A German traveler, Thomas Platter, noted in his *Reisebeschreibung:*

> On the twenty-first of September [1599], I with my companions, after dinner, somewhere about two o'clock, were rowed across the river to see in the straw-thatched house there the tragedy of the first emperor, *Julius Cæsar*, acted extremely well [*gar artlich*] with scarcely more than fifteen persons.[1]

The tragedy was in striking contrast to those studies in boisterous humor with which Shakespeare had just been amusing the public; yet Brutus and Cæsar seem to have met with success hardly less than that attained by Falstaff and Shallow. Leonard Digges thus describes the effect the play produced on the audience:

> So have I seen, when Cæsar would appear,
> And on the stage at half-sword parley were
> Brutus and Cassius — oh, how the audience
> Were ravish'd! With what wonder they went thence!

Julius Cæsar marks the close of the first period of Shakespeare's labors for the Chamberlain's Company. Before his next group of plays appeared, he and his fellow-actors had moved to the Bankside, where in their new and splendid playhouse, the Globe, they began an even more brilliant career as the leading dramatic company of London.

[1] Quoted by Gustav Binz, in "Londoner Theater und Schauspiele im Jahre 1599," *Anglia*, xxii (1899), 458.

CHAPTER XIII

RISE IN FAME AND IN SOCIAL DIGNITY

SHAKESPEARE had been working hard for his fellows, producing on the average three plays a year, besides revamping old manuscripts. As a result of his efforts he had enabled the Chamberlain's Company to rise above its rival, the Admiral's Company, and stand undisputed as the leading troupe in London. He had rendered Burbage immortal in the titular rôles of Richard III, Romeo, and the like, and had increased the fame of Kempe as the leading comedian of the age. The names of these two actors were now household words throughout England. In a play written at Cambridge University, we read: "Who of more report than Dick Burbage and Will Kempe? He is not counted a gentleman that knows not Dick Burbage and Will Kempe. There's not a country wench . . . but can talk of Dick Burbage and Will Kempe." [1] Finally, he had made his fellow-sharers in the company rich through the throngs that daily flocked to see his plays. Yet only four years had elapsed since he gave up his career in pure letters and threw in his lot with the theatre.

What had he earned for himself? First of all let it be observed that, in spite of the general notion of plays as mercenary and ephemeral products, he had won frank recognition as England's chief man of letters. John Weever, who set himself up as a critic, writes in his *Epigrames* (1599):

> *Romeo, Richard*, more whose names I know not,
> Their sugred tongues and power-attractive beauty
> Say they are Saints, although that Saints they shew not,
> For thousands vowe to them subjective duty.

[1] *II Return from Parnassus*, 1601, ed. by W. C. Macray, p. 139.

In the three Parnassus plays, written and acted by the students of Cambridge University between 1597 and 1601, we find not only quotations from Shakespeare's poems, and scraps from *Romeo and Juliet* and *Henry IV*, but also specific mentions of him by name, showing that the young men of the university then recognized him as the most popular writer in England:

Ey, marry sir, these have some life in them! Let this duncified world esteem of Spenser and Chaucer, I'll worship sweet Mr. Shakespeare.[1]

And one of the students in his enthusiasm exclaims:

O sweet Mr. Shakespeare! I'll have his picture in my study at the court.[2]

Francis Meres, scholar and critic, who describes himself as "Master of Arts of both Universities," in attempting in 1598 to evaluate English literature in comparison with classical literature, unhesitatingly placed Shakespeare in the front rank of literary artists, and indicated his position as the greatest living English man of letters.[3] He writes:

As the soul of Euphorbus was thought to live in Pythagoras, so the sweet, witty soul of Ovid lives in mellifluous and hony-tongued Shakespeare; witness his *Venus and Adonis*, his *Lucrece*, his sugared *Sonnets* among his private friends, etc. As Plautus and Seneca are accounted the best for comedy and tragedy among the Latins, so Shakespeare among the English is the most excellent in both kinds for the stage; for comedy, witness his *Gentlemen of Verona*, his *Errors*, his *Love's Labour's Lost*, his *Love's Labour's Won*, his *Midsummer-Night's Dream*, and his *Merchant of Venice;* for tragedy, his *Richard II, Richard III, Henry IV, King John, Titus Andronicus*, and his *Romeo and Juliet*. As Epius Stolo said that the Muses would speak

---

[1] *I Return*, 1600, ed. by Macray, p. 63.
[2] I.e., Inns of Court. *Ibid.*, p. 58.
[3] *Palladis Tamia. Wits Treasury, Being the Second part of Wits Commonwealth. By Francis Meres, Master of Artes of both Universities.* London, 1598.

with Plautus' tongue if they would speak Latin, so I say that the Muses would speak with Shakespeare's fine filed phrase if they would speak English.

It is hard to see how Meres could have used stronger language to express the esteem in which even at this early date Shakespeare was held. He further mentions the poet in six special categories as among those who have "mightily enriched" the English tongue, who have rendered themselves immortal in verse, who are "our best for tragedy," "the best for comedy," "the best lyric poets," "and the most passionate among us."

Did space allow, more witnesses could be cited to the high fame in letters which Shakespeare had achieved by the close of 1598. Those who are interested should consult *The Shakespeare Allusion-Book*, where references to the poet are arranged in chronological order.

At the same time, of course, Shakespeare was attaining wealth. From his position as a full-sharer in the Chamberlain's Company he derived a large and steady income, and from the sale of his plays, from his benefit performances,[1] and from his appearances at Court and elsewhere, he gained not a little in addition.[2] Thus he was now a man of affluence, able to live in the style his tastes dictated. Yet his tastes, we may suspect, were simple, and his manner of living frugal. The author of *Ratsies Ghost* seems to have him specially in mind when he writes of players: "I have heard indeed of some that have gone to London very meanly, and have come in time to be exceeding wealthy"; and he implies that the accumulation of this wealth was the result of careful husbandry: "There thou shalt learn to be frugal, for players were never so thrifty as they are now about London."

But, however simply or frugally he lived, his recog-

[1] See pp. 442–44.
[2] For an estimate of his annual income, see pp. 441–45.

nized position in letters would bring him the acquaintance of distinguished men, and his attractive personality would everywhere win him friends and admirers.[1] As early as 1592 Chettle had been impressed by his gracious demeanor, as had "diverse of worship" with whom Chettle had talked. Ben Jonson bears witness not only to the brilliancy of his intellect, which needed no comment, but also to the essential refinement of his manners:

> Look, how the father's face
> Lives in his issue, even so the race
> Of Shakespeare's mind and *manners* brightly shines
> In his well-turnèd and true-filèd lines.

The old theatrical manager Beeston tells us that "he was a handsome, well-shapt man, very good company, and of a very ready and pleasant smooth wit." Rowe observes that "Besides the advantage of his wit, he was in himself a good-natured man, of great sweetness in his manners, and a most agreeable companion." Affability was indeed a striking characteristic of his nature. John Davies of Hereford addresses him as "Good Will," Anthony Scoloker calls him "friendly Shakespeare," William Barkstead refers to him as "so dear lov'd a neighbor," his actors speak of him as "such a fellow as was our Shakespeare," and even the envious Jonson declares, "I did love the man this side idolatry as much as any."

Gifted with a charming personality, and famed as a poet, he must have been welcome to the society of those gallants of the law Inns and young noblemen of the Court who haunted the theatres and eagerly sought the acquaintance of actors and playwrights. Rowland Whyte, in a letter to Sir Robert Sidney, 1599, wrote: "My Lord Southampton and Lord Rutland came not to the Court.

[1] On Shakespeare's friendships with eminent men in London, see C. M. Gayley, *Shakespeare and the Founders of Liberty*, 1917.

The one doth but very seldom. They pass away the time merrily in going to plays every day." It was customary for these young gentlemen to entertain the players with expensive tavern suppers, at which wit flowed as freely as the wine. Dekker notes that it was the special ambition of young dandies who would like to be thought men of fashion to give banquets to the actors;[1] and Jonson, writing of courtiers, says: "Their glory is to invite players to suppers" — adding that the players were by no means bad company, for they have wit "both at drinking and breaking of jests."[2] No doubt Shakespeare often was a guest at tavern entertainments given by Southampton, or Rutland, or Pembroke, or Sir Walter Ralegh, or Sir John Salisbury. And that he enjoyed these occasions we may well believe, for we have abundant evidence that the creator of Falstaff was convivial in his disposition. Fuller states that "his genius generally was jocular, inclining him to festivity." The tradition of his bout with the Bidford tipplers, ending in a night under the crab-tree, though doubtless apocryphal, testifies to his reputation for conviviality; nor should one overlook the statement that his death was occasioned by his drinking too much with Drayton and Jonson.

Yet he must also have been frequently present at more serious gatherings where literature was the common interest that brought men together. The most famous of these gatherings were those associated with the Mermaid Tavern,[3] reputed by tradition to have been inaugurated by Sir Walter Ralegh. There, "the first Friday of every month, at the signe of the Mermaid in Bread Street,"[4] came together young noblemen, *littérateurs* from the Inns of Court, playwrights, eminent actors, and other

[1] *The Gul's Hornbook*, Dedication.   [2] *Poetaster*, III, i.
[3] Other taverns were also used, especially The Sun, The Dog, The Three Tuns, and The Mitre.
[4] So writes Thomas Coryat.

persons interested in the fine arts, to drink and smoke and to discuss plays and poetry. In these meetings the dominant figure (certainly at a later date) was Ben Jonson, who, with his vast learning in the classics and strong assertive personality, usually overshadowed the gentler and more retiring Shakespeare. Bishop Fuller, however, represents Shakespeare as able to attack the ponderous Jonson, and escape by the nimbleness of his wit:

Many were the wit-combats betwixt him and Ben Jonson, which two I behold like a Spanish great galleon and an English man-of-war; Master Jonson (like the former) was built far higher in learning, solid, but slow in his performances; Shakespeare with the English man-of-war, lesser in bulk, but lighter in sailing, could turn with all tides, tack about, and take advantage of all winds by the quickness of his wit and invention.

Beaumont and Fletcher were also numbered among the guests of the Mermaid; and the former has left us a glowing description of the meetings there:

> What things have we seen
> Done at the Mermaid! heard words that have been
> So nimble, and so full of subtle flame,
> As if that every one, from whence they came,
> Had meant to put his whole wit in a jest,
> And had resolv'd to live a fool the rest
> Of his dull life.

Robert Herrick, who in his younger days was admitted to these gatherings, bears similar testimony to the brilliancy of the conversation:

> We such cluster had
> As made us nobly wild, not mad.

And Keats, in imagination, contemplated the pleasure the poets must have found in each other's company:

> Souls of poets dead and gone,
> What Elysium have ye known,
> Happy field or mossy cavern,
> Choicer than the Mermaid Tavern?

These diversions, we may suppose, were typical **of** Shakespeare's social life in London. Yet he must have reserved to himself many evenings for quiet reading and composition. The wide knowledge of books which incidentally he reveals in his plays is shown by H. R. D. Anders' monograph *Shakespeare's Books;* and the frequency with which he delivered new plays to his company evinces the "copious industry" of his Muse.

As his fame increased, and as his acquaintances multiplied in both literary and fashionable circles, it was natural for him to seek to lift himself in the social ranking of the day. In such a light we must view his efforts to secure a coat of arms. A dignity of this sort was the more necessary in his case because he belonged to the then despised tribe of actors. As has already been pointed out, the profession was new, and in its beginnings had been recruited from the lowest elements of society — from strolling tumblers, jugglers, minstrels, bear-leaders, rope-walkers, and such like itinerant entertainers. And the players, thus recruited from "vagabonds," were at first deemed little better than "rogues." Moreover, their plays were not only crude, but, in order to please the vulgar rabble of the inn-yards, often deliberately obscene; and their performances stirred up the wrath of those interested in the moral welfare of the nation. Thus from the very outset the professional actors acquired a bad reputation. In Elizabeth's reign they were still looked upon as belonging to one of the most disreputable of the professions. In the *II Return from Parnassus* (1601), certain impecunious students, when advised to write for the London actors, indignantly protest: "And must the basest trade yield us relief?" Shakespeare in his *Sonnets* seems to reveal his humiliation at being a player: "Thence comes it that my name receives a brand," he complains; and to his friend, who enjoyed a higher social rank, he says:

> I may not evermore acknowledge thee,
> Lest my bewailèd guilt should do thee shame;
> Nor thou with public kindness honor me,
> Unless thou take that honor from thy name.

Abundant evidence of this general scorn of players is to be found in a comedy by Ben Jonson, who had himself begun as a player, and was still a dramatist, though now writing for the children of Her Majesty's Chapel Royal. In his *Poetaster* (1601), he attacks his former friends, the public actors, and in particular the Lord Chamberlain's Men. One specimen of the abuse he heaps on their profession, put into the mouth of Captain Tucca, will be sufficient:

2 Pyr. 'Tis a player, sir.

Tucca. A player! Call him. Call the lousy slave hither. What, will he sail by and not once strike or vail to a man-of-war? ha! — Do you hear! you player, rogue, stalker, come back here! . . . You slave . . . you rascal. . . you two-penny tear-mouth. . . you stinkard. . . rogue. . . slave. . . gulch. . . you presumptuous varlet. . . vermin!

To this abuse, and more of the same sort, the representative of the Chamberlain's Company is forced meekly to submit.

The frequent use of the word "rogue" in this scene, as well as throughout the whole play, had a specially vicious significance that was not lost on the public. Jonson knew, possibly from experience, where the actors were most sensitive. In the statutes of the day players were classified under the legal heading "Rogues, Vagabonds, and Sturdy Beggars." Thus, in the Proclamation of Henry VIII, 1545, *For Punishment of Vagabonds, Ruffians and Idle Persons*, occurs the phrase: "All such ruffians, vagabonds, masterless men, common players, and evil-disposed persons." In 1572 Parliament issued *An Act for the Punishment of Rogues and Vagabonds*, where again players are put in the same disreputable category "Which said fencers, bearwards, common players in in terludes, minstrels, jugglers, peddlers, tinkers, and petty chapmen, shall wander abroad and have not license from two justices of the peace at the least . . . shall be taken, adjudged, and deemed Rogues, Vagabonds, and Sturdy Beggars." The better grade of players were able to escape the punishment designated for rogues (public whipping and branding) by placing themselves under the protection of some nobleman, but they were not able wholly to escape the odium given by the statutes of the realm to their profession. Even so late as 1598, in *An Act for Punishment of Rogues, Vagabonds, and Sturdy Beggars*, the old classification is maintained, although players patronized by a nobleman are exempted from arrest: "All fencers, bearwards, common players of interludes, and minstrels wandering abroad (other than players of interludes belonging to any baron of the realm, or any other honorable personage of greater degree, to be authorized to play under the hand and seal of such baron or personage) . . . shall be taken, adjudged, and deemed Rogues, Vagabonds, and Sturdy Beggars."

We can readily understand that the wealthy and dignified actors of London resented this classification of their profession, and that their enemies found peculiar delight in taunting them with it. Philip Stubbes, in his attack upon players, demands: "Are they not taken by the Laws of the Realm for rogues and vagabonds?" And Jonson, in his *Poetaster*, does not let slip the opportunity of more than once twitting them with it:

Go, thou art an honest shifter. I'll have the statute repealed for thee.

Methinks if nothing else yet this alone, the very reading of the public edicts, should fright thee from commerce with them.

Throughout the play Jonson constantly applies to the players the epithets "rogues" and "common players" to remind them of their legal status. Shakespeare, it is interesting to observe, did not allow Jonson's ill-mannered attack to pass without rebuke; in *Hamlet*, II, ii, he makes his retort, good-naturedly as we should expect, but firmly. Yet he could not help realizing that as a "common actor" he was looked down upon. Even his warm friend, John Davies of Hereford, in a poem addressed to Fortune, scornfully refers to "stage-players," though taking pains to exempt Shakespeare and Burbage:

> Yet some (W. S., R. B.) she [Fortune] guerdoned not to their deserts,
> But other some were but ill-action all,
> Who while they acted ill, ill stayed behind,
> By custom of their manners, in their mind.[1]

These lines bear an obvious relation to Shakespeare's Sonnet III:

> O! for my sake do you with Fortune chide,
> The guilty goddess of my harmful deeds,
> That did not better for my life provide
> Than public means, which public manners breeds.
> Thence comes it that my name receives a brand,
> And almost thence my nature is subdu'd
> To what it works in, like the dyer's hand.

Davies elsewhere writes:[2]

> Players, I love ye, and your quality,
> As ye are men that pass time not abus'd:
> And some (W. S., R. B.) I love for *painting, poesie*,[3]
> And say fell Fortune cannot be excus'd
> That hath for better *uses* you refus'd. . . .
> And though the stage doth stain pure gentle blood,
> Yet generous ye are in *mind* and *mood*.

In the same apologetic vein Davies addresses a poem —

> *To our English Terence, Mr. Will. Shake-speare.*

> Some say, good Will, which I in sport do sing,
> Had'st thou not played some kingly parts in sport,
> Thou hads't been a companion for a king.

---

[1] In *Humor's Heaven on Earth*, ed. by Grosart, p. 37. A marginal note to the word "some" reads "W. S. R. B." — clearly Shakespeare and Burbage.

[2] *Microcosmos*, 1603, p. 215.

[3] Burbage was famous as a painter as well as an actor; "poesie" refers to

In the face of this general contempt for their profession, the London actors made such efforts as they could to acquire better social standing. Unfortunately some, as was inevitable, sought to rise by a display of their wealth:

> England affords those glorious vagabonds,
> That carried erst their fardels on their backs,
> Coursers to ride on through the gazing streets,
> Sooping it in their glaring satin suits,
> And pages to attend their masterships.[1]

'Slid, other men have wives as fine as players, and as well dressed.[2]

Some with better taste, and more shrewdness, sought to escape from the category of "rogues" by the acquisition of a coat of arms and the right to affix "gentleman" to their names. This was comparatively easy for them to do, since the Heralds' Office was lax in the bestowal of the honor, and a little influence and a liberal use of money might reasonably be counted on to secure the coveted dignity.

Whether or not Shakespeare was the first of the players to make use of this device for improving his social status we do not know; but that it became a common practice with actors is shown in the case of the Chamberlain's Company itself. Augustine Phillips, Thomas Pope, Richard Cowley, John Heminges, and Richard Burbage, besides Shakespeare, all sooner or later secured the right to display arms. William Smith, Rouge Dragon Pursuivant, a soured critic of the College of Heralds, complains that " Phillips the player had graven in a gold ring the arms of Sir William Phillip, Lord Bardolph, with the said Lord Bardolph's coat quartered." [3] Lord Bardolph

Shakespeare. The general allusion, of course, is to Simonides' statement, more familiar in Horace's " *Ut pictura, poesis.*"

[1] *II Return from Parnassus*, V, i; ed. by Macray, p. 144.

[2] *Bartholomew Fair*, I, i.

[3] Cited from his manuscript attack on the College entitled "A brief Discourse of the causes of Discord amongst the officers of arms," page 9, verso. The manuscript is now in the library of Mr. W. A. White, of Brooklyn. The author wishes to express his gratitude to Mr. White for placing this manuscript, and many other treasures, freely at his disposal.

had won fame at the battle of Agincourt.[1] The same critic, Smith, further writes: "Pope the player would have no other arms but the arms of Sir Tho. Pope, Chancellor of the Augmentations." This Sir Thomas Pope was a distinguished courtier and Privy Councillor: after founding Trinity College at Oxford, he died without issue in 1559. Still another critic of the Heralds' Office, Ralphe Brooke, reveals the fact that Richard Cowley, the original actor of Verges in *Much Ado*, had secured from the College a coat of arms that was open to suspicion. Possibly Jonson had in mind this general desire on the part of the actors for heraldic honors when in his *Poetaster* (1601), with the Chamberlain's troupe specially in view, he wrote:

> They forget they are in the statute, the rascals. They are blazoned there! There they are tricked, they and their pedigrees![2] They need no other heralds, i-wis.

In the light of all these facts we see that it was natural enough for Shakespeare to seek a coat of arms. In the earlier half of 1596 he made his application to the College of Heralds. Since his father was still alive, he had to enter the application in his father's name;[3] but this was a mere technicality, and we may suppose that for all practical purposes the officers of the College regarded the application as coming from the distinguished poet.

In the draft prepared by the heralds, four separate reasons are advanced in support of the application.

---

[1] Since Phillips was a comedian we are tempted to wonder whether Shakespeare created for him the rôle of Bardolph in *Henry IV* as a laughing satire on his supposed ancestor. But we do not know when Phillips secured his coat of arms.

[2] Cf. *Histriomastix* (1599), II, 243, 272: "Proud statute rogues! ... Blush not the peasants at their pedigree?"

[3] This seems to have been required; at any rate it gave added dignity to the grant. Moreover if issued to his father it would restore to Mary Arden the right to the Arden arms, and allow Shakespeare to quarter his coat with hers.

The first is that John Shakespeare's "antecessors" had, "for valiant and faithful and ... service," been "rewarded by the most prudent prince, King Henry the Seventh." Scholars have been unable to discover any records verifying this statement, and it may have been a pleasant fiction on the part of the Heralds' Office. Harrison, writing about 1580, declares that a man who is not engaged in a trade "shall for money have a coat and arms bestowed upon him by heralds, who in the charter of the same do of custom pretend antiquity and many gay things." Whether the statement about the poet's "antecessors" was merely a gay thing pretended, or whether it was based on fact, we are unable to say. However, we should not entirely overlook the possibility that Shakespeare in his interview with the officer of the Heralds' College may have mentioned the circumstance that his ancestors on his mother's side had been honored and rewarded by Henry VII. This was true of two of the brothers of his maternal great-grandfather: Sir John Arden had been made Esquire of the Body to Henry VII; Robert Arden had been appointed Yeoman of the Chamber, and had also received from Henry three patents.[1] Shakespeare may not have intended to mislead the herald by obscuring the fact that these ancestors were on his mother's side; or the herald, with his easy conscience, may have deliberately ignored the fact, especially since the coat of arms was in reality to be granted to Shakespeare himself, though technically to his father. Still another possibility is that the "antecessors" referred to in the draft may have been on John Shakespeare's maternal side; but, since we do not know even the name of his mother, we cannot investigate this interesting possibility.

The second reason advanced in favor of the application was that John Shakespeare had married "the daughter,

[1] For details see C. C. Stopes, *Shakespeare's Family*, pp. 26 ff.

and one of the heirs, of Robert Arden, of Wilmecote," who is described as "a gentleman of worship." The accuracy of the statement is obvious, and need not here be further discussed.

The third reason was that, twenty years before, John Shakespeare had applied for a coat of arms by virtue of the fact that he was then "a Justice of Peace, and was Bailiff, officer, and chief of the town of Stratford upon Avon," and that Robert Cook, then Clarenceux King, had actually submitted a "pattern" or sketch of a proposed coat. It is not asserted that the matter went further than the submission of the tentative sketch, although it is distinctly said that John still had this sketch in his possession. That Shakespeare's father held the offices named, and was on that score entitled to a coat of arms, cannot be questioned; and the possibility of his actually having made application to Clarenceux Cook for the dignity has already been considered. There seems to be no substantial reason for doubting the truth of the herald's assertion.

The fourth reason advanced in behalf of the petition is that John Shakespeare "hath lands and tenements, of good wealth and substance £500." John Shakespeare certainly had land and tenements in Stratford, but the estimate of his substance at £500 is an obvious exaggeration. Such exaggerations, however, were conventional with the officers of the College, and we need not suppose that Shakespeare himself was responsible for the statement. What the heralds meant to imply was that the person to whom the grant was made was able to support the dignity. It may be that Shakespeare himself was worth £500, or at least that the heralds thought so; and since they were really making the grant to him, they added this necessary assurance of his pecuniary standing.

Two drafts of the grant have been preserved, each

accompanied by a rough sketch of the coat of arms, and a verbal description: the shield "in a field of gold, upon a bend sable, a spear of the first, the point upward, headed argent"; the crest, "a falcon, with his wings displayed, standing on a wreath of his colors, supporting a spear, armed, headed, and steeled silver"; the motto, "*Non sans droict.*" The use of a falcon in the crest, according to the eminent authority, George Russel French, deserves special notice, "the falcon being one of the badges of Edward the Fourth, father of Henry the Seventh's Consort; no person, therefore, would venture to adopt such a cognizance except by special favour." It may be added that Anne Boleyn had used the falcon, and Queen Elizabeth later had adopted it as her device. The motto, *Non sans droict*, would seem to declare that Shakespeare was entitled to the dignity of arms by clear right.

Neither of the two extant drafts is fully executed; yet there is reason to believe that the grant to Shakespeare was actually made at this time.[1] Three years later, in 1599, he made application, again using his father's name, for the right to quarter his coat of arms with that of his mother, Mary Arden, which by virtue of the previous grant had been restored to her.[2] The College of Heralds, after stating that the applicant had duly "produced" his coat of arms, acknowledged the justice of his present request, and gave him formal permission to quarter his arms "with the ancient arms of the said Arden of Wilmecote." In the margin the clerk roughly sketched the arms of Shakespeare impaled with the arms of the Ardens of Park Hall. But the Ardens of Wilmecote, being descended from a younger branch of the family, had no right to that coat of arms. Either the officers of the

---

[1] See S. A. Tannenbaum, *Was Shakespeare a Gentleman?* 1909.

[2] She had forfeited her right to bear arms through her marriage to "one who was no gentleman."

College discovered the mistake, or Shakespeare himself called their attention to it, and in place of the arms of the Ardens of Park Hall, crossed out, were correctly substituted the arms of the younger branch of the family.[1]

After receiving his coat of arms, Shakespeare, as if properly to support his new dignity, purchased a handsome estate in Stratford. On May 4, 1597, he secured possession of New Place, the largest and possibly the finest mansion in the town; indeed only one other dwelling in Stratford could pretend to vie with it in magnificence, namely the College House, once the seat of the clergy connected with the parish church, and recently, in 1596, acquired as a home by one of the wealthiest and most aristocratic gentlemen of the county, Thomas Combe. New Place had been erected in the latter half of the fifteenth century by Sir Hugh Clopton as his own residence. He refers to it in 1496 as his "great house," and it was regularly called in Stratford, even down to 1767, by the suggestive title "The Great House." Leland, author of the *Itinerary*, writing in 1540, states that it was built of "brick and timber" (i.e., with beams showing for ornamental effects), and that it was "a pretty house." It stood in the heart of the town just opposite the fine old Guild Chapel. Its spacious grounds, almost an acre in extent, included two barns and two gardens. That it was rightly called by the citizens "The Great House" is shown by the fact that it had a frontage of more than sixty feet, while its breadth in some parts was at least seventy feet, and one of its gables was over twenty-eight feet in height. Moreover, it had no fewer than ten fireplaces, and that at a time when fireplaces were a taxed luxury provided for relatively few

[1] For an illuminating discussion of the problems involved, see C. C. Stopes, *Shakespeare's Environment* and *Shakespeare's Family*.

rooms in a mansion.[1] In still another way its size and importance as a dwelling are revealed. When in July, 1643, Queen Henrietta Maria, on her triumphant march to Kineton, accompanied by two thousand foot, a thousand horse, a hundred waggons, and a train of artillery, was joined at Stratford by Prince Rupert at the head of a second body of troops, she held her Court for three days in New Place.

The Reverend Joseph Greene has recorded a description of the house by an aged resident of Stratford named Richard Grimmitt: "This Richard said he in his youth . . . had been often . . . in the Great House, near the Chapel in Stratford, call'd New Place; that, to the best of his remembrance, there was a brick wall next the street, with a kind of porch [i.e., a gatehouse] at that end of it next the Chapel, when they cross'd a small kind of green court before they enter'd the house, which was bearing to the left, and fronted with brick, with plain windows consisting of common panes of glass, set in lead, as at this time." [2]

It has been suggested that Shakespeare's ability to return to his native town, which he had left a few years before in poverty, and purchase one of its handsomest mansions was due to the bounty of the young Earl of Southampton. Rowe, in his life of the poet, 1709, writes: "There is one instance so singular in the magnificence of this patron of Shakespeare's that, if I had not been assured that the story was handed down by Sir William Davenant, who was probably very well acquainted with his affairs,[3] I should not have ventured to have inserted; that my Lord Southampton at one time gave him a

[1] See Halliwell-Phillipps, *Outlines*, ii, 110.

[2] Halliwell-Phillipps, *Outlines*, i, 132.

[3] Davenant was named for Shakespeare, and the poet probably was his godfather. In his youth Davenant lived as a page in the household of Fulke Greville, Lord Brooke, seven miles from Stratford.

thousand pounds to enable him to go through with a purchase which he heard he had a mind to." [1] And according to a resident of Stratford, writing in 1759, "the unanimous tradition of this neighbourhood is that by the uncommon bounty of the Earl of Southampton he was enabled to purchase houses and land in Stratford." This so-called "tradition," however, may be merely an echo of the statement in Rowe's widely-read life of the poet. The notion that Southampton made Shakespeare a generous gift of money in return for the dedication of *Venus and Adonis* and *Lucrece* is well within the bounds of probability. It was customary for a person accepting the dedication of a book to give the author a pecuniary reward,[2] and Shakespeare himself speaks of "the warrant" he had received of the Earl's "honourable disposition." But that the sum amounted to £1000 can hardly be believed. Nor is it necessary to suppose that at this date Shakespeare had to look to his patron for money with which to effect the purchase of a home. The profession of acting was very lucrative, and Shakespeare was a full-sharer in the most successful troupe in London. He would have little difficulty in carrying out unaided a transaction involving only £60.

The small sum he paid for New Place suggests that at the time of the purchase it was in a state of decay. Nor is supporting evidence of this entirely lacking. At some date after 1549 [3] the statement is made that the mansion was "in great ruin and decay, and unrepaired, and it doth still remain unrepaired." In 1597 it may have been in an even worse condition.[4] Theobald was informed by

[1] Oldys also records the tradition; see British Museum Addit. MS. 12523, p. 127.

[2] The minimum reward expected by an author was £2, but this amount was often exceeded by generous patrons.

[3] When Dr. Thomas Bentley, President of the College of Physicians, died, who had occupied New Place on a long lease.

[4] The owner, Clopton, was in pecuniary embarrassment so serious that he

Sir John Clopton, a descendant of the original builder of the house, that Shakespeare "repaired it to his own mind." Possibly the load of stone which the Corporation of Stratford purchased from the dramatist in 1598 to mend the old Clopton Bridge [1] was left over from the work done on New Place.

Henceforth this beautiful mansion served as his country residence.[2] Some scholars have inferred that Shakespeare and his family did not occupy the house until 1611, basing the inference on the fact that in 1609 Thomas Greene is mentioned as residing there. This Thomas Greene was Shakespeare's cousin, who moved from London to Stratford in 1601. He may well have had lodgings for a time at New Place, for the building was too large for Mrs. Shakespeare and her two young daughters, and Shakespeare's absence in London for the better part of each year made the residence of his Cousin Greene at New Place desirable as a protection for the family. Moreover, in a return dated February 4, 1597–98, Shakespeare is actually described as a householder in Chapel Street, and is declared to have then had at New Place a large quantity of corn and malt.[3] How much time he could spend each year with his wife and children we do not know; but Aubrey records that "he was wont to go to his native country once a year," and doubtless he found occasion for numerous shorter visits. Certainly from

found it necessary to sell some of his estates; he was hardly in a position to repair New Place. He sold the house to William Bott in 1563, who was soon in trouble; Bott sold it in 1567 to William Underhill for £40.

[1] On January 24, 1598, Abraham Sturley writes to Richard Quiney: "Wm. Wiatt is mending the pavement of the bridge"; Halliwell-Phillipps, *Outlines*, ii, 57.

[2] The house was pulled down about the year 1700 by Sir John Clopton. No picture of it has come down to us. At present the old foundations are the only relics of the building.

[3] Halliwell-Phillipps, *Outlines*, ii, 58. It is worth noting also that before 1602 there were added to the place two orchards (*ibid.*, ii, 105), traditionally said to have been planted by Shakespeare.

this time on the poet regarded New Place as his home and henceforth he describes himself, and is commonly described, as "William Shakespeare, of Stratford-on Avon, gentleman." [1]

Nor was Shakespeare, now that he had become a country gentleman, satisfied with this one piece of property in his native county; at once he sought to regain possession of the valuable Arden estate of Asbies which should have come to him from his mother, and which was unjustly held by Lambert. In the autumn of 1597 he brought suit, in the name of his father and mother, to recover the property. Formal complaint was made in London to Sir Thomas Egerton, requesting a writ of subpœna ordering Lambert to appear in the Court of Chancery. Lambert engaged lawyers, and made reply; Shakespeare's lawyers made counter-replies; but nothing came of the effort, save delay. Twice in 1598, and again twice in 1599, steps were taken by the lawyers on both sides, and by the courts; but without result. In October, 1599, the court ordered that, "If the defendant shew no cause for stay of publication by this day sevennight, then publication is granted." Apparently, however, a further stay was allowed to Lambert. The case dragged along until Shakespeare in despair abandoned the suit, and included "the law's delay" in Hamlet's famous list of justifiable reasons for suicide.

But if he could not regain his lost inheritance of Asbies, he secured by purchase other properties in and about Stratford, until ultimately he became one of the important land-holders of the community. His desire to purchase land seems locally to have been well known. On January 24, 1598, Abraham Sturley, a well-to-do citizen

[1] As Halliwell-Phillipps observes (*Outlines*, i, 134), henceforth "in none of the indentures is he described as a Londoner, but always as 'William Shakespeare, of Stratford-on-Avon, in the county of Warwick, gentleman.'"

of Stratford, High Bailiff in 1596, wrote to his brother-in-law, Richard Quiney,[1] then in London:

Most loving and beloved in the Lord, — in plain English we remember you in the Lord, and ourselves unto you. I would write nothing unto you now but come home. I pray God send you comfortably home. This is one special remembrance from your father's motion. It seemeth by him that our countryman, Mr. Shakespeare, is willing to disburse some money upon some odd yard land or other at Shottery, or near about us. He [your father] thinketh it very fit pattern to move him to deal in the matter of our tithes. By the instructions you can give him thereof, and by the friends he can make therefore, we think it a fair mark for him to shoot at, and not unpossible to hit. It obtained would advance him indeed, and would do us much good. *Hoc movere, et quantum in te est permovere, ne necligas, hoc enim et sibi et nobis maximi erit momenti. Hic labor, hic opus, esset eximie et gloriæ et laudis sibi.*[2]

The letter shows that the people of Stratford were aware of Shakespeare's ambition to advance himself in the social scale; the purchase of the tithes would indeed confer upon him special dignities and privileges. They also were aware of the fact that he had acquired wealth, and were ready to seek from him pecuniary assistance. Nine months later, in the autumn of 1598, Quiney was again in London looking after the affairs of the Corporation of Stratford, particularly the securing from the Court of a new charter for the town, and a relief from the payment of the year's subsidy. In conducting these negotiations he was forced to stay longer in London than he had expected, and having accumulated debts in the city, he made this an excuse to borrow from Shakespeare the large sum of £30. The poet, with characteristic shrewd-

[1] Quiney was a prosperous draper of Stratford, prominent in civic affairs, being twice elected High Bailiff. His son later married Shakespeare's younger daughter Judith.

[2] The use of Latin by Sturley in writing to Quiney shows the effectiveness of the training in the Stratford grammar school. For this interesting letter in full see Halliwell-Phillipps, *Outlines*, ii, 57–58.

ness, did not make the loan himself, but negotiated a loan for Quiney from some money-lending friend on the offer of proper security. Quiney's letter to Shakespeare regarding the transaction is of special interest as the only extant letter addressed to the poet. The inscription on the back of the folded sheet reads:

> To my loving good friend and
> countryman, Mr. Wm. Shakespeare,
> deliver these.

The letter itself, neatly written in a small hand, runs as follows:

Loving countryman: I am bold of you, as of a friend, craving your help with xxx*li.*, upon Mr. Bushell's and my security, or Mr. Mytton's with me. Mr. Rosswell is not come to London as yet, and I have especial cause. You shall friend me much in helping me out of all the debts I owe in London, I thank God, and much quiet my mind, which would not be indebted. I am now towards the Court, in hope of answer for the dispatch of my business. You shall neither lose credit nor money by me, the Lord willing; and now but persuade yourself so, as I hope, and you shall not need to fear, but with all hearty thankfulness I will hold my time and content your friend;[1] and if we bargain further,[2] you shall be the paymaster yourself. My time bids me hasten to an end, and so I commit this to your care, and hope your help. I fear I shall not be back this night from the Court. Haste. The Lord be with you, and with us all, amen! From the Bell, in Carter Lane, the 25 October, 1598.

Yours in all kindness,
RYC. QUYNEY.

The letter, however, seems not to have been delivered; Quiney took it back with him to Stratford among his papers, and since he died there in the year of his office as

---

[1] I.e., the friend of Shakespeare who was to make the loan.

[2] Apparently Shakespeare was bargaining with Quiney about the purchase of "some odd yard land or other" near Stratford. If this purchase was consummated, Shakespeare himself could pay his friend and subtract the sum from the amount due to Quiney for the land.

High Bailiff, it was preserved in the corporation archives. The reason why the letter was not delivered can readily be guessed. On that same day, October 25, Quiney got into direct communication with Shakespeare — either he thought it wiser to see him in person about so important a matter, and wrote the letter to leave in case he found the dramatist not at home,[1] or Shakespeare paid a visit to Quiney at his inn. By whatever means they met, Shakespeare good-naturedly agreed to secure the money for Quiney, for before the day was over Quiney had written the news to his brother-in-law. On November 4 Sturley wrote back to Quiney:

> Your letter of the 25 of October came to my hands the last of the same at night per Greenway,[2] which imported . . . that our countryman, Mr. Wm. Shak[espeare], would procure us money; which I will like of as I shall hear when and where and how; and I pray let not go that occasion if it may sort to any indifferent conditions.[3]

Quiney's father, Adrian Quiney, writes to him about this time:

> If you bargain with Wm. Sha., or receive money therefor, bring your money home that you may; and see how knit stockings be sold; there is great buying of them at Aysshome. Edward Wheat and Harry your brother's man were both at Evyshome this day sennight, and as I heard bestowed 20*li.* there in knit hose; wherefore I think you may do good, if you can have money.[4]

The outcome of these proposed transactions is unknown to us; but the letters show the high respect the

[1] It will be observed that the letter has no address, as it probably would have had if sent by a messenger.

[2] Greenway was the Stratford carrier who delivered letters from London.

[3] Halliwell-Phillipps, *Outlines*, ii, 59. It is generally assumed that Sturley is referring to some loan that Shakespeare was to make to the Corporation of Stratford. But the evidence, I think, shows that Shakespeare was making a personal loan to Quiney and Sturley so as to enable them to carry out some private speculation.

[4] Halliwell-Phillipps, *Outlines*, ii, 59.

citizens of Stratford had for the pecuniary standing of Shakespeare, and the confidence they felt in the willingness of their "loving countryman" to help them in their need.

But from those persons who had no occasion to experience his kindness, his rise to social dignity through his coat of arms and his purchase of lands did not escape caustic comment. The following quotations may have been intended to refer to actors in general, yet at this early date, so far as we know, they fitted Shakespeare more aptly than any other.

Ben Jonson, in his savage attack on the Lord Chamberlain's Men in *Poetaster* (1601), says to Histrio: "What, you are proud, you rascal, are you proud? ha? You grow rich, do you? and purchase?" And here we may again quote his bitter reference to actors seeking heraldic honors: "They forget they are in the statute, the rascals. They are blazoned there! There they are tricked, they and their pedigrees! They need no other heralds, i'wis." It is not to be wondered at that in return for this attack Shakespeare gave Jonson "a purge that made him beray his credit." [1] The anonymous author of *The Return from Parnassus* (1601) says of London actors:

> With mouthing words that better wits have framed,
> They purchase lands, and now "Esquires" are named.

Henry Crosse, in *Virtue's Commonwealth* (1603), writes: "And as these copper-lace gentlemen grow rich, they purchase lands." And the ghost of the famous highwayman Gamaliel Ratsey, according to the pamphlet entitled *Ratsie's Ghost* (1605), advises a poor strolling actor to hurry to London: "And when thou feelest thy purse well lined, buy thee some place of lordship in the country,

---

[1] So we are informed in *II Return from Parnassus* (1601), ed. by W. C. Macray, p. 138.

that growing weary of playing, thy money may there bring thee to dignity and reputation." [1]

Even if these remarks were not aimed directly at Shakespeare, they included him in their purview, for at this early date he was perhaps the most conspicuous example of a player who had come to London in poverty, had grown rich, had tricked himself out with heraldic honors, and had purchased lands in the country. He must have felt the edge of all this satire; yet, when troubled by his "disgrace with Fortune and men's eyes," he could find ample consolation in his friends, and in his esteem with those whose good opinion, he knew, was most to be desired.

[1] Some of these passages have been thought to refer to Edward Alleyn, who purchased a splendid estate at Dulwich for about £10,000. But Alleyn made his initial purchase there on October 25, 1605. Shakespeare's fellow actor, Augustine Phillips, bought an estate at Mortlake in Surrey in 1604–05. Richard Burbage also "purchased," for at his death in 1619 he was said to be worth £300 in land. Although the dates of these purchases are later than Shakespeare's, they show the general tendency among actors to acquire estates.

CHAPTER XIV

THE ERECTION OF NEW PLAYHOUSES; THE GLOBE

SINCE Shakespeare's life was now centred in the London playhouses, and since both his personal and his literary career were bound up with the fortunes of his troupe, we must turn next to certain events in the theatrical world deeply affecting the Chamberlain's Men: the construction of the Blackfriars Playhouse, later occupied by them; the building of the Swan Playhouse to compete with them; and, finally, the erection of the Globe to serve henceforth as their permanent home.[1]

It will be recalled that James Burbage instead of purchasing the land on which he built the Theatre in 1576 merely leased it for a term of twenty-one years. Unless renewed, the lease would expire in April, 1597, he would lose his profitable investment, and the Chamberlain's Men would be driven from their playhouse. For ten years he had been pleading with the owner of the land, Gyles Alleyn, for an extension of the demise, but without success; and when at last his tenure was entering upon its last year, he realized that he must at once do something to safeguard his interests and the interests of the Chamberlain's Company. He resolved, therefore, to build a theatre elsewhere, and to have it ready for the actors on or before the expiration of the lease.

But his fertile mind, which had already created the existing type of playhouse — a circular tower-like structure, with the centre open to the sky — now conceived of a new type of theatre, better adapted to the comfort

[1] For a complete and fully-documented account of these events, see my *Shakespearean Playhouses*, 1917.

of actors and audience alike. Experience had revealed to him at least three objections to the playhouses then in existence. First, they were at too great a distance from the centre of London's population. Difficult of access under the best of circumstances, they were at a serious disadvantage in bad weather, when audiences sometimes shrank to a mere handful. This is why the troupes persistently tried during the winter months to secure the use of an inn-yard, which, though smaller and more poorly equipped, was at least accessible to the public. But permission to act in the city was hard to get, for the Common Council took the position that, "if in winter . . . foulness of season do hinder the passage into the fields to plays, the remedy is ill conceived to bring them into London." [1] Secondly, all the playhouses were in localities associated with immorality, for now the suburb to the north of the city, as well as the Bankside, was recognized as the home of the London stews. This naturally reflected unfavorably upon the players, and upon the drama itself. In view of the constant attack on theatrical performances, business insight suggested the desirability of moving playhouses to more respectable communities. Thirdly, the buildings, being open to the air, were exposed to all the inconveniences of the weather. So long as the audience could not be protected from the rain and heat of summer, or the snow and cold of winter, there would necessarily be a diminution in the profits of both the actors and the proprietor.

With characteristic energy and originality, Burbage laid plans for a new theatre that would be free from these objections. His mind turned to the liberty of Blackfriars, "scituated in the bosome of the Cittie," within a short distance of St. Paul's Cathedral, the centre of London life. At the dissolution of the monasteries the

[1] The Malone Society's *Collections*, i, 172.

land belonging to the Blackfriars passed into the possession of the Crown, and hence, though in the city, was not subject to the ordinances of the Common Council; as Stevens observes in his *History of Ancient Abbies, Monasteries*, etc.: "All the inhabitants within it were subject to none but the King. . . . Neither the Mayor, nor the sheriffs, nor any other officers of the city of London had the least jurisdiction or authority therein." Thus Blackfriars being, on the one hand, in the very heart of London, and, on the other hand, wholly free from the annoying ordinances of the Mayor and Aldermen, was an ideal site for a playhouse.

Furthermore, the precinct was one of the most fashionable in the city. Here, in various buildings of the old monastery, resided many distinguished noblemen, including: Henry Brooke, Lord Cobham, Lord Warden of the Cinque Ports; Sir Thomas Cheney, Treasurer of the Queen's Household; George Carey, Lord Hunsdon, Chamberlain of the Queen's Household; Sir William More, Chamberlain of the Exchequer; and others. Obviously a playhouse in this aristocratic district would escape the odium that attached to the playhouses in the disreputable sections of Shoreditch and the Bankside.

But there were drawbacks. A playhouse here would prove a costly undertaking. When in 1576 Burbage erected the Theatre he was a poor man, and could not have stretched his lean purse so far; now that he was no longer a poor man he could, though not without running "far into debt," meet the greater expense demanded. A more serious difficulty lay in the fact that the land in Blackfriars was entirely covered with buildings (except for the small garden-plots attached to the residences of a few wealthy inhabitants), so that the erection of a new structure specially designed as a theatre was impracticable; it was necessary to make use of some building already in existence. Burbage visited the district, and inspected the available structures. Among these he found one that he thought would be suitable for his purpose, the ancient Frater, or dining-hall, of the monks. The hall was of great size, built of solid stone, with walls three feet thick, windows "wrought as a chirche," a flat roof covered with lead, and a ceiling lofty enough to admit of the construction of galleries.[1]

On February 6, 1596, he purchased this excellent building for £600, and quietly set about converting it into a theatre. By tearing out a partition he was able to secure an auditorium sixty-six feet in length by forty-six feet in breadth, including a stage at the southern end; and around the sides and back he was able to erect one or more galleries. He also provided facilities for heating the building with sea-coal fires; and he furnished illumination for the actors by means of chandeliers hung over the stage, and, possibly, by footlights. The German traveler, Gerschow, specially noted that at Blackfriars "alle bey Lichte agiret, welches ein gross Ansehen macht"; and the obvious advantage of artificial light for producing beautiful stage-effects must have contributed not a little to the charm of the plays there presented.[2] No money seems to have been spared in making the theatre sumptuous in all its appointments. The Frater alone, before any changes were instituted, cost £600, and the alterations and equipment must have called for an outlay of at least £300 more. In every respect the building was made the finest, as it was unquestionably the most fashionable, theatre known to Englishmen before the Restoration.

[1] For a detailed description of the Frater and its surroundings see the writer's illustrated article, "The Conventual Buildings of Blackfriars, London, and the Playhouses Constructed Therein," *Studies in Philology*, xiv, 64.

[2] See Pepys' *Diary* under the date March 19, 1665–66.

But trouble was in store for the unsuspecting Burbage. As soon as the aristocratic inhabitants of the district discovered that he was planning to operate a "public" theatre in their midst, they were outraged, and promptly took steps to prevent it. In particular they prepared and sent to the Privy Council late in 1596 a strongly-worded petition against the undertaking, pointing out that a "common playhouse" would be "a very great annoyance" to "all the noblemen and gentlemen thereabout inhabiting." Among the signatures to the petition were the names of the Lord Chamberlain, the patron of Shakespeare's troupe, and Richard Field, Shakespeare's printer friend. This need not surprise us, however, for Shakespeare and the Chamberlain's Company were not directly concerned with the enterprise. The erection of the theatre was a business speculation on the part of an individual, James Burbage, who alone had invested money in it. But it is more than likely that in preparing this "common playhouse" at such cost he expected the Chamberlain's Men, under the leadership of his son Richard, to occupy it after they were driven from the Theatre. Without such an expectation he would hardly have ventured on so costly a project, for the only other public troupe regularly acting in London, the rival Admiral's Company, was comfortably housed in Alleyn and Henslowe's Rose.

In response to the petition of the fashionable inhabitants of Blackfriars, the Privy Council issued an order by which they flatly "forebade the use of the said house for plays." This was a sad blow to Burbage, who had invested a small fortune in the building, and had even run "far into debt" in order to equip it as a playhouse. To the Chamberlain's Men, too, the order must have brought keen disappointment, for with the prospect of early expulsion from the Theatre, they could not look forward to establishing themselves in the splendid roofed-in Blackfriars, "scituated in the bosome" of the metropolis.

In the midst of his difficulties, possibly in a measure overcome by them, James Burbage died in February, 1597, just two months before Alleyn's twenty-one year lease expired, bequeathing his troubles to his sons. To his elder son, Cuthbert, he left the Theatre,[1] which was abandoned by the actors within a few months, and to his younger son, Richard, he left Blackfriars, which could not be used for plays at all.

The Chamberlain's Men, however, had other things to disturb them besides the impending loss of their playhouse and the dissipation of their hopes of being able to move into Blackfriars. Hitherto a virtual monopoly of acting in London had been enjoyed by themselves and the Lord Admiral's Men; but now this monopoly, it seemed, was to be challenged by a third great city company, with the largest playhouse in England, the best of noble patronage, and liberal pecuniary backing.

A London goldsmith, Francis Langley, having become aware of the profits being made at the playhouses, decided as a speculation to erect a theatre of his own. In the Manor of Paris Garden, situated on the Bankside to the west of the Rose, he selected a site near the river, and there set up "the largest and the most magnificent playhouse" in London, to which he gave the name "The Swan." Aside, however, from its greater size and its more splendid appearance, it differed in no essential respect from the three open-air theatres already in existence. A Dutch traveler, Johannes de Witt, who visited London in the summer of 1596, has left the following description of the city's playhouses:

There are four amphitheatres in London [the Theatre, Curtain, Rose, and Swan] of notable beauty, which from their di-

---

[1] Unless Cuthbert's purchase of it from Hide in 1589 was *bona fide*.

verse signs bear diverse names. In each of them a different play is daily exhibited to the populace. The two more magnificent of these are situate to the southward beyond the Thames, and from the signs suspended before them are called the Rose and the Swan. The two others are outside the city towards the north on the highway which issues through the Episcopal Gate, called in the vernacular Bishopsgate.[1] . . . Of all the theatres,[2] however, the largest and the most magnificent is that one of which the sign is a swan, called in the vernacular the Swan Theatre,[3] for it accommodates in its seats three thousand persons, and is built of a mass of flint stones (of which there is a prodigious supply in Britain),[4] and supported by wooden columns painted in such excellent imitation of marble that it will deceive even the most cunning. Since its form resembles that of a Roman work, I have made a sketch of it above.

Langley, the goldsmith, however, was not familiar with theatrical affairs, and after completing his splendid playhouse he seems to have had difficulty in finding a troupe of actors to occupy it in successful competition with the two famous companies at the smaller and less pretentious Rose and Theatre. Doubtless he derived very little profit in letting the Swan to occasional or inferior troupes, that would draw small audiences, or would spend the better part of each year in travel.

But at last, early in 1597, he secured the organization of a new city company under the leadership of the eminent Gabriel Spencer. In addition to Spencer, some of the best actors of London were induced to join the organization, including Robert Shaw, Richard Jones, William Bird, Thomas Downton, and Ben Jonson. Pos-

[1] *Viâ quâ itur per Episcopalem portam vulgariter* Biscopgate *nuncupa'am.*
[2] *Theatrorum.*
[3] " *Id cuius intersignium est cygnus (vulgo* te theatre off te cijn)." Mr. Wallace proposes to emend the last clause to read: "te theatre off te cijn off te Swan," thus making "cijn" mean "sign."
[4] De Witt was certainly wrong in stating that the Swan was built of flint stones. Possibly the plastered exterior deceived him; or possibly in his memory he confused this detail of the building with the exterior of the church of St. Mary Overies, which was indeed built of "a mass of flint stones."

sibly Jonson had already, like Shakespeare, shown ability in refurbishing old plays, and was counted upon to help in writing as well as in acting. The company thus formed secured the patronage of the Earl of Pembroke. Gabriel Spencer certainly, and possibly other members of the troupe, had been connected with the old Pembroke's Company, and probably were ambitious of reëstablishing that once-famous organization in the esteem of London playgoers.

The new Pembroke's Company entered into an agreement with Langley (each sharer becoming bound for the sum of £100) to play at the Swan for one year, beginning February 21, 1597. Langley thereupon "disbursed and laid out for making the said house ready, and providing of apparel fit and necessary for their playing, the sum of £300 and upwards."

Here was a troupe with a name once illustrious in the theatrical world, comprising some of the ablest actors in England, enjoying the patronage of no less a nobleman than the Earl of Pembroke, occupying the largest and handsomest playhouse in London, and managed by a person of wealth who was disposed to be liberal and even extravagant in supplying them with costumes and stage-equipment. The Chamberlain's and Admiral's companies could not but have been disturbed by the prospect of serious competition.

All went well with the Pembroke's Men until near the end of July, when they put on the boards a satirical play entitled *The Isle of Dogs*. The plot was conceived and partly written by Thomas Nashe, the "young Juvenal" of the age; but the satirical portions were heightened and added to by Ben Jonson and one or two other members of the troupe described as "inferior players." The title was taken from a foul, marshy island just below London called the Isle of Dogs. Apparently, for the play is not extant, on this little island Nashe created a kingdom of and by dogs, and under a thin disguise attacked the English government, or at least certain persons high in authority. The exact nature of the offense cannot now be determined, but Nashe himself informs us that "the troublesome stir which happened about it is a general rumor that hath filled all England." The Queen seems to have been highly incensed. On July 28 the Privy Council ordered the arrest of the authors of the play, and of the actors who had taken part in its performance. Nashe saved himself by precipitous flight, but his lodgings were searched, and his private papers turned over to the authorities. Gabriel Spencer and Robert Shaw, as leaders of the troupe, and Ben Jonson as one of the "inferior players" who had a share in writing the play, were thrown into prison. The rest of the company fled into the country, the speed with which they moved being indicated by the fact that we find them in Bristol a few days later, with the Privy Council vainly asking where they are.

A special commission was appointed by the Council to examine the players and mete out to them condign punishment. Among other things the commission was directed to discover "what copies they have given forth of the said play, and to whom," and to destroy all such copies. They did their work so well that no text of *The Isle of Dogs* has been preserved.[1] The Council further ordered that "no plays shall be used within London, or

[1] Possibly a copy was formerly preserved in a volume of miscellaneous manuscripts at Alnwick Castle, though we cannot be sure. If it ever was there it has since disappeared. On a blank page still remaining in the volume is written "By Thomas Nashe and inferior players." This page is further interesting because some contemporary has idly scribbled over it the name of Shakespeare, with a quotation from *Lucrece*, and the title of two of his plays, *Richard II* and *Richard III*. Apparently no significance is to be attached to these scrawls; they merely indicate the general fame of Shakespeare as a writer.

about the city, or in any public place, during this time of summer." This was a serious blow to the Chamberlain's Men, who were compelled to leave the city during the most profitable months of the year when Falstaff was crowding their house with large audiences, and to go on a tour of the country. But the Privy Council did not stop with this. It ordered that all playhouses in and about London should "be plucked down" to the ground. Fortunately this drastic order, possibly an expression of the Queen's hot temper, was not carried into effect. We may easily guess why. Both the Lord Chamberlain and the Lord Admiral were prominent members of the Privy Council. Ever alert to protect the interests of their "servants," they knew that the players could not maintain an existence without playhouses; and they knew, too, that the Queen herself would not welcome the destruction of the great city troupes which alone were able to supply her with the entertainments she was passionately fond of. So, in all probability, secret instructions were issued to the sheriffs not to carry into effect that part of the order which called for the demolition of the playhouses.

These were uncomfortable times for the actors. But the Queen's anger gradually cooled, and ultimately punishment was limited to the actual offenders. The Pembroke's Company was permanently dissolved by the Council, and the Swan playhouse was closed for dramatic performances throughout the life of the Queen.

More important still, the Privy Council ordered that henceforth license to act in the city should be granted to two companies only, and that these companies should be the Lord Chamberlain's Men, and the Lord Admiral's Men. Upon the passing of this ordinance the chief actors of the Pembroke's Company, including Gabriel Spencer, Robert Shaw, and Ben Jonson, joined the Admiral's Men at the Rose. The other members of the Pembroke's Company, finding themselves without employment, resolved to defy the order of the Privy Council, and began to act again in the city. But the news of this coming to the Privy Council, on February 19, 1598, the Council dispatched a peremptory order to the Master of the Revels, who had general supervision of the drama, and also to the Justices of both Middlesex and Surrey, "to require you, upon receipt hereof, to take order that the aforesaid third company may be suppressed, and none suffered hereafter to play but those two formerly named, belonging to us, the Lord Admiral and Lord Chamberlain." Thus, through the erection of the Swan and the episode of *The Isle of Dogs*, the two older companies became more strongly than ever intrenched in their monopoly of acting in the city.

In obedience to the order of the Privy Council forbidding plays in or near London during the summer of 1597, the Chamberlain's Men had gone upon a tour of the provinces; but on November 1, when the inhibition was raised, they returned to the city. Cuthbert Burbage's lease of the land on which the Theatre stood had now expired, and he was having serious trouble with Gyles Alleyn, who for puritanical reasons did not wish the building to be longer used for plays. The Chamberlain's Men, therefore, moved into the adjacent Curtain, while the owner of the Theatre carried on further negotiations with Alleyn in the hope of inducing him to renew the lease on something like reasonable terms. But the Curtain was smaller than the Theatre, probably had not been altered to meet the demands of more modern acting, and in general was ill-suited to the needs of the great Chamberlain's Company. The inadequacy of its accommodations seems to be glanced at in the Prologue to *Henry V:*

> But pardon, gentles all,
> The flat unraised spirits that hath dar'd
> On this unworthy scaffold to bring forth
> So great an object. Can this cockpit hold
> The vasty fields of France? or may we cram
> Within this wooden O the very casques
> That did affright the air at Agincourt?

The Merry Wives, *Henry V*, and *Julius Cæsar* were first presented at this playhouse during 1598–99; and Romeo, as well as Falstaff, we are told, won "Curtain plaudities." Still another notable event marking the company's temporary stay there was the production, in September, 1598, of *Every Man in his Humor*. In connection with this play Shakespeare, according to tradition, was able to show to its author, Ben Jonson, a small bit of kindness which the latter never forgot.

Jonson, if we may believe his own statement, was of gentle birth: "His grandfather . . . served King Henry VIII, and was a gentleman. His father lost all his estates under Queen Mary, having been cast in prison and forfeited; at last turned minister. He himself was posthumous born a month after his father's decease."[1] The widow subsequently married a bricklayer in London, and young Ben learned to handle the trowel and lay chimneys. But he had also received an excellent general education and a thorough grounding in the classics under the tuition of William Camden at Westminster School. Later, as did Shakespeare, he threw in his lot with the drama, and became both actor and playwright, thereby endeavoring to improve his pecuniary condition and win a place in the world of letters. Always conscious of his gentle birth, he was unduly sensitive about being called the son of a bricklayer, with the result that his enemies never ceased to twit him with lime-and-mortar jests.

As already stated, he was a member of the unfortunate

[1] William Drummond's *Conversations with Ben Jonson.*

Pembroke's Company, and had a finger in the composition of *The Isle of Dogs*. After the suppression of that company several of its leading actors joined the Admiral's Men under Henslowe at the Rose. The great Gabriel Spencer appears to have taken for the time being the place of Edward Alleyn as their chief performer. And along with Spencer came Ben Jonson. Though an "inferior player" (he was never good as an actor), he rapidly developed as a playwright, and was engaged in composing several plays, mainly in collaboration with other and more experienced dramatists working for Henslowe. In December, 1597, he submitted to Henslowe the plot of an original play, and on the promise of completing it at an early date, secured an advance payment of £1. Before delivering the finished manuscript, however, he seems to have quarreled with the Admiral's Men, and left them.[1] Accordingly, he took the manuscript of his next play, *Every Man in his Humor*, to the rival Chamberlain's Company at the Curtain. The play was of a new type, now famous as the comedy of humors, and the manager of the Chamberlain's Men, so tradition states, declined to accept it. Shakespeare then intervened in behalf of his fellow-dramatist, looked over the manuscript, and persuaded the players to try it; and shortly it was put on the boards with Shakespeare himself in one of the leading rôles. The tradition is thus narrated by Rowe:

His acquaintance with Ben Jonson began with a remarkable piece of humanity and good nature; — Mr. Jonson, who was at that time altogether unknown to the world,[2] had offer'd one of

---

[1] This may explain Henslowe's subsequent entry in his *Diary:* "unto Mr. Chapman on his play book, and two acts of a tragedy of Benjamin's plot, the sum of £3."

[2] It is true that at this time Jonson's reputation as an author was not great, his previous work having been in collaboration, but he was not "wholly unknown" as a playwright

his plays to the players in order to have it acted; and the persons into whose hands it was put, after having turn'd it carelessly and superciliously over, were just upon returning it to him with an ill-natur'd answer that it would be of no service to their company, when Shakespeare luckily cast his eye upon it, and found something so well in it as to engage him first to read it through, and afterwards to recommend Mr. Jonson and his writings to the publick. After this they were profess'd friends.

We need not accept all the details with which Rowe has garnished the story, yet the tradition that Shakespeare's intervention led to the presentation of *Every Man in his Humor* by the Chamberlain's Company seems to be supported by other evidence. For example, when Jonson published the play he associated Shakespeare's name with its performance in an apparently significant way. He placed on a special leaf the following statement:

This Comoedie was first

Acted in the yeere

1598

By the then L. Chamberlayne

his Servants

The principall Comoedians were

Will. Shakespeare	Ric. Burbage
Aug. Philips	Joh. Hemings
Hen. Condell	Tho. Pope
Will. Slye	Chr. Beeston
Will. Kempe	Joh. Duke

It has been thought that by placing the name of Shakespeare at the head of the first column, with the name of the great actor Burbage relegated to the head of the second column, Jonson meant to indicate his special debt to Shakespeare for the appearance of the play on the stage.

If in truth Shakespeare was responsible for the production of *Every Man in his Humor*, its author had special reason to be grateful to him, for the comedy proved to be one of the great successes of the day, instantly making Jonson, then in his twenty-seventh year, famous, and launching him upon a notable career as a dramatist.

Possibly Shakespeare's kindness to Jonson went beyond merely rescuing *Every Man in his Humor* from oblivion. Shortly after that play had attained its phenomenal success on the stage (it is described as "new" on September 20, 1598 [1]), a quarrel arose between its author and Gabriel Spencer. We do not know the cause, but it may have concerned Jonson's desertion of the Admiral's Company, his sale of *Every Man* to the Chamberlain's Company, and his failure to complete the manuscript of the play for which Henslowe had made him an advance payment of £1. And we may suspect that in the heat of the argument that followed, Spencer very unwisely called Jonson a bricklayer. Jonson, an expert swordsman, promptly challenged him to a duel. The challenge was accepted, and on September 22, 1598, these two eminent members of the theatrical profession met by appointment in the Fields near the Theatre. Spencer came with a weapon ten inches longer than had been agreed on, but Jonson was in no mood to quibble over such a trifle. At the outset Jonson was wounded in the arm; but ultimately he succeeded in killing his opponent, "giving then and there to the same Gabriel Spencer with the aforesaid sword a mortal wound of the depth of six inches and of the breadth of one inch, in and upon the right side of the same Gabriel, of which mortal blow the same Gabriel Spencer . . . then and there died instantly." On September 26 Henslowe wrote to Edward Alleyn, then in Sussex: "I will tell you some [news], but

---

[1] On this date Tobie Mathew wrote to Dudley Carleton: "There were with him divers Almains, whereof one lost out of his purse at a play 300 crowns a new play called *Every Man's Humor*." (*State Papers, Domestic Series*. cclxiii, 67.)

it is for me hard and heavy. Since you were here with me I have lost one of my company which hurteth me greatly, that is Gabriel, for he is slain in Hogsdon Fields by the hands of Benjamin Jonson, bricklayer; [1] therefore I would fain have a little of your council if I could." [2]

Jonson was promptly arrested and thrown into prison. Unluckily for him the Queen at this time was making a special effort to suppress dueling. A true bill of manslaughter was returned against him, he was put on trial, pleaded guilty, and thus stood condemned to be hanged. Jonson, however, claimed the right of clergy, scanned his "neck verse" to the satisfaction of the court — for he was one of the best Latin scholars in England — and so managed to escape the gallows. [3] But his property was confiscated to the Crown, and he was branded on the thumb with the felon's mark, a large capital T standing for Tyburn prison. As the record of the court summarized his case: "He confesses the indictment, asks for the book, reads like a clerk, is marked with the letter T, and is delivered according to the statute."

For the newly famous playwright these were dark hours; and it may be that in connection with his imprisonment and trial Shakespeare further befriended him. When in 1601 Jonson (who was naturally given to quarrels) fell out with the Chamberlain's Men, and wrote in *Poetaster* his bitter attack upon them, Dekker, assisted by the actors, retorted in *Satiromastix*. Among the reproaches heaped on him was the following charge of ingratitude: "Thou . . . should'st have been hang'd, but for one of these part-takers, these charitable copper-

---

[1] In September, 1598, Jonson was well-known as a playwright. Henslowe's anger at him is reflected in this contemptuous reference to his early trade. Possibly it echoes, also, the cause of the duel between Spencer and Jonson.

[2] J. P. Collier, *Memoirs of Edward Alleyn*, p. 51.

[3] To escape execution through benefit of clergy one had to demonstrate his knowledge of Latin, usually by reading the first verse of the twenty-first Psalm, vulgarly called the "neck verse."

lac'd Christians, that fetched thee out of purgatory." Which "one" of the Chamberlain's players assisted Jonson in his trouble, and helped him out of prison, is not stated; but it may well have been his friend Shakespeare. We know that Jonson always maintained for Shakespeare the deepest affection: in his *Timber* he declared, "I lov'd the man, and do honor his memory on this side idolatry as much as any"; and in a poem prefixed to the First Folio he called him "my beloved."

Every Man in his Humor, acted in the autumn of 1598, was among the last new plays the Chamberlain's Men brought out at the Curtain, for within a few months they had moved to a house especially built for them on the Bankside as a solution of the difficulty the Burbages were having over the Theatre.

For nearly a year Cuthbert had been desperately prosecuting his negotiations with Alleyn. By the terms of the old lease he had a right to tear down the Theatre and move the timber, benches, and stage-equipment to another place, provided he did so before the expiration of the twenty-one years; if, however, he allowed the building to stand one day after the lease expired, it legally passed into the possession of Alleyn. Upon a verbal agreement with Alleyn, he had allowed the Theatre to stand after the lease expired, in order to carry on further negotiations, for Alleyn now professed himself ready to sign a renewal, although he would not make clear his terms. This was not without danger to Cuthbert, for if Alleyn should repudiate his verbal agreement and seize the building as his own, he could hold it by law. This was precisely what Alleyn was scheming to do; for when, at last, he stated his conditions he made them so preposterous that they could not possibly be accepted.

After Cuthbert declined to consider these terms, Alleyn, near the close of 1598, resolved to seize the building, claiming that now, since the owner had "suffered the same there to continue till the expiration of the said term . . . the right and interest of the said Theatre was, both in law and conscience, absolutely vested" in himself; and he proposed "to pull down the same, and to convert the wood and timber thereof to some better use." Luckily the Burbages "got intelligence" of this treachery, and luckily, too, Alleyn was called away into the country, not to return until after the Christmas holidays. This gave Cuthbert his opportunity to save the building. He consulted his brother Richard, and together they laid plans to outwit the crafty Alleyn, and at the same time provide the Chamberlain's Company with its much needed playhouse.

But a playhouse suitable to the uses of the Chamberlain's Company would have to be large and sumptuous, and the Burbages, already saddled with two theatres, and heavily in debt on account of Blackfriars, would need assistance. Moreover, they desired to make sure that the Chamberlain's Men would permanently occupy the building after it was completed. In order to accomplish these two ends, they devised a brand-new scheme of playhouse ownership: they proposed to form a stock company to finance the erection of the building, and to admit into this stock company the leading actors of the Chamberlain's troupe. Such a scheme would not only provide the necessary funds, but also tie the Chamberlain's Men to the building. Furthermore, it would allow the chief players to share in the profits from the ownership of a structure which their efforts alone made valuable. Hitherto theatres had been operated by shrewd business men who were not themselves actors, and who leased their buildings to the companies on hard terms, taking all, or at least a large share, of the income from the galleries. As a result they had long reaped an unduly rich harvest from the labors of the players. The new plan would remedy this state of affairs by making the actors themselves the proprietors of their theatre.

The opportunity of participating in the scheme was possibly, though we do not know, offered to each of the full-sharers in the Chamberlain's troupe; and those who were able to advance the necessary money, or were willing to risk investment in the enterprise, we may suppose, were admitted to the syndicate. However that may be, only five sharers actually joined the two Burbages in their undertaking — William Shakespeare, John Heminges, Augustine Phillips, Thomas Pope, and William Kempe. All the members of this syndicate, it will be observed, were members also of the Chamberlain's troupe, except Cuthbert Burbage, who had long been closely associated with the players, and now stood ready to supply the materials of the old Theatre towards the erection of the new structure; and the intention was to keep the ownership of the playhouse in the hands of the actors. To that end the builders legally bound themselves in such a way as to prevent any member from disposing of his share to an outsider.

It will be observed, too, that relatively few members of the Chamberlain's troupe were members of the syndicate. The syndicate, indeed, was strictly a business organization made up of men of substance, who were required to advance considerable capital, and to assume the necessary risks of a speculative venture. It was thus entirely distinct from the troupe. Its members, as owners of the building, stood in the relation of landlords to the players, and were known by the technical name of "housekeepers." The players, with their organization of sharers, hirelings, etc., were technically known as the "company." The "company" of course, had to pay the "housekeepers" a suitable remuneration for the use of the building. It was agreed that, in return for providing the building, the "housekeepers" should receive one half the income from the "galleries"; the "company," for supplying and acting the plays, was to receive the other half of this income, plus all the takings at the doors. Thus the two organizations, though entirely distinct, the one a business, the other a professional organization, were interlocking. Their interests were closely bound up together. And to perpetuate this common interest it was the intention from time to time to admit leading actors to be sharers in the building as soon as their attainments made their permanent connection with the playhouse desirable.

The scheme thus evolved had many advantages. In the first place, it prevented the troupe from shifting from one playhouse to another, often to the serious loss of the proprietors. In the second place, it guaranteed the sustained excellence of the company. Too often good troupes were weakened by the desertion of a few leading members who could be tempted to join rival organizations. In the third place, it tended, like all profit-sharing schemes, to elicit from each member his full energy; and, by offering the younger actors the hope of ultimate admission into the syndicate, it stimulated them to their best efforts. Finally, the plan brought the leading members together in bonds of close friendship that lasted throughout life. Heminges, who acted as business-manager, was universally loved and trusted, and he generously gave his fellows the benefit of his shrewd business judgment. The "gentle" Shakespeare was admired and revered by all. Indeed, a study of the numerous documents relating to the lives of these men is inspiring because of their loyalty and devotion to each other. The pious effort of Heminges and Condell, the last survivors, to publish the works of their "friend and fellow" Shakespeare is but one out of many expressions of this splendid comradeship.

According to the original organization of the "house-keepers" there were to be ten shares in the stock company.[1] The two Burbages, who were to supply most of the material, were to hold between them one half of the shares, and the rest were to hold the other half. The distribution of the shares, therefore, was as follows:

Cuthbert Burbage	2½
Richard Burbage	2½
William Shakespeare	1
John Heminges	1
Augustine Phillips	1
Thomas Pope	1
William Kempe	1

All the expenses of erecting and maintaining the building, and likewise all profits from its use as a playhouse, were to be divided among the sharers according to their several holdings.

The first question presenting itself to the members of the syndicate was, Where should the new playhouse be erected? Doubtless they gave the question much thought. The precinct of Blackfriars, though in every respect admirable, obviously was not to be considered; they were under the necessity of remaining in the suburbs. Their experiences in Shoreditch had not been happy, and they probably desired to get closer to the centre of London. So they turned their eyes to the Bankside, a section that had become the chief amusement-resort of the citizens. Here were situated the Rose and the Swan, and the great Bear Garden for the baiting of bears and bulls; and thither each day, by boat, or over the bridge, thousands of persons flocked in search of entertainment. The Swan, it was realized, had been

[1] For the subsequent history of the stock company, see the writer's article, "The Housekeepers of the Globe Playhouse," *Modern Philology*, May, 1919.

poorly placed; for it was so remote from London Bridge that audiences were forced to use boats in order to reach it, or to walk an unduly long distance if they made use of the bridge. This mistake had to be avoided. Close to the end of the bridge, and hard-by the fine old church of St. Mary Overies (now Southwark Cathedral), they found a plot of land that met their approval. From the owner, Sir Nicholas Brend, they secured a lease of the property for thirty-one years, beginning on December 25, 1598.

Three days later, on December 28, Gyles Alleyn being still absent in the country, Richard and Cuthbert Burbage, having engaged the services of a master-carpenter, Peter Street, with his twelve workmen, gathered at the Theatre, and began to tear down the building. We know that the widow of James Burbage "was there, and did see the doing thereof, and liked well of it," as was also a special friend of the Burbages, "William Smith, of Waltham Cross, in the County of Hartford, gentleman." We may suspect that among the interested and satisfied spectators was also William Shakespeare, together with the other venturers associated in the enterprise.

The episode is best described in the language of the angry Gyles Alleyn:

The said Cuthbert Burbage, having intelligence of your subject's purpose herein [to seize the building], and unlawfully combining and confederating himself with the said Richard Burbage and one Peter Street, William Smith, and diverse other persons to the number of twelve [workmen], to your subject unknown, did about the eight and twentieth day of December, in the one and fortieth year of your highness reign . . . riotously assemble themselves together, and then and there armed themselves with diverse and many unlawful and offensive weapons, as, namely, swords, daggers, bills, axes, and such like; and so armed did then repair unto the said Theatre, and then and there armed as aforesaid, in very riotous, outrageous.

and forcible manner, and contrary to the laws of your high ness realm, attempted to pull down the said Theatre. Where upon, diverse of your subject's servants and farmers, then going about in peaceable manner to procure them to desist from tha their unlawful enterprise, they, the said riotous persons afore said, notwithstanding procured then therein with great vio lence, not only then and there forcibly and riotously resisting your subject's servants and farmers, but also then and there pulling, breaking, and throwing down the said Theatre in very outrageous, violent, and riotous sort.

The workmen, under the expert direction of the master-carpenter, Peter Street, carried the timber and other stuff from the old Theatre to the tract of land that had just been leased from Sir Nicholas Brend — as Gyles Alleyn puts it, they "did then also, in most forcible and riotous manner, take and carry away from thence all the wood and timber thereof unto Bankside, in the Parish of St. Mary Overies, and there erected a new playhouse with the said timber and wood."

The playhouse thus erected was an entirely new building, towards the construction of which the timber from the old Theatre merely contributed; much new material, of course, had to be supplied. Nearly a quarter of a century had elapsed since James Burbage had designed the Theatre, the first structure of its kind, and much progress had been made both in effective stage craft and in dramatic art. Doubtless many improvements were possible, in the stage as well as in the auditorium, to provide better facilities for the actors, and greater comfort for the spectators. In designing such improvements, Peter Street had the advice and help of the players, including Shakespeare with his fertile imagination; we need not wonder, therefore, that he succeeded in producing a playhouse that was notable for its excellence, and that won for him a reputation as a builder of theatres. To the new playhouse the actors gave the name "The

Globe." Dekker punningly writes: "How wonderfully is the world altered! And no marvel, for it has lyen sick almost five thousand years: so that it is no more like the old *Theatre du munde*, than old Paris Garden is like the King's Garden at Paris. What an excellent workman, therefore, were he that could cast the *Globe* of it into a new mold." And Henslowe and Alleyn, in erecting their magnificent Fortune Playhouse, 1600, immediately sent for Peter Street, and frankly made use of the Globe as the model of their new theatre. The details of the contract they signed with the builder give ample testimony to the excellence of the planning that went into the design of the Globe:

With such-like stairs, conveyances, and divisions, without and within, as are made and contrived in and to the late-erected playhouse . . . called the Globe. . . . And the said stage to be in all other proportions contrived and fashioned like unto the stage of the said playhouse called the Globe. . . . And the said house, and other things before mentioned, to be made and done, to be in all other contrivations, conveyances, fashions, thing, and things, effected, finished, and done according to the manner and fashion of the said house called the Globe.

Apparently Henslowe and Alleyn, and the actors of the Admiral's Company, felt that the Globe could not be bettered.

The playhouse was situate in Maiden Lane, thus described by Strype in his edition of Stow's *Survey of London*: "Maiden Lane, a long straggling place, with ditches on each side, the passage to the houses being over little bridges, with little garden-plots before them, especially on the north side, which is best both for houses and inhabitants." In certain of these garden-plots,[1] and near one of the ditches, or "sewers" as they were called,

[1] See *The Site of the Globe Playhouse*, published by the London County Council, 1921.

the Globe was erected; and, like the other houses there situated, it was approached over a bridge. In February, 1606, the Sewer Commission ordered that "the owners of the playhouse called the Globe, in Maid Lane, shall before the 20 day of April next, pull up and take clean out of the sewer the props or posts which stand under their bridge on the north side of Maid Lane." The ground on which the building stood was marshy, and the foundations were made by driving piles deep into the soil. We can thus understand Jonson when he writes: "The Globe, the glory of the Bank ... Flanked with a ditch, and forced out of a marish."

In shape the building was polygonal, with three galleries surrounding an open "yard," as in the case of all public playhouses. The frame, we know, was of timber, the exterior of plaster, and the roof of thatch. In front of the main door was suspended, it is said, a sign of Hercules bearing the globe upon his shoulders, under which was the motto *Totus Mundus Agit Histrionem*.[1]

The earliest representation of the building is probably to be found in the Delaram view of London set in the background of an engraving of King James on horseback. This view, which presents the city as it was in 1603 when James came to the throne, shows the Bear Garden at the left, polygonal in shape, the Rose in the centre, circular in shape, and the Globe at the right, polygonal in shape. The building is again represented in Visscher's view of London, which, though printed in 1616, presents the city as it was several years earlier.

The cost of the finished Globe is not exactly known. Mr. Wallace observes that it was erected "at an original

---

[1] So Malone states. Oldys records an early anecdote on the subject: "Verses by Ben Jonson and Shakespeare, occasioned by the motto to the Globe Theatre, *totus mundus agit histrionem*." Shakespeare apparently makes a punning allusion to this sign in *Hamlet*, II, ii, 378; cf. also his "All the world's a stage," *As You Like It*, II, vii, 139.

cost, according to a later statement, of £600, but upon better evidence approximately £400." [1] I am not aware of the "better evidence" referred to, nor do I know whether the estimate of £400 includes the value of the timber and materials of the old Theatre furnished by the Burbages. If the Theatre cost nearly £700, and the second Globe £1400, the sum of £400 seems too small. We may safely assume that the cost of the Globe was not far from £600. Since William Kempe had withdrawn from the syndicate before a year had gone by, and the shares had been reduced from ten to eight, Shakespeare must have contributed to its erection approximately £75.

Nor do we know exactly when the Globe was opened to the public. On May 16, 1599, a post-mortem inquisition of the estate of Sir Thomas Brend, father of Sir Nicholas, was taken. Among his other properties in Southwark was listed the Globe playhouse, described as "*vna domo de nova edificata . . . in occupacione Willielmi Shakespeare et aliorum.*" Besides indicating the conspicuous part Shakespeare took in the erection of the playhouse, this statement suggests that the building was either completed or nearing completion on May 16. Unquestionably before the end of the summer of 1599 the Lord Chamberlain's Men had moved from the Curtain to their new home, "the glory of the Bank."

To celebrate this occasion the actors, we may suppose, used a new play, possibly Ben Jonson's *Every Man out of his Humor* (a sequel to his very successful *Every Man in his Humor*). In the Epilogue he speaks of "the happier spirits in this fair-fitted Globe," and in the Induction he makes allusion to the elaborately-carved pillars in the galleries: "A well-timbered fellow! He would have made a good column, an he had been thought on when the house was a-building."

[1] The London *Times*, October 2, 1909.

Henceforth this "fair-fitted" playhouse was the home of the Chamberlain's Men; and here, in a theatre of which he was one of the proprietors, Shakespeare's plays were to be introduced to applauding audiences. More than any other building it is associated with the greatest achievements of his career, and with the noblest triumphs of English dramatic art.

CHAPTER XV

JOYOUS COMEDIES; *HAMLET*

WITH the building of the Globe Shakespeare had almost reached the summit of his remarkable career. It may be worth our while to glance back in rapid survey over his achievements. Coming to London unknown and in poverty, he had earned recognition as one of England's greatest poets; he had made himself the most successful playwright of his age; he had acquired wealth, heraldic honors, and a splendid country home in Stratford; and by sheer force of genius he had placed his company in a position of undisputed supremacy in the dramatic world. And he was now just thirty-five years of age. It is not strange, therefore, that in the exhilaration of success he should produce some of his finest and most exuberant plays. He celebrated the first year of his company's stay at the Globe by composing a magnificent comic trilogy, the very titles of which reflect the buoyancy of good health and a consciousness of worldly success — *Much Ado About Nothing, As You Like It,* and *What You Will.*

The first of these comedies, *Much Ado,* was probably acted by the Chamberlain's Men shortly after they opened the Globe in the early summer of 1599. For the main theme Shakespeare used an Italian love-romance based on one of the novels of Bandello; but then, as now, the chief appeal the play had for the public lay in the comic scenes, English in color and spirit, which the dramatist spun from his own rich imagination. In particular, Benedick and Beatrice, with their superabundant joy in life, took the fancy of theatre-goers, and at once made the play a favorite. Leonard Digges wrote:

> Let but Beatrice
> And Benedick be seen, lo, in a trice,
> The cockpit, galleries, boxes, all are full.

We need not wonder that when the play was presented at Court in 1613, it was described in the Treasurer's accounts as *Benedicte and Betteris*.[1] Yet Dogberry, a study in colossal stupidity created especially for William Kempe, scored a success hardly less notable, and established the pompous constable with big words and little wit as a stock figure on the stage. Perhaps the best indication of the sustained popularity of Shakespeare's written-down "ass" is found in a comedy by Henry Glapthorne, 1639, entitled *Wit in a Constable*, which attempts to show that in one instance, at least, a constable was able to display some gleams of intelligence.

Much Ado About Nothing was quickly followed by *As You Like It*, probably acted at the Globe in the autumn of 1599. For the main theme, as in the case of its predecessor, Shakespeare made use of a foreign love-romance, taken almost without change from Lodge's pastoral story of *Rosalynde;* and to this he added from his own invention comic scenes and characters essentially English in spirit. Again we have an outburst of sheer joy in life, typified by such characters as Rosalind and Orlando; and again the good-natured laugh at human stupidity, provoked this time by Touchstone and Audrey. Furthermore, in "the melancholy Jaques" with his humorous philosophizing on life and his studied pose as a malcontent, we have a new type that in favor with theatre-goers shared honor even with Rosalind and Touchstone. Marston, realizing its effectiveness, at once

---

[1] The actors had probably christened the play with this title for the occasion.

developed the type in his play entitled *The Malcontent* (1600); and from now on the "cynical railer" enjoyed something like a vogue on the stage.[1]

In the performance of the play, according to an early tradition, Shakespeare himself assumed the rôle of the faithful servant Adam. An "old man"[2] in the days of the Restoration, "stricken in years" and his memory "weakened with infirmities," spoke of "having once seen him in one of his own comedies, wherein being to personate a decrepit old man, he wore a long beard, and appeared so weak and drooping and unable to walk that he was forced to be supported and carried by another person to a table, at which he was seated among some company, and one of them sung a song." If this rather doubtful tradition can be accepted, we have at least the satisfaction of knowing that the rôle was well-enough acted to make a lasting impression on the mind of the spectators. In still another way the play has a personal interest. Shakespeare inserted a deft allusion to his early friend and master, Christopher Marlowe, calling him with some display of affection "dead shepherd." This he accomplished by quoting a line from Marlowe's *Hero and Leander*, just issued from the press:

> Dead shepherd, now I find thy saw of might:
> "Who ever loved that loved not at first sight?"

It is significant that this is the only allusion Shakespeare made to a contemporary poet. That he should break his custom in this one instance may be taken as a possible indication of close relations with Marlowe in early days when as a young "upstart" from the country he was struggling to find a place in the theatrical world.

[1] See E. E. Stoll, "Shakespeare, Marston, and the Malcontent Type," *Modern Philology*, iii, 281.

[2] Said, but inaccurately, to have been one of the poet's brothers. This tradition is more fully discussed on pages 426–27.

The third member of the comic trilogy was probably composed late in the year, and brought out at the Globe in November or December, 1599, under the title *What You Will*. The substitution of another title can readily be explained. On January 6 the Chamberlain's Men were called upon to present a play at the annual Twelfth Night revel before the Queen and her guests, commonly the most notable of all the Christmas entertainments. In 1596, 1597, and 1598 Shakespeare's troupe had been complimented with the invitation to furnish the play, and now for a fourth time it was summoned to grace the festivities. The Twelfth Night revels of 1600 were unusually splendid; the Admiral's Men also were pressed into service, and the children of the Chapel were paid "for a show, with music and special songs prepared for the purpose." [1] Possibly it was in honor of this grand occasion that Shakespeare rechristened the comedy with the otherwise irrelevant title *Twelfth Night*.[2] His retention of the older title, *What You Will*, however, serves to reveal the essential kinship of the play with the two other members of the trilogy.

For the main theme, as in *Much Ado* and *As You Like It*, Shakespeare made use of a foreign love-romance, ultimately derived from Italian sources; and this he set off with purely English comic material drawn from his own fertile brain. Again, too, we have the combination of joy in life, and laughter at human stupidity; Olivia and Viola provide the one, Malvolio the other. The appeal that the cross-gartered gull had for the audience is shown by the fact that the play was sometimes acted under the title *Malvolio*, and by many contemporary allusions. For example, when in February, 1602, the Chamberlain's

---

[1] See Peter Cunningham, *Revels*, p. xxxiii.

[2] Samuel Pepys, writing on January 6, 1663, justly complains that the play is "not related at all to the name or day."

Company presented the comedy before the members of the Inner Temple, one of the students, John Manningham, wrote in his diary: "At our feast we had a play called *Twelfth Night, or What You Will.* . . . A good practise in it to make the steward believe his lady widow was in love with him, by counterfeiting a letter as from his lady, in general terms, telling him what she liked best in him, and prescribing his gesture in smiling, his apparel, etc., and then when he came to practise making him believe they took him to be mad." Manningham fails to mention the other characters at all; yet to modern spectators no less "a good practise in it" is Viola in her page's rôle, with her irrepressible girlhood shining through the disguise.

The success attained by the Chamberlain's Men with such excellent plays as *Much Ado*, *As You Like It*, and *What You Will*, must have told heavily on the fortunes of the rival Admiral's Company. Moreover, the new and splendid Globe within a few feet of the old and now obsolete Rose would attract the populace by its smarter appearance and more luxurious accommodations. The Admiral's Men naturally felt themselves at a serious disadvantage. So, before the lapse of a year, Henslowe and Alleyn decided to build for their company a playhouse that would surpass the Globe both in size and magnificence. At the same time they resolved to move away from the dangerous proximity of the Globe and the powerful Chamberlain's organization.

Where could they erect their new home? Obviously not in Blackfriars, nor yet in Shoreditch which the Chamberlain's Company had just abandoned. They decided on a new suburb outside of Cripplegate to the northwest of the city. Here, on December 22, 1599, they secured a suitable building lot, and then sent for Peter Street, the builder of the Globe. In drawing up the plans for their new structure they found they could not improve on the playhouse erected by the Chamberlain's Men; yet desiring originality of some kind, they determined on a building not polygonal as was the Globe, but square. This, as they later discovered, was a mistake, and when their building was destroyed by fire in 1621, they re-erected it in the conventional circular shape.

The contract which they signed with Street on January 8, 1600, still preserved among the papers of Henslowe, furnishes us with exact knowledge of many details of the structure. Since the building was a close copy of the Globe — differing chiefly in being square instead of polygonal — these details are of great value as affording some notion of the architectural economy of Shakespeare's more famous playhouse. From the document, too long for quotation in full, I summarize below the main specifications:

Foundation. "A good, sure, and strong foundation, of piles, brick, lime, and sand, both without and within, to be wrought one foot of assize at the least above the ground."

Frame. "The frame of the said house to be set square, and to contain fourscore foot of lawful assize every way square without, and fifty-five foot of like assize square every way within."

Materials. "And shall also make all the said frame in every point for scantlings larger and bigger in assize than the scantlings of the said new erected house called the Globe."

Exterior. "To be sufficiently enclosed without with lath, 'ime, and hair."

Stairs. "With such like stairs, conveyances, and divisions, without and within, as are made and contrived in and to the late erected playhouse . . . called the Globe. . . . And the staircases thereof to be sufficiently enclosed without with lath, lime, and hair."

Height of Galleries. "And the said frame to contain three stories in height; the first, or lower story to contain twelve foot of lawful assize in height; the second story eleven foot of lawful assize in height; and the third, or upper story, to contain nine foot of lawful assize in height."

Breadth of Galleries. "All which stories shall contain twelve foot of lawful assize in breadth throughout. Besides a jutty forward in either of the said two upper stories of ten inches."

Protection of Lowest Gallery. "The lower story of the said frame withinside . . . to be paled in below with good, strong, and sufficient new oaken boards." "And the said lower story to be also laid over and fenced with strong iron pikes."

Divisions of Galleries. "With four convenient divisions for gentlemen's rooms, and other sufficient and convenient divisions for two-penny rooms . . . And the gentlemen's roomes and two-penny rooms to be ceiled with lath, lime, and hair."

Seats. "With necessary seats to be placed and set, as well in those rooms [i.e., Gentlemen's and Two-Penny Rooms] as throughout all the rest of the galleries."

Stage. "With a stage and tiring-house to be made, erected, and set up within the said frame; with a shadow or cover over the said stage . . . which stage shall contain in length forty and three foot of lawful assize, and in breadth to extend to the middle of the yard of the said house. The same stage to be paled in below with good, strong, and sufficient new oaken boards. . . . And the said stage to be in all other proportions contrived and fashioned like unto the stage of the said playhouse called the Globe."

Columns. "All the principal and main posts of the said frame and stage forward shall be square, and wrought pilasterwise, with carved proportions called satyrs to be placed and set on the top of every of the said posts."

Roof. "And the said frame, stage, and staircases to be covered with tile."

Miscellaneous. "To be in all other contrivations, conveyances, fashions, thing and things, effected, finished, and done, according to the manner and fashion of the said house called the Globe."

To their new playhouse Henslowe and Alleyn gave the name "The Fortune." No pictorial representation of the building has come down to us; yet from the details cited in the contract we can readily imagine how it looked — a hollow structure eighty feet square, and approximately forty feet high; the galleries, seventeen and a half feet deep, enclosing an open yard fifty-five feet square; a red tile roof, and a turret and flagpole rising high above the stage. Over the main entrance was placed a handsome sign representing Dame Fortune.

Into this building, which in size, and probably in decoration, surpassed the Globe, the Admiral's Men moved in November, 1600. Thus within little more than a year the two city companies changed homes. Both were now housed in new and commodious theatres, the one to the north, the other to the south of the city; and the rivalry between them continued as of old.[1]

But no longer were they to enjoy their previous monopoly of entertaining the London public. At once they were called upon to face competition of a new sort, this time from child-actors. The choir-boys of the Queen's Chapel Royal and of St. Paul's Cathedral had long been accustomed to present plays, mainly for the amusement of the sovereign or distinguished individuals. From 1577 to 1584 they had been allowed to give their plays before the public in a small hall in the Blackfriars precinct.[2] After the closing of this hall in 1584, the Paul's Boys continued to act in their singing-school near the Cathedral until 1590, when they were suppressed.

About the end of the century, however, both these child-troupes again revived their performances before the public. In the closing months of 1598, or the early months of 1599, the Paul's Boys were allowed to reopen their singing-school to small and select audiences. They engaged John Marston and Thomas Dekker to write plays for them, and began to compete, though in a very limited way, with the Chamberlain's and Admiral's

[1] For the full history of the Fortune see my *Shakespearean Playhouses*, 1917.

[2] At first the Windsor boys, later the Paul's boys, were associated with the boys of the Chapel Royal at Blackfriars. For a full history of their connection with public performances see my *Shakespearean Playhouses*.

companies. In *Jack Drum's Entertainment* (1600), we read:

> I saw the Children of Paul's last night,
> And troth, they pleased me pretty pretty well.
> The apes in time will do it handsomely.

And they did. Paul's playhouse became very fashionable with gentlemen, who were willing to pay the higher prices charged in order to escape the noisy rabble that haunted the public theatres:

> I' faith, I like the audience that frequenteth there
> With much applause. A man shall not be choak't
> With the stench of garlic, nor be pasted
> To the barmy jacket of a beer-brewer.[1]

But far more serious competition for the adult actors was to come from the children of the Queen's Chapel Royal. In the autumn of 1600 they secured the use of the handsome Blackfriars Theatre which James Burbage had fitted up in 1597, and which the Privy Council had closed for public plays. Henry Evans, who had managed these boys during their former occupancy of the small upstairs hall in Blackfriars, hit upon a shrewd scheme for avoiding the order of the Privy Council. He proposed to have the children give what he was pleased to call "private" performances, though these were such merely in name. The order of the Privy Council would then be interpreted to apply only to "public" performances by "common" actors. But Evans mainly counted, no doubt, on the fact that the Privy Council would not be disposed to interfere with the doings of the royal choristers, members of the Queen's own household, especially if it were known that the Queen sanctioned their proceeding; and unquestionably Evans had Elizabeth's consent before going far with his undertaking.

---

[1] *Jack Drum's Entertainment*, acted at Paul's in 1600.

On September 2, 1600, he secured from Richard Burbage a lease of the Blackfriars Theatre for twenty-one years, agreeing to pay £40 a year as rental. And in a short time he and Nathaniel Giles, Master of the Chapel Children, had a large and well-trained company of boy-actors performing at this theatre. The boys could act well, with a grace and charm that often made them more attractive than the adult players. Middleton advises a new arrival in London "to call in at Blackfriars, where he should see a nest of boys able to ravish a man." Ben Jonson gives eloquent testimony to the power of one of these Chapel children, little Salathiel Pavy, to portray the character of old men. While assuming such rôles, Salathiel died at the early age of twelve, and Jonson wrote the following elegy on him:

> Years he numbered scarce thirteen
>   When fates turned cruel;
> Yet three filled zodiacs had he been
>   The stage's jewel,
> And did act, what now we mourn,
>   Old men so duly
> As, sooth, the Parcæ thought him one,
>   He played so truly.

Thus Death, thinking Salathiel to be indeed an old man, gathered him in his scythe. The mistake was not discovered until too late; and then Heaven, well pleased with him, refused to give him up.

Furthermore, to expert acting these boys of the Chapel added the charms of expert vocal and instrumental music, in which they had been carefully trained. The Duke of Stettin-Pomerania, who upon his grand tour of European countries in 1602 attended a play at Blackfriars, gave high praise to the musical powers of the children: "For a whole hour before the play begins, one listens to charming instrumental music played on organs, lutes, pandorins, mandolins, violins, and flutes; as, indeed, on this occasion a boy sang, *cum voce tremula*, to the accompaniment of a bass-viol, so delightfully, that, if the Nuns at Milan did not excel him, we had not heard his equal in our travels."

Finally, to write plays for them Evans engaged the two eminent poets, George Chapman, whose translation of Homer was receiving the applause of the world, and Ben Jonson, whose recent comedies, *Every Man in his Humor* and *Every Man out of his Humor*, had lifted him into the front rank of popular dramatists.

With the handsomest theatre in the city, with excellent acting, with charming musical accompaniment, and with the famous playwrights Chapman and Jonson, the children began their performances before the public late in 1600, or early in 1601, charging high prices of admission and catering to aristocratic audiences. The innovation took London by storm. At last the Admiral's and the Chamberlain's companies had competition that seriously affected their long and comfortable monopoly of playing.

Perhaps the most interesting evidence of the success of the innovation is to be found in the words of Shakespeare himself; for the popularity of the child-actors, it would seem, forced even the Chamberlain's Company to close the Globe for a time, and to go on a tour of the country.[1] Shakespeare alludes to this in *Hamlet*, where the traveling players that visit Elsinore are in reality the Chamberlain's troupe. Hamlet, astonished that they should leave the city, questions them closely as to the cause.

---

[1] This cannot be absolutely proved by the provincial records, but seems to be established on other grounds. A. W. Pollard, *Shakespeare Folios and Quartos*, 1909, p. 73, says that the company "is heard of as acting at Aberdeen as late as October," 1601; but the evidence on which he bases this assertion is not conclusive. See J. T. Murray, *English Dramatic Companies*, i, 104, note 3.

Hamlet. What players are they?

Rosen. Even those you were wont to take delight in, the tragedians of the city.[1]

Hamlet. How chances it they travel? Their residence, both in reputation and profit, was better both ways.

Rosen. I think their inhibition comes by the means of the late innovation.

Hamlet. Do they hold the same estimation they did when I was in the city? Are they so followed?

Rosen. No indeed they are not!

Hamlet. How comes it? Do they grow rusty?

Rosen. Nay, their endeavour keeps in the wonted pace; but there is, sir, an aerie [i.e., nest] of children, little eyases [i.e., fledglings], that cry out on the top of question, and are most tyrannically clapped for it. These are now the fashion, and so berattle the "common stages" — so they call them — that many wearing rapiers are afraid of goose-quills and dare scarce come thither.

Hamlet. What! are they children?

The passage ends with the question from Hamlet: "Do the boys carry it away?" which gives Rosencrantz the opportunity to pun on the well-known sign of the Globe: "Ay, that they do, my lord, Hercules and his load, too." The form this passage takes in the pirated first quarto is hardly less interesting:

> *Gil.* Yfaith, my lord, novelty carries it away,
> For the principal public audience that
> Came to them are turned to private plays,
> And to the humor of children.

And Jonson, in his *Poetaster* (1601), makes Histrio, who represents the Chamberlain's Company, say:

O, it will get us a huge deal of money, captain, and we have need on't; for this winter has made us all poorer than so many starved snakes; nobody comes at us, not a gentleman, nor a ———.

Still other evidence might be quoted to show that the competition of the two children's companies seriously affected the prosperity of the public troupes.

---

[1] In 1601 Shakespeare had begun his tragic period, and the Chamberlain's Company was acting *Julius Cæsar* and *Hamlet*.

This competition, however, did not stimulate Shakespeare to increased productivity; on the contrary we observe, beginning with the year 1600, a gradual letting-down of effort on his part. Whereas heretofore he had been producing on an average about three plays a year, he now begins to produce on an average about one play a year. His plays, to be sure, have a greater depth, but that alone is not sufficient to explain the slowness with which they appeared; nor can it be supposed that by winning greater popularity with London audiences they made up for their paucity in number.

And along with this diminished productivity there is noticeable also a distinct change in the mood of the plays; or, to put it in other words, immediately after writing the joyous trilogy of comedies in 1599, Shakespeare began to study the darker sides of human character, and to produce his great series of tragedies. Many scholars have supposed that this was due to some deep personal sorrow, or to some bitter experience in the life of the poet, which for a time made him pessimistic about human nature, and plunged him — to use the phrase most commonly employed — "into the depths." But if this be the case, we may with Browning exclaim, "the less Shakespeare he," for complete objectivity as an artist has been regarded as one of his crowning merits. It seems more reasonable to suppose that with the passing of youth, and the coming of the harder and more subtle intellect of middle-age, the dramatist sought to probe into those festering "imposthumes" of life which, as he had observed, oft breaking within, show no cause without why the world is filled with unhappiness. And if this led him to the production of his great tragedies, with such personages as Iago and Edmund, Goneril and Lady Macbeth, Cleopatra and Volumnia, we have no right to complain. That he did not easily and at once arrive at the secret of great tragedy can readily be understood — he had no guides among his contemporaries. For a time he seems to have been groping through sordid material for the true effects of pity and fear; but ultimately the vision flashed upon him in the nobility and purity of Lear and Cordelia, of Othello and Desdemona, set, like stars in darkest night, against a background of human nature superlatively corrupt. Accordingly — if we accept this theory, and we have no evidence for any other — we may assume that Shakespeare, in the full maturity of his powers, felt at last ready to attempt tragedy, the most difficult and lofty type of dramatic art; and that ambition, rather than melancholia, led him to the production of his masterpieces.

After *Twelfth Night*, in 1600 or 1601, though the precise date cannot be determined, Shakespeare delivered to his troupe *All's Well that Ends Well*, a revision of an earlier play of about 1596, usually identified by scholars with the *Love's Labour's Won* mentioned by Francis Meres in 1598. The reader familiar with Shakespeare cannot fail to note the presence of lines and scenes of an early date mingled with lines and scenes that bear the stamp of greater maturity. The main theme, a foreign love-romance taken from the *Decamerone*, set off by the addition of the comic characters Parolles, Lafeu, and the Clown, drawn from the poet's own invention, suggests a superficial kinship with the comic trilogy of 1599. But now joy in life gives place to a sombre consideration of the unpleasant elements in human nature, and the innocent laughter we derive from Touchstone and Dogberry finds no counterpart in the humor of Parolles. The absence of contemporary allusion to the play suggests that it did not please in its own day. Nor does it now. Something in the moral quality of the story repels the reader. Yet Helena, the maiden who loves not wisely but too well, is rendered so pure and true that Coleridge declared her to be "the loveliest of Shakespeare's characters."

In 1601, too, Shakespeare put on the boards another revision of an old play, *Hamlet*, which had demonstrated its effectiveness through more than a decade of popularity. The original play had been composed at least as early as 1589, for in that year Nashe used it as the type of tragic rant: "He will afford you whole *Hamlets*, I should say handfuls of tragical speeches." [1] This early drama had never been printed, and the stage-manuscript doubtless perished in Shakespeare's revision; but its general character and even the main outlines of its plot are discernible in a crude German adaptation, *Der bestrafte Brudermord*,[2] and in the mutilated 1603 quarto of *Hamlet*. Even in Shakespeare's finished revision as represented in the second quarto of 1604 the chief features of the older play are still retained. Its plot was of the bloody, melodramatic type which Kyd had rendered popular in *Hieronimo*, and its style clearly showed the influence of Seneca that prevailed in the tragedies of this early date. Most scholars attribute the first draft to Kyd himself, but it is unwise to be positive on the slender evidence we possess. Indeed, the very closeness with which the play, even as it emerges in Shakespeare's revision, copies the famous *Hieronimo*, at times echoing its phraseology, suggests that it might have been a slavish imitation of Kyd rather than an original work by that versatile author.[3]

The old *Hamlet*, it appears, had belonged to the Pem-

---

[1] Address "To the Gentlemen Students of both Universities," prefixed to Robert Greene's *Menaphon*, 1589.

[2] The result of the travels of English actors on the Continent. For a translation of this play see Furness' Variorum edition of *Hamlet*.

[3] One must not confuse the "additions" to *Hieronimo*, or, as it is now called, *The Spanish Tragedy*, with the work of Kyd. The additions represent Hieronimo as really mad, and show, I think, the influence of Shakespeare's popular revision of *Hamlet*.

broke's Men; but when that troupe was dissolved in 1593–94 the manuscript was purchased, along with *The Taming of the Shrew*, *Titus Andronicus*, and other plays, by the Chamberlain's Company. From Henslowe's *Diary* we learn that the Chamberlain's Men acted the play once during their brief stay of ten days at Newington Butts in 1594:

> 9 of June, 1594. Rd. at *Hamlet*, viiis.

After leaving Henslowe, they carried the play with them to the Theatre, where they occasionally performed it with success. It may be that Shakespeare then took the opportunity slightly to touch up the manuscript, for in the final draft we discover passages that resemble his early style. And we have evidence of a special revival of the play about 1595; Lodge, in his *Wit's Miserie* (1596), writes: "As pale as the visard of the ghost which cried so miserably at the Theatre, like an oyster-wife, *Hamlet, revenge!*"

Shakespeare's first revision of the play in 1601 seems not to have been thorough, yet it was adequate enough to attain sensational popularity, and led him shortly to a further and more complete reworking of the piece. Dekker, in *Satiromastix*, acted late in 1601, makes Captain Tucca exclaim: "My name's Hamlet revenge." [1] It may be, of course, that the allusion is to the ancient play, but more likely it was inspired by the popularity of Shakespeare's revision. And the Admiral's Men at the Fortune promptly made an attempt to revive the equally famous old tragedy of revenge, *Hieronimo*, now called *The Spanish Tragedy*, as a rival attraction.

---

[1] The rest of the passage, "Thou hast been at Paris Garden, hast not?" does not show, as many have thought, that *Hamlet* had been acted at the Swan. Tucca suddenly turns and addresses this question to Ben Jonson, and it refers to Jonson's having acted in *The Isle of Dogs* at the Swan in Paris Garden, to his great misfortune.

For this purpose they engaged Ben Jonson himself to freshen up the manuscript. Henslowe, acting as manager for the troupe, records in his *Diary:*

> Lent unto Mr. Alleyn the 25 of September, 1601, to lend unto Benjamin Jonson upon his writing of his additions to *Hieronimo* [i.e., *The Spanish Tragedy*] the sum of xxxxs.

Since Henslowe paid only from £6 to £8 for a new play, the sum of £2 indicates that Jonson's alterations were thoroughgoing. Bills were, of course, posted all over the city announcing the revival at the Fortune of this popular old tragedy of revenge with additions by the great dramatist Jonson. The play must have been a success, for in June, 1602, we find Henslowe paying Jonson for still further additions. It is probable also that Marston, in the sequel to his *Antonio and Mellida*, entitled *Antonio's Revenge* (tentatively entered in the Stationers' Registers on October 24, 1601, and published in 1602), shows the influence of the popularity of Shakespeare's *Hamlet*. Many passages, some apparently interpolations, were designed to take advantage of the contemporary interest in ghosts crying for revenge; and echoes of both *Hamlet* and *The Spanish Tragedy*, even of Jonson's additions, are observable. The appeal such echoes might have to London audiences would largely depend on fresh familiarity with the two famous revenge plays at the public theatres.

Furthermore, the great stir that *Hamlet* made started a vogue in tragedies of revenge. In 1602 Chettle wrote *Hoffman, or A Revenge for a Father;* in 1602–03 Tourneur wrote *The Atheist's Tragedy, or The Honest Man's Revenge*, which seems to have been intended as a reply to *Hamlet*, for the author refuses to give a son the right of revenge for his father, advancing instead the principle, "Leave revenge unto the King of Kings," and attempting to prove that "Patience is the honest man's revenge." About 1605 Chapman wrote *The Revenge of Bussy d'Ambois*, and about 1606 Tourneur *The Revenger's Tragedy*. Until the closing o the theatres in 1642 the type maintained its popularity, and in addition colored many plays that do not strictly fall within its category.

The success of *Hamlet* must have enabled the Chamberlain's Men to emerge from any temporary eclipse in public favor caused by "the late innovation" at Blackfriars. As Anthony Scoloker wrote: "Faith, it should please all, like *Hamlet*." Not only did it please all in London, who could attend its numerous performances at the Globe, but, we are told, the actors were called upon to present it before "the two universities of Cambridge and Oxford." That this was a signal honor deeply appreciated by playwrights is shown by Ben Jonson's satisfaction when his *Volpone* was similarly presented before "the two most famous universities"; in dedicating the play to them he declares: "I now render myself grateful, and am studious to justify the bounty of your act."

Naturally this popularity would make *Hamlet*, which had never been printed in any form, a desirable item to the publishers. But the actors were careful of their manuscripts, and preserved them safely under lock and key. As a rule only one complete copy of a new play was in existence, namely the author's original manuscript bearing the official license of the censor. From this original manuscript the playhouse copyist made for each member of the company taking part in the performance an actor's part, giving only the lines each was required to memorize, with the cue from the preceding speaker. No actor, therefore, had a full copy of the text, so that the danger of the play's falling into the hands of a printer was slight.

Yet, in spite of these precautions, the success of *Hamlet* led to the theft of the play in mangled form, and the issue in 1603 of an exceedingly corrupt text. This annoying occurrence must have been in the minds of Heminges and Condell when they framed their complaint against "stolen and surreptitious copies, maimed and deformed by the frauds and stealths of injurious impostors." [1]

The thief seems to have been one of the hirelings employed by the Chamberlain's Company. Although we do not know his name, we can trace the rôles he assumed in the play. [2] He acted in succession as Marcellus, Voltimand, one of the traveling players, one of the soldiers in Fortinbras' army, the second grave-digger, the churlish priest, and one of the ambassadors from England. Most of these rôles were unimportant, but they kept him on the stage through a large part of the performance, and enabled him to patch up a "maimed and deformed" copy to sell to an unscrupulous publisher. To his own speeches, which were fairly exact reproductions of what Shakespeare wrote, he added from ready but inaccurate memory the utterances of the other actors in the scenes in which he appeared. He was also familiar, though to a less extent, with certain other scenes which he might overhear after making up and while waiting his cue to come on, or in which he might possibly have been used as a mere "super." In the case of numerous scenes, however, he had no such sources of knowledge; and in these cases he was forced to resort to some transcript of the old play in its unaltered form. [3] The resultant hodge-podge of a text would fully justify Heminges and Condell in describing it as a "fraud," and in branding the compiler as an "injurious impostor."

[1] Prefixed to the First Folio of Shakespeare, 1623.
[2] For a fuller discussion, with bibliographical references, see Chap. XXVIII.
[3] It has been suggested that this was an abridged transcript prepared for the company's use while traveling.

Apparently the actors discovered the treachery of the hireling, and in order to prevent his disposal of the copy to some publisher, resorted to the device of having their printer friend, James Roberts, who had helped them before in similar cases, take the genuine playhouse manuscript to the Stationers' Hall and there copyright it in his own name. This he did on July 26, 1602: "James Roberts, Entered for his copy . . . a book called *The Revenge of Hamlet, Prince of Denmark*, as it was lately acted by the Lord Chamberlain his servants." Roberts, it will be understood, was taking this step in behalf of the players, and had no intention of actually printing the play; his sole purpose was to prevent any one else from securing a license to do so.

In this he was successful; but he was not successful in preventing the issue of the stolen text, for the hireling managed to sell his copy to two publishers unscrupulous enough to defy the laws of the Stationers' Company, Nicholas Linge and John Trundle.[1] Without a license they issued the play in May, 1603, with the title: "The Tragicall Historie of Hamlet, Prince of Denmarke. By William Shake-speare. As it hath beene diverse times acted by his Highnesse servants in the Cittie of London: as also in the two Universities of Cambridge and Oxford, and else-where."

Shakespeare must have been greatly provoked that the play, which had won him fame both in London and at the universities, should be offered to the reading public in so corrupt a form. Yet he had no recourse at law, and the only way he could protect his reputation was to issue a correct and authorized edition. This, however, he did not at once do. The death of Elizabeth, with the coming of James and the resultant distraction, and

---

[1] Trundle seems to have made himself especially disliked by the playwrights and actors, and is satirized in several plays.

especially the outbreak of the plague, caused him to defer action. The pirated edition appeared in May, 1603; on May 26 the theatres were closed by the plague, and they remained closed for six months. Shakespeare may have utilized this interval of leisure further to improve the play. No doubt he had been astonished at the success it had attained as a result of his hasty revision, and felt stimulated to give it further and more careful reworking before offering it to critical readers.[1] Late in 1604, however, he sent to the press his authorized edition.[2] The title-page states that the tragedy was "enlarged to almost as much again as it was," and gives assurance to the purchaser that the text is printed "according to the true and perfect copy." There is every reason to believe that the printer set up the type from a manuscript furnished by Shakespeare.[3]

Thus at last the world was supplied with a trustworthy edition of the play, and readers were able to judge of its merits as literature. They were not disappointed. Even Gabriel Harvey, the censorious scholar of Cambridge, acknowledged that it had in it "to please the wiser sort"; and Harvey's judgment has been unanimously approved by literary critics of subsequent ages.

On the stage *Hamlet* still maintains the popularity which marked its first appearance; yet the Hamlet we

---

[1] In the first quarto Polonius appears as Corambis, Guildenstern and Rosencrantz as Gilderstone and Rossencraft, Reynaldo as Montano, and the order of the scenes is different.

[2] Some copies bear the date 1604, others 1605, indicating that the book was issued late in 1604.

[3] Curiously enough, the volume was published by Linge, who had issued the pirated edition. Perhaps he was the leader in that enterprise, and agreed to suppress the corrupt edition, only two copies of which are extant. He engaged James Roberts to print the play. They must have come to terms whereby Roberts in return for the privilege of printing the play transferred the copyright to Linge, for later we find Linge selling the copyright to another publisher. The text of the First Folio was set up from a different manuscript, that used by the actors.

see to-day is probably not the Hamlet that Shakespear
conceived, and that in the hands of Burbage won suc
plaudits from Elizabethan audiences. The rôle has bee
subjected to the whims of several generations of actors
who have gradually built up the modern interpretatio
of the character. One illustration will suffice to mak
this clear. In the play as originally presented Hamle
first appears to the audience neatly dressed in black
as became a mourner and one who had always bee
the "glass of fashion." But when he begins to feig
madness, he suddenly becomes foul and slovenly of dress
His uncle describes the change as nothing less than
"transformation":

> Since nor the *exterior*, nor the inward man
> Resembles that it was.

When Hamlet impetuously rushes into Ophelia's close
after having several times been denied access to her
she is greatly shocked at the change in his dress:[1]

> *Oph.* O, my lord! my lord! I have been so affrighted!
> *Pol.* With what, i' the name of God?
> *Oph.* My lord, as I was sewing in my closet,
> Lord Hamlet, with his doublet all unbraced,
> No hat upon his head, his stockings foul'd,
> Ungarter'd and down-gyved to his ancle,
> Pale as his shirt . . .

And Anthony Scoloker, who had seen the play on the
stage, writing in 1603–04, compares the mad Daiphantus
to Hamlet in these terms:

> Puts off his clothes, his shirt he only wears,
> Much like mad Hamlet.[2]

When a man entered the stage "in his shirt" [3] he was

---

[1] This has been supposed to be the affectation of a forlorn lover, but it
goes far beyond that.
[2] *Daiphantus*, published in 1604.
[3] So the stage directions read. Cf. *The Spanish Tragedy*, where Hieronimo

supposed to be at the limit of deshabille. Hamlet's slovenliness of dress is, of course, in perfect keeping with his feigned rôle of a madman, and must have made a profound impression upon the audience, as it did upon Ophelia.[1] But the modern actor represents Hamlet as throughout the play exquisitely groomed in black velvet, with an attractive gold chain about his neck — still, though mad, the "glass of fashion."

We cannot sufficiently regret the absence of Shakespeare himself to drill our actors in the representation of his plays. That he was painstaking in such matters, and exacting in the extreme, is indicated by the advice, put into the mouth of Hamlet, to the traveling actors in Elsinore; and that he was successful as his own stage manager we have abundant evidence. John Downes, book-keeper and prompter at the Restoration theatres, writes of Betterton's performance of *Hamlet* in accordance with the instructions of Sir William Davenant:[2]

The Tragedy of *Hamlet; Hamlet* being Perform'd by Mr. Betterton; Sir William (having seen Mr. Taylor of the Black-Fryars Company Act it, who being Instructed by the Author Mr. Shaksepear) taught Mr. Betterton in every Particle of it; which by his exact Performance of it, gain'd him Esteem and Reputation Superlative to all other Plays.

This "correct" representation of *Hamlet* came to Betterton indirectly: Shakespeare personally instructed Richard Burbage; after Burbage's death in 1619, Joseph

roused out of his "naked bed" enters "in his shirt." Was Edmund Gayton really thinking of "mad Hamlet" when he wrote in his *Festivous Notes*, p. 17: "This roguing Queane had watch'd her Uncle, and seen him act Jeronimo [i.e., Hieronimo] in his short shirt, and now thinking him quite lost, discovers his mad pranks to the Curate"?

[1] Tourneur, in *The Revenger's Tragedy* (III, v), written under the influence of *Hamlet*, makes Vindici say:

> Surely wee're all mad people, and they
> Whome we thinke are, are not; we mistake those:
> 'Tis we are mad in *scence*, they but in *clothes*.

[2] *Roscius Anglicanus*, p. 21.

Taylor assumed the rôle;[1] Davenant had seen Taylor act the part, and, after the Restoration, attempted to instruct Betterton "in every particle of it." The success his instruction enabled Betterton to achieve is revealed by contemporary criticism. Samuel Pepys writes on August 24, 1661: "To the Opera, and there saw *Hamlet, Prince of Denmarke*, done with scenes very well; but above all Betterton did the Prince's part beyond imagination"; on May 28, 1663: "There saw *Hamlet* done, giving us fresh reason never to think enough of Betterton"; and again on August 31, 1668: "Saw *Hamlet*, which we have not seen this year before, or more; and mightily pleased with it; but above all with Betterton — the best part, I believe, that ever man acted!" And Pepys' enthusiasm was shared by numerous other men of letters. Steele described Betterton's performance of Hamlet as "the force of action in perfection." Rowe declared that "Betterton performed the part as if it had been written on purpose for him, as if the author had conceived it as he played it." Possibly Rowe did not know that under Davenant's instruction Betterton was actually attempting to play the rôle "in every particle" as the author himself had conceived it.

With Shakespeare's guiding hand the difficult scene of Hamlet's leaping into the grave would doubtless prove one of the most effective moments in the play. So it was when Burbage acted under the author's tutelage. In the mind of the person who wrote the *Funeral Elegy on the Death of the Famous Actor Richard Burbage*, the scene stood out among his greatest achievements:

> Oft have I seen him leap into the grave,
> Suiting the person, which he seemed to have,

[1] James Wright, in *Historia Histrionica* (1699), says: "Burbage, Heminges, and others of the older sort, were dead before I knew the town; but in my time, before the wars, . . . Taylor acted *Hamlet* incomparably well."

> Of a sad lover with so true an eye,
> That there, I would have sworn, he meant to die.

Even in the hands of Betterton the scene called for special comment from Steele, who observes that it is one of the "circumstances which dwell strongly upon the minds of the audience." To-day the leaping into the grave is commonly omitted.

Perhaps Shakespeare did not specially concern himself with the way in which the clowns might render the humorous grave-digging episode, yet their comic business must at least have had his approval; it is interesting, therefore, to note an early traditional representation of the scene, which is peculiarly Elizabethan in spirit. A Frenchman, who saw this in London in 1811, has left the following description: [1]

After beginning their labour and breaking ground for a grave, a conversation begins between the two grave-diggers; — the chief one takes off his coat, folds it carefully, and puts it by in a safe corner; then, taking up his pickaxe, spits in his hand, gives a stroke or two, talks, stops, strips off his waistcoat, still talking, folds it with great deliberation and nicety, and puts it with the coat; then an under-waistcoat, still talking; another, and another; — I counted seven or eight, each folded and unfolded very leisurely in a manner always different, and with gestures faithfully copied from nature; — the British public enjoys this scene excessively, and the pantomimic variations a good actor knows how to introduce in it are sure to be vehemently applauded.

How old this traditional representation of the scene is we cannot say, but it seems to have gone back at least to the days of Betterton and Davenant. And it was imitated in the Restoration, if not previously in the Elizabethan, performances of Webster's *Duchess of Malfi*, written with distinct reminiscences of Shakespeare's plays, and acted by the Globe company about 1611.

[1] I quote the passage from Halliwell-Phillipps, *Outlines*, ii, 320.

The 1708 quarto, valuable for the fulness of its stage-directions, notes that in Act V, Scene ii, when the comic doctor removes his gown, he "puts off his four Cloaks one after another." Possibly Anthony Scoloker was thinking of this farcical representation of the grave-digging episode when in 1603–04 he cited the play of *Hamlet* as a triumphant example of those tragedies in which the broadly comic and the deeply pathetic are placed side by side: "Like friendly Shakespeare's tragedies, where the comedian rides when the tragedian stands on tip-toe." [1]

Though a few of the personal instructions from Shakespeare may have come down through Burbage, Taylor, Davenant, Betterton, and later stage-tradition to the present time, most of them doubtless have been lost or modified beyond recognition. We may have no reason to complain at the modern performance of *Hamlet*, for our actors succeed in maintaining the original popularity of the play; yet it is well to bear in mind the possibility that the Elizabethan representation differed in many essential ways from that of Henry Irving or Forbes-Robertson, and their imitators.

Successful as *Hamlet* is on the stage, it is no less popular as a closet drama. The subtle, elusive personality of the young Prince of Denmark, and the eternal mystery of life which seems to brood over the plot, exercise upon readers a spell that makes the tragedy one of the most fascinating in the English language. Tennyson's dictum, "*Hamlet* is the greatest creation in literature that I know of," merely reflects the universal esteem in which the play is held by lovers of poetry.

[1] As to the Elizabethan impersonation of the Ghost, cf. Randolph in *Hey for Honesty*: "Her looks are as terrible as . . . the Ghost in *Hamlet*."

CHAPTER XVI

THE ESSEX REBELLION, AND THE WAR
OF THE THEATRES

THE year 1601 held for Shakespeare other things than the gratifying success of *Hamlet*. Its early months were marked by a sensational occurrence which must have deeply stirred him, and which involved his troupe in a perilous experience.

The gallant soldier, Robert Devereux, Earl of Essex, who had endeared himself to the hearts of the people by his spectacular expeditions to Cadiz and the Azores,[1] had in 1599 been appointed Lord Deputy of Ireland for the specific purpose of subduing the rebellious islanders and bringing peace to that unfortunate land. On March 27, with his staff and a splendid retinue of attendants, he set out for his new post. His progress through the streets of London took the form of a triumphal procession, the populace everywhere flocking to see and applaud their hero. Stow tells us that "the people pressed exceedingly to behold him, especially in the highways, for more than four miles' space, crying and saying, *God bless your Lordship! God preserve your honour!* etc., and some followed him until the evening, only to behold him." By his side

---

[1] Spenser, in *Prothalamion*, goes out of his way to celebrate Essex. The passage begins thus:

> Yet therein now doth lodge a noble Peer,
> Great England's glory, and the world's wide wonder,
> Whose dreadfull name late through all Spaine did thunder,
> And Hercules' two pillors standing neere
> Did make to quake and feare.
> Fair branch of Honor! Flower of Chevalrie!
> That fillest England with thy triumphys fame,
> Joy have thou of thy noble victorie!

rode his dear friend, the Earl of Southampton, as one of his captains.

Shakespeare was keenly interested in the expedition, and seems fully to have shared the popular confidence in its ultimate success. In a Chorus prefixed to the last act of *Henry V* he gave expression to this confidence in words that suggest high admiration for Essex, if not indeed personal affection:

> How London doth pour out her citizens,
> The mayor and all his brethren in best sort,
> Like to the senators of the antique Rome,
> With the plebeians swarming at their heels,
> Go forth and fetch their conquering Cæsar in:
> As, by a lower, but loving, likelihood,
> Were now the general of our gracious empress, —
> As in good time he may, — from Ireland coming,
> Bringing rebellion broachèd on his sword,
> How many would the peaceful city quit
> To welcome him!

But Essex, like other great men who have attempted to solve the Irish problem, lamentably failed, and the following year he returned to London to be put on trial for his conduct of affairs in the island. In August, 1600, he was deprived of all his offices in the State, and his public career, hitherto so brilliant, was clouded in official disgrace. This downfall he attributed, not without cause perhaps, to his political enemies who were then in favor with Elizabeth; and he schemed to use force to overthrow these men, and reëstablish himself in power. In a daring plot to seize by violence the reins of government he interested several great noblemen, including Shakespeare's friend and patron the Earl of Southampton.[1] The date set for the uprising was Sunday, February 8, 1601.

---

[1] For details see C. C. Stopes, *The Life of Henry, Third Earl of Southampton*, 1922, pp. 186–234.

The main hope of the conspirators was that, when the banner of Essex was raised in the streets, the populace would rally to the support of their hero. And in order to prepare the public in advance for conduct so revolutionary, they planned to have the Chamberlain's Company at the Globe act Shakespeare's *Richard II*, in which was represented "the deposing and murder" of an English sovereign.[1] One might here suspect the hand of the Earl of Southampton, who doubtless was familiar with Shakespeare's plays,[2] and aware of Shakespeare's personal sympathy with Essex. However that may be, certain of the conspirators interviewed the Globe actors, and requested them to present *Richard II* on the afternoon of February 7 — that is, on the day preceding the fateful morning set for the revolt. Augustine Phillips, a leading member of the Chamberlain's Company, subsequently testified:

Sir Charles Percy, Sir Jostlyne Percy, and the Lord Montegle, with some three more, spake to some of the players in the presence of this examinant, to have the play of the deposing and killing of King Richard the Second to be played the Saturday next, promising to give them xls. more than their ordinary to play it, when this examinant and his fellows were determined to have played some other play, holding that play of King Richard to be so old and so long out of use that they should

---

[1] It is curious that the quarto of *Richard II* issued by Wise in 1597 from the players' copy omitted the deposition scene. Possibly Wise used his own judgment, for the scene might well have brought him into trouble with the censors of the press. The scene, however, remained in the actors' version, and was added to the edition of 1608.

[2] C. C. Stopes, *op. cit.*, p. 106, calls attention to what may be a significant letter written by Sir Walter Ralegh from Plymouth, July 6, 1597, to Sir Robert Cecil: "I acquainted my Lord Generall [Essex] with your letter to mee, and your Kind acceptance of your entertainment. He was also wonderfull merry att your consait of Richard II. I hope it shall never alter, and whereof I shalbe most gladd if it is the trew way to all our good, quiet, and advancement, and most of all for her sake, whose affairs shall truely fynd better progression."

have small or no company at it;[1] but, at their request, this examinant and his fellows were content to play it . . . and so played it accordingly.

At noon on the day of the arranged performance the plotters met at dinner, and after dinner proceeded in a body to the Globe. Sir Gelly Merrick later testified that "he dined at Gunter's in the company of the Lord Montegle, Sir Christopher Blount, Sir Charles Percy, Ellys Jones, and Edward Bushell,"[2] and others "whom he remembreth not; and after dinner that day, and at the motion of Sir Charles Percy and the rest, they went all together to the Globe." There the play was duly acted, with the conspirators, probably from a box, watching the effect upon the audience, and loudly applauding the deposition scene. What influence, if any, the performance had upon the public we cannot say; but that the Chamberlain's Men were unaware of the part they were taking in a bold attempt to overthrow the government is certain.

On the following morning, Sunday, February 8, about eleven o'clock, the Earl of Essex, accompanied by the Earl of Southampton, the Earl of Rutland, the Earl of Bedford, and other "knights and gentlemen of great blood, to the number of some sixty," passed through Ludgate into London, marching "on foot, armed some with swords, some with targets, and some few with French pistols," and in the main streets of the city raised the banner of Essex. The populace, however, did not rally to their support; and it soon became obvious that

[1] This, I think, may be regarded as an *ex parte* statement, for *Richard II* was probably not unpopular. It was still being acted at the Globe as late as 1611, when it was witnessed by Forman; and in 1631 it was chosen by Sir Henry Herbert for his benefit performance.

[2] All these men were close personal friends of Essex, and intimately concerned in the revolt; see C. C. Stopes, *op. cit.* Sir Charles Percy, son of the Earl of Northumberland, was familiar with Shakespeare's plays; see above, p. 227.

the rebellion was doomed to failure. Some of Essex's followers, observing this, took occasion to slip away from him; and Essex and his friend Southampton, realizing their own danger, hastily retreated to Essex House on the banks of the Thames, where they prepared to defend themselves to the death. Here they were immediately besieged by the Queen's forces, the Lord Burghley assaulting the house from the land side, and the Lord Admiral from the river side. At six o'clock in the afternoon parleys were held with the Earl of Southampton, who was boldly pacing the roof with a sword drawn in his hand.

All London was seething with excitement; and Shakespeare, we can hardly doubt, was profoundly moved by the stirring events of the day, as well as by the grave peril of his friend Southampton.

The upshot — for we cannot linger over details — was that the conspirators were arrested and put on trial for treason. Both Essex and Southampton were sentenced to the block; but later Southampton's sentence was reprieved on the ground that he had acted merely through love of his friend, and he was sent to close confinement in the Tower, where he remained during the rest of the Queen's life.

Nor did the actors at the Globe wholly escape. They were brought before the authorities, and made to explain their performance of *Richard II*. Yet no real blame could be fastened upon them, and, possibly through the influence of their patron, the Lord Chamberlain, and their other friends at Court, they were not subjected to any punishment.[1] The Queen, however, did not forget the episode, and ever afterwards felt a strong resentment at the play. In August, 1601, she exclaimed to Lambard: "I am Richard the Second, know ye not that?"

[1] Sir Gelly Merrick, who paid the actors £2 to present the play, was among those executed.

And with what seems to be hysterical exaggeration she declared to him that "this tragedy was played forty times in open streets and houses."

On the morning of February 24, Essex was led to the block. With fine irony, Elizabeth summoned the Chamberlain's Men to entertain Her Majesty on the evening before; and, as though further to show her indifference to the fate of her one-time favorite, on the morning of the execution she amused herself by playing on the virginals.

Shakespeare, we may feel sure, had no part in this luckless conspiracy; but he seems not to have forgiven Elizabeth for her heartless treatment of the unfortunate Essex, and her long imprisonment of Southampton. This may perhaps explain why he refused, in spite of several protests, to write, as did so many poets, an elegy on the great Queen who had taken such delight in his plays, or to express any grief at her death.

The summer that followed was destined to bring him another unpleasant experience, the so-called "War of the Theatres," growing out of the "Poetomachia." The chief personages in the "Poetomachia" were Ben Jonson, on the one hand, and John Marston and Thomas Dekker, on the other; and the trouble originated in a private quarrel between Jonson and Marston.[1]

Marston, formerly a spendthrift gallant of the Middle Temple, began his career as a poet with the publication in 1598 of a volume of "snag-tooth'd" *Satires*, followed immediately by a second volume of the same character, *The Scourge of Folly*, in both of which he attempted to lash the sins of the day. The satires are chiefly remarkable for the use of an uncouth "gallimaufry of words," which often produces the effect of a deafening verbiage

[1] This theatrical quarrel has been studied by J. H. Penniman, *The War of the Theatres*, 1897, R. A. Small, *The Stage Quarrel*, 1899, and J. H. Penniman, *Poetaster and Satiromastix*, 1913. I have chosen to give my own interpretation of the facts.

without much apparent meaning. Yet they brought Marston no little reputation. John Weever, in his *Epigrams* (1599), writes:

> Marston, thy Muse enharbors Horace's vein;
> Then some Augustus give thee Horace's merit!

And Charles Fitzgeoffrey, in *Affaniæ* (1601), thus addresses him:

> Gloria, Marstoni, satirarum proxima primae,
> Primaque, fas primas si numerare duas!

But Jonson, with his surer judgment, realized that the satires were bad; and probably in his conversation with literary men ridiculed Marston's obscurity of thought and absurdities in diction. If so, it must be said, he was fully justified.

When the Paul's Boys opened their little private theatre late in 1598 or early in 1599, and engaged Marston and Dekker as playwrights, Marston at once furbished up for them an old academic play entitled *Histriomastix*. Again he made use of his strange "gallimaufry of words" to split the ears of the public. Jonson was just putting on the boards of the Globe his *Every Man out of his Humor*, a play avowedly designed to tax the follies of the time; and he took the occasion to insert what he probably intended to be a good-natured ridicule of the "fustian" language of Marston:

Now, sir, whereas the ingenuity of the time, and the soul's synderisis are but embrions in nature, added to the paunch of Esquiline, and the intervallum of the zodiac, besides the ecliptic line being optic and not mental, but by the contemplative and theoric part thereof, doth demonstrate to us the vegetable circumference, and the ventosity of the tropics, and whereas our intellectual or mincing capreal, according to the metaphysics — as you may read in Plato's *Histriomastix*.

The parody of Marston's style, in words and phrases culled from his works, was very clever; and the mention of *Histriomastix* by name made it impossible for the audience to miss the identity of the victim. But Jonson did not stop with this. In another scene he humorously alluded to Marston's second volume of satires, *The Scourge of Villany:*

And how dost thou, thou *Grand Scourge* or Second Untruss of the time?

Marston, sensitive to criticism, seems to have been deeply resentful, and to have exhibited, in the taverns of London and other places where literary men gathered, an open hostility to Jonson, in which he was seconded by his friend and fellow-laborer Thomas Dekker. Jonson was made aware of their attacks upon him; and in his next play, *Cynthia's Revels*, produced at Blackfriars in 1600, he introduced, as a digression, Marston and Dekker under the names of Anaides and Hedon,[1] and represented them as backbiting him in literary company. He made Hedon (i.e., Marston) say:

Well, I am resolv'd what I'll do. . . . Marry, speak all the venom I can of him; and poison his reputation in every place where I come . . . and if I chance to be present where any question is made of his sufficiences, or of anything he hath done private or public, I'll censure it slightingly and ridiculously.

Anaides (i.e., Dekker) is made to say that he likewise will speak detractingly of Jonson whenever possible. But to their attempts at backbiting Jonson retorted with characteristic arrogance:

> I think but what they are, and am not stirred,
> The one [Marston] a light, voluptuous reveler,[2]
> The other [Dekker] a strange arrogating puff,
> Both impudent and ignorant enough.

The satire on Marston in this play was so obvious that, as Dekker declared, it was no wonder that, out of an

[1] The identification is verified by Dekker in *Satiromastix*, I, ii, 183–95.
[2] In *Poetaster* Jonson again contemptuously describes Marston as a reveler; see Act III, Scene iv, line 72.

audience of five hundred, four hundred "should all point with their fingers in one instant at one and the same man." [1] Marston therefore answered the attack in his *What You Will*, acted by the Paul's Boys late in 1600.[2] In this play he gave a full-length portrait of Jonson as Lampatho, taking the name from Jonson's own description of himself in *Cynthia's Revels:* "Foh! he smells all lamp-oil with studying." In what were probably savage terms,[3] he ridiculed Jonson's arrogance and insolence, and caustically referred to the failure of *Cynthia's Revels* at Court.

Jonson was furious, and challenged Marston to a duel. This put Marston in an embarrassing situation, for Jonson was one of the best swordsmen in England, known already to have killed two men in duels. Under the circumstances he ignored the challenge. Jonson thereupon sought him out, and ultimately found him in one of the taverns of London. Marston, who must have been expecting such an occurrence, drew a pistol. Jonson promptly "took his pistol from him" — so he boasted to William Drummond of Hawthornden — and then gave him a beating.[4]

Not content, however, with drubbing his opponent in private, Jonson desired to settle the score before the theatrical audiences of the city. To this end he began to write, for the performance at the Blackfriars, *Poetaster*,

---

[1] *Satiromastix*, I, ii, 290–91.

[2] The date can be fixed by internal evidence, especially the reference to *Cynthia's Revels* (1600), and the absence of any allusion to *Poetaster* (1601).

[3] It should be remembered that the play as we have it was rewritten by Marston. Jonson had unmercifully satirized its diction in *Poetaster* (1601), which led Marston carefully to revise it before publishing it in 1607. Since he was then on friendly terms with Jonson, he doubtless omitted much of the original abuse. There is enough left, however, to make clear the nature of Marston's attack.

[4] See Drummond's *Conversations*, and cf. Jonson's *Epigram* No. 68. That the episode preceded *Poetaster* is clear from passages in the play; see especially (Belles-Lettres Series) II, i, 115–18; II, ii, 176; II, ii, 188.

in which he planned to celebrate contemporary London under the name, conventional in Elizabethan satire, of Rome, pompously representing himself as the great Quintus Horatius Flaccus, "poet and priest to the Muses," and Marston as Crispinus, "an ignorant poet-aster." At the end of the play, as a climax, he proposed to give Marston a pill which should make him vomit up on the stage before the London public his grotesque diction, "words able to bastinado a man's ears," such as "oblatrant — furibund — fatuate — conscious dampe — prorumped — snarling gusts — spurious snotteries — obstupefact." He was at work on the play — for he was slow in composition — nearly four months,[1] during which time he must have freely talked about it, and have taken the tavern-gossips into his confidence. Thus his enemies were well-informed of his intentions, and even learned much about the plot of his "comical satire." Marston, after his recent experience with Jonson, thinking prudence to be the better part of valor, took no steps towards a counter-attack. But Dekker bravely came to the defense of his friend. He was just finishing for the Paul's Boys a comedy on William Rufus, and upon the shoulders of this play he foisted a sub-plot lampooning Jonson. Taking a cue from *Poetaster*, he introduced Jonson as Horace, Marston as Crispinus, and himself as Demetrius. He also stole thunder from Jonson by using Captain Tucca, whom Jonson had created as a vainglorious braggart. Finally, he rechristened the play with the title, *Satiromastix, or The Untrussing of the Humorous Poet*. News of Dekker's purpose coming to Jonson while he was still engaged on *Poetaster*, he inserted Dekker in the play as a second "poetaster," and made other efforts to counter the expected attack.

So far this was merely a private quarrel between Jonson,

---

[1] According to his own statement some fifteen weeks.

on the one hand, and Marston and Dekker, on the other—or what Dekker himself aptly termed the "Poetomachia." But a second quarrel, between Jonson and the Chamberlain's Company, became involved with the "Poetomachia," so that we have to consider the two together.

Jonson was exceedingly vain of the fact that he was writing for the children of the Chapel Royal. They were not "common players," but members of the Queen's household; their theatre was finer than the public houses, and situated not in the vulgar suburbs but in a most aristocratic locality; and they charged higher prices of admission, and drew their audiences from fashionable circles. With unpardonably bad taste he took occasion in the plays he wrote for the children to emphasize the superiority of Blackfriars, and to sneer at the "common actors." In this he seems to have been further inspired by the animosity he had for some unknown reason developed towards the Lord Chamberlain's Men, who had recently brought out his *Every Man in his Humor* and *Every Man out of his Humor*. It was his arrogant and ill-natured attacks upon the public actors in general, and the Chamberlain's Company in particular, that led to the open quarrel between the Blackfriars and the Globe. This is known as the "War of the Theatres." [1]

In his very first play for the children of the Chapel, *Cynthia's Revels* (1600), Jonson began to draw his invidious distinction between the elegant and fashionable Blackfriars Theatre and what he was pleased to call the "public theatres" or "common stages."

'Slid, the boy takes me for a piece of perspective. . . . Sir Crack, I am none of your fresh pictures that use to beautify the decayed dead arras in a public theatre.

---

[1] In *Raven's Almanacke* (1609), Dekker writes: "The contention of the two houses (the gods be thanked) was appeased long ago, but a deadly war between the three houses [Globe, Fortune, Red Bull] will I fear burst out like thunder and lightning," etc.

Furthermore, he speaks scornfully of the sort of plays acted on the "common stages," and sneers at those gentlemen who "will press forth on common stages and brokers' stalls."

It is not strange that Shakespeare, in behalf of the Chamberlain's Men, should make a protest against this ill-natured attack upon the "common stages" and "common players." In the passage in *Hamlet* dealing with the Blackfriars children, reference to which has already been made, he uttered his protest as follows:

Rosencrantz. These [children at Blackfriars] are now the fashion, and so berattle the "common stages" — so they call them [1] — that many wearing rapiers [i.e., men of fashion] are afraid of goose-quills [i.e., Jonson's pen], and dare scarce come thither.

Hamlet. What! are they children? . . . Will they pursue the quality [of acting] no longer than they can sing? Will they not say afterwards, if they should grow themselves to be "common players" — as is most like if their means are no better, — their writers do them wrong to make them exclaim against their own succession? [2]

Jonson, however, continued his sneers at the "common stages" and "common players," and in writing his next play, *Poetaster* (1601), became even more virulent. In Act I, Scene ii, Ovid Senior says to the poet, Ovid Junior: "Yes, sir! I hear of a tragedy of yours coming forth for the common players." Whereupon Tucca adds: "They are grown licentious, the rogues, libertines, flat libertines. They forget they are in the statute" — referring to the well-known statute which listed "common players" with Rogues, Vagabonds, and Sturdy Beggars. Ovid Senior then observes to his son: "Methinks if nothing else yet this alone, the very reading of the public edicts, should fright thee from commerce with them."

[1] The phrase quoted appears in *Cynthia's Revels* (1600), but not in *Poetaster* (1601).

[2] Shakespeare's anticipation came true, for three of these boy-actors, Nathaniel Field, William Ostler, and John Underwood, later joined the "common players" at the Globe.

But the self-respecting Ovid Junior, jealous of his good name, replies with some heat:

> They wrong me, sir, and do abuse you more
> That blow your ears with these untrue reports.
> I am not known unto the *open stage*,
> Nor do I traffic in their theatres.

The Chamberlain's Men, bent upon revenge, allied themselves with Marston and Dekker. The latter was then, as has been stated, preparing for the Paul's Boys his attack on Jonson called *Satiromastix, or The Untrussing of the Humorous Poet*, in which Jonson was to be fetched upon the stage and scurrilously abused. The Chamberlain's Men arranged with Dekker that *Satiromastix* should be acted simultaneously by the Boys at Paul's and by themselves at the Globe. Furthermore, the play being in process of composition, the Chamberlain's Men assisted in devising some of the cruelest scenes. As Jonson makes Demetrius (i.e., Dekker) say in *Poetaster*, IV, iii, 145: "Wee'll all join, and hang upon him like so many horse-leeches, the players and all. We shall sup together soon, and then wee'll conspire, i' faith." Even Shakespeare seems to have been induced to put a finger in the play. Jonson later [1] wrote as follows:

> What they have done against me
> I am not moved with . . .
> Only amongst them I am sorry for
> Some better natures, by the rest so drawn,
> To run in that vile line.

If Shakespeare had a hand in *Satiromastix*, we may suspect that he is responsible for the scene which represents Jonson in the pangs of composing one of his odes. The passage is free from the gross scurrility and personal abuse that mark the other satirical scenes, and as humor has a merit that cannot be attributed to the play as a

[1] In an Apologetical Dialogue subsequently added to *Poetaster*.

whole. Jonson, as every one in London knew, was slow at composition, and had to hammer out his verses with great effort, with the burning of many candles, and with inspiration drawn from numerous classical authors; that, and nothing else, is laughed at in this scene:

SCENE 2

Horace sitting in a study behind a curtain, a candle by him burning, books lying confusedly. To himself.

Horace. To thee, whose forehead swells with roses,
Whose most haunted bower
Gives life and scent to every flower,
Whose most adorèd name incloses
Things abstruse, deep, and divine,
Whose yellow tresses shine
Bright as Eoan fire,
O me, thy priest, inspire!
For I to thee and thine immortal name,
In — in — in golden tunes —
For I to thee and thine immortal name
In — sacred raptures flowing — flowing — swimming — swimming —
In sacred raptures swimming,
Immortal name — game — dame — tame — lame, lame, lame!
Pux! — hath shame — proclaim — oh! —
In sacred raptures flowing, will proclaim, not —
O me, thy priest, inspire!

Jonson, learning that the Chamberlain's Men were to have a share in *Satiromastix*, inserted in his *Poetaster* some special abuse aimed at them in the character of Histrio. Captain Tucca says to Histrio: "I would fain come with my cockatrice one day and see a play, if I knew where there were a good bawdy one. But they say you have nothing but Humors, Revels, and Satires" (alluding to Jonson's Blackfriars plays — *Cynthia's Revels*, a study in "humors," and *Poetaster*, described on the title-page as "a comicall satire"). Histrio promptly corrects him: "No, I assure you, Captain, not we. They are on the other side of Tyber [i.e., the Thames]. We [on the Bankside, where only the Globe was in operation as a playhouse] have as much ribaldry in our plays as can be, as you would wish, Captain; all the sinners in the suburbs [i.e., the occupants of the licensed stews on the Bankside] come and applaud our action daily." Tucca, thus learning that Histrio is connected with the Chamberlain's Company, angrily exclaims: "I hear you'll bring me o' the stage there; you'll play me, they say; I shall be presented by a sort of copper-laced scoundrels of you. Life of Pluto! if you stage me, stinkard, your mansions shall sweat for't, your tabernacles, varlet, your *Globes*." Not content with such general abuse, Jonson proceeds to lampoon five particular members of the Chamberlain's Company under the then no doubt easily identified descriptions of "your eating player," "the villanous out-of-tune fiddler Aenobarbus," "Æsop, your politician," [1] "Frisker, the zany," [2] and "Your fat fool." [3] And it would seem that he even took a fling at Shakespeare, who had recently acquired heraldic honors and purchased an estate at Stratford: "What, you are proud, you rascal, are you proud? ha? You grow rich, do you, and purchase?"; and with reference to a coat of arms: "They forget they are in the statute, the rascals. They are blazoned there! There they are tricked, they and their pedigrees! They need no other heralds, i-wis."

If Jonson's abuse of the players was severe, the lam-

[1] An allusion to the share the Globe actors had in the Essex conspiracy? Æsop is again referred to in Act V, Scene iii, as a politician.

[2] Probably Will Kempe, who danced a morris all the way to Norwich in 1600.

[3] Possibly the comedian who took the rôle of Falstaff and for whom Shakespeare designed the rôle of Ajax. In his Apologetical Dialogue Jonson says:

> Now, for the Players, it is true I tax'd 'hem,
> And yet but some; and those so sparingly
> As all the rest might have sat still, unquestioned,
> Had they but had the wit or conscience
> To think well of themselves. But impotent they
> Thought each man's vice belong'd to their whole tribe:
> And much good doo't 'hem.

pooning of Jonson by Dekker and the Chamberlain's
Men was worse. As Shakespeare observed, there was
"much throwing about of brains." The public seems
to have enjoyed both the *Poetaster* at Blackfriars and
Satiromastix at Paul's and the Globe. Rosencrantz
declares: "Faith, there has been much to-do on both
sides: and the nation holds it no sin to tarre them to
controversy: there was, for a while, no money bid for
argument, unless the poet and the player went to cuffs
in the question."

Further details of the quarrel are unknown to us; but
a contemporary writer seems to give Shakespeare credit
for putting an end to it. In *II Return from Parnassus*,
composed late in 1601, occurs the following colloquy
between the two leading actors of the Globe:

> *Kempe.* . . . . O that Ben Jonson is a pestilent fellow! He brought up
> Horace, giving the poets a pill; but our fellow Shakespeare hath given
> him a purge that made him bewray his credit.
> *Burbage.* It's a shrewd fellow, indeed!

Shakespeare's purge, whatever it was, seems to have
been effective. Very soon after we find the "War of the
Theatres," and along with it the "Poetomachia," a
matter of the past. Jonson and his old enemy Dekker
are lovingly writing a play together; Marston dedicates
The Malcontent to Jonson in affectionate terms, "Ben-
jamino Jonsonio, poetæ elegantissimo, gravissimo, amico
suo, candido et cordato"; Jonson assists Marston in the
composition of *Eastward Hoe;* and the Chamberlain's
Men, in order to show that they too had "buried the
hatchet," act his *Sejanus* at the Globe.

Still another distressing experience was reserved for
Shakespeare in this memorable year. In the first week of
September his father died at Stratford at the age of at
least seventy. We may suppose that the glover's later
years were, through the dramatist, rendered free from

pecuniary embarrassment, and that he was happy in the success achieved by his illustrious son. Sir John Mennes, it will be recalled, described him as a merry-cheeked old man, still in his shop, who said, "Will was a good honest fellow, but he darest have crackt a jest with him at any time." Such property as the father had, except for the dower-rights of the widow, came to the poet. The bulk of the estate consisted of the two houses in Henley Street, namely, the family home and the adjacent Wool Shop. Shakespeare's mother continued to occupy the eastern house, which had been her residence since her marriage; the western house, the Wool Shop, was, it seems, let by the poet for commercial use.

If Shakespeare was in Stratford at or soon after the death of his father, he probably returned to London in time to take part in the usual Christmas performances at Court. The Queen, though now in failing health, summoned the Chamberlain's Men to amuse her at Whitehall on December 26 and 27, 1601. Two days later, on December 29, the Lord Chamberlain had the honor of entertaining her at his private house in Blackfriars, where after dinner he had his company of actors to present a play. Sir Dudley Carleton writes on December 29: "The Queen dined this day privately at my Lord Chamberlain's. I came even now from the Blackfriars, where I saw her at the play with all her *candidæ auditrices*." Three days later Shakespeare and his fellows again presented a play before the Queen, this time at Court and on her own summons. Thus within a week the Chamberlain's Men appeared before Her Majesty four times — ample evidence that they had not suffered a permanent loss of royal favor through their unlucky part in the Essex plot.

CHAPTER XVII

THE PASSIONATE PILGRIM AND LOVE'S MARTYR

SHAKESPEARE, as we have seen, had definitely abandoned the composition of non-dramatic literature; yet just at the turn of the century appeared two volumes of lyrical verse with which his name was associated, though in different ways.

The first bore the title: "The Passionate Pilgrime. By W. Shakespeare. At London. Printed for W. Jaggard, and are to be sold by W. Leake, at the Greyhound in Paules Churchyard. 1599." It is mainly significant as showing the eagerness of publishers to secure something from the pen of the dramatist, and the confidence they had in the potency of his name on the title-page to "vent" a work.[1] In all probability Jaggard had come into possession of a small commonplace-book, such as Elizabethan gentlemen were fond of making. From various sources its owner had copied into its blank leaves songs and sonnets — for the most part amorous — that pleased him, including two sonnets from Shakespeare's unpublished cycle, and two sonnets from *Love's Labour's Lost*,[2] all four, no doubt, with Shakespeare's name appended; and in addition, verses by Griffin, Barnfield, Marlowe, and others, some with, some perhaps without, the author's name attached. Collections of this character[3] frequently fell into the hands of publishers and

---

[1] The publisher of the first quarto of *Othello* says: "The author's name is sufficient to vent his work."

[2] Not transcribed from the printed play (unless from the pirated and corrupt first quarto of which no copy is extant), but, apparently, from some manuscript then circulating among gallants.

[3] They were very common; the present writer has two such commonplace-books, with poems by Jonson, Donne, and other well-known writers, and many verses with no names attached.

were made the basis of piratical issues, a noteworthy instance being Tottel's Miscellany.

When Jaggard realized that he had two sonnets from Shakespeare's famous cycle, he decided to make capital of the fact. For his volume he devised the title *The Passionate Pilgrime* (using "Pilgrime" in the well-known sense of "Lover" [1]), added the statement "by W. Shakespeare," and carefully put in the display-window his two prize poems. Apparently he hoped to deceive the unwary into supposing that here at last they were able to purchase the "sugared sonnets" which the master had so long allowed to circulate among his "private friends." With the two authentic sonnets from that cycle Jaggard associated the two sonnets from *Love's Labour's Lost,* and certain other poems which he thought might with some show of plausibility be attributed to Shakespeare, namely: four sonnets on the theme of Venus and Adonis, almost certainly by Griffin, who had already printed one of them in his *Fidessa;* four short love-poems (the author of which has not been identified), written in the six-line stanza familiar in *Venus and Adonis;* the sonnet "If music and sweet poetry agree," printed by Barnfield in his *Poems in Diverse Humours;* and a song, "Crabbed age and youth," often found in early anthologies. These fourteen poems made up what Jaggard was pleased to call "The Passionate Pilgrime, by W. Shakespeare." Then he slyly inserted a second title-page, *Sonnets to Sundry Notes of Music,* without any author's name, following which he printed verses by Barnfield, Marlowe, and other writers.[2] Obviously he intended the book-

[1] As used, for example, by Romeo in addressing Juliet. The lady beloved was commonly called "saint." In this connection it is interesting to observe that Thomas Nashe, in *Jack Wilton,* describes sonneteers as "passionate lovers."

[2] It is curious that this second section contained, doubtless unsuspected by Jaggard, a genuine poem by Shakespeare, Biron's address to Rosaline, extracted from *Love's Labour's Lost.*

buying public to suppose that the whole volume was by Shakespeare; only on closer inspection would the purchasers discover that merely the first section actually was attributed to the master.

Jaggard had but twenty short poems. In order to make this slender collection into a sizable volume he used a diminutive type-page with wide margins of paper, he inserted at the top and bottom large ornamental devices, and, finally, he resorted to the unusual scheme of printing on only one side of each leaf. By these clumsy expedients he managed to stretch his material into a book of sixty pages.

Because of the presence, no doubt, of Shakespeare's name on the title-page, the volume met with a ready sale. A second edition was called for, of which no copy has come down to us, and a third edition appeared in 1612. In this third edition, Jaggard, still embarrassed by his scanty material, added two long amorous poems, the epistles of Paris to Helen, and of Helen to Paris, impudently extracting them from Thomas Heywood's *Troia Britanica*, a work he had himself published in 1609. Since this enlarged edition bore on the title-page the assertion "newly corrected and augmented, by W. Shakespeare," Heywood felt called upon to defend himself against the possible charge of having plagiarized from that more distinguished author a portion of his *Troia Britanica*. Accordingly, in the same year, 1612, he added to his *Apology for Actors* an explanation to the reading public:

Here, likewise, I must necessarily insert a manifest injury done me in that work [*Troia Britanica*] by taking the two epistles of Paris to Helen, and Helen to Paris, and printing them in a less volume [*The Passionate Pilgrime*] under the name of another [William Shakespeare], which may put the world in opinion I might steal them from him, and he, to do himself right, hath since published them in his own name: but, as I must acknowledge my lines not worth his [Shakespeare's] patronage, under whom he [Jaggard] hath published them, so the author [Shakespeare], I know, much offended with Mr. Jaggard, that altogether unknown to him presumed to make so bold with his name.

Shakespeare may have gone further than merely expressing his resentment privately to Heywood. At any rate Jaggard at once canceled the objectionable title-page, and issued the remainder of the sheets with a new title-page from which the name of Shakespeare was omitted.

The second work with which the dramatist's name was associated is interesting in an entirely different way. In the latter months of 1601 there appeared a volume by an obscure provincial writer, Robert Chester, entitled *Love's Martyr: or Rosalin's Complaint. Allegorically shadowing the truth of Love, in the constant Fate of the Phœnix and Turtle*, at the end of which Shakespeare affixed a poem — the only time he is known to have contributed to the published work of another author.

Chester in all probability was a domestic retainer — a chaplain or a tutor — in the household of a wealthy country gentleman. John Salisbury, Esq., of Lleweni, County Denbigh, Wales.[1] Since *Love's Martyr* was dedicated to Salisbury, and solely designed to celebrate him, and since Shakespeare contributed his poem not as a compliment to Chester, or to Chester's work, but as an expression of his personal esteem for Salisbury, we must glance for a moment at this man who won for himself a place among the dramatist's London friends.

Salisbury was born in December or January, 1566–67, and thus was approximately of the same age as Shake-

[1] The lives of Chester and of Salisbury are sketched in an excellent volume by Professor Carleton Brown, *Poems by Sir John Salisbury and Robert Chester*, 1913. *Love's Martyr* has been edited by A. B. Grosart for the New Shakspere Society, 1878.

speare. On one side he came of royal blood, though with the bend sinister, for his mother, the famous Catherine of Berain, was the granddaughter of Sir Roland Velville, illegitimate son of King Henry VII. In 1581 he entered Oxford University. In 1586, upon the execution of his elder brother for complicity in the Babington plot, he became the heir of Lleweni. A few months later he married Ursula Stanley, illegitimate daughter of Henry Stanley, Earl of Derby and King of Man, and at Lleweni established a home that was noted for its hospitality to men of letters. Salisbury, himself a poet, was conspicuous for his generous patronage of the native poets, among whom was Robert Chester. Numerous verses by various local bards are extant celebrating his liberality and his kindly interest in their work.

In 1595, at the age of twenty-eight, he left his country estate in Wales, came to London, and entered the Inner Temple of Law; and he spent the greater part of the next ten years in the metropolis, frequenting the theatres and the Court. He won the friendship of the Earl of Pembroke, Sir Robert Cecil, and other noblemen of power, and enjoyed the favor of the Queen herself, who made him one of her Esquires.

Moreover, in London he continued to show his deep interest in literature, and became the patron of several playwrights, numbering among his friends not only Shakespeare but also Chapman, Marston, and Jonson. In a collection of his manuscripts now preserved at Christ Church, Oxford, there is a poem entirely in Jonson's autograph, signed in full by the great dramatist. Presumably Jonson lent the poem to Salisbury to read, and Salisbury forgot to return it. After Jonson's death it was discovered, and printed in the folio of 1640 with the statement: "Writ in Queen Elizabeth's time, since lost, and recovered." If Salisbury had the privilege of looking over

Jonson's poems in manuscript, we may suppose that he was one of those choice "friends" who had the privilege of reading Shakespeare's *Sonnets* in manuscript.

In 1597 he was appointed, on Pembroke's recommendation, Privy Council Deputy for the County of Denbigh; and in June, 1601, at the age of thirty-four, he was knighted by the Queen's own hand. Shortly after this event, and possibly to some extent in celebration of it, the volume entitled *Love's Martyr* was issued.

For years Chester, under the stimulus of his master's kindly interest, had been composing verse at Lleweni, and in 1601 he sought, we may infer, to have some of his work published in London. Apparently Sir John encouraged him in this ambition, and offered to see a volume of his poems through the press. In gratitude Chester not only dedicated the volume to Sir John, but attempted to fuse all the poems (originally composed at various times on unrelated subjects) into a single long poem celebrating the marriage of his patron and patroness. At the beginning of the volume he placed a eulogy, written about 1587, on the union of Salisbury, described as the Turtle, to Ursula Stanley, described as the Phœnix. Dame Nature comes weeping to a parliament of the gods on Olympus, expressing her fear that the beautiful Phœnix will decay, —

> And from her ashes never will arise
> Another bird her wings for to display.

The gods are astounded at the description of the Phœnix (as they well might be [1]), and Jove orders Dame Nature

---

[1] Her teeth are hewed from rich crystal rocks. . . .
When the least whistling wind begins to sing
And gently blows her hair about her neck,
Like to a chime of bells it soft doth ring.

t is obvious that this whole description of a beautiful woman — a good example of that "descending description" so popular with Elizabethan writers — was an inset poem, originally composed as a separate exercise; note

to "leave Britania," cross "over the mountain tops
to Paphos Isle (Wales), and there, in a vale (Lleweni
"environed with a high steepie mountain," find Salis
bury, "true honor's lovely squire," who will be a suitab
match for "such beauty that all beauty was excelling.
The gods and goddesses loudly applaud this decree from
thundering Jove, and Dame Nature hastens away to pu
it into effect. The "allegory" thus developed Chest
determined to use for the purpose of giving unity to th
whole volume. Accordingly, the poems that follow, o
miscellaneous and often incongruous subjects, he linke
by clumsy devices to the Phœnix-Turtle and Dame Na
ture theme, with a resultant hotch-potch that is, to sa
the least, astonishing.

At the end of the first poem we suddenly descen
from the heights of Greek Olympus and the immediat
presence of all the pagan deities to hear the poet in h
humble capacity as the family chaplain utter a piou
prayer — strangely put into the mouth of Venus —
Jehovah, Christ, God of Israel, for his mistress, wh
now is described as "a silver dove" instead of a phœni
Next, in order to enable him to introduce various oth
unrelated poems, he devised a long dialogue betwee
Dame Nature and the Phœnix, interweaving therein
metrical history of early England, then a description
certain famous cities, then an account of the nine fema
worthies, then, with a special apology to the indulge
reader — much needed by that long-suffering individu
— a narrative of the "Birth, Life, and Death of Kir
Arthur," followed by miscellaneous epistles, oration
and epitaphs dealing with that sovereign, and a tedio
pedigree of Arthur, all of which in spirit and in co

its reference to Jove, Vesta, Juno, Venus, and an Angel, all incongruous
its present setting. The description of a terrestrial paradise (pp. 9–11)
also apparently an inset, clumsily made to serve as a description of Wa

ent are totally out of keeping with the Phœnix-Turtle *motif*.[1] Immediately after this digression into the field of English history, we come upon some love-ditties, supposedly sung by Dame Nature and the Phœnix, likewise quite out of harmony with all that precedes. But our astonishment reaches a climax when the author next drags in, as if by the ears, a long metrical treatise on herbs, trees, fishes, stones, beasts, insects, reptiles, and birds, with their respective "virtues" and "secrets." The discussion of birds happily enables him to return to the original Phœnix-Turtle story, and he narrates the marriage of his patron and patroness, which, with the Arabian Phœnix in mind, he curiously represents as a death. The Pelican then advances to sing the glory of their unparalleled love; and in a *Conclusion* the author himself makes the announcement that from the matrimonial ashes of the two birds has arisen a new Phœnix. The reference, presumably, is to the birth of Salisbury's first child, Jane. The *Conclusion*, one might think, should end the volume. But Chester could not resist the temptation to add two more long poems, of which he was doubtless proud because of their ingenuity, the first a series of "Cantoes" on the letters of the alphabet, the second a collection of fifty-eight poems of varying length built up on short love posies such as were then used in rings. By slightly altering these, he was able to hitch them also to the Phœnix-Turtle allegory.

It is hard to imagine a more incongruous or ridiculous compilation. Yet apparently Sir John, in order to please Chester, as well, we may suspect, as to see himself celebrated in verse, was resolved to have it published. Furthermore, he seems to have called upon his distinguished

[1] How incongruous the volume is may be illustrated by the fact that the publisher, not readily disposing of the work, offered the unsold copies in 1611 under the new title *The Annals of Great Brittaine, or A Most Excellent Monument, wherein may be seene all the antiquities of this Kingdome.*

literary friends in London to honor the volume wi
some verses of their own. This they agreed to do; b
instead of complimenting the author, Chester, th
wholly ignored that impossible creature, and celebrat
Sir John himself. In this respect the volume is uniqu
so far as I know, in Elizabethan literature.

Following the long and tedious poem by Chest
which fills no fewer than 167 pages, comes a blank pag
and then a new and formal title, running thus: "Her
after Follow Diverse Poeticall Essaies on the Form
Subject; viz. The Turtle and Phœnix, Done by the Be
and Chiefest of our Moderne Writers, with their Nam
Subscribed to their Particular Works: Never befo
Extant. And (now first) Consecrated by them all Ge
eraily to the Love and Merite of the True-Noble Knigh
Sir John Salisburie." The contributors were the fo
eminent playwrights, William Shakespeare, John Mar
ton, George Chapman, and Benjamin Jonson, and
writer who signed himself "Ignoto."

The first poem, called *Invocatio*, and signed "*Vatu
Chorus*" (i.e., "Chorus of the Poets," meaning all t
poets contributing the following verses), explains t
purpose they have in writing, namely to celebrate t
generosity and nobility of Sir John Salisbury:

> That we may give a round to him
> In a Castalian bowl crown'd to the brim.

The second poem, likewise signed "*Vatum Chorus*," a
addressed *To the Worthily Honor'd Knight, Sir Jo
Salisburie*, requests him to accept the following vers
for their sincerity:

> No mercenary hope did bring them forth,
> They tread not in that servile gate,
> But a true zeal, born in our spirits,
> Responsible to your high merits.

The first poem, very brief, is signed "Ignoto." The second is signed "William Shake-speare." Then follow in succession poems signed "John Marston," "George Chapman," and "Ben Jonson."

Ignoto, in fourteen lines, vaguely observed that only from the death of one phœnix is another phœnix born. Marston described in grandiloquent terms the beauty of that offspring, "which now is grown unto maturity" (Jane Salisbury would be fourteen years old in 1601), "a most exact, wondrous creature, arising out of the Phœnix and Turtle Dove's ashes." Chapman praised Salisbury's constancy to his mate:

> She was to him the analis'd world of pleasure,
> Her firmness cloth'd him in variety.

Jonson, after a humorous invocation, celebrated likewise Sir John's fidelity to his wife:

> O, so divine a creature,
> Who could be false to?

And in an *Ode* 'ενθουσιαστική he described in extravagant terms the "illustrate brightness" of Lady Salisbury.

The verses Shakespeare contributed, though ostensibly on the theme of the Phœnix and the Turtle, are not closely related to that theme as Chester had developed it. Indeed Shakespeare seems not to have read Chester's tedious poem far enough to have unraveled its cryptic meaning, or to have discovered that from the ashes of the dead birds, whose death was merely an allegorical representation of matrimony,[1] there came noble offspring. Accordingly, in his haste jumping to the conclusion that the two birds died in reality "leaving no posterity," he wrote a graceful funeral song, in which, in the meta-

---

[1] I cannot accept Sir Sidney Lee's opinion (*Life*, p. 272) that Shakespeare's poem was not penned for Chester's book, but was "either devised in an idle hour with merely abstract intention, or it was suggested by the death within the poet's own circle of a pair of devoted lovers."

physical style of John Donne, he played with the idea that marriage makes two into one and that "one is no number." The concluding lines of the "*Threnos*" may be slyly humorous when the poet calls upon his reader to repair to the urn and —

> For these dead birds sigh a prayer.

The whole undertaking on the part of these distinguished London poets reminds one, at least in a way of the commendatory poems which many writers contributed to Coryat's *Crudities*. Jonson begins jocularly "We must sing too?" and all the poets seem to try in a sly way to be as obscure as Chester himself. But, of course the contributors restrained themselves in order rightly "to gratulate an honorable friend."

The episode may be taken as illustrating Shakespeare's good nature in humoring the vanity of a country knight who had been a generous friend to the theatres and the London playwrights. And Sir John's abiding affection for the poet is indicated in lines recently found among papers belonging to the Salisbury family.[1] Addressing Heminges and Condell as "my good friends," the writer declares that in publishing the First Folio they have given to England a treasure more glorious than "Cortés, with all his Castelyne associates," digged from the richest mines of Mexico. Though the lines could not have been written by Sir John, who died in 1612, they were produced by some member of his family, probably by his son, Sir Henry, who, being admitted to the Middle Temple in 1607, was no doubt familiar with his father's distinguished friend, and so came to be numbered among those who, as he puts it, "loved the dead" playwright.

[1] See Sir Israel Gollancz, "Contemporary Lines to Heminges and Condell," in *The Times Literary Supplement*, Thursday, January 26, 1922, p. 56.

CHAPTER XVIII

WORCESTER'S MEN; *TROILUS AND CRESSIDA*

'OR many years the Chamberlain's and the Admiral's
ompanies were the only adult troupes "allowed" by the
'rivy Council to perform regularly in London. But in
he spring of 1602 the Earl of Worcester's Men and the
.arl of Oxford's Men, who had been "joined by agree-
nent together in one company," thereafter called
Vorcester's Men, secured through the "suit of the Earl
f Oxford" the permission of the Queen likewise to play
1 the city.[1] On March 31, 1602, the Privy Council,
nder special orders from the Queen, wrote to notify
he Lord Mayor of the "allowance" of the new company,
dding: "And, as the other companies that are allowed,
amely, of me, the Lord Admiral, and the Lord Cham-
erlain, be appointed their certain houses, and one and
o more to each company, so we do straitly require that
his third company be likewise [appointed] to one place.
.nd because we are informed the house called the Boar's
Iead [an inn situated in Whitechapel without Aldgate]
; the place they have especially used, and do best like of,
ve do pray and require you that the said house, namely
he Boar's Head, may be assigned unto them."

This new company was in part composed of actors
vho had seceded from the Chamberlain's Men soon after
he Globe was erected — William Kempe, Christopher
3eeston, John Duke, and Robert Pallant, all excellent
ctors, favorably known to the public. With them were

---

[1] For the history of this company see my *Shakespearean Playhouses,*
p. 157–59, 294–309.

associated Robert Lee, who had as early as 1593 belonged to the Chamberlain's Company, and who now was ranked among the best players of the day, Thomas Greene, whose fame as a comedian was not much inferior to that of William Kempe,[1] John Lowin, whose ability later made him one of the leading members of the Globe Company, and Richard Perkins, whose fine acting was praised by John Webster.[2] As their playwright they secured Thomas Heywood, called by Charles Lamb "a prose Shakespeare," who for many years had been industriously writing for the Admiral's Men. As the chief dramatist for this new company he was destined to produce some of his most successful plays, for example his *Ages*, which, we are told, thronged the theatre "with numerous and mighty auditories." To secure his services the actors gave him a position among them as a full-sharer, so that he bore to his company much the same relation that Shakespeare did to the Chamberlain's organization. In addition to Heywood, who was their regular playwright, they occasionally employed the well-known dramatists Henry Chettle, Thomas Dekker, John Day, Wentworth Smith, Richard Hathaway, and John Webster.

After securing their license as a city company, Worcester's Men occupied, in accordance with the order of the Privy Council, the Boar's Head in Whitechapel; but an inn-yard remote from the centre of population put them at a serious disadvantage, and six months later they

---

[1] See *Greene's Tu Quoque*. Heywood wrote: "There was not an actor of his nature [i.e., a comedian] of better ability, ... more applauded by the audience, of greater grace at Court, or of more general love in the city."

[2] Webster, in publishing *The White Devil*, affixed at the end an expression of his appreciation to the company for its excellent performance of the play: "Whereof, as I make a general acknowledgment, so in particular I must remember the well approved industry of my friend Master Perkins, and confess the worth of his action did crown both the beginning and end." A portrait of Perkins now hangs in the Dulwich Picture Gallery.

secured the use of the Rose playhouse recently abandoned by the Admiral's Men.[1] At the same time they engaged Henslowe, with all his experience, to serve as their business-manager.

The Chamberlain's Men could hardly have welcomed the competition of this excellent troupe housed so near them. Its organization, too, followed close on the appearance of the two child-companies at St. Paul's and Blackfriars. Thus before the end of Elizabeth's reign there were no fewer than five troupes of actors, at five several playhouses, all catering to the patronage of London audiences. Yet the Globe had little difficulty in maintaining its sovereignty over theatre-goers, largely through the prestige of Shakespeare. In 1609 we have printed testimony to the superior drawing-power of "this author's comedies, that are so fram'd to the life that they serve for the most common commentaries of all the actions of our lives, shewing such a dexterity and power of wit that the most displeased with plays are pleased with his comedies. And all such dull and heavy-witted worldlings as were never capable of the wit of a comedy, coming, by report of them, to his representations, have found that wit there that they never found in themselves, and have parted better-witted than they came, feeling an edge of wit set upon them more than ever they dreamed they had brain to grind it on. So much and such savored salt of wit is in his comedies that they seem, for their height of pleasure, to be born in that sea that brought forth Venus."[2]

The same writer adds that "amongst all there is none more witty than" *Troilus and Cressida*. This play, we may feel reasonably sure, was composed in 1602. Shake-

[1] Within a few years they moved to a new and larger playhouse, the Red Bull, erected for them to the north of the city.

[2] "A never writer to an ever reader," prefixed to the 1609 quarto of *Troilus and Cressida.*

speare had long been interested in the story of Troy, which he first met in Virgil and Ovid. Even so early as *Lucrece* the fascination it had for him is apparent, and innumerable references in his plays — in *Hamlet*, for example — show how deeply it had stirred his imagination.[1] It would be strange were it otherwise; for the beauty of Helen, the bravery of Hector, the craft of Ulysses, the treachery of Sinon, the fickleness of Cressida, and the woes of old Hecuba are without parallel in literary annals. The story had gripped the heart of the world from the days of Homer, and had graced the pens of many poets — Euripides and Sophocles, Ovid and Virgil, Chaucer and Lydgate, to mention only a few. On the Elizabethan stage, too, it had proved astonishingly popular. Between the years 1559 and 1599 our records, which are far from complete, show that it had received dramatic handling at least twenty-nine times. And the appearance of two volumes of Chapman's translation of Homer in 1598 greatly increased this popularity with theatre-goers. In 1599 the Admiral's Men produced *Brute* (apparently a two-part play dealing with Brutus), *Troy's Revenge*, *Agamemnon*, *Orestes Furies*, and *Troilus and Cressida* (by Dekker and Chettle[2]). And we have much other evidence of the extraordinary interest in the Troy story at the close of the century.

At last Shakespeare turned his hand to the theme, working, apparently, from some earlier play on the subject, portions of which he embodied in his later scenes with very slight alteration.[3] Some scholars think that he

---

[1] The passages in *Lucrece* and *Hamlet* are adaptations from the second book of Virgil's *Æneid*.

[2] This play is not extant, but the stage "plot" is preserved; see W. W. Greg, *Henslowe Papers*, pp. 142, 144. Some scholars think that about this same time the Admiral's Men produced Heywood's two plays called *The Iron Age* dealing with the siege of Troy.

[3] See the able article by J. S. P. Tatlock, "The Siege of Troy in Eliza-

was merely seeking to take advantage of the vulgar popularity of the subject, and felt no deep interest in his task; yet it cannot be doubted that he put his heart into much of the play, and one is tempted to believe that he wrote many scenes not to agitate the "clapper-claws" of the "hard-handed multitude," but rather to please himself. *Troilus and Cressida* could hardly be expected to succeed on the stage, and there is grave doubt whether the Chamberlain's Men ever put it on the boards. How unsuitable it is for representation is indicated by the fact that it is known to have been performed only three times, in Munich (1898), in Berlin (1904), and in London, (1907). Even as a closet drama it has few admirers. It is not loved, as *Lear* and *Cymbeline* are loved; some critics even find it repulsive. Yet, coming as it did from Shakespeare at the mature age of forty, it is in some respects one of the most remarkable works we have from his versatile pen.

Our first reference to the play is in February, 1603, when the Chamberlain's Men took steps to prevent its publication. This action may have been due to the imminent danger of a pirated edition; but the danger of piracy would in large measure depend on the success of the play, and *Troilus and Cressida* could hardly tempt any one to run the risks involved in stealing it; moreover, the troupe, after its recent experience with *Hamlet*, would guard the manuscript with redoubled precautions. It seems more likely that since the play was not then to be staged, the author had allowed private transcripts to be made for circulation among his friends, and that the actors, in view of a possible future presentation of the play, desired to prevent any one of these transcripts from falling into the hands of a publisher. Whatever the

bethan Literature, Especially in Shakespeare and Heywood," in *Publications of the Modern Language Association of America*, xxx, 673.

cause, on February 7, 1603, their printer friend, James Roberts, took the playhouse copy to the Stationers' Hall, and secured a blocking license: "7 Februarii. Master Roberts. Entred for his copy, in full court holden this day, to print, when he hath gotten sufficient authority for it, the book of *Troilus and Cressida*, as it is acted by my Lord Chamberlain's Men." Roberts' purpose, of course, was merely to prevent any one else from publishing the work. The phrase "as it is acted by my Lord Chamberlain's Men" may be simply a glance at the future, or a conventional tag inserted to identify the play by mention of the troupe that owned it.[1] The phrase "when he hath gotten sufficient authority for it" may indicate that the Stationers' Company understood the arrangement between Roberts and the actors, or it may indicate that the manuscript had not yet been submitted to the Master of the Revels, and did not bear the signature of that official, which it must have before it could be printed.[2]

Our next reference to the play is in 1609. On January 28 of this year two young publishers, Bonian and Walley, secured from the wardens of the Stationers' Company (who seem to have forgotten Roberts' entry) a new license to print "a booke called the history of Troylus and Cressida," and shortly afterwards they issued it with the stereotyped phrase on the title-page, "as it was acted . . . at the Globe." It may be that, since the play was by Shakespeare, they assumed, as was natural, that it had been acted by his company. But after publishing it they were informed that in reality *Troilus and Cressida* never had been presented on the stage; and they hurried to

---

[1] A play with the same title was owned by the Admiral's Men.
[2] On this point see my edition of *The Dramatic Records of Sir Henry Herbert*, pp. 39–42. It would cost the actors £1 to have the manuscript licensed for acting, an expense they would hardly incur unless they intended to put the play on the stage at once.

make capital of so remarkable a fact. They cut out the title-page as originally issued, pasted in a double sheet with the signature ¶, containing a fresh title-page, and a notice to the public announcing their astonishing discovery. The second title-page omitted the former statement that *Troilus and Cressida* had been acted; and the notice, with the flamboyant heading "A never writer to an ever reader, News," literally shouted to the book-buyers: "You have here a new play, never stal'd with the stage, never clapper-clawed with the palms of the vulgar, . . . not . . . sullied with the smoaky breath of the multitude."

The publishers then congratulated the reader on the great privilege of acquiring a copy of the play, "since by the grand possessors' wills I believe you should have prayed for them, rather than been prayed." The allusion is commonly supposed to be to the actors, but "grand" is a strange adjective to apply to them; and the reference may be to the poet's friends — gentlemen of fashion interested in the theatre — who had been allowed to make transcripts for their private examination. The copy that Bonian and Walley sent to the printer was not the actors' manuscript (which later became the basis of the Folio text), but was an accurate transcript of what Shakespeare wrote. The evidence is not decisive, yet the presumption clearly favors the theory that the play, as the publishers declared, never was acted, that in view of this fact it was allowed to circulate in transcripts among certain "grand possessors," and that in 1609 one of these transcripts fell into the hands of Bonian and Walley.

Critics have found few plays of Shakespeare so puzzling as *Troilus and Cressida*, mainly because they ignore its literary pedigree, and approach it with the point of view of the Greeks. Furnivall calls it "a deliberate debasing of that Homer Chapman englisht"; and Lloyd, in a similar tone, describes it as "a profanation of Homeric poetry," adding: "It is difficult at first to restrain a feeling of indignation at the travesty he thus commits himself to. . . . The change was deliberate. Was it malicious?" And the assumption that the play is a deliberate travesty of the Homeric story has led many scholars to attempt to interpret it as "an important biographical document." Some have advanced the theory that Shakespeare was at enmity with Chapman, and wrote in savage antagonism to his highly-praised translation of Homer; others have connected the play with the "War of the Theatres," and suggested that the author was bent on lashing the insolent Jonson; still others hold that he was giving vent to his personal resentment at womankind in general resulting from his experiences with the Dark Lady of the *Sonnets*.

But all difficulty vanishes when we realize that Shakespeare is handling the Troy story, not as told by Homer, but as told by mediæval writers, who had transformed it both in substance and in kind.[1] For this transformation there was an obvious reason. The Romans traced their establishment as a nation to the Trojans; so did other peoples of western Europe, including the French and the British — the descent of the latter from Brutus, the great-grandson of Æneas, who supposedly founded Troynovant (i.e., London) on the banks of the Thames, constituted one of the proudest chapters in the history of England as accepted in Shakespeare's time. Thus it was only natural for mediæval writers to glorify not the Greeks but the Trojans; and in doing so they represented the Trojan heroes as superior to the Greeks both in loftiness of soul and in military prowess; the Greeks — as the old proverb contemptuously declared — were all

---

[1] See H. E. Rollins, "The Troilus-Cressida Story, from Chaucer to Shakespeare," *Publications of the Modern Language Association of America*, xxxii (1917), 383.

liars, or at least deceitful, who triumphed over the nobler and more chivalrous Trojans through craft rather than valor. This biased view led to an early modification of the Homeric account of the siege of Troy, and the production of such versions as Dictys' *Ephemeris Belli Troiani*, of the second century of the Christian era, and Dares' *Historia de Excidio Troiæ*, of the sixth century, which became the chief authorities for mediæval writers. Moreover, in order further to glorify the exploits of a race destined to found the nations of western Europe, the legend was greatly expanded. For example, the Troilus and Cressida episode was added by the Frenchman Benoît de Sainte-More in his *Le Roman de Troie*, about 1184. At the same time the story underwent a profound transformation in character. The supernatural element, with the machinery of the gods from Olympus, was omitted, and for the atmosphere of classical times was substituted the atmosphere of the Middle Ages. The heroes of Troy became knights of chivalry, gleaming in mediæval armor, fighting in the service of their ladyloves, and observing the elaborate code of honor celebrated in romances.

Shakespeare, it should be remembered, was dealing with the legend as it was conceived by writers sympathetic with the Trojans, and as it was altered in character under the influence of chivalric romance. The sources of his play make this clear. The Troilus and Cressida episode, created by Benoît in the twelfth century, and retold by Guido della Colonna in his *Historia Destructionis Troiæ* (1287), had been selected for special treatment by Boccaccio in *Il Filostrato* (1341–46), whence it passed directly to Chaucer (1377–85). Shakespeare found it ready to his hand in Chaucer's telling; and for the details of the siege he made use of Caxton's translation (1475) of Raoul Lefevre's *Recueil des Histoires de Troie*, a work

based on Guido, and ultimately on Dictys and Dares.
It is true that he — or it may be the author of the old
play he was using — was familiar with Homer,[1] whence
he drew Thersites; yet Shakespeare was not at all concerned with the classical treatment of the theme; instead
he was attempting to dramatize a mediæval story well
known to his age.[2]

The bitterest criticism has been aimed at his supposed
debasement of the character of Cressida. But here again
he was merely following a well-established literary tradition. In the sixteenth-century editions of Chaucer,
which he naturally would use, there was added to *Troilus
and Creseyde* a sixth book written by Robert Henryson,
entitled *Testament of Creseid*, dealing with Cressida's life
after her infidelity to Troilus. Though not unsympa-
thetically treated, she is represented as having at last de-
generated into a common prostitute in the Greek camp,
finally stricken with a loathsome disease, and dying amid
miserable surroundings. And to the Elizabethans Cressida became the very type not only of fickleness in woman
but of absolute moral depravity.[3] The phrase "Cressid's
kind" was proverbial for a woman of ill fame. The traditional opinion of her may be illustrated by a passage
from the university poem, *Willobie his Avisa* (1594):

> Though shameless callets may be found
> That soil themselves in common field
> And can carry the whore's rebound,
> Yet here are none of Cressid's kind.

Pistol in *Henry V*, surely no scholar, merely echoes the
common opinion when he exclaims: "To the spital go,

[1] Not in Chapman's English rendering, for some details are drawn from
books of Homer not yet translated by Chapman.
[2] Heywood does the same thing in his *Iron Age*, which should be read by
every student of *Troilus and Cressida*.
[3] See, for example, Gascoigne's *Posies*, 1575. Chaucer prophesied as
much: see Book V, stanzas 151–52.

and from the powdering tub of infamy fetch forth the lazar kite of Cressid's kind."

Such, then, was the story as Shakespeare found it out-lined for him by tradition. And he used his material as he used the old chronicles in producing his historical plays; his task as a dramatist was merely to breathe into the personages the breath of life, and give to the incidents a logical motivation from character. Thus it is unnecessary to think with some scholars that he is attacking Chapman; or with others that he is satirizing Jonson under the name of Ajax — he found Ajax the comic character that he left him.[1] Still less need we suppose that in Cressida he is giving venomous expression to his disillusionment at womankind; for we make of the drama a poor thing indeed if we do not allow a great literary artist to portray so well-known and conventionalized a story without accusing him of dragging before the public his own more sordid experiences. We may be sure that the play has no more significance for the student of Shakespeare's life than his other plays.

When we turn from shallow hypotheses like these to the veritable records of his private life we discover that in May, 1602, he purchased from William and John Combe one hundred and seven acres of valuable arable land near Stratford, for which he paid the goodly sum of £320.[2] And a few months later, in September, 1602, he purchased a house with about a quarter of an acre of land, in the heart of the village and adjoining his estate of New Place. These purchases, together with his recent

[1] In the play Ajax is notable for corpulency; Jonson was at this time equally notable for the opposite. Dekker, in *Satiromastix* (1601), calls him a "pigmy," twice applies to him the adjective "little," and declares that the Roman poet "Horace was a goodly corpulent gentleman, and not so lean a hollow-cheekt scrag as thou art."

[2] In his absence the transaction was effected by his brother Gilbert: "Sealed and delivered to Gilbert Shakespeare, to the use of the within-named William Shakespeare."

inheritance from his father of two houses in Henley Street, made him now one of the largest property-owners in Stratford.

The inference from all this is plain. One cannot say enough in condemnation of that specious type of scholarship which seeks to disclose the life of so practical a man and objective a poet as Shakespeare by a closet examination of his plays. No doubt he put much of himself into his work, as every artist must do, and especially the dramatist; but he drew from his great store of wisdom and sympathy, not from his temporary moods and petty troubles. To say that when he set himself to the task of writing a tragedy he was necessarily in a misanthropic, or pessimistic, or melancholy state of soul, or ready to lay bare his private experiences, is as foolish as it is unjust. Yet the insistence of writers upon the "autobiographical importance" of *Troilus and Cressida* will not down; some have even declared that the interpretation of the play constitutes "the chief problem in Shakespeare." This common error alone justifies so long a discussion here of a play so little loved.

CHAPTER XIX

THE COMING OF JAMES; ROYAL FAVOR

THE rapidly failing health of the aged Queen caused most of the Court festivities to be omitted during the Christmas season of 1602–03. Elizabeth, indeed, had withdrawn from London to her palace at Richmond in search of quiet; yet on February 2, 1603, she summoned thither her favorite troupe, the Chamberlain's Men, to entertain her with a play. This proved to be the last time she was to call upon them. On March 19 the Privy Council, in view of her sinking condition, ordered the discontinuance of dramatic performances in the city; and on the morning of March 24, she quietly passed away at Richmond.

Many poets wrote tributes suitable to the memory of so great a Queen; but Shakespeare, in spite of the obvious favor she had always shown him and his troupe, maintained a complete silence. The fact did not escape comment. Henry Chettle, whom we met at the outset of the poet's career in London, now again crossing his path, expressed regret that the dramatist had forborne to —

> Drop from his honied Muse one sable tear
> To mourne her death that graced his desert,
> And to his laies opened her royal ear;

and with an obvious allusion to *Lucrece* he added the injunction:

> Shepherd, remember our Elizabeth,
> And sing her rape done by that Tarquin, Death.

A second writer, who remains anonymous, likewise reproved Shakespeare for his silence:

You Poets all, brave Shakespeare, Jonson, Greene,[1]
Bestow your time to write for England's Queene.
Lament, lament, lament, you English Peeres.

A third writer, "I. C., gent.," refers to the author of the poem just quoted:

As he that calde to Shakespeare, Jonson, Greene,
To write of their dead noble Queene.[2]

Shakespeare, however, refused to invoke his Muse, and allowed the death of the Queen who had so "gracèd his deserts" to pass, not only without the sable tear of a formal elegy, but without a single reference to her of any kind.[3] Perhaps, as has been suggested, he felt estranged from her as a result of her heartless treatment of Essex, and her long imprisonment of Southampton. If such were the case, his sincerity would keep him from any expression of pretended grief. And in justice to him it should be added that if he failed to lament the death of Elizabeth, he had the good taste to refrain from celebrating, as did so many ambitious poets, the accession of James.

The advent of James, however, was an event of the greatest moment to him and his fellows. The new sovereign arrived in London on May 7; ten days later he issued an order taking the Chamberlain's Men under his own patronage, and bestowing upon them the new title, "The King's Men." On May 19 he furnished them with a

[1] Since Robert Greene died in 1592, the writer must be referring to Thomas Greene, the leading comedian of the Earl of Worcester's Men, and a poet. He was, for example, the author of *A Poet's Vision and a Prince's Glorie*, 1603, a congratulatory poem to King James.

[2] The writer of this poem refers, not to Chettle, as Sir Sidney Lee thinks (*Life*, p. 374), but to the anonymous writer whose lines I have quoted. The anonymous writer was clearly referring to Thomas Greene, as I have indicated; but "I. C., gent.," not understanding this, supposed that he was referring to Robert Greene, long dead. Hence his jeer at the anonymous writer for craving "helpe of Spirits in their sleeping graves."

[3] There is no good reason for supposing that in Sonnet 107 he refers to her death. But even if he does, the reference is colorless. See above, p. 164.

formal Patent licensing them to act henceforth under his royal protection, "as well within their now usual house called the Globe, within our County of Surrey, as also within any town-halls, moot-halls, or other convenient places within the liberties and freedom of any other city, university town, or borough whatsoever within our said realms and dominions," and significantly declaring to all officers and others concerned: "What further favor you shall shew to these, our servants, for our sake, we shall take kindly at your hands." The Patent singled out nine players for special mention, and merely referred to the others as "the rest of their associates." The nine persons mentioned are noted in the following order:

> Lawrence Fletcher
> William Shakespeare
> Richard Burbage
> Augustine Phillips
> John Heminges
> Henry Condell
> William Slye
> Robert Armin
> Richard Cowley

Fletcher's name was placed first, not because he was the most distinguished actor, or occupied the highest position in the Globe company, but, it would seem, because he happened to be a favorite with King James, before whom he had often acted in Scotland, and under whose patronage he had recently served as leader of "His Majesty's Players";[1] James doubtless brought him to London, and added him to the new royal troupe. Thus the position of Shakespeare second in the list, above Burbage, Heminges, and the rest of the company, evinces his recognized importance in the Globe organization. By way of emolument, to each player there was granted an annual

[1] See J. T. Murray, *English Dramatic Companies*, i, 104, note 3; and Dibdin, *Annals of the Edinburgh Stage*, p. 21.

stipend of £3 6s. 8d., which was supplemented, of course, by the usual payments and "rewards" when the company acted at Court.[1]

Thus from now on Shakespeare and his fellows are known, not as The Chamberlain's Men, but as The King's Men, or His Majesty's Servants. They had the right to wear, and probably on all formal occasions did wear, the royal livery, consisting of scarlet doublet, hose, and cloak, with the King's arms and cognizance

ENTRY IN THE LORD CHAMBERLAIN'S BOOKS OF THE GRANT OF RED CLOTH TO THE KING'S COMPANY OF PLAYERS, MARCH, 1604

embroidered on the sleeve. Warrants were issued at regular intervals ordering such liveries "to be delivered unto His Majesty's Players . . . to each of them the several allowances of four yards of bastard scarlet for a

---

[1] This fact is revealed by a folio manuscript entitled "The Officers of England, Collected in Anno 1608," sold at the Anderson Galleries in New York, 1921. Under the entry "Players of Enterludes" we read: "The fee to every of them £3.6.8." That this fee prevailed in the days of Mary and Elizabeth we know from other records; see J. T. Murray, *English Dramatic Companies,* i, 3, and 4 (note 1).

cloak, and a quarter of a yard for crimson velvet for the capes," the total cost of each livery being £5 13s. 4d.[1]

Somewhat later, three other London troupes were likewise taken under the protection of the royal family. The Admiral's Men, who long had been the chief rivals of the Chamberlain's Men, were placed under the patronage of the youthful Prince Henry, then ten years of age, and received the new title The Prince's Men; the Worcester's organization was assigned to Her Majesty, and designated The Queen's Men;[2] and, finally, the child-actors at Blackfriars were put under the care of the Queen also, with the title The Children of Her Majesty's Revels. The Paul's Boys alone were not honored with royal favor.

Furthermore, King James, following a precedent established by Elizabeth, appointed the leading members of the King's Company, the Prince's Company, and the Queen's Company, to the honorary rank of Grooms of the Royal Chamber. This was a title of courtesy that carried some distinction for the holders; and on one occasion at least, as we shall see, the post required Shakespeare and his fellows to assist in the official entertainment of foreign ambassadors. Thus with the beginning of the new reign the actors, who had long suffered under the legal designation of "rogues," acquired a conspicuous, and we may suppose a grateful, recognition of the dignity of their profession.

On May 5, 1603, all the city companies had been ordered to cease playing "now at the King's coming"; but on May 9 the inhibition was lifted, and they were allowed to resume their performances before the public. His Majesty's Servants thereupon presented at the

[1] See Ernest Law, *Shakespeare as a Groom of the Royal Chamber*, 1910, pp. 39–40.

[2] This company had moved from the Rose to the Curtain; but, shortly after, it caused to be erected for itself a large new playhouse, The Red Bull, in keeping with its dignity as Her Majesty's Players.

Globe as a new play Jonson's Roman tragedy, *Sejanus His Fall*. That in the performance Shakespeare took one of the principal rôles Jonson himself tells us. Affixed to the 1616 folio edition of the play is the statement:

> This Tragœdie was first
> acted, in the yeere
> 1603.
> By the King's Maiesties
> Servants.
> The principall Tragœdians were,

Ric. Burbadge	Will. Shake-speare
Aug. Philips	Ioh. Heminges
Will. Sly	Hen. Condel
Ioh. Lowin	Alex. Cooke

By placing Shakespeare's name at the head of the second column Jonson gives it a significance almost equal to that of Burbage's. And it is just possible, though we cannot feel at all sure, that Shakespeare had a hand in the composition of some of the scenes.[1] When Jonson published the play he inserted a notice "To the Readers" saying: "I would inform you, that this book, in all numbers, is not the same with that which was acted on the public stage; wherein a second pen had good share: in place of which I have rather chosen to put weaker, and, no doubt, less pleasing, of mine own, than to defraud so happy a genius of his right by my loathed usurpation."

Perhaps one reason[2] why Jonson kept the name of his collaborator from being associated with the published work was the fact that the play on its presentation was unmercifully damned.[3] As Jonson himself states, it

---

[1] Some scholars, on no better evidence, think that Chapman was the man who assisted Jonson. The truth is, we do not know.

[2] There may be a second reason. Jonson told Drummond of Hawthornden that "he was called before the Council for his *Sejanus*," but whether as a result of its performance or of its publication is not clear.

[3] Not because it was poor as literature, for it is among Jonson's best tragedies, but, we may suspect, because its display of erudition made it caviar to the general.

"suffered no less violence from our people here than the subject of it did from the rage of the people of Rome." And Fennor wrote:

> They screwed their scurvy jaws, and looked **awry**,
> Like hissing snakes, adjudging it to die.

The failure of *Sejanus* must have meant a considerable pecuniary loss to the players. But they did not have long to concern themselves with either failure or success. The plague broke out in the city, and soon became so violent that on May 26, 1603, all theatres were closed, and the actors hurried into the country. We can trace the King's Men in their progress to Richmond, Bath, Coventry, Shrewsbury, and other towns.[1]

Nor were the players the only ones affected; the King was forced to defer indefinitely his formal entry into London. For a time he took up his residence at Wilton, the beautiful country-seat of the Earl of Pembroke, Shakespeare's friend and patron, to whom the actors dedicated the First Folio in recognition of his having "prosecuted" the author while alive "with so much favour." Thither the King's Men were summoned, and on December 2 they acted a play before His Majesty, receiving therefor £30. Shortly after this, the plague still raging in London, James moved his Court to Hampton. The King's Men went with him, and there presented six plays, on December 26, 27, 28, January 1, February 2, and February 18, receiving in payment £53. In addition, on February 8 the King gave Burbage as a "free gift" £30, "for the maintenance of himself and the rest of his company."

The plague at last beginning to subside, James announced his purpose of making his royal entrance into

---

[1] By October 21 they were back in London for a time; see W. W. Greg, *Henslowe Papers*, p. 59.

London on March 15, 1604. Great preparations were made to render this a magnificent spectacle. Triumphal arches were erected in the streets, and people crowded the thoroughfares from the Tower to Whitehall. To each of the leading members of the King's Company — Shakespeare's name heads the list, and Fletcher's is relegated to third place — were issued four-and-a-half yards of "red cloth" with which to make themselves suitable liveries "against His Majesties Royall Proceeding through the Citie." Extant documents do not note the presence of any actors in the procession; but the grant of liveries to the players was made for that specific occasion, and Shakespeare and his eight fellows may have taken part in it under their more dignified title of Grooms of the Royal Chamber.[1]

Three-and-a-half weeks later, on April 9, the Privy Council ordered the lifting of the ban against acting, and the King's Men resumed their regular performances before the public.[2]

The death of Elizabeth, the inhibition of acting, the advent of James, the plague, the traveling of the troupe, the long stay at Wilton and Hampton, the royal entry of James, and other such distractions naturally interfered with Shakespeare's production of new plays. Nevertheless, he seems to have found time to compose one comedy, *Measure for Measure*. For some reason, not easily comprehended, he had become interested in an early play by Whetstone, *Promos and Cassandra*, 1578, and had resolved to make use of its theme in a drama of his own. By way of preparation he studied both the ancient play and Whetstone's prose rendering of the same story in his *Heptameron of Civil Discourses*, 1582; and he also went

---

[1] In a document in the Record Office there are specially noted as present in the procession "Messengers of the Chamber," and other such officials.

[2] See W. W. Greg, *Henslowe Papers*, p. 61.

to Whetstone's original source and read the narrative in Geraldi Cinthio's *Hecatommithi*. Not content even with this, he seems to have examined Cinthio's untranslated Latin play, *Epitia*, from whence he drew the name Angelo. Out of these scattered materials he wrought *Measure for Measure*, delivering the manuscript to his actors in 1603 or early in 1604.[1]

Though technically a comedy, the play has none of the bright and cheerful atmosphere that we find in *As You Like It*, *Much Ado*, or *Twelfth Night;* and the genial humor embodied in Touchstone, Dogberry, and Malvolio is entirely wanting. Instead, the tone is sombre, and the plot concerns unpleasing, even sordid, aspects of human nature. Coleridge declares that it is the only play of Shakespeare's that we may actually call painful. Yet, in spite of a disagreeable theme, it is, like *Troilus and Cressida*, "a wonderful piece of work," which not to have read discredits any traveler in Shakespeare's dramatic world. Dowden is of the opinion that nowhere in Shakespeare "can greater speeches and scenes be found"; and Pater has admirably set forth its beauties in a glowing appreciation.

While reading Cinthio's *Hecatommithi* in preparation for his *Measure for Measure*, Shakespeare came upon the narrative of the Moor of Venice and Desdemona. Crude and horrible as the story was, he saw in it great dramatic possibilities, and he promptly worked it into his tragedy of *Othello*. The material never had been dramatized, and Shakespeare was thus able to mold the plot in accordance with his own theories of dramatic art. The result is what we might expect; as a model of tragic composition *Othello* is almost without a flaw. Landor places

---

[1] Allusions to James' dislike of crowds (I, i, 67–72; II, iv, 27–30), indicate that it was completed after the coming of that sovereign, and we know that it was performed at Court on December 26, 1604.

it at the summit of all creations of man's imagination; and Macaulay, in his enthusiasm, declared that it was perhaps the most perfect work of art in existence. If Shakespeare reached the apex of his popularity with theatre-goers by the production of *Hamlet*, he may be said to have reached the apex of his dramatic art in the production of *Othello*. And if for several years he had been groping through sordid material for the true effect of tragedy, he at last found it in the sweetness of Desdemona and the nobility of Othello.

The play doubtless was offered to the London audiences at the Globe in the autumn of 1604; we know that it was presented at Court before His Majesty on November 1 of that year. At once it took a powerful hold on the public; and Burbage, through his emotional interpretation of "the grieved Moor" thronged the theatre with applauding audiences.

Shortly after this Shakespeare and his fellows were called upon to close the Globe for a time, and, in their capacity as Grooms of the Royal Chamber, to assist in extending the hospitality of the Government to certain distinguished foreign visitors. In August, 1604, there arrived in London an Ambassador Extraordinary from the Court of Spain, with the high-sounding title "Don John de Velasco, Constable of Castile and Legion, Duke of the Citie of Fryas, Earle of Haro, Lord of the Townes of Villapano and Pedraca de la Syerra, Lord of the House of Velasco, and of the Seven Infants of Lara, Great Chamberlain unto Philip III King of Spain, Councellor of State, and Warre, and President of Italy." With him came also a special Ambassador from Archduke Albert of Austria; and the two ambassadors, we are told, were "accompanied with Marquesses, Earles, Barons, Knights, and Gentlemen to the number of one hundred persons." This notable commission was empowered by King

Philip III to negotiate a treaty of peace between Spain and the new English sovereign, a treaty much needed after years of animosity following the Armada, during which the two nations openly preyed on each other's commerce.

The Ambassador from the Archduke of Austria, with his retinue, was entertained at Durham House, in the Strand. The far more important Spanish Ambassador, with his suite, was lodged in Somerset House, one of the royal residences, and, next to Whitehall, the most splendid palace in London. To do honor to the visitors, the house was specially furnished with some of the most beautiful tapestries and other treasures in the possession of the Crown.[1]

To "wait and attend" on the Spanish guests, Shakespeare and eleven other members of the King's Company were ordered to take up residence at Somerset House in their capacity as Grooms of the Chamber. They were not to appear as actors at all,[2] but as Court officials, and they were expected merely to furnish courteous attendance on the foreign visitors. They began their residence at Somerset House on August 9, assisted in the welcome to the Spanish Ambassador upon his arrival there after a triumphal progress up the river, and throughout the next two weeks acted as grooms in waiting to the guests of the nation. Mr. Ernest Law describes them as "a group of twelve gentlemen in red doublets and hose, with cloaks of the same, embroidered in gold with the King's cypher crowned; and among these was one, more notable than the rest, who may well have been, then or later, pointed out to the Ambassador, a certain interesting individual, known to the King and all the Court.

---

[1] For an admirable account of the incidents briefly treated in this chapter, see Ernest Law, *Shakespeare as a Groom of the Chamber*, 1910.

[2] They gave no plays, nor was any attempt made to entertain the visitors with dramatic performances.

the intimate associate of several prominent nobles, one of His Majesty's Grooms of the Chamber, and the foremost poet and dramatist in England, no other, in fact, than William Shakespeare."

At the end of two weeks, the treaty having been completed and properly drawn up for the signatures of the contracting parties, the Ambassadors, with their followers, went in grand procession to Whitehall Palace, and there in the Chapel formally took oath with King James faithfully to observe all the articles agreed upon. This ceremony over, the King entertained the Ambassadors at a State dinner in the large Banqueting House.

Shakespeare, with his fellow Grooms of the Chamber, may — we cannot tell — have accompanied the Spanish Ambassador in the procession from Somerset House to Whitehall. He may, also, have been a witness to the signing of the treaty in the Chapel, and have helped in the service of the State dinner held with unusual splendor in the Banqueting House. This great structure, originally erected by Queen Elizabeth,[1] was admirably adapted to such spectacles as now took place there. Holinshed thus describes it in his *Chronicle*:

On the south-west side of Her Majesty's palace of Whitehall, made in manner and form of a long square three hundred thirty and two foot in measure about. . . . This house had two hundred ninety and two lights of glass. The sides within the same house were made with ten heights of degrees for people to stand upon; and in the top of this house was wrought most cunningly upon canvas works of ivy and holly, with pendants made of wicker rods, garnished with bay, rue, and all manner of strange flowers garnished with spangles of gold; as also beautified with hanging toseans made of holly and ivy, with all manner of strange fruits, as pomegranates, oranges, pompions, cucumbers, grapes, carrots, with such other like, spangled with gold, and most richly hanged. Betwixt these works of bays and

---

[1] See my *Shakespearean Playhouses*, pp. 385-87.

ivy were great spaces of canvas, which was most cunningly painted, the clouds with stars, the sun and sun-beams, with diverse other coats of sundry sorts belonging to the Queen's Majesty, most richly garnished with gold.

A description of the ceremonies which on this occasion took place in the Banqueting House has been preserved in a Spanish pamphlet printed in 1604.[1] A few excerpts will help us to understand the pomp with which the diplomats were entertained in London, and to visualize the scenes among which Shakespeare was now moving.

The audience-chamber was elegantly furnished, having a buffet of several stages filled with various pieces of ancient and modern gilt plate of exquisite workmanship. A railing was placed on each side of the room in order to prevent the crowd from approaching too near the table. At the right hand, upon entering, was another buffet containing rich vessels of gold, agate, and other precious stones. The table might be about five yards in length, and more than one yard broad. The dishes were brought in by gentlemen and servants of the King, who were accompanied by the Lord Chamberlain; and before placing them on the table they made four or five obeisances. The Earls of Pembroke and of Southampton officiated as gentlemen-ushers.

Their Majesties [the King and Queen] with the Prince [of Wales] entered after the Constable [of Spain] and the others, and placed themselves at their throne, and all stood in a line to hear the grace said, the Constable being at the King's side, the Count de Villamediana on the Queen's.

Their Majesties washed their hands in the same basin, the Lord Treasurer handing the towel to the King, and the High Admiral to the Queen. The Prince washed in another basin, in which water was also taken to the Constable, who was waited upon by the same gentlemen. They took their seats.... The principal noblemen of the Kingdom were likewise at the table. ... There was plenty of instrumental music, and the banquet was sumptuous and profuse.

---

[1] Reprinted in W. B. Rye, *England as Seen by Foreigners*, 1865, pp. 118 ff.

The first thing the King did was to send the Constable a melon, and half a dozen of oranges on a very green branch, telling him that they were the fruit of Spain transplanted into England. To which the latter, kissing his hand, replied that he valued the gift more as coming from His Majesty than as being the fruit of his own country. He then divided the melon with Their Majesties, and Don Blasco de Aragon handed the plate to the Queen, who politely and graciously acknowledged the attention. Soon afterwards the King stood up, and, with his head uncovered, drank to the Constable the health of Their Spanish Majesties. . . .

Immediately afterwards, the Constable, seeing that another opportunity might not be afforded him, rose and drank to the King the health of the Queen, from the lid of a cup of agate of extraordinary beauty and richness, set with diamonds and rubies, praying His Majesty would condescend to drink the toast from the cup, which he did accordingly . . . and the Constable directed that the cup should remain in His Majesty's buffet. At this period the people shouted out: *Peace, peace, peace! God save the King! God save the King!* . . . The Constable rose a second time, and drank to the Queen the health of the King, from a very beautiful dragon-shaped cup of crystal, garnished with gold, drinking from the cover; and the Queen standing up gave the pledge from the cup itself.

The dinner, prolonged in this fashion, lasted "about three hours," with the drinking of many healths, and the making of speeches. At last —

The cloth having been removed, every one immediately rose up; the table was placed upon the ground, and Their Majesties standing upon it, proceeded to wash their hands.

The dinner was followed by a grand ball:

In the mean time dancing had begun in the said chamber. . . . There were present at this ball more than fifty ladies of honour, very richly and elegantly dressed, and extremely beautiful, besides many others who, with the noblemen and gentlemen that were present at the dinner, were already engaged in dancing. After a little while the Prince [Henry, aged ten] was commanded by his parents to dance a galliard, and they pointed out to him the lady who was to be his partner; and this he did with much sprightliness and modesty, cutting several capers in the course of the dance. The Earl of Southampton then led out the Queen, and three other gentlemen their several partners, who all joined in dancing a *brando*. In another, Her Majesty danced with the Duke of Lennox. After this they began a galliard, which in Italy is called a *planton;* and in it a lady led out the Prince, who then led out another lady whom Their Majesties pointed out to him. After this a *brando* was danced; and that being over, the Prince stood up for a *correnta*, which he did very gracefully.

At the conclusion of the dancing, which followed immediately after dinner, certain outdoor entertainments were provided:

Hereupon the ball ended, and all then took their places at the windows of the room which looked out upon a square, where a platform was raised, and a vast crowd had assembled to see the King's bears fight with greyhounds. This afforded great amusement. Presently a bull, tied to the end of a rope, was fiercely baited by dogs. After this certain tumblers came, who danced upon a rope, and performed various feats of agility and skill on horseback.

This concluded the entertainments provided for the guests of the nation:

Their Majesties now retired, being accompanied by the Constable and the other noblemen to their apartment; before entering which, many compliments passed on both sides, and Their Majesties and the Prince shook hands with the Constable and the Count; and the other Spanish cavaliers kissed hands and took their departure. The Constable and the others upon quitting the ball-room were accompanied by the Lord Chamberlain to the farthest room, and by the Earl of Devonshire and other gentlemen to their coaches; more than fifty halberdiers lighting them with torches until they reached home.

Shakespeare's duties, however, were not yet over. The next morning "the Constable awoke with a slight attack of lumbago," which kept him in bed several days, during which time His Majesty called to see him. At last, on August 27, after James had bidden him a formal farewell, he took his departure for Spain; and Shakespeare and his fellows were able to return to their ordinary business of acting plays.

In return for their services the government paid them the sum of £21 12s. This, of course, was supplemented by various perquisites, and by the special gifts of the Spanish Constable. Stow in his *Chronicle* observes that the Constable upon his departure "gave very bountifully unto all that attended him." We should like to know what present the Spanish Ambassador bestowed on the most distinguished member of the little group that entertained him. Mr. Law has suggested that perhaps it was the "broad silver-gilt bowl" which the dramatist left in his will to his younger daughter Judith. It seems, however, quite as likely to have been the sword which he bequeathed to Thomas Combe, the wealthiest and most aristocratic gentleman he numbered among his friends in the later years of his retirement at Stratford. Apparently this weapon was one of the poet's finest and most cherished possessions, a genuine Toledo blade, we may suppose, with an ornate and jeweled hilt — as he writes in *Othello* (which he may even then have been composing),

A sword of Spain, the ice-brook's temper.

On November 1, in the great Banqueting House just described, Shakespeare and his fellows presented *Othello* before His Majesty. This initiated for the King's Men a period of remarkable popularity at Court, unprecedented in theatrical history. During the Christmas season that followed they were called upon to present no fewer than eleven plays before the royal family; and from this time on their performances at Whitehall far

utnumbered those of all the other troupes combined.
thello, however, was the only play acted in the Ban-
ueting House. That great building, though admirably
uited for State functions, was entirely too large for
rivate dramatic entertainments at which only the royal
amily and a limited number of invited guests were to be
resent. Accordingly, for subsequent plays James made
se of the "Great Hall" of the palace, a room approxi-
ately ninety feet in length and forty feet in breadth.
here, on November 4, the King's Men gave *The Merry
Vives of Windsor*, on December 26, *Measure for Measure*,
nd on December 28, *The Comedy of Errors*.

On New Year's Day the King was to be entertained
y the Children of the Queen's Revels with Chapman's
ll Fools, and on Twelfth Day with a grand masque.
But at some date before the masque was to be held, that
s "between New Year's Day and Twelfth Day," the
Queen expressed a desire to see a play, and Sir William
Cope on short notice was charged with the duty of fur-
ishing Her Majesty with a suitable performance. The
laborate preparations then being made for the produc-
ion of the masque at Whitehall probably rendered a
ramatic entertainment there impossible, so that Cope
ad to arrange for a performance in the private home of
ome nobleman. He sent for Burbage, and requested him
o have the King's Men present a "new play" before the
Queen. Burbage, after informing him that the King's
Men had no new play which the Queen had not seen,
ecommended *Love's Labour's Lost*, which was just being
evived, and which he felt sure would please Her Majesty.
Cope took Burbage's advice, and promptly dispatched
im with a letter to Lord Cranborne, the King's Secre-
ary, for further directions. The letter is as follows:

SIR, — I have sent and been all this morning hunting for
layers, jugglers, and such kind of creatures, but find them

hard to find; wherefore, leaving notes for them to seek me, Bu
bage is come, and says there is no new play that the Queen ha
not seen, but they have revived an old one called *Love's L*
bour's Lost, which for wit and mirth, he says, will please her e
ceedingly. And this is appointed to be played to-morrow nig
at my Lord of Southampton's, unless you send a writ to remo
the *corpus cum causa* to your house in Strand. Burbage is m
messenger ready attending your pleasure.

Yours most humbly,
WALTER COPE.[1]

Whether the play was acted at Southampton's hous
or at Cranborne's house in the Strand, does not appear
but that it was acted somewhere is shown by an entr
(not hitherto understood) in the *Revells Booke An° 160*
"Between New Year's Day and Twelfth Day, a play
Love's Labour's Lost, by His Majesty's Players."

The masque out of the way, on January 7 the King
Men presented *Henry V*, on January 8, *Every Man o*
of his Humor, on February 2, *Every Man in his Humo*
on February 10, *The Merchant of Venice*, on February 1
The Spanish Maz, and on February 12, *The Merchant*
Venice (repeated by special command of the King).

The superiority of the Globe company over the oth
London companies is demonstrated by the fact tha
during this Christmas season of unusual Court revel
the Prince's Men were not called upon at all, and tl
Queen's Men and the Children of Blackfriars were calle
upon for but one play each, whereas the King's Me
were called upon for no fewer than eleven performance
Furthermore, the supremacy of Shakespeare over a

---

[1] The letter is endorsed "1604" (i.e., 1604–05), but without month or da

[2] Cope's letter is vague; perhaps we should not entirely ignore the pos
bility that the actors had been engaged by Southampton to entertain hims
and his private guests on the very evening when the Queen desired a pla
and that a writ from the King's Secretary was needed to cancel that engag
ment and remove the play to Cranborne's house. The probabilities, ho
ever, favor the interpretation I have given above.

ther playwrights is shown by the choice of his plays for ight representations before the royal family, as compared with two by Jonson, one by Heywood, of the Queen's Company, and one by Chapman, of the Blackfriars Company.

During the following Christmas season, the King's Men presented ten plays before Their Majesties. And between 1603 and 1616, although our records are incomplete, we know of at least one hundred and eighty-seven occasions on which Shakespeare's troupe was summoned to give performances at the Court.[1] This extraordinary popularity of the King's Company was almost wholly due to Shakespeare, and constitutes a remarkable testimony to the reputation he enjoyed in his own lifetime. Well might Jonson write:

> Sweet Swan of Avon, what a sight it were
> To see thee in our waters yet appear,
> And make those flights upon the banks of Thames
> That so did take Eliza and our James!

In *Othello* Shakespeare had worked with material never before cast into the dramatic mold; in his next effort he was content to revamp an old play that already had served its turn in entertaining London audiences. *King Leir*, for so the old play was called, was probably in existence before the plague of 1592–94; Henslowe records its performance by the Queen's and Sussex' Men in April, 1594, at which time it is not marked by him as new. As a result of the disastrous years of the plague the original manuscript, which belonged to the Queen's Men, was sold to a publisher, who duly entered it in the Stationers' Registers on May 14, 1594. So far as we know, however, it was not then printed, and it sinks out of view until May 8, 1605, when it was again entered in the

[1] I take the figures from an unpublished doctoral dissertation by Miss Mary Steele.

Stationers' Registers, and shortly after was published with the title *The True Chronicle History of King Leir and his three daughters, Gonorill, Ragan, and Cordella.*[1] I seems likely that Shakespeare bought a copy of the old play, and, seeing in it possibilities of an effective tragedy at once set about rewriting it for his company.[2] There i some evidence that he was engaged on the task in th autumn of 1605; for example, the allusion to the eclipse may refer to the eclipse of October, and certain passage are supposed to relate to the Gunpowder Plot in Novem ber of this year.

As was his custom, Shakespeare was not content with examining merely the old play, but went directly to the account of King Lear in Holinshed's *Chronicle;* and h also read the story as told by Spenser in *The Faeri Queene.* Moreover, in handling the theme he exercise much originality, as instanced by the facts that in spit of all his sources he gives to his tragedy an unhappy ending, that from his own creative imagination he drew the figure of the Fool, and that he added the importan sub-plot of Gloucester, which he found in Sidney's *Arca dia.* Yet the old play seriously handicapped him, for it story was disjointed, its action rambling, and its theme essentially epic in nature, ill-suited to dramatic treat ment. It was indeed a poor bottle to contain the fine new vintage of Shakespeare's brain. But if *Lear* is defective in those qualities of technique which make *Othello* almost flawless, in other respects it is one of the noblest achieve ments of the poet's genius; indeed, it is so well loved that many scholars call it his greatest play.

[1] H. Dugdale Sykes, in *Sidelights on Shakespeare*, 1919, pp. 126–42, give strong evidence for the belief that the author was George Peele.

[2] There is, of course, the other possibility, that the play had actually bee printed in 1594, and that the republication in 1605 was occasioned by the ap pearance of Shakespeare's popular revision; but this seems the less likely for if the play already existed in printed form, the publishers of 1605 woul hardly have entered it again in the Stationers' Registers.

In all probability it was acted before the public at the Globe throughout most of 1606; we know that it was performed at Whitehall on December 26 of that year to open a brilliant Christmas season in which the King's Men were called upon to appear at Court many times.

The favor James so obviously showed to the Globe actors led Shakespeare next to write for them a play that would be a graceful compliment to their royal master, and at the same time familiarize Englishmen with the Scottish ancestors of the new sovereign. Accordingly, drawing his material from Holinshed's *Chronicle of Scotch History*, he dramatized the reign of Macbeth,[1] with special emphasis on the "noble Banquo," founder of the Stuart dynasty. In one scene James himself is represented — in the vision of Kings descended from Banquo, carrying "two-fold balls and treble sceptres" as Kings of England and Scotland, and rulers of England, Scotland, and Ireland. In various other ways, too, Shakespeare paid deference to the tastes of the new sovereign, or flattered his idiosyncrasies; for example, in the representation of the evil power of witches, the description of the King's ability to heal by touch, and the allusion to the Gunpowder Plot.

The evidence clearly points to the conclusion that *Macbeth* was put on the stage of the Globe in 1606; and it seems to have attained at once the popularity it now enjoys among playgoers. In 1610 the well-known astrologer, Dr. Simon Forman, attended a performance of it at the Globe, and made certain notes regarding it in his Diary:

In Mackbeth at the Glob, 1610, ♄ the 20 of Aprill, ther was to be observed, firste howe Mackbeth and Bancko,[2] 2 noble men

---

[1] In Kempe's *Nine Days' Wonder*, 1600, there is an allusion to an earlier play on this subject, but of this play nothing else is known.

[2] The spelling "Bancko" probably indicates Shakespeare's pronunciation of the name.

of Scotland, ridinge thorowe a wod, the[r] stode before them
women feiries or nimphes, and saluted Mackbeth, sayinge
tyms unto him, Haille Mackbeth, King of Codon; for tho
shalt be a kinge, but shalt beget no kinge, &c. Then sai
Bancko, What, all to Mackbeth and nothing to me? Yes, sai
the nimphes, Haille to thee, Banko, thou shalt beget kinges
yet be no kinge.

The statement that Macbeth and Banquo came upo
the stage "riding through a wood" shows the way i
which the play was then staged. No doubt there was a
actual scenic representation of a forest; and it is quit
likely that both men appeared on horseback.[1] Forma
also reveals the fact that Banquo's ghost had objectiv
existence:

The next night, beinge at supper with his noblemen whom h
had bid to a feaste, to the which also Banco should have com
he began to speake of Noble Banco, and to wish that he we
ther. And as he thus did, standing up to drincke a carouse t
him, the ghoste of Banco came and sate down in his cheier be
hind him. And he turninge about to sit down again, sawe th
goste of Banco, which fronted him so that he fell into a grea
passion of fear and fury.

Forman's minute details of the position and movemen
of the personages are of interest as indicating the Eliza
bethan mode of acting the scenes. In the course of hi
notes he gives a long and on the whole accurate summar
of the plot, closing with the paragraph:

Observe also howe Mackbetes quen did rise in the night in
her slepe, and walke and talked, and confessed all, and the doc
tor noted her wordes.

---

[1] Middleton, in *The Mayor of Queenborough*, makes one of the players say:
"We have a play wherein we use a horse." In *Summer's Last Will and Testament* occurs the stage-direction: "Enter Bacchus riding upon an ass." In
The Witches of Lancashire appear the directions: "Enter drum beating before, Skimington and his wife on a horse ... Parnell pulls Skimington off the
horse." Illustrations might be multiplied. In some cases a hobby-horse
of canvas might have been used, but not in all cases, nor is it likely to have
been used in this case.

No doubt the play was among those presented at Court during the Christmas season of 1606–07, if not on an earlier special occasion. Celebrating as it did James' ancestry, and catering to his tastes, it must have proved highly gratifying to that vain monarch. We should like to know the circumstances under which it was performed at Whitehall, but no record of the event has been preserved. Was it the subject of the letter which, according to a well-founded tradition, His Majesty is said to have addressed to the dramatist? In the Preface to Lintot's edition of *Shakespeare's Poems*, 1709, appears the statement: "King James the First was pleased, with his own hand, to write an amicable letter to Mr. Shakespeare; which letter, though now lost, remained long in the hands of Sir William Davenant, as a credible person, now living, can testify." The "credible person" referred to was, in all probability, the Duke of Buckingham, who died in 1721. We find in his commonplace-book the following statement: "King James the First honoured Shakespeare with an epistolary correspondence, and I think Sir William Davenant had either seen or was possessed of His Majesty's letter to him." And Oldys, in a marginal note to his copy of Fuller's *Worthies*, states that the Duke of Buckingham told Lintot he had seen it in the possession of Davenant.

CHAPTER XX

PERSONAL AFFAIRS, 1602–07

WHEN we think of the high position Shakespeare had now attained in theatrical, literary, and courtly circles, and call to mind the handsome country home he had provided for himself and his family in Stratford, we naturally wonder where he lived while in London. As we have already seen, in the nineties he was residing, possibly with his wife and children, in the Parish of St. Helen's, where he supported an establishment of some dignity, if we are to judge by comparative assessments. In 1596, however, he seems to have sent his family back to Stratford, and to have taken lodgings on the Bankside, near his fellow-actors Pope and Phillips. In 1601 or 1602 he moved again, this time securing rooms in the home of a French Huguenot named Christopher Mountjoy in Silver Street.[1] One may indulge in the pleasant speculation that he was informed of this lodging by his printer friend Richard Field, who was closely associated with the French Huguenots in London. The Vautrollier printing house had a special license to employ six foreign printers, who most naturally would be Frenchmen. Moreover, Field had married a French widow, Jacqueline Vautrollier, who through her association with the Huguenot church would come to know the Mountjoys. And in or shortly before 1600 Field himself had moved to Wood Street, where he was living as a near neighbor to this French family.

[1] For this information we are indebted to the researches of Professor C. W. Wallace. See his article, "Shakespeare and His London Associates," in *University Studies*, Lincoln, Nebraska, x, 261, where the significant documents are printed; and cf. his popular article in *Harper's Magazine* for March, 1910.

Christopher Mountjoy was born at Cressy, France, and came to England with the flight of the Huguenots after the Massacre of St. Bartholomew. He early settled in Silver Street, where he plied his trade as a tire-maker, or manufacturer of head-dress for women. His house was a large one — we are told that, after the death of his wife and the marriage of his only child, it was "divided into two tenements" — standing on the north-east corner of Mugwell (now Monkwell) and Silver Streets. On the opposite corner was Neville's Inn, a "great house," says Stow, "builded of stone and timber, now called the Lord Windsor's House, of old time belonging to the Nevilles." Close by was the Barber-Surgeons' Hall, and the Church of St. Olaf's. Stow describes Silver Street as having "diverse fair houses"; and it was one of the more respectable residence sections of London. The hairdressing shop was on the ground floor, as was customary, and the lodgings on the upper floors.[1]

Mountjoy seems to have done a thriving business. Not only were both he and his wife industrious in their craft, but they had at least two apprentices whose names we know, and may have employed others. Their only child, Mary, also, was required to work in the shop with the apprentices, by which means she was, in the words of her father, brought "to a good perfection" in the trade. The reputation the establishment enjoyed among women of fashion in London is possibly indicated by the following allusion in Jonson's *Silent Woman* (IV,ii, 94–95):

All her teeth were made i' the Blackfriars, both her eyebrows in the Strand, and her hair in Silver Street.

Mountjoy was thus a tradesman of means; we are in-

[1] Ben Jonson lived for a time "without Temple Barre, at a combemaker's shop," according to Aubrey.

formed that he was "amongst his neighbors thought to be a sufficient man in estate, and ability." [1]

In one or more rooms on the upper floors of Mountjoy's house Shakespeare found lodgings, apparently from 1601–02 until 1606–07, or during the golden period of his career as playwright. In many ways the location was admirable for him. It was near the heart of the city, and within a short walk of St. Paul's Cathedral, the home of the book-trade, and the general meeting-place of all Londoners. He must have spent much time haunting Paul's Churchyard, where he could search out the newest books as they came fresh from the press or were imported from the Continent; and in the great "Mediterranean Isle" of the Cathedral, Duke Humphrey's Walk, as it was popularly called, he could greet his friends, or study human nature as it exhibited its foibles, from the lowest classes grouped about the servingmen's pillar, to the silken gulls strutting up and down in outlandish costumes. [2]

In still another way his residence with the Mountjoys may have proved advantageous to him. The entire establishment was made up of persons born in France, who spoke among themselves their native tongue. Since Shakespeare doubtless already possessed a fair reading knowledge of French, it seems likely that he availed himself of the chance to acquire some facility in speaking the language as well. Perhaps young Mary Mountjoy helped him, with the aid of some beginner's manual of conversation he had bought in Paul's Churchyard. In

---

[1] It may be of some interest to readers to know that in the Subsidy Rolls, 1599 and 1600, he was assessed £5 on his goods, the same sum that Shakespeare was assessed while a householder in the Parish of St. Helen's. But, as he was an alien, the rate of his assessment was double that applied to Shakespeare.

[2] For a vivid account of the stir of life in St. Paul's see Thomas Dekker, *The Gul's Hornbook*, 1609.

Henry V there is an amusing scene which may be applied to his halting efforts:

> *Kath.* Alice, tu as esté en Angleterre, et tu parles bien le langage.
> *Alice.* Un peu, madame.
> *Kath.* Je te prie, m'enseignez: il faut que j'apprenne à parler. Comment appellez vous la main en Anglois?
> *Alice.* La main? elle est appellée de hand.
> *Kath.* De hand. Et les doigts?

We can easily imagine the great poet saying to Mary, "Je te prie, m'enseigne." And we may suppose that he learned rapidly, for with his quick wits, his retentive memory, and his earlier acquired ability to read the language, he might soon attain facility in conversing with members of the household in which he now was living.

Before long his kindly interest in the family led him to play the rôle of match-maker on behalf of Mary. The author of *Romeo and Juliet*, as we might expect, did not fail in his efforts; but the course of the love-affair he engineered not running smooth, he was later haled into court, and made to serve as a witness in the Mountjoy family quarrels.

This introduces to us another lodger in the Silver Street home, the none too romantic hero of the love-match, Stephen Belott. About 1594 an Englishman, Humphrey Fludd (in 1612 described as "one of the King's trumpetors"), while in France married a French widow named Belott. After his return to London, in 1597, he put his young stepson, Stephen Belott, to board with the Mountjoys; and a year later, in 1598, signed him as an apprentice in the shop to learn the trade of tire-making. The young apprentice, as Shakespeare himself tells us, "did well and honestly behave himself," and proved to be "a very good and industrious servant"; indeed he became so excellent a workman that his service was said to be "to the great profit and advantage" of Mountjoy. Moreover, he demeaned himself in such a way that his master bore towards him "great good will and affection."

At the end of six years, in 1604, having completed the term of his apprenticeship, and being "desirous" of seeing the world, he went "to travel into Spain." Returning in a short time from this journey, he began to work again in the Silver Street establishment, but now with a fixed stipend. Mountjoy became so pleased with Stephen as a workman that he made up his mind that his only daughter, Mary, should marry him, and even went so far as vehemently to declare in Shakespeare's presence that if she refused to marry Stephen she "should not cost him, nor have a groat from him." [1] Stephen tells us that he was "moved and earnestly solicited" by both Monsieur and Madame Mountjoy "to consent to his marriage of their daughter." But in spite of their earnest solicitations he held off, though, as a serving-woman then employed in the house testified, "there was a show of good-will between" the young people, which the mother "did give countenance unto." Matters halting thus, Madame Mountjoy, so the servant further declares, "did send and persuade one Mr. Shakespeare, that lay in the house, to persuade the plaintiff [Stephen] to the same marriage." Similar testimony was given by a near neighbor and friend, Daniel Nicholas, the son of Sir Ambrose Nicholas:

This deponent sayeth he heard one, William Shakespeare, say that the defendant [Mountjoy] did bear a good opinion of the plaintiff [Stephen], and affected him well when he served him; and did move the plaintiff by him, the said Shakespeare, to have a marriage between his daughter, Mary Mountjoy, and the plaintiff; and for that purpose sent him, the said Shake-

---

[1] For evidence that Shakespeare was responsible for this statement, see Wallace, "Shakespeare and His London Associates," pp. 286, 288.

speare, to the plaintiff to persuade the plaintiff to the same, as Shakespeare told him, this deponent.

Upon various promises of Mountjoy relating to the dowry, transmitted through Shakespeare, Stephen at last agreed to consider the match. But being a shrewd man of business, he requested Daniel Nicholas and Nicholas' wife to interview Shakespeare, in order later, if necessary, to serve as witnesses to the details of the contract. The visit Nicholas and his wife made to Shakespeare is thus described by Nicholas himself:

This deponent sayeth that the plaintiff [Stephen] did request him, this deponent, to go with his wife to Shakespeare to understand the truth, how much and what the defendant [Mountjoy] did promise to bestow on his daughter in marriage with him the plaintiff; who did so. And asking Shakespeare thereof, he answered that he [Mountjoy] promised if the plaintiff [Stephen] would marry with Mary, his, the defendant's, only daughter, he, the defendant, would, by his promise, as he [Nicholas] remembered, give the plaintiff with her in marriage about the sum of fifty pounds in money, and certain household stuff.

According to Stephen, however, Mountjoy promised to give him "threescore pounds, or thereabouts, for a portion," and "would likewise, at the time of his decease, leave unto" Stephen and his wife "the sum of two hundred pounds more." Shakespeare could not remember the precise sums of money Mountjoy had promised to pay. His account of what happened, as taken down by the court scribe in 1612, may be quoted in full.

William Shakespeare, of Stratford-upon-Avon, in the County of Warwick, gentleman, of the age of xlviii years, or thereabouts, sworn and examined the day and year abovesaid, deposeth and sayeth:

1. To the first interrogatory, this deponent sayeth he knoweth the parties, plaintiff and defendant, and hath known them

both, as he now remembereth, for the space of ten years or thereabouts.

2. To the second interrogatory this deponent sayeth he did know the complainant [Stephen] when he was servant with the defendant [Mountjoy], and that during the time of his, the complainant's, service with the said defendant, he, the said complainant, to this deponent's knowledge, did well and honestly behave himself; but to this deponent's remembrance he hath not heard the defendant [Mountjoy] confess that he had got any great profit and commodity by the service of the said complainant. But this deponent sayeth he verily thinketh that the said complainant [Stephen] was a very good and industrious servant in the said service. And more he cannot depose to the said interrogatory.

3. To the third interrogatory this deponent sayeth that it did evidently appear that the said defendant [Mountjoy] did, all the time of the said complainant's service with him, bear and show great good will and affection towards the said complainant [Stephen]; and that he hath heard the defendant [Mountjoy] and his wife diverse and sundry times say and report that the said complainant was a very honest fellow. And this deponent sayeth that the said defendant [Mountjoy] did make a motion unto the complainant [Stephen] of marriage with the said Mary in the bill mentioned, being the said defendant's sole child and daughter, and willingly offered to perform the same if the said complainant should seem to be content and well like thereof. And further this deponent sayeth that the said defendant's wife did solicit and entreat this deponent to move and persuade the said complainant [Stephen] to effect the said marriage; and accordingly this deponent did move and persuade the complainant thereunto. And more to this interrogatory he cannot depose.

4. To the fourth interrogatory this deponent sayeth that the defendant [Mountjoy] promised to give the said complainant [Stephen] a portion [1] in marriage with Mary his daughter, but what certain portion he remembereth not, nor when to be paid,[2] nor knoweth that the defendant [Mountjoy] promised the

---

[1] After this word appears the phrase "of money and goods," stricken out in the original. Possibly when Shakespeare looked over the clerk's summary of his testimony before signing it, he caused this to be omitted.

[2] Following this word appears the phrase "if any sum were promised," stricken out in the original, possibly at Shakespeare's instigation.

plaintiff [Stephen] two hundred pounds with his daughter **Mary** at the time of his decease; but sayeth that the plaintiff [Stephen] was dwelling with the defendant in his house, and they had amongst themselves many conferences about their marriage,[1] which afterwards was consummated and solemnized. And more he cannot depose.

5. To the fifth interrogatory this deponent sayeth he can say nothing touching any part or point of the same interrogatory, for he knoweth not what implements and necessaries of household stuff the defendant gave the plaintiff in marriage with his daughter Mary.

WILLM SHAKP.[2]

Such were the preliminary negotiations, which, as it appears, proved satisfactory to both Stephen and Mary. "In regard Mr. Shakespeare had told them that they should have a sum of money for a portion from the father, they were made sure by Mr. Shakespeare, by giving their consent, and agreed to marry [giving each other's hand to the hand (stricken out in the original)], and did marry" — on November 19, 1604, in the adjacent Church of St. Olaf's, in Silver Street. Shakespeare the matchmaker, we may suppose, was present, or at least took some part in the festivities of the day.

Shrewd old Mountjoy planned that Stephen and Mary should thereafter "continue and work in their trade to the benefit" of the paternal establishment. He later declared that he made the payment of the dowry dependent upon two years of service by both the groom and the bride. But to his distress, at the end of "half a year or thereabouts," Stephen and his wife left the Silver Street house, engaged an apprentice of their own, and started a rival tire-shop to their "better preferment." Mountjoy thereupon bestowed upon the young married

[1] Obviously at some of these Shakespeare was present. French was probably used.

[2] Shakespeare was required to sign the clerk's summary of his testimony after reading it over for possible errors.

people certain "household stuff," indifferently valued by outsiders at £5, and scornfully itemized by Stephen as follows: "One old featherbed; one old feather bolster; a flock bolster; a thin green rug;[1] two ordinary blankets, woven; two pairs of sheets; a dozen of napkins of coarse diaper; two short table-cloths; six short towels, and one long one; an old drawing-table; two old joined stools; one wainscot cubbard; one twisting wheel of wood; two pairs of little scissors; one old trunk, and a like old trunk; one bobbin box." Mountjoy also presented them with "ten pounds of ready money to put into their purse." Beyond this, however, the father, though a man of some means, was not disposed to be generous to the young couple, either then or later. One witness testified that "he hath often heard Mary, the defendant's wife, often in her life time urge her husband, the defendant, to give something more unto the plaintiff [Stephen] and his wife than he had done before; whereunto the defendant, Mountjoy, would commonly answer her that he would not promise them anything, because he knew not what he should need himself."

Stephen and his young wife, thus abandoning the parental roof, moved to the parish of St. Sepulchre's, and secured lodgings in the house of one George Wilkins. It is quite possible that this was the playwright[2] who wrote for the Globe actors *The Miseries of Enforced Marriage*, and who, it is almost certain, was the main author of *Pericles* and, as some scholars think, the collaborator in *Timon of Athens*. The evidence is too doubtful to warrant any conclusion, yet we should like to believe that the poet, still taking an interest in the wel-

[1] I.e., a table-cover.

[2] In the legal document Wilkins is described as victualer, or innkeeper, which may have been then, or earlier, his chief occupation. Such legal descriptions mean little; for example, the great Globe actor, John Heminges, describes himself in his will as "citizen and grocer of London."

fare of the young people he had induced to marry, directed them to the home of one of his friends.

In May of this year, 1605, Shakespeare and the other members of his troupe suffered a great personal loss in the death of Augustine Phillips, who had been associated with the company since its organization, and was one of the original builders of the Globe. He enjoyed an enviable reputation as an actor,[1] and seems also to have been a musician of some accomplishment (in his will he disposes of his "base viall, citterne, bandore, and lute"). In official records he was dignified with the title "gentleman," and, as we have already seen, he had secured from the College of Heralds a coat of arms. For many years his home had been on the Bankside just a few steps from the Globe, where, no doubt, Shakespeare often enjoyed his hospitality. Like most of the King's Men he acquired considerable wealth.[2] Shortly before he died he purchased an estate at Mortlake, in Surrey, more in keeping with his dignity, and directed that his body be buried there, "in the chauncell of the parish church." In his will, of which Heminges and Burbage were the executors, he left sums of money to several of his friends for the purpose of buying memorial rings. It is significant that he mentions Shakespeare first: "Item, I give and bequeathe to my fellow, William Shakespeare, a thirty shilling piece in gold." He left the same sums to Christopher Beeston, now a member of the Queen's Company, and to Henry Condell, and lesser sums to the other full-sharers in the Globe organization. Nor did he forget even the hirelings, to whom he gave £5, "to be equally distributed amongst them." His will is an interesting document, revealing a

[1] See Thomas Heywood, *Apology for Actors*, 1612, edition of 1841, p. 43.
[2] See his will, reproduced in full by J. P. Collier, *Memoirs of the Principal Actors in the Plays of Shakespeare*, 1846, pp. 85–88.

generous and high-minded character that compels our admiration.

Two months later, on July 24, 1605, Shakespeare executed the most important business transaction of his life: for the sum of £440 he purchased the lease of a large portion of the tithes of Stratford, Old Stratford, Bishopton, and Welcombe. Abraham Sturley had suggested a purchase of this nature as early as 1598, with the significant comment, "It obtained would advance him indeed." The tithes were originally the property of the ecclesiastical members of the College at Stratford. In 1544 they had been leased for a period of ninety-two years to a certain William Barker. After the dissolution of the College in 1553 King Edward had granted the tithes to the Corporation of Stratford, subject, however, to the ninety-two year lease just mentioned.[1] Barker had disposed of the lease to other parties, so that by the time Shakespeare made his purchase the tithes were distributed among approximately forty owners. Shakespeare's portion — it was relatively large, consisting of more than a quarter of the whole — was estimated to bring him in annually the sum of £60; but out of this sum he was required to pay to the Corporation of Stratford £17, and to one John Barker £5, so that his net annual income was reduced to £38. On the other hand, there was a fair expectation that this income would increase with time; and that it did increase is revealed by the fact that in 1624 the Corporation purchased from his heirs the tithes of that year for £90.

In October, 1605, the King's Men were at Oxford. Apparently their frequent visits to the university towns [2]

---

[1] The history of the tithes will be found embodied in the deeds of sale to Shakespeare and in the bill of complaint, printed in Halliwell-Phillipps, *Outlines*, ii, 19 and 25.

[2] They were at Oxford, so far as our imperfect records show, in 1604, 1605, 1606, 1607, 1610, 1613; but no doubt their visits were more frequent than the records indicate.

were welcome to both faculty and students, who must have been glad of the opportunity to see the great Globe actors present the plays which the Court and the literary circles of London so loudly acclaimed. During the visits of the King's Men to Oxford, as well as on his frequent pilgrimages to and from Stratford, Shakespeare is said to have lodged at the Crown Inn, kept by John Davenant and his wife Jane. Davenant was a man of property who occupied various civic offices including those of Bailiff and Mayor. Aubrey tells us that "he was exceedingly respected," and that he was "a very grave and discreet citizen." Anthony à Wood states that he "was seldom or never seen to laugh," yet, he adds, he was "an admirer and lover of plays." Aubrey describes Davenant's wife as "a very beautiful woman, and of very good wit, and of conversation extremely agreeable." We know on contemporary evidence that husband and wife were devoted to each other; and this mutual affection, combined with comfortable means, must have made their home a happy one.

This home, it would seem, became for Shakespeare a pleasant retreat, where he often lingered as a welcome guest. The Oxford antiquarian already cited, Anthony à Wood, states that Davenant was "an admirer" of Shakespeare, and that Shakespeare "frequented his house in his journeys between Warwickshire and London." Aubrey writes: "Mr. William Shakespeare was wont to go into Warwickshire once a year, and did commonly in his journey lie at this house in Oxon., where he was exceedingly respected."

In the Davenant family there were five sons and three daughters. The eldest son, Robert, was born in 1604. Later he became a fellow of St. John's, Oxford, a Doctor of Divinity, and a well-known clergyman. The second son, born in March, 1606, was named by his parents

William in honor of their illustrious friend, who is said to have acted as the boy's godfather. We may believe that after this event Shakespeare was more often than before an honored guest in the Davenant home. An interesting glimpse of the poet among the children of the family is furnished by a brief note in Aubrey's manuscript jottings: "I have heard Robert [Davenant the eminent divine,] say that Mr. W. Shakespeare has given him a hundred kisses." Could we ask for better evidence of the sort of man the dramatist was in private life? Or can we be surprised that young William, at the age of twelve, wrote a tender "Ode in Remembrance of Master William Shakespeare"?

It is pleasing to contemplate this happy relationship between the poet and the family that gave him so delightful a harborage on his travels. Yet an unfortunate result was the springing up — though not until many years later — of a bit of gossip reflecting on the moral character of Shakespeare and Mrs. Davenant. The scandal, one needs hardly say, took the form of insinuating that Shakespeare was not only the godfather of young William but the real father as well. The origin of such a rumor can readily be understood. William Davenant came to be an eminent dramatist, knighted by King Charles, and created Poet Laureate of England. Thus it was natural for idle gossips to whisper jestingly among themselves that for his dramatic and poetic gifts he was indebted to no less a person than his immortal godfather.

Moreover, Sir William himself, in his vanity to be thought a second Shakespeare, seems to have been not unwilling to have the story believed — at least according to Aubrey, who is the first to record the gossip:

Now Sir William would sometimes when he was pleasant over a glass of wine with his most intimate friends — e.g. Sam

Butler (author of *Hudibras*), &c. — say that it seemed to him that he writ with the very spirit that Shakespeare [did], and seemed contented enough to be thought his son.[1]

Aubrey originally added, "He would tell them the story as above, in which way his mother had a very light report," but crossed the passage out. Perhaps his conscience checked him, and made him realize that this was merely his own invention tagged on to render his story more effective;[2] for it is hard to believe that Sir William would give to his own mother a "light report."

The story was doubtless gathered by Aubrey from the gossipy tables of that convivial circle in London which he haunted in search of biographical items. Anthony à Wood, the Oxford antiquarian, to whom Aubrey supplied his manuscript notes in 1680, entirely rejected the story. Gerard Langbaine, another resident of Oxford, who devoted years to a close study of the English dramatic poets, makes no mention of it in his lives of either Davenant or Shakespeare. Early in the eighteenth century, however, it was developed into a tradition,[3] with certain amusing anecdotes added which can easily be traced to other sources. Thus, so far as we can discover, the scandal was of late origin, first appearing long after the death of both Shakespeare and Mrs. Davenant, and rejected by those earlier writers best qualified to judge of its accuracy.[4]

---

[1] Halliwell-Phillipps, *Outlines*, i, 216, and C. I. Elton, *William Shakespeare, his Family and Friends*, p. 47, independently suggest that Davenant had in mind merely that literary sonship which Jonson made so real and valuable to young poets. If so, the story may have grown from this by misinterpretation.

[2] Such was the natural bent of his mind; for example he writes: "Ben Jonson had one eye lower than the other and bigger, like Clun the player; perhaps he begot Clun."

[3] Gildon, in his revised edition of Langbaine, 1699, seems to glance at it. Hearne noted it in his commonplace-book, 1709. It reappears in Jacob's *Poetical Register*, 1719, in Joseph Spence's *Anecdotes*, 1728–30, in Oldys' manuscripts, and in other places.

[4] It is significant that the scandal is not remotely glanced at by any of the

We have still further reason for giving little credence to the story. Mrs. Davenant, it appears, enjoyed an excellent reputation in Oxford, and she and her husband lived happily together with singular devotion to each other. It is noteworthy that John Davenant ordered in his will that he should be "buried in the parish of St. Martin's in Oxford, as near my wife as the place will give leave where she lieth." An anonymous eulogist thus celebrated husband and wife:

> He had choice gifts of nature and of art;
> Neither was Fortune wanting on her part
> To him, in honors, wealth, or progeny;
> He was on all sides blest. Why should he die?
> And yet, why should he live, his mate being gone,
> And turtle-like sigh out an endless moon?
> No, no; he loved her better, and would not
> So easily lose what he so hardly got.
> He liv'd to pay the last rites to his bride,
> That done, he pin'd out fourteen days and died.
> Thrice happy pair! Oh could my simple verse
> Rear you a lasting trophy o'er your hearse,
> You should vie years with Time. Had you your due,
> Eternity were as short-liv'd as you.
> Farewell, and in one grave, now you are dead,
> Sleep undisturb'd, as in your marriage bed.

Still another elegy bears witness to the undisturbed happiness of this marriage:

> If to be great, or good, deserve the bays,
> What merits he whom great and good doth praise?
> What merits he? Why a contented life,
> A happy issue of a virtuous wife,
> The choice of friends, a quiet honor'd grave.
> All these he had; what more could Dav'nant have?[1]

The evidence cited above should not lightly be ignored in favor of a late tradition which obviously owes its

numerous writers on the death of Davenant, though in comparing him with Shakespeare they call the older poet his "brother" and "cousin." See *An Allusion-Book to Ben Jonson*, especially pp. 338, 339, 340, 359.

[1] I quote these poems from Halliwell-Phillipps, *Outlines*, ii, 49.

origin to gossip and its vogue to salacious fancy. We can readily understand how the story might arise in the taverns of Caroline London when cups were flowing too freely; and in view of all the facts which so clearly discredit the scandal, we should not entertain it without grave doubt.

In 1606 Shakespeare's residence with the Mountjoys — for presumably he still maintained lodgings there — was disturbed by domestic troubles affecting that unhappy family. Madame Mountjoy — who seems to have been an admirable woman — died in October, and Stephen and Mary were persuaded to return to keep house for the widower, and join with him "as partners in their said trade of tireing." But their return soon led to further quarrels, for Mountjoy was self-seeking, and Stephen, perhaps, too exacting. Stephen lent his father-in-law £2, who, instead of repaying the sum, claimed to have paid for him a brewer's bill amounting to £3. There followed other quarrels over the expenses of transacting the tire-making business, with the result that at the end of half a year, in the spring of 1607, Stephen and Mary again moved away to open up a shop of their own. This apparently disrupted Mountjoy's home, and he made his house into two tenements, letting one half to other persons. Shakespeare doubtless left at this time, if he had not already departed.

Yet he maintained an interest in Stephen and Mary, and was sometimes a visitor at their newly-established shop; for Stephen's young apprentice, William Eaton, aged nineteen (who declared that he first met Stephen about June, 1607), testified as to certain conversations he had subsequently heard Shakespeare hold with his master. Stephen's family rapidly increasing — he tells us that he and Mary had "lived together by the space of these five years, and have had diverse children betwixt them, to the great increase of their charge, and are likely to have many more" — he naturally desired a settlement of the dowry which Mountjoy never had paid. Nor was this all that distressed him. Old Mountjoy, now freed from the restraining influence of his wife, began rapidly to dissipate his property in immoral living. He borrowed much money, and even went so far as to sell "his plate, and some household stuff." Stephen, therefore, began to worry, not only about the payment of the dowry of £50, but also about the special settlement of £200 payable at his father-in-law's death.[1] Both these payments were further jeopardized by Mountjoy's increasing estrangement; diverse persons had heard him declare that he intended to leave his daughter and her husband not "the value of one penny."

At last, Stephen brought suit against his father-in-law for the immediate payment of the dowry long overdue, or for a bond guaranteeing the ultimate payment of the £200. The suit dragged along until 1612, when Shakespeare was haled into court as a witness, and made to recount his share in the marriage arrangements.

The case was finally referred to the "reverend and grave overseers and elders of the French Church in London," to which the contending parties belonged. The church authorities, after due investigation, reproved Mountjoy for his dissipated life, and rendered a decision in favor of Belott. But Mountjoy, scorning their decision,

---

[1] There may be in *Timon of Athens*, I, i, 111–52, an echo of this Mountjoy episode. The Old Athenian declares:

> One only daughter have I, no kin else . . .
> If in her marriage my consent be missing,
> I call the gods to witness, I will choose
> Mine heir from forth the beggars of the world,
> And dispossess her all.

And when Timon asks "How shall she be endowed?" the father replies

> Three talents on the present, in future, all.

continued his profligate career. The subsequent history of the case is unknown to us.

Shakespeare, as has been suggested, had probably moved away from the Mountjoy house in 1606 or 1607. Whither he moved we do not know; but Malone states that he had in his possession a document which gave "the strongest presumptive evidence" that in and before 1608 the dramatist was living on the Bankside in Southwark, near the Globe.[1] And evidence tending to confirm Malone's inference may be found in the circumstance that on December 31, 1607, Shakespeare's youngest brother, Edmund, who had joined him in London and entered the profession of acting, was buried in St. Saviour's Church, Southwark, in a place of honor within the chancel.

The poet was also, no doubt, spending much of his time at Stratford. His two daughters were now grown women, both somewhat past the age at which it was then customary for young ladies to marry. Of these, the elder, Susanna, seems to have been the father's favorite; and with good reason, for she was clearly the more tractable and stable of the two. How well-educated she was we do not know, but at least she was able to sign her name to legal documents, whereas her younger sister, Judith, was forced to make use of a mark. Moreover, according to the epitaph on her tomb in the Stratford Church, she inherited some of her father's intellectual power, and was generally regarded by those who knew her as "witty above her sex." She was also charitable by nature. We are told that she "wept with all — that wept, yet set herself to cheer them up with comforts cordiall"; and we are assured that "her love shall live, her mercy spread" long after her death.

On June 5, 1607, this favorite daughter, Susanna,

[1] *Inquiry*, p. 215.

being then twenty-four years of age, was married to John Hall, thirty-two years of age, who had recently settled in Stratford to practise medicine. The groom was in every respect worthy of alliance with the Shakespeares. He came of a family enjoying heraldic honors, and himself bore arms, sable three talbots' heads erased or. Not only did he hold the degree of Master of Arts, but he had traveled on the Continent, and, it seems, had secured his medical training at foreign universities.

He had an excellent knowledge of French, and he kept his diary and his medical notes in Latin. As a practising physician he soon acquired a wide reputation throughout Warwickshire and the adjacent counties. Dr. Bird, Linacre Professor at Cambridge University, referred to him as being "in great fame for his skill far and near"; the Stratford clerk in entering his name in the burial register of the church adds the comment "*medicus peritissimus*"; and his epitaph declares that he was "*medica celeberrimus arte*." Among his patients he numbered virtually all the families of distinction in Warwickshire, being summoned even to Ludlow Castle, forty miles distant, to attend the Earl and Countess of Northampton. In his treatment of diseases he was credited with displaying considerable originality. Dr. James Cooke wrote: "Mr. John Hall had the happiness to lead the way to that practice, almost generally used now by the most knowing, of mixing scorbutics to most remedies. It was then, and I know for some time after, thought so strange that it was cast as a reproach upon him by those most famous in the profession." In 1677 his medical notes were published in London with the title: *Select Observations on English Bodies, or Cures Both Empiricall and Historicall, Per-*

*formed upon Very Eminent Persons, in Desperate Diseases,
First Written in Latine by Mr. John Hall, Physician,
Living at Stratford-upon-Avon in Warwickshire, Where
He Was Very Famous, as Also in the Counties Adjacent.*
The volume must have been well received by the medical
profession, for new editions appeared in 1679 and 1683.

After their marriage, Susanna and her husband established an attractive little home not far from New
Place. The house they occupied, known as Hall's Croft,
is still preserved in Stratford, where it is an object of
interest to tourists. We may suppose that this "famous"
physician, with his intellectual curiosity, his Continen-
tal experiences, and his enthusiasm for science, proved a
congenial soul to Shakespeare. And Susanna, with her
ready wit and her charitable heart, must have made
Hall's Croft a pleasant haven of refuge to her father
from the noise and stir of London theatres. Shortly, too,
there was added to the home another attraction for the
dramatist: on February 8, 1608, a daughter was born to
the Halls, later christened Elizabeth. This was the only
grandchild Shakespeare lived to know, and his fondness
for her is clearly revealed in his will.

CHAPTER XXI

DRAMATIC LABORS, 1607–09; ACQUISITION
OF BLACKFRIARS

BUT we must return to Shakespeare's labors as a dramatist for His Majesty's Servants at the Globe. In 1607
he produced for them his second Roman tragedy, *Antony
and Cleopatra*. Having already handled the youthful
career of Mark Antony in one of his most successful
plays, *Julius Cæsar*, it was natural for him to complete
the story, and show the hero in his decline and fall. Yet
his interest was not altogether in the noble Roman; the
Egyptian Cleopatra shares titular honors with Antony,
and is reserved alone for the glorious finale of the fifth
act. Indeed, the greatness of the play lies mainly in the
subtle portraiture of "the serpent of old Nile." The
material Shakespeare found in North's Plutarch, whence
he had drawn the plot of *Julius Cæsar*. It has often been
observed that he follows the episodic narrative closely,
with unusual care for historical accuracy. This fact indicates, as Professor Bradley points out in his admirable
study,[1] that the play, though ranked among the tragedies, belongs in technique to that peculiarly Elizabethan
type known as the chronicle. It is not designed so
much to produce in us the emotions of pity and fear, as
to excite our wonder; and hence we do not find ourselves
constantly exclaiming with the broken-hearted Othello,
"The pity of it, Iago! O Iago! The pity of it, Iago!"
but rather declaring with the smiling Enobarbus that
not to have seen it would have "left unseen a wonderful
piece of work." It is in truth a splendid historical pag-

[1] *Oxford Lectures on Poetry*, 1909.

eant, full of moving armies, of battles on land and sea, of varied action rapidly shifting from Italy to Greece and to Egypt — and in the midst of it all, "staged to the view," two of the most amazing personages the world has ever seen.

To this same year, 1607, we may assign *Pericles* and *Timon of Athens*. Neither play, however, was written by Shakespeare alone, nor was his share in them relatively large. In *Pericles* his task seems to have been merely to touch up a purchased manuscript — to add passages here and there, and insert a few scenes, especially near the end — in order to make the piece more suitable for presentation by his company. The early Shakespearean editor, George Steevens, thus happily puts the case: "The play of *Pericles* was in all probability the composition of some friend whose interest the 'gentle Shakespeare' was industrious to promote. He therefore improved his dialogue in many places; and, knowing by experience that the strength of a dramatic piece should be augmented towards its catastrophe, was most liberal of his aid in the last act."

It seems well-nigh certain that the original author was George Wilkins; and Professor Wallace would have us believe that Wilkins, as Steevens surmised, was a friend of the poet, by identifying him with the "George Wilkins, victualer," to whose house Stephen Belott and his wife Mary moved in 1604.[1] Of Wilkins, the playwright, we know little, save that in 1607 he suddenly appears as a dramatist for the King's Men, and a hack-writer for the printers. His first work, it seems, was *Three Miseries of Barbary, Plague, Famine, Civill Warre*, a pamphlet of

[1] There are no grounds for this identification beyond the similarity of the name, Shakespeare's known friendship for Belott and Mary, and the probable association of Wilkins with *Pericles*. It is strange that Wilkins disappears as a writer after 1607–08, whereas the victualer gave testimony at the Mountjoy trial in 1612.

fifteen leaves printed without date. In 1607 he issued in collaboration with Thomas Dekker *Jests to Make You Merry*, a pamphlet of thirty-one leaves. In the same year he published two plays, each described on the title-page as then being acted by the King's Men at the Globe, *The Miseries of Enforced Marriage*, and *The Travailes of Three English Brothers* (in which he was assisted by John Day and William Rowley). The following year, 1608, he issued the story of *Pericles* made into a prose romance. From now on we hear nothing of him either in connection with the stage or the press.[1]

The attribution of *Pericles* to Wilkins rests on the following facts: he was writing for the King's Men in 1607; the play bears a general resemblance in versification to *The Miseries;* certain of its odd jests, and many unusual turns of thought or expression find close parallels in his known works; and, finally, in 1608 he issued under his own name the story of the play in the form of a prose novel, claiming the plot as "a poor infant" of his brain. The evidence, cumulative in force, seems to place the matter beyond a reasonable doubt.[2]

The play, as carefully revised by Shakespeare, won a sensational popularity. An anonymous poet in 1609 thus alludes to the crowds that thronged the Globe to see its performance:

[1] H. Dugdale Sykes, in *Sidelights on Shakespeare*, 1919, gives reasons, little short of conclusive, for attributing to Wilkins *A Yorkshire Tragedy*, 1608, a share in *Law Tricks*, 1608, and the first section of the prose tract, *Two Most Unnatural Murders*, 1605, telling the story of *A Yorkshire Tragedy*. Was Wilkins also responsible for the prose novel, *The Historie of Hamblet*, 1608, issued by Thomas Pavier, who in the same year published *A Yorkshire Tragedy* and printed the prose novel of *Pericles?*

[2] See N. Delius, "Ueber Shakespeare's *Pericles*," Shakespeare *Jahrbuch*, iii, 175–204; Robert Boyle, "On Wilkins' Share in the Play called Shakespeare's *Pericles*," *The New Shakspere Society's Transactions*, 1882, pp. 323–40; and *The Nation and Athenæum*, xxix, 298; cf. also H. T. Baker, "The Relation of *Pericles* to George Wilkins' Novel," *Publications of the Modern Language Association of America*, 1908, xxiii, 100. The most thorough and convincing study, however, is that by Sykes, quoted above.

> Amazed I stood to see a crowd
> Of civil throats stretched out so loud;
> (As at a new play) all the rooms
> Did swarm with gentles mixed with **grooms,**
> So that I truly thought all these
> Came to see *Shore,* or *Pericles.*[1]

And in the Prologue to Robert Tailor's *The Hog Hath Lost His Pearl,* 1614, the actors express a hope that their comedy will prove a like success:

> And if it prove so happy as to please,
> Wee'l say 't is fortunate, like *Pericles.*[2]

So popular was the play that unscrupulous publishers made efforts to steal the text for a pirated issue. In order to prevent this the actors had their printer friend, Edward Blount, carry the manuscript to the Stationers' Hall on May 20, 1608, and enter a blocking license. At the same time, as already stated, Wilkins took advantage of the great interest in the drama to prepare and issue in 1608 a prose novel giving to the public in this form the story which was creating such a sensation at the Globe. The title of the novel runs in part: *The Painful Adventures of Pericles, Prince of Tyre. Being the True History of the Play of Pericles.* But all efforts to forestall publication proved futile. In the following year, 1609, Henry Gosson secured a corrupt and mangled text, probably taken down in the theatre by shorthand, and issued it with the title *The Late and Much Admired Play Called Pericles, Prince of Tyre.*

In this, as well as in subsequent editions, the drama was attributed on the title-page solely to "William Shakespeare." But when Shakespeare's actor friends, Heminges and Condell, came to issue a "complete" —

[1] *Pimlyco, or Runne Red-Cap,* 1609.
[2] Ben Jonson, on the failure of his *New Inn,* 1629, took occasion to satirize the popularity of *Pericles.* For many other allusions to the play see *The Shakespeare Allusion-Book.*

so they called it — and authentic collection of his works
they rejected *Pericles*, even though one of the publishers
of the Folio owned the copyright. They knew that in
the main it was not the composition of the master, and
could not in fairness be attributed to him. Yet we cannot
doubt that his hand appears in many scenes, and that
much of its excellence is due to the magic skill of his pen.
This is the conclusion not only of scholars but of modern
poets as well. Dr. Furnivall records the opinion of Tennyson thus:

He asked me during our talk whether I had ever examined
Pericles with any care. I had to confess that I'd never read it,
as some friends of mine whom I considered good judges had
told me it was very doubtful whether Shakespeare wrote any of
it. Mr. Tennyson answered: "Oh, that won't do. He wrote all
the part relating to the birth and recovery of Marina, and the
recovery of Thaisa. I settled that long ago. Come up-stairs
and I'll read it to you." Up-stairs to the smoking-room in Sea-
more Place we went; and there I had the rare treat of hearing
the poet read in his deep voice — with an occasional triumphant "Is n't *that* Shakespeare? What do you think of *that?*"

Timon of Athens, assigned to this same year, presents
greater difficulty, for it is hard to understand the exact
connection Shakespeare had with its production. The
most plausible theory is that while he was reading the
life of Antony in North's Plutarch he came upon the
account of Timon, and started to work the story into a
play. After sketching its main outlines, however, he
realized that the material was unsuited to a great drama,
and turned over what he had composed to some inferior
writer,[1] who completed the tragedy by padding it out
to the proper length.[2] It is true that Heminges and Condell included it in the First Folio; yet originally they seem

[1] Some scholars have suggested that this writer was George Wilkins. I
can discover in the play no indication of Wilkins' hand.
[2] See E. H. Wright, *The Authorship of Timon of Athens*, 1910.

to have intended to omit it, for the same reason that they omitted *Pericles*. When, however, they encountered an unexpected difficulty with *Troilus and Cressida* which compelled them to remove that play bodily from the section of "Tragedies" after a part of it had been set up and printed off, they inserted *Timon of Athens* to fill the awkward gap thus created in the pagination.[1] For this purpose they could not use *Pericles*, which was a comedy rather than a tragedy, though they might well have felt that its extraordinary fame rendered its inclusion more desirable than that of the far less successful *Timon of Athens*.

Shakespeare, it is obvious, utilized the account of Timon which Plutarch parenthetically inserted in the *Life of Mark Antony*. He drew also, directly or indirectly, from the only other classical version of the story, Lucian's *Misanthropos*. And it is almost certain that by some means, not now clear, he was familiar with the plot of the unpublished play of *Timon*, which contained the figure of the loyal steward and the episode of the banquet, neither of which appears in the classical sources.[2] The dramatist who expanded the plot as outlined by Shakespeare added nothing of significance.

If the play was acted — and we have no reason to suppose that it was not — it could hardly have attained any great popularity. To-day it is not a favorite with readers. Yet the scenes composed by Shakespeare, sketchy as they are, add to our conception of his versatile genius. As Verplanck writes:

To borrow an illustration from the often used parallel between the Shakespearean and the Greek drama, and the admir-

---

[1] See the writer's article "*Timon of Athens* and the Irregularities in the First Folio," in *The Journal of English and Germanic Philology*, 1908, vii, 53–63.

[2] See the writer's article, "The Timon Plays," in *The Journal of English and Germanic Philology*, 1910, ix, 506–24.

able architectural works of their respective ages, I would say
that *Timon* is not, indeed, like one of the massive yet graceful
columns which give support or solidity, as well as beauty and
proportion, to the classic portico, but rather resembles one of
those grand adjuncts — cloister, or chapel, or chapter-house —
attached to the magnificent cathedrals of the Middle Ages; and
like one of them, might be removed without impairing the solemn sublimity of the sacred edifice, or robbing it of many of its
daring lighter graces; yet not without loss of the portion of the
pile, majestic and striking in itself, and by its very contrast
adding to the nobler and more impressive beauty of the rest
an effect of indefinite and apparently boundless grandeur and
extent.

Late in 1608 Shakespeare joined with others in securing for the King's Men the use of the Blackfriars playhouse as a winter home.[1] The acquisition of this excellent theatre was made possible by the indiscretions of
the managers of the Children of the Queen's Revels. In
1605 they allowed the boys to put on the stage a play
which ridiculed the horde of Scotchmen who had followed James to London in search of political advancement, and satirized the King's creation of innumerable
Knights as a means of raising money. One of the little
actors was actually made, it seems, to mimic the royal
brogue: "I ken the man weel; he is one of my thirty-
pound knights." The King in his anger punished the
managers, and closed the playhouse; and the Queen
promptly took away her patronage from the troupe.

After a time the boys, now with the plain title The
Children of Blackfriars, were allowed to reopen their
theatre. But in 1608 they once more gave offense by
acting a play in which they brought King James on the
stage as drunk and swearing at his attendants. And a
few days later they created an embarrassing diplomatic
situation by presenting Chapman's *Conspiracy and Trag-*

[1] For a more detailed account see my *Shakespearean Playhouses*, pp. 182-
233.

edy of Charles, Duke of Byron, introducing before the audience the French Queen, and representing her as boxing Madame de Verneuil on the ears. The French Ambassador made a vigorous complaint to the English government, with the result that James gave orders for the immediate and permanent suppression of the Blackfriars Children. This marked the end of the boy-troupe which had so long been a thorn in the flesh of the adult players.

Henry Evans, having leased the building from Burbage for a period of twenty-one years at an annual rental of £40, found himself in a serious predicament, with an expensive playhouse on his hands for which he had no possible use. He naturally was desirous of surrendering the lease, and for this purpose interviewed Burbage. It was then that Burbage conceived the brilliant idea of converting Blackfriars into a winter home for the King's Men. The Globe, though admirably adapted to summer performances, was uncomfortable and difficult of access during the bitterly cold months of the year.[1] The luxury of a winter home, enclosed and heated, and situated in the very heart of the city, must have appealed to the members of the King's Company, who, now strongly entrenched in royal favor, felt no fear of the order of the Privy Council forbidding the use of Blackfriars for "public plays."

Burbage at once proceeded, as he had done in the case of the Globe, to organize a syndicate of "housekeepers," distinct from the "company of players," to secure the lease from Evans, and manage the building as a winter house for the King's Men. The new syndicate was made up of the following persons, sharing equally in the enter-

---

[1] The winter of 1607–08 was one of the severest on record. The Thames was frozen over, and long remained so. See Howes' continuation of Stow's *Annales*, p. 891.

prise: Richard Burbage, Cuthbert Burbage, William Shakespeare, John Heminges, Henry Condell, William Slye, and Henry Evans. The seven sharers took over the lease of Blackfriars in August, 1608, at the old rental of £40 *per annum*, each agreeing to pay the sum of £5 14*s*. 4*d*. annually. The building, we are told, had run "far into decay for want of reparations," and probably the housekeepers were called upon to spend a goodly sum in fitting it up for the more exacting demands of His Majesty's Players; but doubtless it was ready for occupancy during the winter of 1608–09. Henceforth the King's Men were accustomed to act at the Globe from about the last week in April until the first week in November, and at Blackfriars during the rest of the year.

The plan was designed to obviate the pecuniary losses often caused by a severe winter. Edward Kirkham, a man experienced in theatrical finances, offered to prove to the court in 1612 that the King's Men "got, and as yet doth, more in one winter in the said great hall [of Blackfriars] by a thousand pounds than they were used to get on the Bankside." And Kirkham's testimony to the popularity of the King's Men in their winter home is borne out by a petition to the city authorities made by "the constables and other officers and inhabitants of Blackfriars" in June, 1619. They declared that to the playhouse "there is daily such resort of people, and such multitudes of coaches (whereof many are hackney-coaches, bringing people of all sorts), that sometimes all our streets cannot contain them, but that they clog up Ludgate also, in such sort that both they endanger the one the other, break down stalls, throw down men's goods from their shops, and the inhabitants there cannot come to their houses, nor bring in their necessary provisions of beer, wood, coal, or hay, nor the tradesmen or shopkeepers utter their wares, nor the passengers go to the common water stairs without danger of their lives and limbs." "These inconveniences" were said to last "every day in winter from one or two of the clock till six at night."

As one might infer from the above complaint, Blackfriars became exceedingly fashionable. Even the Queen did not hesitate occasionally to engage the building for private performances before herself and her invited guests.[1] At a sitting of the Privy Council in 1633 (the King being present) we hear of "the discommodity that diverse persons of great quality, especially Ladies and Gentlewomen, did receive in going to the playhouse of Blackfriars by reason that no coaches may stand" there. And a glimpse of high society at the theatre is given in a letter written by Garrard, January 25, 1636: "A little pique happened betwixt the Duke of Lenox and the Lord Chamberlain [the Earl of Pembroke and Montgomery] about a box at a new play in the Blackfriars, of which the Duke had got the key, which, if it had come to be debated betwixt them, as it was once intended, some heat or perhaps other inconveniences might have happened."

The possession of this splendid theatre in the very heart of the city gave the King's Men a decided advantage over their less fortunate rivals, and marked an important step in the long history of English playhouses. Gradually the theatres crept into the city, and, at the same time, the old style of unroofed amphitheatre passed away.

For performance at Blackfriars Shakespeare soon had ready a new play. In North's translation of Plutarch's *Lives*, whence he had just drawn *Antony and Cleopatra*, he found the fascinating, though not altogether pleasing, story of Caius Marcus, known as Coriolanus, and his

[1] See my *Dramatic Records of Sir Henry Herbert*, pp. 65, 75, 76, 77.

mother Volumnia. And shortly after finishing *Antony and Cleopatra* he set to work dramatizing this strange story, having it ready for the actors late in 1608 or early in 1609. We may view *Coriolanus* as in theme a companion-study to its immediate predecessor: both plays show a strong man whose career is tragically wrecked by the influence of a woman, in the case of Antony by a mistress, Cleopatra, in the case of Coriolanus by a mother, Volumnia. Yet the two plays are entirely different in kind: *Antony and Cleopatra* is a loosely-constructed history, "brooched" with two lovers that stand out peerless both in their lives and in their deaths; *Coriolanus* is a carefully-wrought tragedy, which as an organic work of art vies with *Othello*. In their different ways, each is an astonishing product of Shakespeare's genius; and together with the earlier *Julius Cæsar*, they form a group of Roman plays not elsewhere matched in literature.[1]

[1] The three plays have been made the subject of an admirable study by M. W. MacCallum, *Shakespeare's Roman Plays*, 1910.

CHAPTER XXII

TRAGI–COMEDY AND ROMANCE

Coriolanus marks the point where Shakespeare's production of plays begins seriously to diminish. Possibly he no longer worked under the double spur of necessity and ambition, for he was both rich and famous; and he may have desired to spend more leisure with his family in his attractive home at Stratford-on-Avon. But the King's Men had to have a supply of new plays, and for this purpose they began to take on other writers. They had always been ready to purchase good manuscripts from the free-lances — for example, Wilkins, Day, Rowley, Dekker — but, like the other city companies, they desired to have also "regular poets," whose industry could be counted upon, and whose plays were available to the public only at one theatre. In 1609 they secured the service of two promising young dramatists, Francis Beaumont and John Fletcher.

Both these men were of aristocratic birth. Beaumont belonged to the younger branch of an ancient titled family; his father was one of the Queen's Justices of the Court of Common Pleas; [1] his mother was "connected with several of the most influential noble families of England and Scotland"; [2] and his two brothers and his uncle were knights. He himself was reared at Grace Dieu, the beautiful country estate of the Beaumonts, was educated at Oxford University, and later entered the

---

[1] Dyce, Rigg (in D.N.B.), Macaulay (in C.H.E.L.), and other scholars state that he was knighted, and the *Inner Temple Records* on one occasion gives him the title "Sir." But this seems to be an error. See C. M. Gayley, *Beaumont the Dramatist*, 1914.

[2] Gayley, *op. cit.*, pp. 16–17, 421.

Inner Temple. From his father, the Justice, and from his brother, Sir Henry, who died in 1605, he inherited a competence, so that his labors for the theatre were probably inspired by a sheer love for dramatic composition. Fletcher was the son of Richard, later Bishop of London, "a comely and courtly prelate" who lived, we are told, in the Queen's "gratious aspect and favour," until without royal permission he married Lady Baker, relict of Sir Richard Baker, and sister-in-law of Thomas Sackville, Lord Buckhurst, kinsman of the Queen. John was educated at Cambridge, and, it seems, traveled for a time on the Continent. Thus Beaumont and Fletcher, each with a university training, and each thoroughly familiar with the life of the upper classes, were of the "newer stamp" now demanded by a drama which was more or less subservient to the Court. They were close friends of the Damon and Pythias type, living together in one house on the Bankside, sharing, if we may believe tradition, all things in common, and writing mainly in collaboration. Their plays proved to be especially popular with courtly audiences, for they understood the tastes, and pictured with great effectiveness the life, of the higher ranks of society. The products of their industrious pens, together with manuscripts the troupe bought from other writers, gradually relieved Shakespeare from the burden of composing a larger number of plays than he naturally felt disposed to attempt. And, as we shall see, he availed himself of this opportunity to withdraw more and more to the quiet of Stratford and the pleasures of his garden and orchard.

Coriolanus is further significant as Shakespeare's last effort at tragedy, for from now on he devotes himself to the composition of tragi-comedy and romance. Many scholars have sought to explain this change on purely subjective grounds. Having already assumed that the dramatist began to write tragedies because of some distressing experience in his own life which rendered him melancholy and even misanthropic, they necessarily account for his sudden turning to light fanciful themes by arguing that at last he had emerged from the dark clouds of melancholia, and that now in the sunshine of a new faith in man he mellowed into a kindly and happy frame of mind. But to explain Shakespeare subjectively is always dangerous. As has been already suggested, he probably directed his attention to tragedy at the zenith of his maturing powers because he knew that this was the noblest form of dramatic art, that an *Othello* was superior to an *As You Like It*, a *King Lear* to a *King Henry IV*. And doubtless we can find a reason outside of personal moods to explain his cultivation of a new type of play; for, it should be remembered, the popular drama, more than any other form of literature, is subject to external influences.

Upon examining contemporary theatrical history we discover that in turning to romance and tragi-comedy Shakespeare merely followed the trend of the day, yielding, as a successful playwright must, to changes imposed by altering conditions. The Age of Elizabeth was no more. And the great Elizabethan drama, after lighting up the first few years of the succeeding reign, had passed away too, giving place to the new Jacobean drama, differing in substance and in kind. During the reign of "the Fairy Queen," who was English in every fibre of her being, sharing in full measure the sympathies and intellectual interests of her people, the drama had been essentially national. Playwrights wrote for the masses assembled in open-air theatres, who applauded what they liked, and vociferously condemned what they disliked, even at times wrecking the stage in their disapproval. They alone constituted the jury before which the success of a play was tried. Elizabeth stood aloof. When a play pleased the citizens and apprentices of London, she summoned that play to Court; and what pleased the London audiences — Falstaff, for example — invariably pleased Her Majesty; for, as has been aptly declared, "Elizabeth was England, and England was Elizabeth." The dramatists thus did not have to consider the Court; they kept always before them the middle classes, upon whose favor their success and prosperity solely depended.

But with the coming of the foreigner James, who had little understanding of and no sympathy with the popular feeling of the English, this state of affairs was altered, and the drama slowly but surely underwent a profound transformation. The first thing the new sovereign did was to take the actors under royal patronage, dress them in scarlet liveries, and make them, in a measure at least, adjuncts of Whitehall to furnish entertainment to himself and his pleasure-loving favorites. Thus there grew up a close and intimate relationship between the Court and the drama. Gradually the plays ceased to be national in the fuller sense of the word, and in place of catering solely to the tastes of the middle classes, with their love of obvious morality and their rather broad sense of humor, began to reflect the tastes, the interests, and the moral standards of the polite and decadent society that grew up about the Stuarts.

In its superficial aspects this society was perhaps the most brilliant in Europe. Extravagant, pleasure-loving, almost barbaric in its splendor, it excited the astonishment of foreign visitors. Zorzi Giustinian, the Venetian Ambassador, after witnessing a performance at Whitehall in 1607–08, wrote to the Doge and Senate: "But what beggared all else . . . was the wealth of pearls and jewels that adorned the Queen and her ladies, so abundant and splendid that in every one's opinion no other court could have displayed such pomp and riches." [1]   Horatio Busino likewise was astonished at the magnificence of this society.   Describing an audience gathered to witness a masque, he writes: "Every box was filled, notably with most noble and richly arrayed ladies, in number some six hundred and more, according to the general estimate, the dresses being of such variety in cut and color as to be indescribable . . . strings of jewels on their necks and bosoms, and in their girdles and apparel, in such quantity that they looked like so many queens; so that at the beginning, with but little light, as that of the dawn of the evening twilight, the splendor of their diamonds and other jewels was so brilliant that they looked like so many stars." [2]   And John Chamberlain in a private letter to a friend speaks of one fashionable lady as "remarkable for nothing else but for multitude of jewels, wherewith she was hanged, as it were, all over." [3]   Beneath a splendor of this sort there was naturally a shallowness of intellectual interests, a loss of the sense of values, and a flippancy towards the more serious problems of life.

The influence exerted by such a society upon the drama which it patronized was quickly evinced. Almost at once we note a lowering of the intellectual level. Studies of men struggling in the bonds of external circumstance or in the toils of internal conflict, suffering and disaster exciting pity and fear, subtle analyses of human nature, revelations of moral grandeur, or portrayals of gross turpitude — these things did not interest the audiences which now sat in judgment on the success of plays. Indeed, such dramas as had deeply moved the Elizabethan

---

[1] *Calendar of State Papers, Venetian*, xi, 86.
[2] Anglipotrida, in *Calendar of State Papers, Venetian*, xv, 111–12.
[3] J. B. Nichols, *The Progresses of King James the First*, iii, 464.

public were too heavy to please the Jacobean Court. As Middleton and Dekker observe in 1610:

> Tragic passion, and such
> Grave stuff, is this day out of fashion.

Accordingly, the dramatists began to cultivate the type of play called tragi-comedy, which made a pretense at "grave stuff," but invariably ended with a happy solution that provided light entertainment without disturbing the deeper emotions or puzzling the mind. And since the Court was passionately fond of masques, fanciful in theme, bizarre in setting, lyrical in character, we observe the appearance also of this element in the drama,[1] leading particularly to the cultivation of that type of play we call romance, of which *The Tempest* is a good example.

In the production of tragi-comedies and romances — perhaps we should add the hybrid form romantic tragi-comedy — the recognized leaders were Beaumont and Fletcher, the young dramatists recently engaged by the Globe Company. Their plays, mirroring the superficial and brilliant life of the Court, and catering to the tastes of the upper classes, attained greater success with artificial emotion and pleasing surprises than did the serious tragedies of Shakespeare with their compelling interest in character, and their moral earnestness. As William Cartwright wrote to Fletcher: "Shakespeare to thee was dull." It is thus not strange that Shakespeare, finding his plays old-fashioned, should turn from tragedy to the now popular romance and tragi-comedy.

But the development of new types of plays was not the only change wrought in the drama by the influence of the Court. There came also a lowering of the moral level. The society which grew up about James enter-

[1] Mary Sullivan, *Court Masques*, 1913, p. 175, observes that "the last word concerning the effect" of Court masques "upon the plays and playwrights of the public theatres will not be said for many a day."

tained lax standards of the relations between the sexes.
One need cite only the notorious case of Somerset and
the Countess of Essex, who, in order to enjoy their illicit
love, sought to make away with the Earl of Essex, and
who, when Sir Thomas Overbury dared to reprove them,
threw him into the Tower of London and poisoned him,
not without a suspicion of connivance on the part of
the King. Superficially this moral decadence expressed
itself in two ways: first, in a fondness for the *risqué*, appearing especially in that obscene innuendo which marked
the conversation of men and women; secondly, in a sentimental and often morbid interest in love to the exclu-
sion of other emotions.

The Jacobean drama inevitably began to reflect these
aspects of Court society; and again Beaumont and Fletcher were the leaders. As Flecknoe wrote: "Fletcher was
the first who introduced that sly obscenity in his plays."
But the decadent influence struck deeper than this. It
affected the very plots themselves, as dramatists began
to deal almost wholly with love, more or less sentimental
in kind, and to create situations that excited artificial
or even morbid emotions. Thomas Heywood, stout old
Elizabethan that he was, wrote in protest: "Now the
common argument intreats of puling lovers and crafty
bawds." This tendency, the beginnings of which appear
in Beaumont and Fletcher, ultimately led to that sad
decadence of the English drama which finds its climax
in the problem plays of Ford and Shirley.

Shakespeare's moral fibre was too strong to let him be
drawn into either the sly obscenity of wit or the morally
unwholesome plot. He met the new fashions only half-
way. He began to dramatize light and fanciful stories,
in which the passion of love, romantic, but not sentimental or pathological, took the place of the more serious
issues he had handled in his tragedies; but he insisted on

maintaining the lofty ethical ideal which had characterized his earlier plays, and which we must believe was
inherent in his nature.

Of the new types of play now popular the first essayed
by Shakespeare was a tragi-comedy, *Cymbeline*, composed late in 1609 or early in 1610. Though very different
in form and spirit from the great tragedies, *Hamlet*,
Othello, *Lear*, and *Macbeth*, it is worthy to be classed
among the best products of his mature genius. That
noble Shakespearean scholar, Horace Howard Furness,
who, after a life-long study of the plays in preparing his
Variorum edition, was well qualified to judge, wrote of
Cymbeline that it is "the sweetest, tenderest, profound-
est of almost all the immortal galaxy." And this is the
opinion of many other lovers of the poet. Tennyson declared that he could not read the play without its bringing
tears to his eyes. Lying on his death-bed, and suffering
the exhaustion of approaching dissolution, he was heard to
call feebly for his copy of Shakespeare; and with trembling
hands he turned the leaves until he exclaimed, "I have
opened it." Those about the bed discovered that he had
succeeded in opening the volume at his favorite *Cymbeline*. And the play was buried with him. As his son
writes: "We placed *Cymbeline* with him, and a laurel-
wreath from Virgil's tomb, and wreaths of roses, the flower
which he loved above all flowers."

As these testimonies indicate, although Shakespeare
had bowed to the will of the Court in writing a new style
of play, he refused to be contaminated by the moral
decadence which was poisoning virtually all his contemporaries. The purity and sweetness of *Cymbeline* thus
stand as a tribute to the innate purity and sweetness of
Shakespeare as a man.

The plot he derived from two sources. In his familiar thumb-worn copy of Holinshed's *Chronicle*, whence he

had drawn so many plays, he found the story of an early British King, Cunobeline; and in the *Decamerone* of Boccaccio he found the story of Imogen, Posthumus, and Iachimo under the names Ginevra, Lomellino, and Ambrogiuolo. Boccaccio's work had not yet been printed in an English translation, but Shakespeare could have read it either in the original Italian or in a French version. From these two sources, with important changes suggested by his better taste, and with many additions from his brooding imagination, he wove the stories of Cymbeline and Imogen.

He did not, however, complete his play without assistance — an action so foreign to his practice hitherto (for neither *Pericles* nor *Timon of Athens* offers a parallel case) that we are tempted to suspect that failing health may have rendered help necessary, or at least desirable. Whatever the cause, he entrusted to an inferior poet certain less important scenes. Dr. Furness, with his usual acumen, writes:

> Regarded broadly, I believe that the Imogen love-story and all that immediately touched it interested Shakespeare deeply; the Cymbeline portion was turned over to the assistant, who at times grew vainglorious and inserted here and there, even on the ground sacred to Imogen, lines and sentiments that shine by their dulness. Nay, one whole character was, I think, confided to him. It is Belarius — who bored Shakespeare.

After an interval of about a year, in the latter part of 1610 or the early part of 1611,[1] Shakespeare produced *The Winter's Tale*, a tragi-comedy embodying, as its title suggests, the qualities of a romance. It was, in truth, a mere dramatization of a prose romance, *Pandosto*, published twenty-two years earlier by Robert Greene. A new edition of *Pandosto* appeared in 1609, which possibly caught the poet's eye on the bookstalls, and led him to

---

[1] Simon Forman witnessed the play at the Globe on May 15, 1611.

buy a copy. Observing that the story could be made into a tragi-comedy such as then pleased the Court, he promptly set his hand to casting it into dramatic form. And the success his play achieved with courtly audiences is attested by the record of its performances at Whitehall. It was acted in the great Banqueting House there on November 5, 1611, and was one of the dramas selected for presentation in 1613 before the Princess Elizabeth and the Prince Palatine on the occasion of the festivities celebrating their marriage. Even so late as 1634 it was still popular. Sir Henry Herbert notes that "*The Winter's Tale* was acted on Thursday night at Court, the 16 of January, 1633[4] by the King's players, and *liked*."

In 1611 Shakespeare composed the beautiful, masque-like romance to which he gave the title *The Tempest*. The story was suggested to him by the wreck of certain English sailors on an unknown island, whence they escaped late in 1610 to astound the ears of the public with narratives of their strange experiences. The facts in the case are as follows.

In 1609 a fleet of ships was dispatched to Virginia for the purpose of establishing a colony at Jamestown. "A most dreadful Tempest" arose, "such a storm as if Jonas had been flying unto Tarsish," so preternatural in its fury that "the experience of the sea-captains was amazed, the skill of the mariners confounded." The chief ship, containing the Lieutenant-Governor of Virginia and Sir George Somers, the Admiral, was separated from the rest of the fleet, and driven upon the rocks of the "still-vexed Bermoothes," where it became "fast lodged and locked for further budging." Not a soul was lost, however, and all succeeded in reaching the shore without mishap, taking with them various articles, including, we may suppose, a bountiful supply of the "strong waters" which the sailors had freely imbibed in their despair.

The shipwrecked voyagers, given up by their companions as lost, were compelled to remain on the island nine months. They found the place exceedingly beautiful, and "the air so temperate and the country so abundantly fruitful" that they were "well refreshed, comforted, and with good satiety contented." But, according to their reports, they were constantly alarmed by strange noises, which made them believe that the island was "a prodigious and enchanted place," "given over to devils and wicked spirits." No news coming from the ill-fated vessel, the English public mourned all on board as lost. But, as one of the survivors observed, the story was soon changed into a "tragical-comedy." Under the direction of Sir George Somers, the sailors constructed two small boats, in which the whole party boldly put to sea, and, after further interesting experiences, managed to reach Virginia in May, 1610.

The report of their safe arrival in the New World was first brought to London in September, 1610, where it created a profound sensation. No fewer than five accounts of their thrilling adventures were published and eagerly bought from the bookstalls. Shakespeare may have read several of these, including Jourdain's narrative entitled *A Discovery of the Bermudas, Otherwise Called The Isle of Devils;* and he seems also to have had access to a confidential letter written by William Strachey, Secretary for the Council in Virginia, to "an Excellent Lady" in England, July 15, 1610, which remained unpublished until 1625.[1] The story with all its circumstantial details fired his imagination, and led him to create a sea-voyage, a tempest, and an enchanted island as a setting for a beautiful love-romance. Where he secured this love-

[1] See C. M. Gayley, *Shakespeare and the Founders of Liberty in America,* 1917. Cf. also J. D. Rea, "A Source for the Storm in *The Tempest,*" *Modern Philology,* 1919, xvii, 279.

romance is not clear, though a parallel may be found in one of the novels of the Spanish *Noches de Invierno* of Antonio de Eslava, published in 1609. Eslava seems to have drawn the novel from the Spanish romance *Espejo de Principes y Caballeros*, 1562, which was translated into English under the title *The Mirrour of Knighthood*, printed in nine volumes at different dates from 1578 to 1601. If Shakespeare came upon the story in Eslava, or in *The Mirrour of Knighthood*, his following of it is not close. It would seem that the dramatist, more than was his custom, drew from his own fancy; and this may explain the wonderful charm the play has for lovers of poetry.[1]

The songs which graced *The Tempest* were set to music by Robert Johnson, one of the most eminent composers of the day; and the scores he wrote for "Full fathom five" and "Where the bee sucks" have been preserved. Since at this date Johnson was in the employ of the Prince of Wales, who granted him a yearly stipend of £40, we may possibly see in his collaboration with the King's Men further evidence of the close relations then existing between the drama and the Court.[2] Other evidence is to be found in the play itself. Not only were its masque-like effects well-designed to please a Courtly audience, but certain allusions were inserted for the gratification of royal ears. And that *The Tempest* was successful in its performances at Whitehall can hardly be doubted. It was acted with special magnificence in the great Banqueting House [3] on November 1, 1611, to usher in the

---

[1] H. D. Gray, *Modern Language Notes*, 1920, xxxv, 321, suggests a possible source for *The Tempest* in the Commedia dell' Arte of Italian actors visiting London.

[2] He seems to have been earlier connected with the Globe orchestra. For the King's Men he composed the music to songs in Middleton's *Witch*, and in several plays by Beaumont and Fletcher. In 1611 he entered the service of the King.

[3] See Ernest Law, *Shakespeare's "Tempest" as Originally Produced at Court*, [n. d.].

revels of the season; and it was among the plays selected for presentation during the celebrations following the marriage of the King's daughter, Elizabeth, to the Elector Palatine.[1]

Thus with *Cymbeline*, *The Winter's Tale*, and *The Tempest*, Shakespeare fully demonstrated his ability to produce plays of the "newer stamp." Differing widely from his true histories, his uproarious comedies, and his profound tragedies, they add to our astonishment at his "infinite variety."

[1] Possibly it was revised in order to grace the betrothal of the Princess Elizabeth on December 27, 1612. See W. J. Lawrence's interesting article, "The Masque in *The Tempest*," *Fortnightly Review*, June, 1920. For a general discussion of the relations between Shakespeare and Beaumont and Fletcher, see A. H. Thorndike, *The Influence of Beaumont and Fletcher on Shakespeare*, 1901.

CHAPTER XXIII

LAST LABORS FOR THE KING'S MEN

WITH *The Tempest* in 1611 Shakespeare had written his last complete play. It is hard to understand why he should thus virtually cease composition at the age of forty-seven when all London with her loudest "O yes!" was crying "This is he!" It was not the time of life at which a successful man likes to give up his activity. Othello, though he had "somewhat descended into the vale of years," upon realizing that he must abandon his profession, exclaimed in agony of soul:

> Farewell the plumèd troop and the big wars
> That make ambition virtue! O, farewell!
> Farewell the neighing steed, and the shrill trump,
> The spirit-stirring drum, the ear-piercing fife,
> The royal banner, and all quality,
> Pride, pomp and circumstance of glorious war! . . .
> Farewell!

Why should Shakespeare, at the peak of maturity, bid farewell to the spirit-stirring life of the London theatres, and to his glorious career as England's most applauded poet? We can, I think, best explain this on the theory that his health was impaired; he had, indeed, only five years of life remaining. And if his strength was failing, he could now relax his efforts, for Beaumont and Fletcher were supplying his company with plays that enabled it to maintain its superiority over all rivals. Possibly he had contemplated retiring in the autumn of 1609. His cousin, Thomas Greene, then living with the poet's family at New Place, wrote in his Diary on September 9, 1609, in allusion to a change in his residence: "the rather that I perceive I might stay another year at New Place." We know that by June, 1611, Greene had moved to a house on the bank of the Avon. It may be, therefore, that in the spring of 1611 Shakespeare temporarily withdrew to Stratford with a view to recuperating his energies under the watchful care of his son-in-law, the eminent physician John Hall. We have documentary evidence that he was in Stratford in 1611: in September of that year the citizens made a collection "towards the charge of prosecuting the Bill in Parliament for the better repair of the highways," and among the seventy names of persons who made contributions we find that of the poet. Throughout the remainder of 1611 and all of 1612 we have no evidence to indicate his presence in London, nor does he seem to have busied himself with literary work of any sort.

This raises the question, When did Shakespeare retire from acting? "A question to be asked," for in his day he was not only a distinguished poet but a distinguished actor as well. Probably his labors on the rush-strewn stages of the Theatre, the Curtain, the Globe, and the Blackfriars playhouses occupied the greater part of his time and energy, as they certainly produced the major share of his income. The reason for our tendency to overlook his career as an actor is not far to seek. Gerard Langbaine, the first to write a sketch of his life, says: "He was both a Player and a Poet — but the greatest Poet that ever trod the Stage"; and it is his greatness as a poet that has in modern times overshadowed his successful career as a player.

Yet in his own day, men never forgot that he was also an actor. As late as 1640 an anonymous admirer printed "An Elegy on the Death of that famous Writer and Actor, Mr. William Shakespeare." He was, indeed, numbered among the better performers in an age when histrionic art kept pace with playwriting. It was as an actor that he scored his earliest successes in London. In 1592 Henry Chettle wrote: "Myself have seen his demeanour, no less civil than he excellent in the quality he professes." Apparently Chettle could find no stronger comparison. In 1594 he was chosen as one of the few full-sharers in the Chamberlain's Company, the best troupe in England. In 1595 the Court Treasurer, in recording a payment of money to the Chamberlain's Men for performances before the Queen, singled out the three actors, "William Kempe, William Shakespeare, and Richard Burbage," as adequately identifying the troupe. In the list of "the principal comedians" who took the chief rôles in Ben Jonson's *Every Man in his Humor*, 1598, Shakespeare stands at the head of the first column, with Burbage heading the second column; and in a similar list prefixed to *Sejanus*, 1603, he again tops one of the two columns, this time exchanging places with Burbage. In the royal patent, 1603, establishing the King's Company of Players, he is named before Burbage, Heminges, and the rest, as also in the various grants of red cloth for liveries. And, finally, in the Folio of 1623 he stands first in the list of the "Principal Actors in All These Plays." Clearly we cannot afford to ignore his labors as one of the "principal actors" in the leading company of the Elizabethan age.

Of the various rôles he assumed during his long career on the stage we have little definite knowledge, for information of this character was preserved only by accident. We have, however, the testimony of his friend, John Davies of Hereford, that sometimes he acted "kingly parts." In a poem entitled "To Our English Terence, Mr. Will. Shakespeare," Davies writes:

> Some say, good *Will*, which I in sport do sing,
> Hadst thou not played some kingly parts in sport,
> Thou hadst been a companion for a king.

From this it has been inferred, and no doubt rightly, that Shakespeare assumed parts that involved a dignified bearing. Such rôles would be in keeping with what we know of his personal manners, with Chettle's glowing praise of his "civil demeanour," and with the epithet "gentle" commonly applied to him by his contemporaries.

As to his style of acting, perhaps some notion may be gleaned from his advice to the players put into the mouth of Hamlet:

Speak the speech, I pray you, as I pronounced it to you, trippingly on the tongue; but if you mouth it, as many of your players do, I had as lief the town-crier spoke my lines. Nor do not saw the air too much with your hand, thus; but use all gently: for in the very torrent, tempest, and — as I may say — whirlwind of passion, you must acquire and beget a temperance that may give it smoothness. O, it offends me to the soul to hear a robustious periwig-pated fellow tear a passion to tatters, to very rags, to split the ears of the groundlings, who for the most part are capable of nothing but inexplicable dumb-shows and noise. I would have such a fellow whipped for o'er-doing Termagant. It out-herods Herod. Pray you avoid it. . . . Be not too tame, neither; but let your own discretion be your tutor. Suit the action to the word, the word to the action; with this special observance, that you o'erstep not the modesty of nature; for anything so overdone is from the purpose of playing, whose end, both at the first and now, was and is, to hold, as 'twere, the mirror up to nature.

We can well believe that Shakespeare tried to follow these principles in his own acting, keeping ever in mind that one judicious spectator whose approval, he tells us, should "o'erweigh a whole theatre of others." And in a goodly measure he must have succeeded. Theatrical managers and actors themselves are competent judges of histrionic ability; the experienced Elizabethan manager Beeston, and the eminent performer Mohun, long after the poet's death, informed Aubrey that Shakespeare "did act exceedingly well."

For further information regarding his career as a player we are dependent on late and untrustworthy gossip. Nicholas Rowe, writing in 1709, says that according to a tradition he acted "the Ghost in his own *Hamlet*," adding that it was regarded as "the top of his performance." If we accept this story, we may suppose that Shakespeare assumed the rôle because he did not care to entrust it to another; and there are some reasons for thinking that he may have acted the part of the Player King in addition.[1]

A second tradition is perhaps even less trustworthy. William Oldys, professing to derive his information from the actor John Bowman, writes (about 1750–60) that one of Shakespeare's younger brothers, "who lived to a good old age, even some years, as I compute, after the restoration of King Charles the Second," was accustomed to come to London to witness plays. On one such occasion he was questioned about the rôles assumed by the poet. But, writes Oldys, "he was so stricken in years, and possibly his memory so weakened with infirmities, which might make him the easier pass for a man of weak intellects, that he could give them but little light into their enquiries; and all that could be recollected from him of his brother Will in that station was the faint, general, and almost lost ideas he had of having once seen him act a part in one of his own comedies, wherein, being to personate a decrepit old man, he wore a long beard, and appeared so weak and drooping and unable to walk, that he was forced to be supported and carried by another person to a table, at which he was seated among some company who were eating, and one

[1] See the writer's article, "Some Notes on Hamlet," *Modern Language Notes*, 1913, xxviii, 39.

of them sung a song." The rôle here described is obviously that of the aged servant Adam in *As You Like It*.

One objection to the story is that none of Shakespeare's brothers lived into the Restoration. Edmund died in 1607, Gilbert, it seems, in 1612, and Richard in 1613. Yet, as Halliwell-Phillipps observes, the tradition may include "a glimmering of truth" garbled from still earlier tradition, and foisted upon a supposedly surviving brother of the poet.

When Shakespeare retired from acting we cannot say, for evidence is lacking. Yet we may suspect that it preceded his withdrawal from the less taxing and doubtless more congenial labor of composition; for at best the life of an Elizabethan player was arduous, with the constantly changing bill, the frequent memorizing of rôles, the morning rehearsals,[1] and the afternoon performances, often followed by evening appearances at Court, at the law-schools, in the homes of the nobility, and elsewhere.[2] Edward Alleyn, upon securing a competency, had withdrawn from acting when about thirty-nine years of age; and there was no reason why Shakespeare should not do

[1] Henslowe's contract with the actor Dawes contains the stipulation: "The said Robert Dawes shall, and will, at all times during the said term, duly attend all such rehearsals, which shall the night before the rehearsal be given publickly out; and if that the said Robert Dawes shall at any time fail to come at the hour appointed, then he shall, and will, pay ... twelve pence; and if he come not before the said rehearsal is ended, then the said Robert Dawes is contented to pay two shillings." — W. W. Greg, *Henslowe Papers*, p. 124. John Downes, the prompter, speaks of "attending every morning the actors' rehearsal, and their performances in afternoons." — *Roscius Anglicanus*, p. iii.

[2] How late in the night these might at times extend is suggested in Sir Gerard Herbert's letter to Sir Dudley Carleton describing a performance of *Pericles* at Court "after supper" in 1619: "In the King's Great Chamber they went to see the play of *Pericles Prince of Tyre*, which lasted till two o'clock. After two acts, the players ceased till the French all refreshed themselves with sweetmeats brought on China bowls, and wine and ale in bottles; after, the players began anew." It will be recalled that at Gray's Inn, 1594, the Chamberlain's Men began the play at midnight. See also *Tarlton's Jests*, ed. by J. O. Halliwell, p. 10.

the same, for his services were far less indispensable to his company. Jonson records his name in the list of the performers of *Sejanus*, 1603, but omits it from similar lists of 1605 and 1610. No great significance, however, can be attached to this fact, for an actor would not necessarily have a rôle in all the plays the King's Men presented. As we read in *A Cure for a Cuckold*, II, iii: "There's better law among the players, for a fellow shall have his share, though he do not play that day." The likelihood is that Shakespeare's retirement from the stage was gradual.

But if he ceased at a relatively early date to act — an assumption, we should remember, unsupported by definite evidence — he remained closely associated with the King's Men as one of the patentees of the company, and continued to serve them in the capacity of playwright. For his plays the actors may have paid him a fixed sum for each manuscript upon its delivery, or, in accordance with the custom prevailing at certain theatres, they may have retained him as their "poet" on an annual stipend.[1] The Reverend John Ward, vicar of Stratford,[2] writes: "He frequented the plays in his younger times, but in his elder days liv'd at Stratford, and supplied the stage with two plays every year, and had for it an allowance." Richard Brome was retained by the actors of the Salisbury Court playhouse at a weekly stipend of 15s., in return for which he was expected to supply the

[1] Precisely when this custom arose I have been unable to discover; the earlier custom was to pay a fixed sum for each play. When the children at Blackfriars were disbanded in 1608, Henry Evans, their manager, speaks of having "discharged and set at liberty" the poets employed; see Fleay, *Stage*, p. 246.

[2] Ward settled in Stratford in 1662. A Master of Arts of Oxford, he became a student of Oriental languages and of Old English literature. He was also deeply interested in local history. No fewer than seventeen of his commonplace-books are preserved; extracts from these have been edited by Charles Severn in *The Diary of the Rev. John Ward*, 1839.

company with three plays a year.[1] In 1639 the Salisbury Court actors were paying their dramatist "poet's wages" of 20s. a week.[2] And in *The Actors' Remonstrance* (1643), the players speak of the "annual stipends" of their "ordinarie poets." Whether the King's Men retained Shakespeare on a regular salary, as Ward states, or purchased each play from him at a fixed sum, we do not know. Nor, if he had gradually withdrawn from acting, can we say when he assumed merely the task of supplying his company with manuscripts.

As has already been stated, *The Tempest*, 1611, was his last complete play; and the facts above cited seem to warrant the conclusion that — at least temporarily — he had given up composition, and had retired to Stratford. But early in 1613 we find him back with his fellows in London, and apparently as active in their affairs as he had been in former years. His presence in the city is proved by several bits of evidence.

The first is connected with the wealthy young Francis Manners, patron of actors and playwrights. In 1612 he succeeded to the title of Earl of Rutland, in recognition of which dignity he was called upon to take part in a great tournament arranged to celebrate the King's Accession Day, March 24, 1613. It was customary for each knight to appear in the lists with a splendid accoutrement, the chief feature of which was an *impresa*, a symbolic picture painted on the shield, with a motto below, usually in Latin or Italian, explaining its significance.[3] Since the picture and its motto carried a hidden allusion to the knight bearing the shield, the spectators derived much pleasure in interpreting the meaning, and the most happy

---

[1] See C. E. Andrews, *Richard Brome*, p. 14. At the expiration of his contract the company offered him 20s. a week, but he went to write for the players at the Phœnix.

[2] *The Shakespeare Society's Papers*, iv, 100.

[3] For a description of several *imprese*, see *Pericles*, II, ii.

and ingenious conceptions were long after applauded in Courtly circles. No little importance, therefore, was attached to these *imprese* by the contending knights, who enlisted the services of poets and painters alike in securing effective and beautiful devices. The interest of poets in the subject is shown by Samuel Daniel's translation of the Italian treatise of Paulus Jovius, *Rare Inventions, both Militarie and Amorous, Called Imprese;* and the artistic quality of the painted shields led to a permanent exhibition of *imprese* in one of the long galleries of Whitehall Palace.[1]

On the notable occasion of his first appearance in this tournament, the Earl of Rutland engaged Shakespeare to devise for him a suitable *impresa* and motto, and put the task of pictorially executing Shakespeare's idea into the hands of Richard Burbage, who was an excellent painter as well as actor.[2] In the accounts of the Earl we read:

Item. 31 Martii 1613 to Mr. Shakespeare in gold about my Lord's *impresa* xlivs. To Richard Burbage for painting and making it, in gold xlivs.

Sir Henry Wotton, who witnessed the tournament, wrote a description of it to his friend Sir Edmund Bacon:[3] "Some caparisons seen before adventured to appear again, ... so frugal are the times, or so indigent. The two Riches only made a speech to the King; the rest were content with bare *imprese*, whereof some were so dark that their meaning is not yet understood. ... The two

---

[1] For a description of many of these beautiful English *imprese* see John Manningham's *Diary*, pp. 3–5.

[2] Cf. Middleton's elegy "On the Death of that Great Master in his Art and Quality, Painting and Playing, R. Burbage," and the anonymous elegy "On Mr. Richard Burbage, an excellent both player and painter" (Halliwell-Phillipps, *Outlines*, ii, 88). One of his canvases is now hanging in the Dulwich Picture Gallery.

[3] L. P. Smith, *Life and Letters of Sir Henry Wotton*, ii, 16.

best, to my fancy, were those of the two Earls brothers [William and Philip Herbert, Earls of Pembroke and Montgomery]: the first a small, exceeding white pearl, and the words *Solo candore valeo;* the other a sun casting a glance on the side of a pillar and the beams reflecting, with this motto, *Splendente refulget;* in which there seemed an agreement, the elder brother to allude to his own nature, and the other to his fortune." Since Wotton fails to mention the *impresa* borne by the Earl of Rutland, we must suppose that it did not strike his fancy, or that its meaning was too dark to be intelligible to him.

The second bit of evidence showing that Shakespeare was in London during this year is more prosaic. In March, 1613, merely as a speculation, he purchased, for the sum of £140, a house in the fashionable district of Blackfriars. He did not enter into the transaction, however, without the business advice of his fellow-actor, John Heminges, the shrewd manager of the Globe organization. The documents show that he paid £80 in cash, and allowed the balance, £60, to remain as a mortgage upon the property.

For Shakespeare's return at this time to active participation in the affairs of his company, two possible reasons suggest themselves. It may be that he desired to assist in the grand celebrations at Court following the marriage of the Princess Elizabeth to the Elector Palatine in February, 1613. The King's Men were called upon to present before the royal party no fewer than twenty plays, for which they received £153 6s. 8d. Shakespeare's plays were enumerated as *Much Ado, The Tempest, The Winter's Tale, Sir John Falstaff (The Merry Wives of Windsor?), The Moor of Venice (Othello), Cæsar's Tragedy (Julius Cæsar?), Hotspur (I Henry IV?),* and *Benedicte and Beatrice (Much Ado* repeated?). Doubtless he superintended the performance of all these plays, and he may even have modified one or more so as to render them better suited to a nuptial occasion.

But a second and stronger reason for his return to London may be discovered in the withdrawal of Beaumont from the stage in 1612–13. Fletcher, though an excellent poet, was somewhat lacking in constructive ability, and usually needed the collaboration of a firmer hand to shape his plots and otherwise render them effective on the stage. Beaumont, as it happened, possessed in abundant measure this very quality in which Fletcher was deficient. William Cartwright put the case thus:

> Though when all Fletcher writ, and the entire
> Man was indulged unto that sacred fire,
> His thoughts, and his thoughts' dress, appeared both such,
> That 'twas his happy fault to do too much;
> Who therefore wisely did submit each birth
> To knowing Beaumont ere it did come forth,
> Working again until he said 'twas fit.[1]

And John Dryden declared that Beaumont was "so accurate a judge of plays" that even Jonson "submitted all his writings to his censure, and, 'tis thought, used his judgment in correcting if not contriving all his plots." Aubrey no doubt exaggerated when he said "Master Beaumont's main business was to correct the overflowings of Mr. Fletcher's wit"; yet his statement reflects the generally accepted opinion that in their collaboration Beaumont supplied Fletcher with the critical force necessary to practical success.

Accordingly, when Beaumont withdrew from the stage in 1612–13, Fletcher stood in need of some experienced hand to guide his pen; and although the Globe Company soon engaged Philip Massinger to take Beaumont's

---

[1] Verses prefixed to the First Folio of Beaumont and Fletcher. Cartwright repeats the thought in a second poem contributed to the same volume.

place, we find Shakespeare temporarily setting himself to the task. In the year 1613 he helped Fletcher with *Henry VIII*, probably with *The Two Noble Kinsmen*, and possibly, though we cannot be sure, with the non-extant *Cardennio*.

Cardennio was acted by the King's Men at Court in May, 1613, in connection with the festivities attending the marriage of the Princess Elizabeth; and it was repeated on July 8 of the same year before the Ambassador of the Duke of Savoy. The obvious assumption is that it was both a new and a successful play in the repertory of the King's Men. It was not included by Heminges and Condell in the First Folio of 1623; but this has no significance for Shakespeare's possible minor share in its composition. Since, however, as the two Court performances show, it was a notable play, we find some difficulty in understanding why it was not included in the 1647 Folio of Beaumont and Fletcher. The publisher, Humphrey Moseley (whose trustworthiness in such matters, it should be added, is always open to doubt), declares in an address to the reader: "You will find here no omissions; . . . there is not any piece written by these authors, either jointly or severally, but what are now published to the world in this volume. One only play I must except (for I mean to deal openly); 'tis a comedy called *The Wildgoose Chase*, which hath been long lost, and I fear irrecoverable, for a person of quality borrowed it from the actors many years since, and (by the negligence of a servant) it was never returned." Later, if we may trust Moseley, it was produced "by a person of honor," and was issued in folio, 1651, as a supplement to the collection of 1647. Yet all the while the play may have been reposing in the archives of the Globe Theatre, for it was published by Moseley on behalf of John Lowin and Joseph Taylor, two well-known members of the

King's Company; and, as we know, the actors, after the suppression of the drama, frequently printed manuscripts from their storerooms for their "private benefit." According to Moseley's statement, *The Wild Goose Chase* completed the list of plays written by Beaumont and Fletcher; yet on September 9, 1653, he himself entered in the Stationers' Registers *Cardennio* as "by Fletcher and Shakespeare." Unfortunately, little dependence can be placed on Moseley's assertions, and he had a special tendency to associate every drama acted by the Globe Company with Shakespeare's name. He failed to print *Cardennio*, and no copy of the play has come down to us. Whether Shakespeare, or for that matter Fletcher, had a hand in its composition must therefore remain doubtful.[1]

Much less doubt is to be attached to the next play to be considered, printed in 1634 with the title: *The Two Noble Kinsmen: Presented at the Black-friers by the King's Majesties servants, with great applause: Written by the memorable Worthies of their time; Mr. John Fletcher, and Mr. William Shakspeare, Gent.* To be sure, not all scholars are agreed that Shakespeare had a hand in the play. Yet critics of special acumen in literary matters — for example, Lamb, Coleridge, De Quincey, Swinburne, and Tennyson — have felt the "unmistakable" presence of the master in various scenes; and opinion is now fairly settled that Shakespeare, if he did nothing more, at least revised the manuscript. The date of composition cannot be fixed with assurance, but a reference in Jonson's *Bartholomew Fair*, acted in 1614, to "the play of Palemon" seems to be an allusion to *The Two Noble Kinsmen*, which was based on Chaucer's story of Palamon and Arcite, and to indicate the date 1613.

---

[1] The play was based on *Don Quixote*, a book utilized by Fletcher. Little attention need be paid to *The Double Falsehood* exploited in 1727 by Theobald as a lost play of Shakespeare's, and dealing with the *Cardennio* story.

A third drama of this year, in which Shakespeare unquestionably collaborated with Fletcher, was *Henry VIII*, first acted at the Globe in June, 1613, with the alternate title *All is True*. It was duly included by Heminges and Condell in the First Folio, possibly to round out the English historical plays. Yet in bulk Shakespeare's part in it was not so great as that of Fletcher (or, as some think, of Fletcher and Massinger); of its seventeen scenes, Spedding, whose conclusions are now generally accepted, can assign only six to Shakespeare. Nor can we believe that Shakespeare is responsible for outlining the play; the plot has that looseness of construction which we know to be characteristic of Fletcher.

This was the last labor Shakespeare was to attempt for his company, and definitely marks the end of his career as a writer. Moreover, by a curious trick of Fortune, its initial performance marks also the end of the Globe Playhouse, which had witnessed so many of his triumphs.

The first presentation of *Henry VIII* was set for June 29, 1613. The public must have looked forward to the event with high expectations — a new play by "the memorable worthies of their time, Mr. John Fletcher and Mr. William Shakespeare, Gent." The actors spared no expense in providing scenery and costume befitting a new play by such distinguished authors; and Shakespeare himself, it appears, took special pains to instruct the actors in their parts. John Downes, prompter of the Lincolns-Inn-Fields Theatre at the time of the Restoration, writes in his *Roscius Anglicanus* concerning a revival of the play under the personal direction of Sir William Davenant: "The part of the King was so right and justly done by Mr. Betterton, he being Instructed in it by Sir William, who had it from old Mr. Lowin, that had his Instructions from Mr. Shakespeare himself, that I dare and will aver, none can, or will, come near him in this Age in the performance of that part."

Many noblemen and distinguished men of letters, including Ben Jonson, Sir Henry Wotton, and John Taylor, the Water Poet, were present. The afternoon, we are told, was balmy and full of "sunneshine." Upon the entrance of the King, in the fourth scene of the first act, two cannon were discharged as a royal salute, one of which hurled a bit of its wadding upon the roof of the building and set the thatch on fire. The members of the audience, however, were so interested in the play that they paid no attention to the fire overhead. Soon they were fleeing for their lives; and within "one short hour" nothing was left of the "stately" Globe.

This, the first theatrical disaster in London, created a great stir, and many narratives of the event have come down to us, of which I quote below a few of the more interesting.

Howes, the chronicler, thus writes in his continuation of Stow's *Annals:*

Upon St. Peter's Day last, the playhouse, or theatre, called the Globe, upon the Bankside, near London, by negligent discharge of a peal of ordnance, close to the south side thereof, the thatch took fire, and the wind suddenly dispersed the flames round about, and in a very short space the whole building was quite consumed; and no man hurt: the house being filled with people to behold the play, *viz.* of Henry the Eight.

The eminent statesman, Sir Henry Wotton, in a letter to a friend, gives the following gossipy account: [1]

Now to let matters of state sleep. I will entertain you at the present with what hath happened this week at the Bankside. The King's Players had a new play, called *All is True*, representing some principal pieces of the reign of Henry the Eighth, which was set forth with many extraordinary circumstances of pomp and majesty, even to the matting of the stage; the Knights

[1] From *Reliquiæ Wottonianæ*, ed. of 1672, p. 425.

of the Order with their Georges and Garters, the guards with their embroidered coats, and the like — sufficient in truth within a while to make greatness very familiar, if not ridiculous. Now, King Henry making a masque at the Cardinal Wolsey's house, and certain cannons being shot off at his entry, some of the paper, or other stuff wherewith one of them was stopped, did light on the thatch, where being thought at first but an idle smoke, and their eyes more attentive to the show, it kindled inwardly, and ran round like a train, consuming within less than an hour the whole house to the very ground. This was the fatal period of that virtuous fabrick; wherein yet nothing did perish but wood and straw, and a few forsaken cloaks; only one man had his breeches set on fire, that would perhaps have broiled him, if he had not, by the benefit of a provident wit, put it out with a bottle of ale.

Perhaps, however, the most vivid account is supplied by a contemporary ballad:

A Sonnet upon the Pitiful Burning of the Globe Playhouse in London [1]

> Now sit thee down, Melpomene,
> Wrapt in a sea-coal robe,
> And tell the dolefull tragedy
> That late was played at Globe;
> For no man that can sing and say
> Was scared on St. Peter's day.
>   *Oh sorrow, pitiful sorrow, and yet all this is true.* [2]

> All you that please to understand,
> Come listen to my story;
> To see Death with his raking brand
> Mongst such an auditory;
> Regarding neither Cardinall's might,
> Nor yet the rugged face of Henry the eight.
>   *Oh sorrow, etc.*

---

[1] Printed by Haslewood in the *Gentleman's Magazine*, 1816, from an old MS. volume of poems. Printed also by Halliwell-Phillipps, *Outlines*, "from a manuscript of the early part of the seventeenth century of unquestionable authenticity." Perhaps it is the same as the *Doleful Ballad* entered in the Stationers' Registers, 1613. I print from Halliwell-Phillipps' text, omitting the last three stanzas.

[2] Punning on the title *All is True*.

This fearful fire began above,
A wonder strange and *true*,
And to the stage-house did remove,
As round as taylor's clew,
And burnt down both beam and snagg,
And did not spare the silken flagg.
 Oh sorrow, etc.

Out run the knights, out run the lords,
And there was great ado;
Some lost their hats, and some their swords;
Then out run Burbage, too.
The reprobates, though drunk on Monday,
Prayd for the fool and Henry Condy.
 Oh sorrow, etc.

The periwigs and drum-heads fry'd
Like to a butter firkin;
A woeful burning did betide
To many a good buff jerkin
Then with swolen eyes, like drunken Flemminges
Distressed stood old stuttering Heminges.
 Oh sorrow, etc.

Ben Jonson, who was present, wrote in his *Execration upon Vulcan:*

The Globe, the glory of the Bank,
Which, though it were the fort of the whole parish,
Flanked with a ditch, and forced out of marish,
I saw with two poor chambers taken in,
And razed ere thought could urge this might have been
See the World's ruins! Nothing but the piles
Left.

The players were not seriously inconvenienced by the disaster, for they could move at once to the Blackfriars Theatre in the city; but the housekeepers, who owned the building, suffered a considerable loss. For a time, in view of the fact that their lease of the ground now had only thirteen years to run, they hesitated about rebuilding. But, after some negotiating, they secured an adequate extension of the lease, and at once authorized Heminges to begin the erection of a new Globe. An initial assessment was made of £50 on each share, which was soon raised to £120; and the final cost of the building, according to the statement of one of the sharers, was £1400.

The New Globe was erected on the old site, the builders being able to make use of the original pile foundations; and like its predecessor it was of timber and plaster construction, though the housekeepers, as Jonson humorously remarked, now had the wit "to cover it with tiles." It was ready for occupancy by the King's Men in the early summer of the following year. John Chamberlain writes to Mrs. Alice Carleton on June 30, 1614:

I have not seen your sister Williams since I came to town, though I have been there twice. The first time she was at a neighbor's house at cards, and the next she was gone to the New Globe to a play. Indeed, I hear much speech of this new playhouse, which is said to be the fairest that ever was in England.

Shakespeare was one of the proprietors of the New Globe, and drew an annual income from its profits; but otherwise he had little or nothing to do with it, either as actor or as playwright. From this time on his life centres in Stratford.

CHAPTER XXIV

RETIREMENT TO STRATFORD

HAVING now definitely given up not only acting but also the composition of plays, Shakespeare retired to Stratford, and spent his remaining years in the quiet life of that obscure village. No doubt he made frequent visits to the city to look after his interests there, to meet his old comrades at the theatre, and to renew for a time the more stirring existence he had formerly led. But his London career was run. Possibly, as has already been suggested, he was not a well man; for, though we can readily understand why he might desire relief from the arduous duties of acting, we cannot believe that he would have given up the writing of poetry — "what I most enjoy," he seems to say in his *Sonnets* — before he had passed the forties, had not the condition of his health rendered it imperative. It may be significant that when he came to London in November, 1614, he was accompanied by the physician John Hall. The age at which he died, and the circumstances which provoked his final illness, suggest that he might have been suffering from Bright's disease, or at least from some chronic trouble which gradually sapped his strength.

Yet in his withdrawal from "the brave world" of London and the Court, in which he had long played such a conspicuous rôle, life still held for him reasonable happiness. Rowe puts it thus: "The latter part of his life was spent, as all men of good sense will wish theirs may be, in ease, retirement, and the conversation of friends." In his beautiful home of New Place, surrounded by his family and his early friends, gossiping with the neighbors, and busied with his garden and orchard,[1] he was able to enjoy that slippered ease which he had celebrated in his plays.

Moreover, from his investments he drew an income that would enable him to lead the life of a country gentleman of means. The Stratford vicar, John Ward, states that "he spent at the rate of a thousand a year, as I have heard." This hearsay evidence may be an exaggeration, but doubtless is an exaggeration of a truth. Nor is there anything unusual about the wealth which it implies, for many Elizabethan actors, by thrift and sound business judgment, had become exceedingly rich. Edward Alleyn was able to purchase for approximately £10,000 a country estate, where he lived in grand style. He not only founded and endowed the College of God's Gift, and the Dulwich Picture Gallery, but left funds with which to erect and suitably to endow thirty almshouses. Richard Burbage, who like Shakespeare was a member of the King's Company, died possessed of an annual income of "better than £300" in land alone. And Augustine Phillips, it will be recalled, purchased an estate at Mortlake, Surrey, in 1604.

This naturally raises the question, How wealthy was Shakespeare? The only way to answer the question is to estimate as best we can his annual income from various sources.

In the first place, like Burbage, he was a full-sharer in the King's Company of players. From declarations made by the young actors in 1635, and from the counter-declarations of Cuthbert Burbage, we have fairly exact information as to the value of such a share. According

---

[1] He is said to have planted the orchard himself, and according to tradition set out with his own hands a mulberry-tree, the first of its kind in Warwickshire. "Shakespeare's mulberry-tree" as it was called, after growing to enormous size, was cut down in 1758.

to Burbage "for one whole year last past, beginning from Whitson Monday, 1634, each" of the King's Men "gained severally, as he was a player, and no house-keeper, £180." [1] There is no reason to suppose that in Shakespeare's day the profits of the company were less.[2]

In the second place, he was one of the housekeepers, or proprietors, of both the Globe and Blackfriars. The value of a housekeeper's share in the Blackfriars was cautiously estimated by Cuthbert Burbage, himself a housekeeper, as "above £30" a year. We have no definite statement of the value of a share in the much larger Globe, but may, I think, conservatively reckon this at £50 a year.

In the third place, Shakespeare was the chief play-wright for his company. From contemporary evidence, too extensive to be quoted here, we are justified in concluding that he received, on an average, about £15 a play;[3] and since he wrote, on an average, two plays a year, his income from this source must have been not far from £30 annually.[4]

In the fourth place, it was customary for the company suitably to reward a dramatist after his play had demonstrated its success. In the earlier days they gave him a sum of money by way of bonus; later they gave him the profits of a benefit performance. At the second [5] (in some theatres the third) acting of a new play, the whole takings

[1] Printed in Halliwell-Phillipps, *Outlines*, i, pp. 312–19.

[2] If, as is possible, there were not so many sharers, the profits may have been greater.

[3] Robert Daborne, a third- or fourth-rate dramatist, was receiving from Henslowe in 1613 £20 for a play, and was offered £25 by another company; see Greg, *Henslowe Papers*, pp. 67, 71, 73. The King's Men seem to have been more liberal than the niggardly Henslowe.

[4] The playwright for the Salisbury Court actors received in 1639 the salary of 20s. a week, or £52 a year.

[5] With the King's Men the second day seems to have been set aside for the poet; see the Prologue to *The City Match*, and compare the Herbert benefits later cited.

of the house, minus the necessary daily charges, were presented to the author. This was called "the poet's day." Dekker in a satirical vein accused some playwrights of writing solely with their benefit in mind, "not caring, so he gains a cram'd Third Day"; [1] and in like vein the author of *Lady Alimony* glances at the poet's "fair revenue" from his benefit performance: [2]

> *Timon.* But were our bills posted, that our house may be with a numerous auditory stored? our boxes by ladies of quality and of the new dress crowdingly furnished? our galleries and ground-front answerably to their pay completed?
> *Siparius.* Assure yourself, sir, nothing is a-wanting that may give way to the poet's improvement.
> *Timon.* Thou sayest well; this is indeed the poet's third day, and must raise his pericranium, deeply steeped in Frontiniac, a fair revenue for his rich Timonic fancy.

Naturally the amount arising from this source varied with different theatres, with the popularity of different authors, and with the success of the individual plays. But we can estimate the value of a Globe benefit from the two annual benefits of a similar nature which Sir Henry Herbert, Master of the Revels, was accustomed to receive from the King's Men. On May 25, 1628, he notes: "The benefitt of the first day, being a very unseasonable one in respect of the weather, comes but unto £4 15s. 0d." That Herbert was rightly disappointed is shown by his receiving on favorable days £17 10s., £9 16s., £12 4s., £13, and £15. Perhaps a fair notion of the average sum he derived from his two benefit performances is supplied by the agreement the King's Men made with him in 1633 to pay him thereafter in lieu of his benefits £20 a year. [3] It should be remembered, however, that

---

[1] Prologue to *If It Be Not Good*, 1610.
[2] Hazlitt's edition of Dodsley's *Old English Plays*, xiv, 278. See also Greg, *Henslowe Papers*, p. 75; Davenant's *Playhouse to Be Let;* John Downes' *Roscius Anglicanus*, p. 41.
[3] On Herbert's benefits see my *Dramatic Records of Sir Henry Herbert*, p. 42–45.

Herbert's benefits were secured not from the performance of a *new* play, but from "the second day of a revived play." Shakespeare's benefits were from the second day of a new play, which was far more certain to fill the theatre, and which possibly commanded double prices for admission. On this showing we may safely reckon the value of Shakespeare's benefits as at least £30 a year.

In the fifth place, actors secured a goodly revenue from performances at Court, at the several law-schools, and in the private homes of the nobility. As a rule these performances were in the evening, and did not interfere with the daily profits at the theatres; in cases when performances at Court caused the players to "lose their day at their house," they received suitable extra compensation, ordinarily "£20 apiece for those plays" instead of "£10 apiece for the other." [2] Shakespeare's income from this source is hard to estimate. Sir Sidney Lee reckons it as, on the average, £10 a year, and this probably not far wrong.

In the sixth place, Shakespeare as one of the King's Players received a yearly wage of £3 6s. 8d., and as Groom of the Chamber, £2 12s. 4d. — a total of almost £6 annually from the royal treasury. [3]

Finally, he drew an income from his invested savings

[1] W. J. Lawrence, *The Elizabethan Playhouse*, ii, 101, goes so far as to say that the benefit performances constituted "the chief source of emolument" for the Elizabethan dramatist. For a discussion of the subject see Alwin Thaler, "Playwrights' Benefits, and 'Interior Gatherings' in the Elizabethan Playhouse," *Studies in Philology*, xvi, 187. The custom persisted after the Restoration. Langbaine writes: "Mr. Dryden . . . has got more on the third day than it's probable ever Horace receiv'd from his patron for any one poem in all his life."

[2] See my *Shakespearean Playhouses*, p. 402 ff.; and note the extracts from the Warrant Book printed by Mrs. Stopes in the Shakespeare *Jahrbuch*, xlv. Probably the same sums were paid the actors when they performed elsewhere; for example, the students of the Middle Temple gave them £10 for the evening performance of *Twelfth Night* in 1602.

[3] There seems to be a misunderstanding of the phrase "sworn groom without fee"; see Mary Sullivan, *Court Masques*, 1913, pp. 251–54.

for he seems to have lived economically in London, and his shrewdness in business transactions is proverbial. We know that from the Stratford tithes alone he enjoyed a net annual revenue of £38. How much he received from the lands purchased at Stratford, from the houses he owned there, and from money lent at usury we have no means even of estimating. Perhaps it would be conservative to reckon his income from such miscellaneous sources at £12 annually.

The total of the sums enumerated above, though of course not all were received simultaneously, is £386. This compares favorably with Richard Burbage's annual income of £300 from land alone, and with what we know of the wealth of other actors of the day. It is clear, therefore, that Shakespeare had ample means to provide himself with every necessary comfort.

But more important for his happiness, now that he had forsworn "the full stream of the world to live in a nook," was the companionship of his family, and of his near neighbors and friends.

With him at "the Great House" lived only his wife Anne and his unmarried daughter Judith. There is no reason to suppose that the former was not an affectionate and beloved wife, as she was unquestionably an affectionate and beloved mother. But Judith, we may fear, was a source of disappointment, even of some worry, to her father. Since she could not, like Susanna, write her name, she apparently had declined to accept an education; and in other ways she seems to have been less stable than her elder sister — less attractive too, if we may judge by the fact that she did not marry until her thirty-second year, and then was wedded to a ne'er-do-well.

Not far from New Place was Hall's Croft, the home of Susanna, where, we can have little doubt, the retired poet spent much of his time. With the distinguished physician, John Hall, he would have many intellectual interests in common. With Susanna, too, "witty above her sex," he could indulge in the sprightly gossip which makes up the life of a small town. Nor should we overlook the presence there of his little granddaughter Elizabeth, rapidly growing into the most attractive years of childhood.

At the old home in Henley Street he found pleasant memories of the past, not unmixed with sadness. His father had died there in 1601, his mother in 1608; and now the property had come to him. The house was occupied by his only sister Joan, who had married a hatter named Hart. In the family, besides his sister and brother-in-law, were his three young nephews, William, Thomas, and Michael.

As for his brothers, all were probably dead. The youngest, Edmund, had followed the dramatist to the city and become an actor at the Globe. When he died in 1607, at the age of twenty-eight, Shakespeare had buried him in St. Saviour's Church, now Southwark Cathedral, placing the body in a position of honor within the chancel itself, and paying for "a forenoon knell of the great bell."[1] A second brother, Gilbert, seems to have died in 1612, and is probably to be identified with the "Gilbert Shakespeare, adolescens," whose burial is noted in February of that year.[2] The third brother, Richard, died in February of the following year.

---

[1] No expense was spared in this burial. The fee for a forenoon knell of the great bell was 8s.; and an additional fee of 20s. had to be paid for burial within the church. The fact that the body was placed inside the chancel would indicate Shakespeare's influence with the church authorities.

[2] As Mrs. Stopes, *Shakespeare's Environment*, pp. 333–35, shows, the terms "adolescens," "adolescentulus," and "adolescentula," were loosely applied by the Stratford clerk to persons as old as thirty-three and thirty-four years. It is worth noting, too, that there is no entry in the Stratford registers to show that Gilbert ever was married, and no other record of his

In addition to the immediate members of the family there was living in Stratford Thomas Greene, who refers to the poet as "my cousin Shakespeare." He had received a legal training in the Middle Temple, London, was called to the bar in 1600, and had come to Stratford to practise his profession. In London he probably had seen much of his distinguished "cousin," and upon his arrival in Stratford he took up his residence for a time at New Place. In 1601 he was appointed Councillor for the Corporation; in 1603 he became Steward of the Court of Records; and in 1610 he was made, in addition, the Town Clerk. He was closely associated with Shakespeare in business affairs, and doubtless was reckoned as a member of the family circle.

Outside of this small group of relatives, the poet must have found pleasure in the society of various friends, some of them companions of his boyhood, others his near neighbors. There were, for example, Hamnet Sadler and his wife Judith, for whom the youthful Shakespeare in 1585 had named his twins. Hamnet was now a prosperous tradesman, and had a large family of his own; one of his sons, William, was in all likelihood named in honor of the dramatist. The lifelong friendship between the two men is further indicated by the poet's will; Sadler acted as one of the witnesses, and received a small legacy for the purchase of a memorial ring.

Another intimate friend was Julius Shaw, living only two doors from New Place. His father, a dealer in wool, had probably in earlier days been a friend of John Shakespeare, who attested the *post mortem* inventory of his property. The son continued in the same trade: "Julius Shaw useth the trades of buying and selling wool, yarn,

burial; and there is no indication that there was a second person of the name in Stratford. Moreover, the total absence of allusion to Gilbert in the poet's will is almost conclusive evidence that he was dead before 1616.

and malting." He had prospered, and now was a man of wealth and influence in the town, having been elected burgess, chamberlain, alderman, and high-bailiff. His fellow-officers in the Corporation thought so highly of him that in 1613 they noted in the Council Book "his honesty [and] fidelity," and recorded their "good opinion of him." Shakespeare likewise entertained a high opinion of him, and invited him to act as a witness to the first draft of his will along with the solicitor Collins.

Another close friend was Henry Walker, a mercer, and one of the aldermen of the town. In 1608 he had named his son for Shakespeare, who acted as godfather on the occasion of the baptism. No doubt the poet took a special interest in the little boy; in his will he left him a small bequest: "To my godson, William Walker, xxs. in gold."

Shakespeare's acquaintance, however, was not confined to the tradesfolk of the village. His rank as one of England's most distinguished men of letters, a Groom of the Royal Chamber, and a favorite with the King and the noblemen of the Court, as well as his wealth, brought him social intercourse with the more aristocratic members of the community. To provincial homes like theirs, his wide experience of the world, his charming personality, and his brilliant intellect would naturally make him a welcome visitor. As Nicholas Rowe writes: "His pleasurable wit and good nature engaged him in the acquaintance, and entitled him to the friendship, of the gentlemen of the neighborhood."

Chief among these were the Combes, owning extensive properties in and about Stratford, and numbered among the wealthiest landed gentry of Warwickshire. William Combe resided mainly at Warwick, where he was a large landowner, though he also held property about Stratford. His nephew, Thomas Combe, resided in Stratford in the fine mansion called The College House, the only dwelling in town that could pretend to vie with New Place in grandeur. Thomas' brother, John, likewise a resident of Stratford, was an exceedingly rich old bachelor of usurious tendency. He possessed a striking personality, not altogether unattractive, and with Shakespeare he soon developed a warm friendship. The latter, according to tradition, composed for him a jocular epitaph, satirizing his shrewdness as a money-lender. Upon his death in 1614, the old man revealed his regard for Shakespeare by leaving him the then handsome legacy of £5. With the sons of Thomas Combe, William and Thomas, of The College House, Shakespeare was likewise on intimate terms. In his will he bequeathed to the younger Thomas his sword, apparently one of his most valued possessions.

The family of Reynolds, near kinsmen of the Combes, were also among the poet's close friends. Thomas Reynolds, Gent., who enjoyed heraldic honors, died in 1613; one of his sons, William, who owned much land in and about Stratford, was remembered by Shakespeare in his will with 26s. 8d. for the purchase of a memorial ring. In like manner the poet remembered the two brothers Anthony and John Nash, belonging to a family of high social position in Stratford — according to Halliwell-Phillipps, "one entitled to coat armour, which, as well as the pedigree, were entered by Thomas Nash at the visitation of 1619." Of the two brothers, Anthony was the more wealthy, possessing considerable property at Stratford and Welcombe, and associated with Shakespeare in the ownership of the tithes. The friendship between the families later found expression in the marriage of Anthony's son, Thomas, to Shakespeare's beloved granddaughter, Elizabeth Hall.

So far we have been dealing with Shakespeare's Stratford friendships for which we can cite definite evidence. Yet with almost equal confidence we may assert that he was on terms of familiarity with Sir Henry and Lady Rainsford, who lived at Clifford Chambers just outside the village. Both were famed for their interest in literature, and their generous hospitality to men of letters. They delighted to honor that other Warwickshire poet and playwright, Michael Drayton, often entertaining him for long periods in their home. Like Shakespeare, Drayton was of humble origin, his grandfather being a butcher, and his father a tradesman — according to Aubrey a butcher also. As a boy he was received into the household of Sir Henry Goodere, who, recognizing that he had genius and ambition, treated him kindly, and gave him an education with his own children. As Drayton grew up in this home, he seems to have formed an attachment for Sir Henry's daughter, Anne, although he well knew that she was out of his star. He celebrates her in his beautiful *Idea* sonnets, and elsewhere in his verse. She married Sir Henry Rainsford, of Stratford, but she always continued her liberal patronage of "her poet." Her husband, Sir Henry, grew to be very fond of Drayton; and Clifford Chambers, as Drayton puts it, became "the Muses' quiet port," where he spent much time in the delightful companionship of his patron and patroness. On his visits to Stratford he must have seen much of his old friend and fellow-playwright, Shakespeare, and have introduced him, if introduction were necessary, to the Rainsfords. In the quiet port of Clifford Chambers we can imagine him talking with the retired dramatist "of poets and poesie," as he loved to do with his friend Henry Reynolds:

> My dearly lovèd friend, how oft have we,
> In winter evenings (meaning to be free)

To some well-chosen place us'd to retire;
And there with moderate meat and wine and fire,
Have past the hours contentedly with chat,
Now talk'd of this, and then discours'd of that,
Spoke our own verses 'twixt ourselves; if not,
Other men's lines, which we by chance had got;
Or some stage pieces, famous long before,
Of which your happy memory had store.[1]

We have, however, besides the frequent presence of Drayton at Clifford Chambers, further reasons to suppose that Shakespeare was known to the Rainsfords. They were on terms of the closest friendship with the Combes and other families with which Shakespeare associated. And John Hall was their family physician, often ministering to the health of both Sir Henry and Lady Rainsford; on one occasion, we know, they called him in to treat the poet Drayton, at the time a guest in their home. It is inconceivable that in a small community, and with so many friends in common, the Rainsfords, with their special interest in literature, should not be familiar with the most distinguished poet of the age, then living close at hand.

With still other members of the local aristocracy Shakespeare no doubt was at least formally acquainted. He may have thus known Sir Thomas Lucy, the younger, of Charlecote, and Fulke Greville, Lord Brooke, of Beauchamp Court, nine miles distant. Brooke, indeed, was related to the Ardens, and displayed their arms with his own, as did Shakespeare. Moreover, as Recorder of Stratford he was often in the village, and in his official capacity must sooner or later have come into contact with its most notable citizen. But a genuine bond of sympathy between the two men, if they enjoyed each other's friendship, would be their common interest in poetry. Brooke, who boasted that he was the friend of Sir Philip Sidney,

[1] *To Henry Reynolds.*

had been writing lyric verse from early manhood; Peele in 1590 called him "the Muses' favorer, lover of learning," and declared that he was a "sound judge of poesy." And he was interested in the drama, too; in 1609 he published a play, and he still reserved another by him in manuscript. As a conspicuous member of the Court he must have known Shakespeare in his London career, and as a fellow Warwickshire man may well have taken some pride in his success. According to the author of *State Worthies*, 1670, Lord Brooke desired "to be known to posterity under no other notion than of Shakespeare's and Ben Jonson's master, Chancellor Egerton's patron, Bishop Overall's lord, and Sir Philip Sidney's friend." [1]

But Shakespeare's social life was mainly centred in the members of his own family, and in their friends, men like Sadler, Walker, and Shaw, who could frequently drop in at New Place or Hall's Croft for a pleasant chat — for the most part, we may suspect, dealing with local happenings. And since the poet now was living in a small country town, he naturally took an interest in the petty events that make up the existence of a rural community. To fill out our conception of his years of retirement, therefore, we must record some of the trivial incidents of Stratford life that especially concerned him, although the narrative may seem like a "chronicle of small beer."

In July, 1613, Shakespeare's eldest daughter, Mrs. Hall, became the victim of a cruel and wholly unjust bit of slander. A young scapegrace, named John Lane, junior, reported that "she had the running of the reins, and had been naught with Rafe Smith at [2] John Palmer's."

---

[1] It is interesting that William Davenant, probably Shakespeare's godson, grew up as a page in Greville's household.

[2] The reading is "at," not "and" as often given; see the facsimile in Halliwell-Phillipps, *Outlines*, i, 242.

After five weeks of whispered gossip, news of the story came to the Halls, and Mrs. Hall promptly brought suit against Lane in the Ecclesiastical Court of the diocese for slander, the case being heard at Worcester, July 15, 1613. Among the witnesses called to refute Lane's story was Robert Whatcote, one of Shakespeare's friends, and a witness of the poet's will. Young Lane failed to appear in response to the summons, and Mrs. Hall was fully exonerated by the authorities. Later, on July 27, Lane was excommunicated by the Bishop, thus further vindicating Mrs. Hall, and putting an end to the episode, which at the time must have exceedingly annoyed the poet.

In the spring of 1614 the Corporation honored an itinerant Puritan preacher, then stopping at New Place, with a present of a quart of sack and a quart of claret wine: "Item, for one quart of sack, and one quart of claret wine, given to a preacher at the New Place, xx*d*." This indicates, not, as some have supposed, that Shakespeare was of puritanical leanings, but that his hospitality was bountiful, and his home freely open to strangers sojourning in the village.

On July 9, 1614, a fire broke out in Stratford, which for a time threatened the whole town. The Council wrote: "Within the space of less than two hours [there were] consumed and burnt fifty and four dwelling houses, many of them being very fair houses, besides barns, stables, and other houses of office; . . . the force of which fire was so great (the wind setting full upon the town) that it dispersed into so many places thereof, whereby the whole town was in very great danger to have been utterly consumed." The loss was so heavy that the Corporation sought and secured from King James royal letters patent for a collection throughout the chief towns of the region "towards the new building and re-edifying" of the village. Shakespeare's property, so far as we know, was uninjured; but he must have spent an anxious night, and no doubt was called upon to render assistance of a practical sort to his less fortunate fellow-citizens.

Three days later Shakespeare's friend, John Combe, the old bachelor, died. In his will he left the poet as a remembrance the legacy of £5, and provided the sum of £60 for the erection of a suitable monument to himself in the Stratford Church, which he stipulated was to be set up within one year after his decease. The executors of the will might naturally apply to Shakespeare for information regarding a good London tomb-maker, and Shakespeare may have been responsible for the employment of Garret and Nicholas Johnson, whose establishment was on the Bankside within a stone's throw of the Globe. However that may be, the Johnson brothers came to Stratford, and erected in the church an elaborate tomb, which has received high praise from critics. A few years later they were again called to Stratford, this time to erect a tomb for Shakespeare himself.

After the death of old John, the two young Combes, William and Thomas, were in full management of the extensive Combe estates lying in and near Stratford. Almost at once they began to make trouble by planning to enclose the common fields of the village, to the great alarm and distress of the citizens. This enclosure, the Corporation declared, would lead to "the undoing of the town"; indeed one Alderman went so far as to say that "all three fires were not so great a loss to the town as the enclosures would be." Nor was the Corporation alone affected; Shakespeare's income from the tithes would be seriously impaired.

The Town Council made strenuous opposition to the proposal of the Combes; and Shakespeare's cousin,

Thomas Greene, as Clerk of the Council, took an active part in the prolonged fight against the project. The citizens apparently expected Shakespeare, in view of his personal concern in the matter, to side with them, and perhaps they looked for powerful assistance from him in his influence at Court. On the other hand, the Combes seem to have specially feared his influence. They approached him on the subject, and on October 28, 1614, through their legal agent, William Replingham, agreed to sign articles [1] completely guaranteeing him and his heirs for ever against any pecuniary loss that might result from the enclosures. With characteristic astuteness, Shakespeare deemed it wise to accept this absolute guarantee rather than run the risk of a serious loss in case the Town Council should be unsuccessful in its opposition. And in making the agreement with the Combes he was thoughtful enough to have the name of his cousin, Thomas Greene, who owned some of the tithes, inserted in order likewise to protect him. [2]

After having made this special agreement with the Combes — who, it should be remembered, were numbered among his close friends — Shakespeare seems to have felt that it was improper for him to use his influence at Court against them, or to side actively with the Town Council. Moreover, since the Combes made various offers to compensate the town — offers which bear every evidence of being fair, but which the Council refused to accept — he may have felt that the Council was not justified in its unyielding attitude.

Thomas Greene, however, continued to carry on a bitter fight against the enclosures, not so much, perhaps,

[1] For these articles see Halliwell-Phillipps, *Outlines*, ii, 36.
[2] So I assume. Greene writes in his *Diary:* "Mr. Replyngham, 28 Octobris, article with Mr. Shakespeare, and then I was put in by T. Lucas," i.e., at Shakespeare's request? Mrs. Stopes, however, thinks that the Combes were attempting to bribe Greene.

because he was personally averse to the scheme, as because, in his capacity of Town Clerk, he was legal agent of the Corporation. On November 12 he was dispatched to London to lay the case before the Privy Council. Four days later Shakespeare, attended by the physician John Hall, arrived in London on private business. Greene at once made them a friendly visit, an account of which he thus recorded in his Diary:

Jovis, 17 No[vember, 1614]. My Cousin Shakespeare coming yesterday to town, I went to see him how he did.[1] He told me that they [the Combes] assured him they meant to enclose no further than to Gospel Bush, and so up straight (leaving out part of the dingles to the field) to the gate in Clopton hedge, and take in Salisbury's piece; and that they mean in April to survey the land, and then to give satisfaction, and not before. And he and Mr. Hall say they think there will be nothing done at all.

Shakespeare's failure to take an active part in the Corporation's fight against the Combes no doubt was a source of disappointment to the citizens. The Town Council on December 23 addressed an appealing letter to him, then in London, requesting his aid in the matter, as we learn from the following entry in Greene's Diary: "23rd Dec. 1614. A hall. Letters written, one to Mr. Mannering [steward of the Lord Chancellor, who was lord of the royal manor of Stratford], another to Mr. Shakespeare, with almost all the company's hands to either. I also writ of myself to my Cousin Shakespeare the copies of all our oaths made then, also a note of the inconveniences would grow by the Inclosure." What action, if any, Shakespeare took in response to this almost unanimous petition of the Town Council we do not know.

[1] Does this indicate that his health was not good? The last sentence in the excerpt shows that Hall had accompanied Shakespeare to London.

With the coming of spring, in 1615, the Combes attempted to dig ditches in preparation for enclosing the lands. This led to an open riot in which the Aldermen and even women and children took spades and attempted to fill up the ditches. The matter was then carried before the Lord Chief Justice, Sir Edward Coke, who, siding with the Corporation, ordered "that no enclosure shall be made within the parish of Stratford, for that it is against the laws of the realm, neither by Mr. Combe nor any other, until they shall shew cause at open assizes to the Justices of Assize." In spite of this order the quarrel continued with great bitterness. Shakespeare's last connection with it, so far as our imperfect records go, is found in Greene's Diary, September, 1615: "W. Shakespeare's telling J. Greene [Thomas Greene's brother] that I [possibly an error for "he" [1]] was not able to bear the enclosing of Welcombe."

Ultimately the Corporation secured a complete victory over the Combes, but not until 1618, after the death of the poet.[2] His failure to side with the citizens against his two friends need not disturb us, for we are not fully enough cognizant of the facts to determine either the justness of the conduct pursued by the Town Council, or the propriety of Shakespeare's attitude in the prolonged quarrel.

He seems still to have been ready to purchase land when it came upon the market. Thomas Barber died on August 14, 1615; on September 5 Greene notes in his Diary concerning Shakespeare: "His sending James for the executors of Mr. Barber, to agree as is said with

---

[1] C. M. Ingleby, in his edition of Greene's Diary, points out the frequency with which Greene uses "I" for "he."

[2] For completer details see Halliwell-Phillipps, *Outlines;* C. M. Ingleby, *Shakespeare and the Enclosure of Common Fields at Welcombe,* 1885; C. C. Stopes, *Shakespeare's Environment,* 1914; and H. C. Beeching, in *A Book of Homage to Shakespeare,* 1916, pp. 121–25.

them for Mr. Barber's interest"[1] — probably in land at Shottery.

On February 10, 1616, Judith Shakespeare, then entering upon her thirty-second year, surprised her father, and doubtless the whole town, by suddenly marrying Thomas Quiney, aged twenty-six. The groom came of a good family of Stratford tradesmen, which, however, had seen better days. His father, Richard Quiney, a draper of some education, had been twice honored by his fellow-citizens with election to the office of High Bailiff, and had on several occasions represented the Corporation in London before the Privy Council and the Court. After his death in 1602, the widow kept a tavern; and, though she must have been in straitened circumstances,[2] she

managed to give her children the advantages of an education. Thomas, we know, wrote a beautiful hand, and possessed some knowledge of French; and George, a

[1] See C. C. Stopes, *Shakespeare's Environment*, pp. 86–89. Mrs. Stopes, followed by Lee, *Life*, p. 478, and Beeching, *A Book of Homage to Shakespeare*, p. 125, sees in this a benevolent move on Shakespeare's part to benefit the children of the deceased and others; but the evidence does not warrant this interpretation.

[2] In 1615 she was unable to pay a loan for which Thomas Barber had gone security, and William Combe proceeded unmercifully to prosecute Barber for the sum. See C. C. Stopes, *Shakespeare's Environment*, p. 87.

younger brother, was a Bachelor of Arts of Balliol College, Oxford. That Judith was on friendly terms with the Quiney family is shown by her witnessing in 1611 for Mrs. Quiney and her eldest son, Adrian, the deed of a sale of certain property. The culmination of this friendship was her marriage to Thomas Quiney on February 10, 1616. The match evidently was quickly arranged, the ceremony falling within the period of prohibition (which did not end until April 7), so that a special license from the ecclesiastical authorities was necessary. For some reason this license was not secured, and the Bishop of Worcester promptly summoned both Thomas and Judith to appear before the Consistory Court to explain their failure to comply with the law. Though twice summoned, they did not obey the order, and a decree of excommunication was issued against them, apparently on March 12, 1616. There seems also to have been danger for a time that the marriage might be declared invalid, and their children, therefore, illegitimate. Shakespeare, we may suppose, was greatly distressed by the whole affair, and perhaps was not altogether pleased with the young man his daughter had selected, who turned out to be far from an ideal husband. We seem to find in the poet's will traces of his displeasure at Judith, and evidence of his lack of confidence in his newly acquired son-in-law.

CHAPTER XXV

DEATH AND BURIAL

SHORTLY after the marriage of Judith, Shakespeare was seized with an illness that was to prove fatal. According to the Reverend John Ward, Vicar of Stratford, the attack was induced by a convivial bout held with the two eminent poets Michael Drayton and Ben Jonson: "Shakespeare, Drayton, and Ben Jonson had a merry meeting," writes Ward, "and, it seems, drank too hard, for Shakespeare died of a fever there contracted." We have no reason to reject this story.[1] Drayton was a frequent visitor in Stratford, Jonson was notoriously fond of the cup, and the creator of Falstaff, as is well attested by early writers and tradition alike, was convivial in his disposition. Moreover, if, as has been suggested, Shakespeare was suffering from chronic Bright's disease, the nature of which was then imperfectly understood, we could explain why an indiscretion of this particular kind might provoke a fatal attack.[2]

The meeting described by Ward must have taken place early in March, 1616. On the twenty-fifth of that

[1] Ward, who was a university graduate, could readily verify the story at the mouths of Shakespeare's two nephews then living as his parishioners at the Henley Street home, from Shakespeare's niece, Elizabeth Hall, or from many old residents of the village.

[2] It has been customary to attribute Shakespeare's death to the supposed unsanitary conditions of Chapel Lane. But the bits of evidence upon which this hypothesis is based (cited by Halliwell-Phillipps, *Outlines*, ii, 141–42) relate to a much earlier period; and, as Halliwell-Phillipps admits, "The only later notices of the state of the lane in the poet's time which have been discovered relate to a pigsty which John Rogers, the vicar, had commenced to erect about the year 1613." It is significant that when Rogers began to erect this pigsty, the inhabitants at once lodged complaint, and the Town Council promptly forbade it, in spite of the pleadings of the vicar.

month the poet was so ill that he sent for his lawyer, Francis Collins, to make important changes in his will. This document had originally been prepared in some preceding January — doubtless subsequent to the death of John Combe in July, 1614,[1] certainly anterior to the marriage of Judith in February, 1616, probably, there-fore, either in January, 1615, or January, 1616. It had been drawn up by Collins, a solicitor then residing in Warwick, but formerly of Stratford, where he was held in high esteem.[2] Devised while the poet was, according to legal parlance at least, "in perfect health," and neatly written on three sheets of paper fastened together, it had, I think, been duly published on its completion. At the end the poet signed in a clear bold hand "By me, Wil-liam Shakespeare," and Collins added "Witness to the publishing hereof, Fra: Collyns." At the same time (or it may be later) Julius Shaw, the dramatist's wealthy neighbor and friend, attached his signature, thus mak-ing the customary two witnesses, all that were required by law.[3]

In this original will, Shakespeare's chief problem had been suitably to care for his younger daughter Judith, for she was unmarried, and her elder sister was to re-ceive the bulk of the estate in entail. Provision had to be

[1] Since Combe is not mentioned in the will, whereas his young nephew and heir, Thomas, is.

[2] He transacted much of the legal business for the Combes. The shrewd old John Combe in his will left £10 to Francis Collins, £10 to his little god-son John Collins, and £6 13s. 4d. to Collins' wife Susanna.

[3] See John Godolphin, *The Orphan's Legacy*, ed. of 1674, pp. 3, 41. There is no evidence that the two witnesses had to sign in the presence of each other

made for her in case she remained a spinster, and an adequate dowry provided in case she married. The instructions concerning her extended through most of the first sheet and ran into the first three lines of the second. Her sudden marriage to Thomas Quiney on February 10, 1616, made a revision of this section of the will desirable.

Shakespeare's condition, however, was so critical on March 25 that the preparation of a brand-new will from beginning to end was impossible. Instead, Collins, who had been hastily summoned from Warwick, undertook to rewrite the first sheet relating primarily to Judith, and to make in the rest of the document such small changes as the very sick man might dictate from his bed. Apparently he worked under distressing circumstances, for transcribing from the original draft he wrote " *Vicesimo quinto die Januarii*," but realizing the error, he drew his pen through the word *"Januarii"* and substituted *"Martii."* [1] Then he rapidly copied the opening lines, including the stereotyped words "in perfect health and memory, God be praised." The presence of these words shows either that Collins was in an agitated frame of mind, and working under unfavorable conditions,[2] or

[1] That this first sheet was entirely rewritten on March 25, 1616, and not merely, as commonly stated, altered in date from January 25, 1615–16, to March 25, 1616, is clearly shown by the rest of the heading, which states that this particular March 25 was in the fourteenth year of King James' reign over England, and in the legal year 1616. Now March 25 was the first day of the legal year 1616, and the second day of the *regnal year* 14, so that if the sheet had originally been drawn up on January 25, 1615–16, the month would have fallen in a different legal and *also a different regnal year* from those noted by Collins. Nor is it very likely that the day of the month, the twenty-fifth, would remain the same for January and March. Halliwell-Phillips (*Outlines*, ii, 392, note 377) attempts to explain this: "When March was substituted for January, it is most likely that the day of the month should also have been changed. There was otherwise, at least, a singular and improbable coincidence."

[2] That Shakespeare was not in good health is "painfully manifest" as Sir Edward Thompson says, by the shaking signatures at the bottom of the first two sheets, indicating that he was in "the condition of a dying man." And that his memory was not perfect is evident from his inability to recall

that he felt that, since he was not making a brand-new will but merely altering an earlier one, he ought to preserve the statement as lending greater authority to the document as a whole.[1]

The preliminary matter having been copied, the lawyer wrote: "Item, I give and bequeath," and then turned to the dying poet for further instructions. The first words Shakespeare uttered were blunders, and had to be stricken through with the pen: "unto my son-in-law." For these words, relating to Thomas Quiney, he promptly corrected: "unto my daughter, Judith." But the presence of the crossed-out phrase shows that this first sheet was written after Judith's marriage. The poet then directed that Judith should receive £150 in cash—£100 as "her marriage portion," to be paid within twelve months, and £50 to be paid upon her surrendering to Susanna her right in a certain copyhold tenement in Stratford. He gave her also a further sum of £150, provided "any issue of her body be living at the end of three years next ensuing the day of the date of this my will."[2]

Having thus cared for Judith, he next framed a bequest to his sister Joan Hart, whose husband may then have been desperately ill.[3] He gave her for the term of her life the use of the old family home in Henley Street, and £20 in cash; and to each of her three young sons the sum of £5. A pathetic touch appears in the inability of the sick man to remember the name of one of his nephews,

the name of one of his nephews. Under these circumstances the phrase "God be praised" is highly incongruous.

[1] This may possibly explain his use of the word "Januarii," in a momentary hesitation. As to the phrase "in perfect health," Halliwell-Phillipps rightly observes: "No conscientious solicitor would ever have used the words untruthfully, while the cognate description of a testator as 'being sick in body, but of whole and perfect memory,' is one that is continually met with in ancient wills."

[2] In a later portion of the original will he left to Judith also his "broad silver-gilt bowl."

[3] Hart died before the poet.

so that the lawyer had to leave merely a blank space.

In order to get all this material on the single sheet that was to replace the original first sheet, Collins had to use a much smaller hand, to crowd the letters, and gradually to narrow the space between the lines. Even so, he found it necessary to run over to the top of the second sheet, and place two lines in the blank margin there.

At the head of this second sheet (a part of the original draft of the will) stood three lines relating, it seems, to Judith's dowry:

to be set out for her within one year after my decease by my executors, with the advice and direction of my overseers, for her best profit, until her marriage, and then the same with the increase thereof to be paid unto her.

Obviously these lines, written before Judith married, were no longer pertinent, and hence the lawyer drew his pen through them. But their presence again clearly reveals the fact that the first sheet of the original will was completely rewritten, whereas the second and third sheets were not.[1]

In the remainder of the will the poet dictated a few minor alterations and additions.[2] These Collins was able to take care of by deleting certain words, and by inserting new bequests between the lines.

The very first alteration is significant. By the original will Shakespeare had left to Judith all his plate. But now he ordered her name to be stricken out, and the name of his little granddaughter Elizabeth Hall to be

---

[1] Halliwell-Phillipps, who does not think of the first page as having been rewritten, says (*Outlines*, ii, 393): "It is exceedingly difficult to understand how the long provision commencing *to be sett out*, could have found its way into the manuscript."

[2] We cannot assume that all the alterations and additions were made at this time; some may have been originally made in the first draft. Yet since the poet was now formally revising his will, and had summoned his solicitor from Warwick for that specific purpose, the probability is that most of them were made on this occasion.

substituted. Can it be that, incensed at Judith's marriage to Thomas Quiney, and her excommunication (which was apparently announced on March 12), he took this means of indicating his displeasure? For since she was setting up a home for herself, the gift of household plate would seem doubly appropriate.

The second alteration is also significant. Originally at the head of his bequests to close personal friends to purchase memorial rings stood the name of "Mr. Richard Tyler, the elder." Tyler's name, however, is crossed through, and the name of Hamnet Sadler inserted above in its place. It is unlikely that a very sick man would cancel a trifling bequest to the person whom originally he first thought of in connection with memorial rings, unless that person were now dead, or had subsequently through some act of his ceased to be so highly regarded. The latter possibility seems to have been the case, for according to the Stratford records Richard Tyler the elder did not die until 1636. Thus the change suggests a lapse of time between the first drafting of the will and the revision on March 25, 1616.

Shakespeare also took occasion to add the bequest of memorial rings to "William Reynolds, gent.," and to his special friends in London, Richard Burbage, John Heminges, and Henry Condell.

The next, and most interesting, addition is the oft-quoted: "Item, I give unto my wife my second-best bed, with the furniture," i.e., the hangings, mattress, pillows, and coverlings. This seemingly trivial bequest, together with the fact that Shakespeare's wife is not otherwise mentioned in the will, has led to much speculation, and not a little adverse criticism. Yet the facts may readily be explained by the assumption that at this time Mrs. Shakespeare, now sixty years of age, was an invalid, and that the poet had already made arrangements for her proper care by Susanna and Mr. Hall, who were at once to move into New Place and provide her with a suitable home. Halliwell-Phillipps effectively puts the matter when he suggests "the possibility of her having been afflicted with some chronic infirmity of a nature that precluded all hope of recovery. In such a case, to relieve her from household anxieties, and select a comfortable apartment at New Place where she would be under the care of an affectionate daughter and an experienced physician, would have been the wisest and kindest measure that could have been adopted." This, he observes, is the only theory "consistent with the terms of the will, and with the deep affection which she is traditionally recorded to have entertained for him to the end of her life." The Stratford clerk tells us that she "earnestly" requested to be buried in the same grave with her husband; and the affection in which she was held by her daughter and Mr. Hall is revealed in the inscription they placed over her tomb.

Precisely the same situation we find in the case of Edmund Heywood, the uncle of the playwright Thomas Heywood. A paragraph from his will, executed in 1624, better than anything else, I think, will help us to understand Shakespeare's possible arrangements with respect to his wife.

And whereas my intent and meaninge was to have given and left to Magdalen, my well-beloved wief, with whom I have by the goodness of God lived a long time, the greatest part of myne estate for her maintenance during her lief, and to have beene disposed of by her after her death; But consideringe howe it hath pleased God to vissit her longe with lamenes whereby and by reason of her other weaknes and imperfections which commonlie doth attende auld age, she is nowe unfit to take care of the thinges of this world, I thought it better to dispose of these Temporall blessings with which God hath indowed me, accordinge as it is declared in this my will; And to leave my saide wief to the care of her naturall and onlie child, than to expose her and my substance to strangers that maie happen to regarde it more than her. Neaverthelesse my will and meaning is, And I doe give and bequeath unto my saide wief the some of fiftie poundes, to be paide unto her within one quarter of a yeare after my Decease, together with all her wearinge apparell, and her hatt band set with goulde buttons, and her ringe, to be disposed of as she shall think good. And for her further and better maintenance, I doe will, charge, and command my saide daughter that she shall provide for, keepe, and maintaine my saide wief in such good sorte, manner, and fashion, with meate, drinke, fireinge, apparell, and all other necessaries as is fitt and necessarie for her duringe her lief. And that shee shall contynue in the house during her lief where we nowe dwell.[1]

The loquacious and sentimental Heywood, who wrote his own will, is more communicative about his private affairs than the reticent Shakespeare; yet the circumstances in the two cases may have been parallel. Shakespeare, we may believe, had a clear and definite agree-ment with John Hall and Susanna about providing for the widow, an agreement which made it improper for him to bind them with legal obligations. Such an arrangement, of course, would be fully understood by Mrs. Shakespeare; and we have the satisfaction of knowing that Susanna and Mr. Hall gave her a comfortable home, and cared for her with all solicitude until her death.

In the light of this interpretation Shakespeare's special direction, in the midst of his suffering, that his wife should have the bed in which she was accustomed to lie appears as a bit of affectionate thoughtfulness. The best bed, we may suspect, was an ornate affair reserved for transient guests; the second-best bed, though less expensive, was probably the more comfortable, and the

[1] K. L. Bates, *A Woman Killed with Kindness and The Fair Maid of the West*, Belles Lettres Series, p. cvii.

poet was now thinking in terms not of money but of comfort.

If the reader is not disposed to accept this interpretation of the matter, one may call his attention to the fact that the law allowed the widow a third of all her husband's goods, a dower right in one-third of his real property,[1] and the use of his "capital messuage" during her life.[2] This would be more than adequate for a person of Mrs. Shakespeare's advanced age, and it was both unnecessary and unprofessional for a solicitor to specify such inalienable rights.

The will, as a result of all these alterations, was a crude, patched-up thing.[3] But apparently there was no time for the lawyer to make a fair copy, as under more favorable conditions he would desire to do. Instead — if my interpretation be correct — three new witnesses were called in, making five in all (an unusual number), who signed below the names of the two original witnesses, Francis Collins and Julius Shaw, the former of whom, of course, was rewitnessing the document. The new witnesses seem to have been hurriedly assembled: Hamnet Sadler, the poet's early friend, who would naturally be at hand; Robert Whatcote, a humble farmer, and

---

[1] It has been pointed out (see Lee, *Life*, pp. 457, 486) that in 1613 when Shakespeare purchased a house in Blackfriars, London, and entered into a joint tenancy with Heminges and two other men, the effect was to bar the widow's dower. But we do not know the circumstances that led to this arrangement. Heminges was acting as Shakespeare's business adviser, and he was fond of the joint-tenancy device for legal protection. That there were problems connected with the title to the house is shown by the fact that two years later Shakespeare had to make suit for the recovery of documents necessary to a clear title to his property. And it should not be forgotten that the Blackfriars house represented an investment on his part of only £80.

[2] See Blackstone's Commentaries, ii, 492, and M. M. Bigelow, "The Rise of the English Will," in *Select Essays in Anglo-American Legal History*, iii, 780.

[3] On the freedom formerly enjoyed in revising and republishing wills, see John Godolphin, *The Orphan's Legacy*, ed. of 1674, p. 34.

the friend who had acted as main witness in defence of Mrs. Susanna Hall's reputation; and John Robinson, an inconspicuous person of whom virtually nothing is known.[1] None of these three men, in dignity, wealth, or social standing, was the equal of Collins and Shaw. Moreover, Shakespeare was asked to sign the sheet that had been fully rewritten, and also the second sheet which had been much altered; but he was in such a state of weakness and exhaustion that his hand shook, and his signatures are barely decipherable, showing painful indications that he was, as Sir Edward Thompson observes, a "dying man." The third page had already been signed in a clear hand "By me, William Shakespeare."[2]

So much for the history of the will in its making. It remains for us to consider its contents in more detail.

1. To his younger daughter, Judith, he gave £300, and his broad silver-gilt bowl.

2. To his only sister, Mrs. Joan Hart, he gave the use of the old family homestead in Henley Street during her lifetime, and £20 in cash.

3. To his three young nephews, sons of Mrs. Hart, he gave £5 each.

4. To his eight-year-old granddaughter, Elizabeth Hall, he gave his plate.

5. To his eight-year-old godson, William Walker, he gave 20s. in gold.

6. To the poor of Stratford he gave £10.

7. To his friend, Thomas Combe, of College House, he gave his sword.

8. To his closest friends in Stratford, Hamnet Sadler, William Reynolds, Anthony Nash, and John Nash, he left 26s. 8d. each with which to buy memorial rings.

[1] Except that in 1608 and again in 1614 he brought action for assault against two different persons.

[2] The testator, of course, was required only to acknowledge the will as his. See Godolphin, *op. cit.*, p. 4.

9. To his old fellows in London, Richard Burbage, John Heminges, and Henry Condell, he likewise left 26s. 8d. each with which to buy memorial rings.

10. To the two men whom he asked to serve as overseers of his will, Thomas Russell and Francis Collins, he gave respectively £5 and £13 6s. 8d.[1]

11. He specially stipulated that his wife was to have a certain bed with all its furniture.

12. To his elder daughter, Susanna Hall, he gave all his other property both real and personal, including his capital messuage of New Place.[2] The bequest reads as follows:

Item, I give, will, bequeath, and devise unto my daughter, Susanna Hall, for better enabling of her to perform this my will and towards the performance thereof, all that capital messuage or tenement with the appurtenances, in Stratford aforesaid, called the New Place, wherein I now dwell; and two messuages or tenements with the appurtenances, situate, lying, and being in Henley Street, within the borough of Stratford aforesaid; and all my barns, stables, orchards, gardens, lands, tenements, and hereditaments whatsoever, situate, lying, and being, or to be had, received, perceived, or taken, within the towns, hamlets, villages, fields, and grounds of Stratford upon Avon, Old Stratford, Bishopton, and Welcombe, or in any of them in the said county of Warwick. And also all that messuage or tenement, with the appurtenances, wherein one John Robinson dwelleth, situate, lying, and being in the Blackfriars, in London, near the Wardrobe; and all my other lands, tenements, and hereditaments whatsoever.

Among the "hereditaments whatsoever" were of course included the miscellaneous investments of money, such as the Stratford tithes, and the shares in the New Globe and the Blackfriars playhouses. The tithes had cost him £440. The value of a share in the Blackfriars was

---

[1] The wealthy John Combe in his will gave £5 to Sir Henry Rainsford for his services as overseer.

[2] Subject, of course, to the dower rights of the widow.

estimated in 1615 to be £300,[1] and a share in the Globe must have been worth still more.[2] Possibly it was his holdings in London that led him to appoint "Thomas Russell, Esquire" as one of his overseers. Nothing is known of such a person in Stratford, and Sir Sidney Lee plausibly suggests that he was a London friend: "Shakespeare had opportunities of meeting in London one Thomas Russell, who in the dramatist's later life enjoyed a high reputation there as a metallurgist, obtaining patents for new methods of extracting metals from the ore. For near a decade before Shakespeare's death Russell would seem to have been in personal relations with the poet Michael Drayton. . . . As early as 1608 Francis Bacon was seeking Thomas Russell's acquaintance on the twofold ground of his scientific ingenuity and his social influence."

The bequest of the great bulk of his fortune to Susanna was in accordance with the English custom of establishing with an endowment the eldest line of descendants. The poet's ambition to found a landed family, with such wealth as he had accumulated for ever entailed upon the male heirs, is apparent from the following passage in his will:

To have and to hold all and singular the said premises with their appurtenances, unto the said Susanna Hall for and during the term of her natural life, and after her decease to the first son of her body lawfully issuing, and to the heirs males of the body of the said first son lawfully issuing; and for default of such issue to the second son of her body, lawfully issuing, and to the heirs males of the body of the said second son lawfully issuing; and for default of such heirs, to the third son of the body of the said Susanna lawfully issuing, and of the heirs males

---

[1] See C. W. Wallace in *The Times*, October 4, 1909, quoting the Heminges-Osteler documents.

[2] Not only since the playhouse was larger and more profitable, but also since the sharers owned the building, whereas they merely rented the Blackfriars.

of the body of the said third son lawfully issuing; and for default of such issue, the same so to be and remain to the fourth, fifth, sixth, and seventh sonnes of her body lawfully issuing, one after another, and to the heirs males of the bodies of the said fourth, fifth, sixth, and seventh sons lawfully issuing, in such manner as it is before lymited . . . and for default of such issue, the said premises to be and remain to my said niece [Elizabeth] Hall and the heirs males of her body lawfully issuing; and for default of such issue to my daughter Judith, and the heirs males of her body lawfully issuing.

In this natural desire to establish an endowed family, however, Shakespeare, like Sir Walter Scott, was to be defeated; for in one generation his direct line became extinct, and his property passed to strangers.

The hurried revision of the will on March 25 indicates that the poet was then in a critical condition, yet he lingered for several weeks. Death was also stalking at the old homestead in Henley Street. On April 17, Shakespeare's sister buried her husband, William Hart, in the Stratford churchyard. Six days later, on April 23, the poet breathed his last — as tradition has it, on his birthday. The body lay in state at New Place for two days, and then, on Thursday, April 25, was interred, not in the churchyard, where his father and mother and other kindred had been laid, but in the church itself —

> Where, through the long-drawn aisle and fretted vault,
> The pealing anthem swells the note of praise.

No account of the funeral has come down to us; yet I think we can have little difficulty in imagining the scene. To the tolling of "the surly, sullen bell," the body was borne from New Place to the church, followed by the mourning family. The immediate relatives included the widow, Mrs. William Shakespeare — unless, indeed, by illness she was confined to her bed; his eldest daughter, Susanna, with her husband, the physician Mr. Hall, and their little daughter Elizabeth, aged eight; Judith, with her husband Thomas Quiney; the poet's sister, Mrs. Joan Hart, in widow's weeds, with her three sons aged respectively eight, eleven, and sixteen; and, finally, Thomas Greene, the poet's cousin. Among those gathered at the church we should certainly expect to see Hamnet Sadler and his wife Judith, Julius Shaw, Henry Walker and his little son William, Anthony Nash, John Nash, William Reynolds, Thomas Combe, and possibly Sir Henry and Lady Rainsford. And the people of the town, no doubt, came in full force to do honor to Stratford's most distinguished citizen.

The body was laid in a conspicuous place of honor, just within the chancel rail and before the altar. It is true that by virtue of his ownership of a portion of the Stratford tithes he had a legal right to interment here; yet we can hardly doubt that his fellow-townsmen would have given him this distinction anyway, as one of England's greatest poets, and Stratford's most illustrious son.[1] His body was not laid in a vault, but in a wooden coffin placed in the earth; and on a flagstone over the grave was carved an inscription traditionally said to have been written, or selected, by the poet himself:[2]

> GOOD FREND FOR IESVS SAKE FORBEARE,
> TO DIGG THE DVST ENCLOASED HEARE:
> BLESE BE Y MAN Y SPARES THES STONES,
> AND CVRST BE HE Y MOVES MY BONES.

[1] *A Banquet of Jests*, 1630: "Stratford-upon-Avon, a towne most remarkable for the birth of famous William Shakespeare." *Theatrum Poetarum*, 1675: "William Shakespeare, the glory of the English stage, whose nativity at Stratford-upon-Avon is the highest honour that town can boast of." *Virtue Betrayed*, 1682: "As Homer and our Shakespeare did, to immortalize the places where they were born."

[2] The parish clerk, indeed, stated to Dowdall in 1693 that the verse had been written by Shakespeare "himselfe a little before his death." According

The reason for this curious inscription seems not to be generally understood, though several times clearly stated; for example, by William Hall, a graduate of Oxford, who visited Stratford in 1694 and wrote to his friend, Edward Thwaites, the Old English scholar, a description of the poet's burial-place.[1] After quoting the verses on the flagstone, he observes: "The little learning these verses contain would be a very strong argument of the want of it in the author, did not they carry something in them which stands in need of a comment. There is in this church a place which they call the bone-house, a repository for all bones they dig up, which are so many that they would load a great number of waggons. The poet, being willing to preserve his bones unmoved, lays a curse upon him that moves them; and having to do with clarks and sextons, for the most part a very ignorant sort of people, he descends to the meanest of their capacitys."

The charnel-house referred to by Hall stood in the churchyard, and adjoined the chancel on the north, within a few feet of Shakespeare's grave. The frequent interment of new bodies in the church led to the constant removal of the remains of persons formerly buried there,[2] and these remains were dumped in a miscellaneous heap in the bone-house. The custom was not limited to Stratford. Aubrey[3] notes that Sir John Birkenhead, who was buried in St. Martin's-in-the-Fields, London, specifically ordered in his will that his body be interred in the churchyard; "his reason was because, he sayd, they removed

to William Hall, 1694, "these words were ordered to be cutt by Mr. Shackspeare."

[1] Hall had just taken his Bachelor's degree and was continuing his studies for the Master's degree. Thwaites was later Regius Professor of Greek and Whyte's Professor of Moral Philosophy at Oxford.

[2] For an example of this custom see the writer's article, "The Bones of Ben Jonson," *Studies in Philology*, xvi, 289.

[3] *Brief Lives*, ed. by Andrew Clark, 1898, i, 105; quoted by Lee, *Life*, p. 484.

the bodies out of the church." And Sir Thomas Browne, in *Hydriotaphia*, bitterly complains, for himself and others, of the "tragicall abomination of being knaved out of our graves." The Stratford bone-house seems to have been unusually repulsive. A visitor to the town in 1777 writes:[1] "At the side of the chancel is a charnel-house almost filled with human bones, skulls, etc."; and Ireland in 1795 declares that it contained "the largest assemblage of human bones" he ever had seen. We may suspect that Shakespeare was recalling one of the nightmares of his boyhood when in *Romeo and Juliet* he wrote:

> Or shut me nightly in a charnel-house,
> O'ercover'd quite with dead men's rattling bones,
> With reeky shanks, and yellow chapless skulls;

for it can hardly be doubted that he had often watched the clownish sextons of the church dig up the bones from their quiet graves, and hurl them like loggats into the adjacent charnel.[2] His natural revulsion at the idea seems to find expression in *Hamlet:*[3]

Ham. That skull had a tongue in it, and could sing once. How the knave jowls it to the ground as if it were Cain's jaw-bone! ... Why does he suffer this rude knave now to knock him about the sconce with a dirty shovel? ... Dost thou think Alexander looked o' this fashion i' the earth?

Hor. E'en so.

Ham. And smelt so? pah!

Shakespeare knew that his bones would lie perilously near to the charnel-house; and he knew also that, before many years had rolled by, his place would be claimed by

[1] "Notes of a Visit to Stratford in 1777," printed in Defoe's *Tour*, 1778; quoted by Halliwell-Phillipps.

[2] The Charnel-House was removed at the end of the 18th century; for a drawing of its interior by Captain Saunders see Halliwell-Phillipps, *Life*, 1848, p. 287. Above the bone-house was appropriately enough, "the minister's study."

[3] Gildon, writing in 1699, says: "I have been told that he writ the Scene of the Ghost in *Hamlet* at his House which bordered on the Charnel-House and Churchyard." This tradition would better apply to the grave-digging scene.

some later owner of the village tithes. It was specifically in order to avoid the "abomination of being knaved out" of his grave that he directed the rude verses to be cut on the stone over his body.

In his effort to provide a lasting peace for his bones he was successful. Dowdall, who visited Stratford in 1693, quotes the church clerk, then above eighty years of age, to the effect that "not one" of the sextons, "for fear of the curse abovesaid, dare touch his gravestone," and this even though, as he adds, "his wife and daughters did earnestly desire to be laid in the same tomb with him." [1] Shakespeare's daughter, Susanna, who was buried near him, suffered the very fate he sought to escape: in 1707 her bones were thrown into the charnel-house, and her grave given over to a certain inconspicuous person named Watts, who then happened to be a part-owner of the Stratford tithes. [2] But to this day the bones of the poet have been unmolested. In 1796, workmen who were employed to construct a vault next to his grave testified to the fact that the earth above his body had never been disturbed. They, indeed, in the course of their labors, accidentally dug into one side of his tomb, and opened up a small hole. Peering through this hole, they saw nothing but a hollow space where the coffin had been; and without further effort to pry into the secrets of the grave, they hastily walled up that side of the vault with brick.

Probably the narrowest escape the dead poet suffered was in the early part of the nineteenth century, when, says Halliwell-Phillipps, "a phalanx of trouble-tombs, lanterns and spades in hand, assembled in the chancel in the dead of night, intent on disobeying the solemn

[1] William Hall writes that the sextons "lest they should not only draw this curse upon themselves, but also entail it upon their posterity," had "laid him full seventeen foot deep, deep enough to secure him."
[2] The inscription on her grave was preserved by Dugdale; in 1844 the inscription to Watts was removed, and that to Susanna restored.

injunction that the bones of Shakespeare were not to be disturbed. But the supplicating lines prevailed. There were some amongst the number who, at the last moment, refused to incur the warning condemnation, and so the design was happily abandoned." The church is now carefully locked and guarded, so that a recurrence of the peril is no longer to be feared.

Since the body was laid not in a stone or brick vault but in the ground, it is probable that long ago all that was earthly of the immortal bard has been peacefully compounded with clay. And there, in all likelihood, his dust will lie undisturbed until the Day of Judgment. Such, we may suppose, was the poet's wish.

Yet shortly after his death the suggestion was made in the literary circles of London that his body be transferred to Westminster Abbey. William Basse wrote:

> Renowned Spenser, lye a thought more nye
> To learned Chaucer, and rare Beaumont, lye
> A little neerer Spenser, to make roome
> For Shakespeare in your threefold, fowerfold Tombe.
> To lodge all fowre in one bed make a shift
> Vntil Doomesday.

After penning these lines, however, Basse seems to have realized the greater appropriateness of Shakespeare's being buried alone in single majesty, and he adds:

> Sleepe, rare Tragœdian, Shakespeare, sleep alone.
> Thy unmolested peace, vnsharèd Caue,
> Possess as Lord.

And this sentiment prevailed. Ben Jonson, in reply to Basse, wrote:

> My Shakespeare, rise! I will not lodge thee by
> Chaucer, or Spenser, or bid Beaumont lie
> A little further to make thee a room.
> Thou art a monument without a tomb.

And Milton expressed the same thought in the lines:

What needs my Shakespeare for his honour'd bones
The labour of an age in pilèd stones?
Or that his hallow'd reliques should be hid
Under a star-ypointing pyramid?

The interment in Stratford was indeed appropriate. It was the poet's home. There lay his father, and mother, his brothers and sisters, and his lifelong friends; and there within a short time were to be placed those others who were dear to him. On his left was entombed his wife, on his right, John Hall, Susanna Hall, and Thomas Nash who had married his granddaughter Elizabeth. Not far from him, too, rested his old acquaintance John Combe. The following diagram shows the arrangement of the tombs within the chancel:

John Combe, 1614.					J. Kendall, 1751.	
Judith Combe, 1649.			**ALTAR.**			
Thomas Balsall, 1491.						
Anne Shakespeare, 1623.	William Shakespeare, 1616.	Thomas Nashe, 1647.	John Hall, 1635.	Susanna Hall, 1649.	Francis Watts, 1691.	Anne Watts, 1704.

Shortly after the poet's death steps were taken to erect in the Stratford church a suitable monument to his memory. The execution of the work was placed in the hands of Garret and Nicholas Johnson, of London, who had recently, and possibly on Shakespeare's recommendation, been engaged to design and set up the expensive tomb for John Combe. The eminence they now had attained in their profession is shown by the fact that in 1618 they were called upon to erect a pretentious monument to the Earls of Rutland at Bottesford, Leicestershire. This monument had been executed in London, and transported to Bottesford at great expense.[1] Since the Johnson brothers, whose establishment was within a few feet of the Globe, must have often seen Shakespeare in his habit as he lived, and possibly knew him personally, they were well-qualified for a task which involved representing him in effigy.

In devising his tomb they made free use of the designs they had recently worked out for the more elaborate tomb of the Earls of Rutland. The main feature is a half-length colored effigy of the poet, framed in an arch flanked by two columns, of the Corinthian order, of black marble with gilded bases and capitals. The dramatist is represented as holding a pen in his right hand, presumably engaged in composing a play. In the coloring of the figure, intended to make it resemble life, the hair and beard are auburn, the eyes hazel, the doublet scarlet (to suggest the royal livery?), and the collar and cuffs white.

Above the arch is emblazoned on a large slab the Shakespeare coat of arms and crest in bas-relief. On either side of the slab sit two small undraped figures, the one alert, holding a spade, allegorically representing Labor; the other drooping, with its eyes closed, the right hand resting on a skull, the left holding a reversed and extinguished torch, representing Rest.[2] And surmounting the tomb, upon a rising architectural climax, is a skull betokening Death.

---

[1] The history of Garret and Nicholas Johnson, and of their father who founded the establishment, has been sketched by Sir Sidney Lee, *Life*, p. 494.

[2] These figures are much like those on the Rutland tomb, which Nicholas Johnson explains in his "plot," now preserved by the family, as respectively a "portraiture of Labor," "the other of Rest."

Below the monument, and serving as a base to support
the effigy, is a slab with the following epitaph:

Ividicio Pylivm, genio Socratem, arte Maronem,
Terra tegit, popvlvs Mæret, Olympvs habet.

Stay, Passenger, why goest thov by so fast?
Read, if thov canst, whom envious Death hath plast
Within this monvment, Shakspeare, with whome
Quick nature dide, whose name doth deck y^s Tombe
Far more then cost. Sith all y^t He hath writt
Leaves living art but page to serve his witt.
Obiit Ano. Doi. 1616
Ætatis 53 Die 23 Ap.

CHAPTER XXVI

DESCENDANTS

AFTER the death of Shakespeare, his daughter Susanna and her husband moved to New Place, and thus provided a suitable home for the aging widow. Through the acquisition of the poet's wealth, Hall at once assumed a new importance in the social order of Stratford, and his fame as a practitioner rapidly spread in fashionable circles. About the same time Judith and her husband moved into a dwelling known as The Cage.[1] Here in November a son was born to them, whom they christened "Shakespeare" in honor of his illustrious grandfather, and, we may suspect, not without hope that he might inherit the dramatist's estates left in entail to the eldest male line. With the marriage portion derived from his wife, Quiney set up an ale-house for the dispensing of liquors and tobacco, and became a person of some mark in the village. The following year he was elected to the Town Council, and also appointed one of the Chamberlains of the Corporation.

On August 6, 1623, Shakespeare's widow died at New Place, aged sixty-seven. According to the clerk whom Dowdall interviewed, she "did earnestly desire to be laid in the same tomb" with her husband, but the sextons, in view of the warning verses, dared not open his grave. Her desire, however, was followed as nearly as possible, and she was placed next to the dramatist. On a brass plate affixed to the slab over her body there was inscribed a tribute of affection, composed, it seems, by her daughter Susanna, and turned into Latin by Mr. Hall:

[1] They secured the lease of this house in the summer of 1616. The building, now modernized, is still to be seen in Stratford.

Heere lyeth interred the body of Anne, wife of William Shakespeare, who departed this life the 6th day of August, 1623, being of the age of 67 yeares.

Ubera tu mater, tu lac, vitamque dedisti,
    Væ mihi pro tanto munere saxa dabo,
Quam mallem amoueat lapidem bonus Angelus ore,
    Exeat ut Christi corpus imago tua;
Sed nil vota valent, venias cito Christe, resurget,
    Clausa licet tumulo mater et astra petet.

The Latin verses may be thus rendered in English:

Milk, life, thou gavest. For a boon so great,
    Mother, alas! I give thee but a stone.
O! might some Angel blest remove its weight,
    Thy form should issue like thy Saviour's own.
But vain my prayers; O Christ, come quickly, come!
    And thou, my mother, shalt from hence arise,
Though closed as yet within this narrow tomb,
    To meet thy Saviour in the starry skies.[1]

In 1626, Elizabeth, the only child of Susanna and Mr. Hall, then eighteen years of age, married Thomas Nash, eldest son of Shakespeare's friend Anthony Nash, remembered in the poet's will with a memorial ring. Nash had been well educated, and for a time had studied law at Lincoln's Inn, London. Upon his father's death, however, he inherited considerable wealth, and returned to Stratford to manage his property. After his marriage to Elizabeth he moved into a fine house adjoining New Place, now commonly known as Nash House.

Nine years later, on November 25, 1635, John Hall, the physician who had so successfully healed others, himself succumbed to a fatal illness, and was buried in the Stratford Church near the poet. Over his grave was

[1] Translation by the Reverend J. Jackson.

carved his coat of arms impaled with that of Shakespeare, and below, the inscription:

> Heere lyeth ye Body of John Hall, Gent. Hee marr. Susanna, ye daughter and coheire of Will. Shakespeare, Gent. Hee deceased Nove^r. 25 A^o 1635; Aged 60.

> Hallius hic situs est, medica celeberrimus arte:
>   Expectans regni gaudia læta Dei;
> Dignus erat meritis qui Nestora vinceret annis,
>   In terris omnes sed rapit æqua dies.
> Ne tumulo quid desit, adest fidissima conjux,
>   Et vitæ comitem nunc quoq; mortis habet.

Thomas Nash and Elizabeth now moved into New Place to live with the widowed Susanna; and Nash, at once assuming the position of head of the family, undertook to manage the Hall and Shakespeare properties as well as his own. But it must have been a source of grief to him and his wife that they had no child to inherit their combined fortunes and perpetuate the family which the dramatist had especially endowed

Eliza Nash

in his will. Indeed, under the terms of that will the Quineys were destined, so it seemed for a time, to acquire all the poet's estates; for though little Shakespeare had died at the age of six months, two other children, Richard and Thomas, had grown into sturdy young manhood. In 1639, however, both these young men were suddenly carried away by some contagious disease, Richard at the age of twenty-one, and Thomas at the age of nineteen; and no other children were born to Judith.

Little of note happened in Stratford until July 11, 1643, when Queen Henrietta Maria, with an army of 2,000 infantry, 1,000 cavalry, 100 wagons, and a suitable equipment of artillery, arrived in the village. Her Majesty promptly established her Court at New Place, where, we may believe, she was heartily welcomed by the daughter and granddaughter of Shakespeare, a one-time King's Man, as well as by Thomas Nash, who in the September preceding had shown himself a stout royalist by contributing to the King's cause the largest sum from Stratford. The Queen was shortly joined by Prince Rupert, and the distinguished guests remained at New Place until July 13.

THE SHIELD ON THE TOMB OF THOMAS NASH

(The arms of Nash and Bulstrode quarterly, impaling Hall and Shakespeare quarterly.)

In 1647, Thomas Nash died at the age of fifty-three, and was buried in the Stratford Church by the side of the poet. On the stone over his body was carved an elaborate shield displaying the arms of the Nash, Shakespeare, and Hall families, with the inscription below:

> Heere resteth Y^e Body of Thomas
> Nashe, Esq. He mar. Elizabeth, the
> Daug: & Heire of Iohn Halle, Gent.
> He Died Aprill 4, A. 1647. Aged 53.

The death of Nash left at New Place only the two women, Susanna Hall, aged sixty-four, and her daughter Elizabeth, aged thirty-eight. But within a year and two months Elizabeth sought consolation in a second husband. On June 5, 1649, she married John Barnard, of Abington Manor, a wealthy widower, aged forty-four, with a number of children. The Barnard family belonged to the ancient landed gentry of Northamptonshire. John's tombstone rather pompously describes him as "a man of most noble race, illustrious through his father, his grandfather, his great-grandfather, his great-great-grandfather, and other ancestors, having been lords of this town of Abington for more than two hundred years." By his first wife, the daughter of Sir Clement Edmonds, he had eight children. Doubtless he took his new bride to the ancestral estate of Abington Manor, of which, as he boasted, his family had been the proud possessors for more than two centuries.

Five weeks after Elizabeth's marriage, Susanna Hall died at New Place, and was buried in the Stratford Church by the side of her husband and near her distinguished father. On her tomb were engraved the arms of the Shakespeare and Hall families, with the following inscription below:

> Heere lyeth ye body of Susanna, wife to John Hall, Gent., ye daughter of William Shakespeare, Gent. She deceased ye 11th of July, A.D. 1649, aged 66.

> Witty above her sexe, but that's not all,
> Wise to Salvation was good Mistress Hall;
> Something of Shakespeare was in that, but this
> Wholly of Him with whom she's now in blisse.
> Then, passenger, hast ne're a teare
> To weepe with her that wept with all?
> That wept, yet set herself to chere
> Them up with comfort's cordiall.
> Her love shall live, her mercy spread,
> When thou hast ne're a tear to shed.

Upon the death of her mother, Elizabeth came into possession of all the Shakespeare and Hall estates. Accordingly, John Barnard and his family left their ancient home of Abington Manor, and moved to Stratford to reside at New Place.

In the meanwhile things were not going well with the Quineys. Though Thomas had a good education, and with the aid of his wife's marriage portion had made a fair start in Stratford, he proved a failure at business. In

1630 he had become involved in legal difficulties, withdrew from the Town Council, was fined for swearing, and was again fined for allowing men to tipple in his house. In 1639 he lost his two sons, and thus all hope of coming into possession of the Shakespeare properties. At last, his affairs growing desperate, he left his wife, and in 1652 went to live in London, where his brother had become a successful grocer. Judith, thus deprived of her children and abandoned by her husband, resided in Stratford to the good old age of seventy-seven. By the foresight of her father she probably enjoyed the income from £150, which the executors of his will were required to invest for her benefit: "My will is, and so I devise and bequeath the said hundred and fifty pounds to be set out by my executors and overseers for the best benefit of her and her issue, and the stock not to be paid unto her so long as she shall be married and covert-baron, but my will is that she shall have the consideration yearly paid unto her during her life." [1]

Shortly before the Restoration the Barnards returned to Abington Manor, and New Place was rented to strangers. John Barnard, who, like the Shakespeares and the Nashes, was a stout royalist, was honored by King Charles with a baronetcy on November 25, 1661. Thus Shakespeare's granddaughter arrived at the dignity of being called "Lady" — a dignity which, we may suspect, would have secretly gratified the actor-dramatist. But of Elizabeth's second marriage also there was no issue, so that the poet's fond ambition, as expressed in his will, of establishing a family was to be again and finally defeated.

In 1662 Judith, aged seventy-seven, died in Stratford, and was buried in the churchyard. In 1670 Elizabeth,

---

[1] The proviso that might alter this condition, namely that her husband should assure to her and her heirs £150 in land, could hardly have been effective, for Thomas Quiney was not able to make such an assurance.

aged sixty-two, died at Abington Manor, and was interred with the Barnard family in the church there. With the death of Lady Barnard, Shakespeare's direct line became extinct.

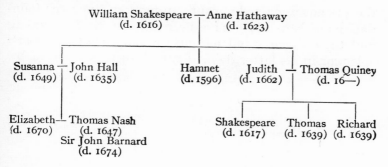

But if Shakespeare has no lineal descendants, there are now many descendants of a collateral line. His three brothers died without issue. His only sister Joan, who married the Stratford hatter, Hart, had three sons and one daughter. The daughter, Mary, died in 1607 at the age of four. One of the sons, Michael, died in 1618 at the age of eleven. A second son, William, moved to London and became an actor; he failed to marry, however, and died in 1639 at the age of thirty-eight. The third and last son, Thomas, married and had four children. Three of these died without issue; but the fourth, George, had seven children, from whom there are to-day numerous descendants in England, Australia, and America.[1]

After Elizabeth's death in 1670 the Shakespeare properties passed to the Barnards.[2] New Place was sold to Sir Edward Walker, Garter King-of-Arms, who resided there until his death in 1677. It then passed, through inherit-

---

[1] For the history of the Hart family see George Russell French, *Shakespeareana Genealogica*, 1869, pp. 367 ff.

[2] But the old homestead in Henley Street was left by Lady Barnard to the Harts, and remained in the possession of the family until 1806.

ance, to the descendants of Sir Hugh Clopton, its original builder. In 1702 it was torn down by Sir John Clopton, and an entirely different structure erected in its place.[1] This second building was demolished in 1759, since when the site has remained vacant. In modern times the foundations of New Place have been exposed by excavation, and these alone stand as mute reminders of the poet's splendor in his latter days at Stratford.

[1] There is no pictorial representation of the earlier house.

CHAPTER XXVII

THE MAKING OF THE PLAYHOUSE MANUSCRIPTS

BEFORE we can intelligently discuss the problems connected with the publication of Shakespeare's plays, we must understand the attitude of contemporary men of letters towards dramatic composition, and the peculiar conditions under which theatrical manuscripts were produced.

Elizabethan critics and poets alike held that while plays written in imitation of Greek and Latin models were a legitimate and even noble species of composition, plays written in the popular style, designed for the "common actors" and the amusement of the rabble, were ephemeral products of a mercenary pen, as art hardly worth serious consideration. Thus the eminent poet Samuel Daniel, though he did not hesitate to publish stately dramas in the classical form, exclaimed with fervency:

> God forbid I should my papers blot
> With mercenary lines . . .
> No, no! My verse respects not Thames nor theatres.

And this was the attitude of literary men in general. It is not to be wondered at, therefore, that the popular dramatists took their work lightly. As a rule they looked upon the manuscript which they prepared for sale to the actors not primarily as literature of a high order, with permanent value as such, but as mainly a utilitarian product for the theatres — a group of situations practicable on the stage, and a collection of speeches adapted to the mouths of actors in the heat of action. Not being at all designed for closet reading, for its proper effect it was vitally dependent on actual stage representation. As Shakespeare's fellow-playwright, Marston, put it: "Comedies are writ to be spoken, not read. Remember, the life of these things consists in action." [1] In other words, the manuscript contributed to the actors by the playwright was regarded as but a part of a more important whole — the whole being a public scenic performance in which the author and the actors collaborated.

And since the object of this scenic performance was to entertain the miscellaneous throng at a theatre, the successful playwright had first of all to consider the means to that end. He could not ignore the restrictions imposed by the Elizabethan stage, [2] or the narrow limitations of the actors. Nor for a moment could he forget the tastes of a public which expressed its likes and dislikes in the most vehement way. As Webster says in a Preface to *The White Devil:* "If it be objected this is no true dramatic poem, I shall easily confess it, *non potes in nugas dicere plura meas, ipse ego quam dixi.* Willingly, and not ignorantly, in this kind have I faulted: for should a man present to such an auditory the most sententious tragedy that ever was written ... yet after all this divine rapture, *O dura messorum ilia,* the breath that comes from the uncapable multitude is able to poison it." [3]

As a result of these inescapable limitations the dramatists usually worked in a practical rather than purely

[1] Address To the Reader, prefixed to *The Fawn* (1606). Webster likewise insists that the "great part of the grace" of his plays "lay in the action."

[2] This, it should be remembered, was not the "picture stage" of modern times, but the "platform stage" inherited from the inn yards, projecting into the middle of the theatre and virtually surrounded by spectators.

[3] The complaint is frequently heard from the dramatists. Thus Thomas Dekker (*A Knight's Conjuring,* 1607) declares that though a playwright "who is worthy to sit at the table of the Sun, waste his brains to earn applause from the more worthy spirits, yet when he has done his best he works but like Ocnus, that makes ropes in hell; for, as he twists, an ass stands by and bites them in sunder, and that ass is no other than the audience with hard hands."

artistic spirit; and since their labor was frankly mercenary, and unsubject to the eyes of readers, they often composed hurriedly and even carelessly.[1] Kirkman informs us that many of Heywood's manuscripts were "written loosely in taverns" on odd sheets of paper; and we are told by Heywood himself in 1633 — long before he had finished his career — that he had produced, or at least had "a main finger" in, two hundred and twenty plays. Naturally, work produced in this fashion was not intended for the press at all, and the authors shrank from a critical examination of their lines. Marston, when his *Malcontent* was published against his will, complains: "Only one thing afflicts me, to think that scenes invented merely to be spoken should be enforcedly published to be read"; and when his *Parasitaster* was similarly given to the press, he writes: "If any shall wonder why I print a comedy, whose life rests much in the actor's voice, let such know that it cannot avoid publishing." To avoid publishing, indeed, was the desire of most Elizabethan play-makers. Jasper Mayne, a dramatist of no mean ability, when his *City Match* was issued in 1639 despite his earnest wishes, affixed a statement to the readers declaring that he "had no ambition to make it this way public, holding works of this light nature to be things which need an apology for being written at all" — not to speak of their being published.

The almost negligible literary value the age set on plays — *nos haec novimus esse nihil*, says Webster — is clearly indicated by the tone of their dedications, or perhaps more effectively by their lack of dedications. It is significant that not one of Shakespeare's plays was thought worthy of a dedication. The publisher, Francis

---

[1] "Henslowe's dramatic accounts for the period 1592 to 1603 show that the playwrights employed by his companies averaged one new play about every two and a half weeks" (to be exact, one in 2.7 weeks). — Alwin Thaler, *Shakspere to Sheridan*, p. 234.

Burton, in offering *The Stately Tragedy of Claudius Tiberius Nero* to Sir Arthur Mannering in 1607, writes: "If custom, right worshipful, had so great a prerogative as that nothing crossing it were at all allowable, then might I justly fear reprehension for this my dedication, having, to my knowledge, but a singular [i.e., single] precedent herein; and the reason wherefore so many plays have formerly been published without Inscriptions unto particular Patrons, contrary to custom in divulging other books, although perhaps I could nearly guess, yet because I would willingly offend none, I will now conceal." Even when at a later date authors, taking courage, ventured to dedicate plays to their friends or patrons,[1] they invariably felt called upon to apologize for so doing, and to justify themselves by citing the custom of antiquity and of other nations — for had not "the greatest of the Cæsars" and "the great princes" of Italy, to cite Webster, deigned to accept such trifles?[2] Heywood in dedicating *The English Traveler* to Sir Henry Appleton in 1633, hopes that he will not "think it any undervaluing" of his worth; and in offering his popular Court success, *Love's Mistress*, to the Earl of Dorset in 1636, he urges that plays are not "so despicable as to be held unworthy the countenance of great men." In a similar vein George Chapman, in dedicating *The Widow's Tears* to Mr. John Reed, expresses doubt "if any work of this nature be worth the presenting"; and in defence of his dedicating *The Revenge of Bussy d'Ambois* to Sir Thomas Howard he resorts to the old excuse that the princes of Italy had deemed the acceptance of a play no "diminution to their greatness." Even Jonson, with

[1] On this point see the Dedication to Chapman's *The Revenge of Bussy d'Ambois*.

[2] Cf. the dedications of *The Devil's Law Case*, *Cæsar and Pompey*, *The Duke of Milan*, *A New Way to Pay Old Debts*, *The Duchess of Malfi*, *The Widow's Tears*.

all his assurance, in offering *Every Man in his Humor* to his old teacher, William Camden, says that "no doubt" some "will esteem all office done you in this kind an injury." And we should not forget that Shakespeare's friends, when dedicating the First Folio to the two Earls of Pembroke and Montgomery, felt it necessary to put his plays in the category of "meanest things," beneath their lordships' serious attention: "We cannot but know their dignity greater than to descend to the reading of these trifles."

Sir Thomas Bodley was merely echoing this well-established attitude toward plays when he stipulated that play-books should not be admitted into the Bodleian Collection. He writes: "Were it so again that some little profit might be reaped (which God knows is very little) out of some of our play-books, the benefit thereof will nothing near countervail the harm that the Scandal will bring upon the Library. . . . The more I think upon it, the more it doth distaste me that such kind of books should be vouchsafed a room in so noble a Library." Was Shakespeare thinking of this general scorn of plays — "baggage-books," Sir Thomas calls them — when he wrote to his friend of the *Sonnets?* —

> My name be buried where my body is
> And live no more to shame nor me nor you.
> For I am shamed by that which I bring forth,
> And so should you, to love things nothing worth.

The first playwright who dared challenge this commonly accepted opinion was the arrogant Ben Jonson. Having painfully sought to observe the laws of dramatic composition as enunciated by classical scholars, and having expended great effort in giving to his comedies and tragedies literary value, in 1616 (the year of Shakespeare's death) he gathered his plays into a single volume and offered them to readers. Yet when he dignified his collection with the title *The Works of Ben Jonson*, there was a general outburst of merriment among men of letters, even among dramatists. Sir John Suckling, in *A Session of the Poets*, wrote:

> The first that broke silence was good old Ben,
> Prepar'd before with Canary wine;
> And he told them plainly he deserved the bays,
> For his were called *Works*, where others' were but plays.

And Thomas Heywood declared with scorn: "My plays are not exposed unto the world in volumes to bear the title of *Works*, as others'." [1] In *Wit's Recreation* (1640) is printed the following epigram:

> Pray tell me, Ben, where does the mystery lurk,
> What others call a *play* you call a *work?*

The same apologetic attitude was held towards Shakespeare's printed plays. In *Conceits, Clinches, Flashes, and Whimsies* (1639), we read:

One asked another what Shakespeare's *works* were worth, all being bound together. He answered, Not a farthing. Not a farthing! said he; Why so? He answered that his *plays* were worth a great deal of money, but he never heard that his *works* were worth anything at all.

Likewise in *Captain Underwit*, attributed to James Shirley:

Underwit. Shakespeare's *works!* why Shakespeare's *works?* . . . They are plays.

And even Leonard Digges, idolatrous admirer that he was, in commending Shakespeare's printed Folio to the public is careful to observe the distinction: "I will not

---

[1] "To the Reader," prefixed to *The English Traveler*. So strongly did Heywood feel on the subject that he repeats the statement in his address "To the Reader," affixed to *The Fair Maid of the Exchange*. For other flings at Jonson's presumption in calling his plays works, see Fitzgeoffrey, *Certain Elegies;* Ferrand, *Erotomania;* Beaumont and Fletcher, ed. by Glover, i, lv; Leonard Digges, *Upon Master William Shakespeare*, prefixed to Shakespeare's *Poems*, 1640; William Sheares, Epistle Dedicatory prefixed to Marston's plays, 1633; and for numerous later references see *The Jonson Allusion-Book.*

say his Workes." Nor, it may be observed, did the publishers of the First Folio grace the title-page with so dignified a term.

Such, then, was the attitude of the literary world toward plays. Naturally it led the popular dramatists to regard their manuscripts as of little worth save for the amusement of public audiences, and gave them an excuse to write with speed rather than painstaking care. This, it will be realized, was quite different from the attitude of the ambitious literary artist — Spenser, for example, who set himself to the task of composing for judicious readers and for all posterity a poem which the world would not willingly let die.

To what extent Shakespeare shared in this prevailing attitude towards dramatic composition we can hardly say. His *Sonnets*, however, rather indicate that he felt his genius handicapped by the necessity of writing for the theatres; and his failure to prepare his plays for publication — as did Ben Jonson — or, so far as we know, to leave instructions regarding their ultimate preservation, seems to indicate that, in a measure at least, he shared the popular notion of their unimportance as lasting contributions to England's treasury of art.

That he, indeed, wore the mantle of dramatic poet lightly was the opinion current among his friends. Ben Jonson says: "I remember the players have often mentioned it as an honour to Shakespeare that in his writing, whatsoever he penn'd, he never blotted out a line." And the Globe actors, Heminges and Condell, in an Address to the Reader prefixed to the First Folio, say: "His mind and hand went together, and what he thought he uttered with that easiness that we [his actors] have scarce received from him a blot in his papers."[1]

---

[1] The publisher of the First Folio of Beaumont and Fletcher, a volume in many ways imitating the First Folio of Shakespeare, declares to the reader:

Yet, one may be sure, Shakespeare was far more pains-taking in the composition of his plays than these broad statements would seem to imply. That at all times he was a conscious artist no one can doubt who has closely studied his plays. And he — as well as Ben Jonson — must have realized that he put into the manuscripts he supplied the actors beautiful poetry and dramatic skill of a high order. It may be that his wonderful power to visualize characters and situations, and a capacity to re-tain long passages in his mind, enabled him to shape his scenes and even to polish his lines before setting them on paper; and this may in a measure explain the astonish-ment of his friends at his facility. Yet he must often have undergone the pangs of authorship, without which no great work of literature is produced. His friend Jonson puts the case clearly. After duly noting the ease with which he composed, "Nature herself" seeming to delight in submitting to "the dressing of his lines," he adds:

> Yet must I not give Nature all. Thy art,
> My gentle Shakespeare, must enjoy a part.
> For though the poet's matter Nature be,
> His art doth give the fashion. And that he
> Who casts to write a living line must sweat,
> (Such as thine are), and strike the second heat
> Upon the Muse's anvil, turn the same,
> (And himself with it) that he thinks to frame;
> Or for the laurel he may gain a scorn.
> For a good poet's made as well as born —
> And such wert thou.

We may therefore believe that within the limits im-posed by the prevailing opinion that plays were not im-portant contributions to the world's store of literature, Shakespeare took his art seriously. At the same time we should remember that he wrote directly for the actors,

"Whatever I have seene of Mr. Fletcher's owne hand, is free from interlin-ing; and his friends affirme he never writ any one thing twice."

and kept mainly in view the audiences gathered in play-houses. And while he sought the approval of judicious spectators, he gave little thought to closet readers, and probably would shrink from that critical examination to which posterity has subjected his every line.

Perhaps in one instance we are able to spy on him at work, and observe for ourselves the manner in which he composed. For it is now, though not certain, at least possible that in one of the Elizabethan playhouse manu-scripts originally belonging to his company we have a scene in his own autograph. This play, entitled *Sir Thomas More*,[1] in the main was the work of Anthony Munday; but it was revamped by several authors, so that the manu-script presents a curious patchwork of cancellations, al-terations, and additions. Thirteen leaves are in the un-mistakable autograph of Munday; the remaining leaves, written in various hands, contain passages or scenes meant to be additions or substitutions. Of these latter, three pages, constituting a neat insertion in one scene, have been with some plausibility assigned to Shakespeare as his contribution to the betterment of the play.[2]

The lines were long ago attributed to Shakespeare by critics on purely literary grounds, and recently this attribution has been ably championed by Sir Edward Maunde Thompson on paleographical grounds.[3] Taking advantage of the new signature of the poet discovered by Professor Wallace, Sir Edward has shown that the scene is probably in the autograph of Shakespeare — a con-

[1] Now preserved in the British Museum as Harleian MS. 7368. It has been reproduced in photographic facsimile by J. S. Farmer, and reprinted, with several facsimiles, by W. W. Greg for The Malone Society.

[2] As the "Johannes-fac-totum" of his company he must have thus touched up many old plays in the stock of the Chamberlain's Men.

[3] *Shakespeare's Handwriting*, Oxford, at the Clarendon Press, 1916. See also the same writer's article, "The Autograph Manuscripts of Anthony Munday," in the *Transactions of the Bibliographical Society*, xiv, 325; and compare W. W. Greg, "Autograph Plays by Anthony Munday," in *Modern Language Review*, viii, 89.

clusion that has since been strengthened by scholars in various ways.[1] Sir Edward writes:

> These three pages, written in the ordinary English cursive script of the Elizabethan period, are obviously the autograph composition of the writer, and not a mere transcript by a copyist. The nature of the first-hand corrections is sufficient proof of this. It is also obvious that the writer was a careless contributor. It has been remarked by Dr. Greg that he shows no respect for, perhaps no knowledge of, the play on which he was at work.[2] In a haphazard fashion he distributes speeches and exclamations among the insurgents, and sometimes he merely attaches the word "other," instead of the actual name of a character to a speech, leaving it to the reviser to put things straight. In one passage, which he has partially altered, he leaves two and a half lines so confused that the reviser has found no way out of the difficulty but to strike them out and substitute a half-line of his own. All these liberties would suggest that the writer was one who held a high place among his fellow contributors to the piecing-out of the play, and that they recognized his superior talent just as much as later critics have done.

So hurried, indeed, was the writer, and so careless, that he not only indicated successive speakers by the tag "other," but at times shortened this into "oth" and even "o"; and Sir Thomas More, in spite of his high position,

[1] See especially J. Dover Wilson in the *News Sheet* of The Bibliographical Society, January, 1919, and Percy Simpson, "The Play of *Sir Thomas More* and Shakespeare's Hand in It," *The Library*, 1917, viii, 79. If I may be allowed to make here a small contribution to the subject, I should point out the following parallels in thought and phraseology. "Whats a watrie parsnip to a good heart? trash, trash . . . our infection will make the city shake, which partly comes through the eating of parsnips. *Clown.* True, and pumpions together" (*More*, 11. 9–16). "This unwholesome humidity, this gross watery pumpion" (*Merry Wives*, III, iii, 43); "like ravenous fishes" (*More*, 1. 86), "as ravenous fishes" (*Henry VIII*, I, ii, 79); "spurn you like dogs" (*More*, 1. 135), "I spurn thee like a cur" (*J. Cæsar*, III, i, 46), "away unpeachable dog, or I'll spurn thee hence" (*T. of Athens*, I, i, 281), "And foot me as you spurn a stranger cur" (*M. of Ven.* I, iii, 119), "your mountainish [=barbarous] inhumanity" (*More*, 1. 140), cf. *T. N.* IV, i, 52, *Hen. V*, IV, iv, 20, V, v, 36, *Merry Wives*, I, i, 164.

[2] Cf. his ignorance of the contents of Chester's *Love's Martyr*, discussed above, p. 341.

appears as "moo." The stage-manager, or reviser, was under the necessity of changing these into proper catch-names; thus for the first "other" he substituted "Geo. Bett," for the second "other," "Bett's Clown," for the third "oth," "William," and so on.

As to the author's manner of composing as indicated by the handwriting, Sir Edward says:

There is a decided distinction between the writing of the first two pages and that of the third page. The text of the former is evidently written with speed. . . . The rapid action of the hand is indicated, for example, by the prevalence of thin long-shafted descending letters (*f* and long *s*), which are carried down often to unusual length and end in a sharp point, and by a certain dash in the formation of the other letters, both in the text and in the marginal names of the characters. These signs of speed generally slacken in the course of the second page, in the second half of which the long-shafted descending letters give place to some extent to a more deliberate and heavier style of lettering. This change seems to be coincident with the change in the character of the composition — the change from the noisy tumult of the insurgents to the intervention of [Sir Thomas] More with his persuasive speeches, requiring more thought and choice of language on the part of the author. The full effect of this change in the style of the composition is manifest in the more deliberate character of the writing of the third page.

There are surprisingly few alterations, and, with one exception, these were promptly made, usually by drawing the pen through the word or letters just written, and immediately adding thereafter the correction. If I understand the alterations, they may be classified as follows. In three cases an accidental slip of the pen is instantly corrected; *mv* is corrected to *nv*, *ar* to *as*, *yo* *yo* to *yo*. In four cases other, and usually better, words are substituted; *watery* is changed to *sorry*, *helpe* to *advantage*, *god* to *he*, *only* to *solely*. In ten cases the drift of the thought is suddenly changed while a line was in composition; the best example is the following, the canceled words being enclosed in brackets:

> Go you to France or Flanders,
> To any German province, [to] Spain, or Portugall,
> Nay any where, [why you] that not adheres to England,
> Why you must needs be strangers.

Other cases are *theise* changed to *the state*, *ar*[*e?*] to *or*, *sh*[*ould?*] to *Charge*, *le*[*nt?*] to *solely lent*, *his* to *and*, *that* to *make*, *th*[*e?*] to *a*, *saying* to *say*, *their* to *your;* and, possibly, *in* to *no* and *y* to *noyce*, though these last two changes may be due to slips of the pen. In one notable instance, however, the poet had serious difficulty, and after several attempts gave up, and left the lines in an unfinished state. The case will serve to illustrate what Jonson said about striking "the second heat upon the Muse's anvil." The writer first set down —

> Is safer wars than ever you can make,
> Whose discipline is riot; why even your wars
> Cannot proceed but by obedience.

Then observing that he had used the noun "wars" in two successive lines, he struck out the second "wars" and substituted the word "hurly." The lines now read:

> Is safer wars than ever you can make,
> Whose discipline is riot; why even your hurly
> Cannot proceed but by obedience.

The change not satisfying him, he experimentally inserted above, after the word "riot," the phrase "In, in to your obedience." This alternative pleasing him no better, he gave up, and left the passage in an imperfect form. The stage-manager, not being able to solve the difficulty, drew his pen through all three lines, and substituted the tame and prosaic phrase: "Tell me but this."

The method of composing revealed in these three pages probably indicates the manner in which Shakespeare worked — swiftly, with minor alterations almost instantly made, and a few passages hammered out with effort. This would justify the actors in saying: "His mind and hand went together, and what he thought he uttered with that easiness that we have scarce received from him a blot in his papers," as well as Jonson's assertion that occasionally he had to sweat, and "turn" the line he sought to frame.

That normally Shakespeare did not take the trouble to recopy the first draft of his plays is indicated by the passage just quoted from his actors, and by Jonson's statement that he "never blotted out a line." Yet playwrights, we know, were expected to furnish the theatre with a clean manuscript. Robert Daborne writes to Henslowe:

MR. HENSLOWE: —

You accuse me with the breach of promise. True it is I promised to bring you the last scene, which that you may see finished I send you the foul sheet and the fair I was writing, as your man can testify. . . . I will not fail to write this fair, and perfect the book, which shall not lye on your hands.

Yours to command,

ROBERT DABORNE.[1]

It is clear that Daborne was expected to supply a "fair" copy. Writing with difficulty, he was forced to transcribe his scenes from the "foul sheets"; the master, with his greater ease at composition, seems not to have been under this necessity — at least so far as his actors knew, for we must not forget Jonson's pertinent warning.

We may suppose, therefore, that for the most part Shakespeare, composing with facility, wrote with great speed, revising the lines as he jotted them down; and the manuscript thus produced, in his own autograph, he delivered to his company.

But before the company could proceed to a stage-performance of the play it had to secure for the manuscript the official license of the censor. A commission issued by

[1] W. W. Greg, *Henslowe Papers*, p. 78; cf. pp. 69, 72, 73.

Elizabeth in 1581 had placed the control of the drama in the hands of the Master of the Revels. By virtue of this commission Edmund Tilney, who was then Master, assumed the right to censor all plays and license them for public representation. "No play is to be played but such as is allowed," he informed the actors, and the evidence of such allowance, he stipulated, was to be a statement to that effect written and signed by the Master "at the latter end of the said book they do play." [1] Later the Master's assistant, Hayward, wrote:

That the Master of His Majesty's Office of the Revels hath the power of licensing all plays, whether tragedies, or comedies, before they can be acted, is without dispute; and the design is that all prophaness, oaths, ribaldry, and matters reflecting upon piety, and the present government may be obliterated before there be any action in a public theatre.

Accordingly, when the company received the manuscript of a play from Shakespeare, it first submitted it to the Master of the Revels to be "perused and licensed." In the case of the manuscript of *Sir Thomas More*, just examined, the Master refused to license the play without drastic revision. After making various notes during the course of his reading, he jotted down the following instructions on the first page:

Leave out . . . the insurrection wholly, and the cause thereof, and begin with Sir Thomas More at the mayor's sessions, with a report afterwards of his good service done, being Sheriff of London, upon a mutiny against the Lombards, only by a Short report and not otherwise, at your own perils.

E. TYLLNEY.

Tilney read all Shakespeare's earlier plays. How much need he had to censor them — one thinks at once of *Richard II* with its deposition scene — we cannot tell; but

[1] For a history of the Office of the Revels and the powers of the Master, see my *Dramatic Records of Sir Henry Herbert*.

the poet could not have composed without having ever in mind this official's watchful eye. In 1597 Tilney's nephew, Sir George Buc, was appointed Deputy-Master, and gradually took over all the duties of the office; after 1607 he seems to have had sole charge of licensing plays, and in 1610, upon the death of Tilney, he succeeded to the office, a position he held until 1622. Thus all Shakespeare's plays were submitted to the scrutiny of Tilney or his nephew Buc.

Some notion of Tilney's censorship of plays may be gained from his comment on *Sir Thomas More;* an excellent notion of how Buc exercised his power may be had by examining the prompt-copy of *The Second Maiden's Tragedy*.[1] Such mild oaths as "life" and "heart" he carefully excised; and the line "Your king's poisoned" evoked from him a heavy black cross in the margin, a vigorous deletion, and the substitution of the less offensive words "I am poisoned." At the end he wrote in a large bold hand:

This Second Maiden's Tragedy (for it hath no name inscribed) may, with the reformations, be acted publickly. 31 October, 1611.

G. BUC.

But a much better notion of the attitude of the Master of the Revels toward plays and their authors may be secured from the fuller records of Sir Henry Herbert, who succeeded Buc in the office, and governed himself by the precedents already established. At the end of Shirley's *The Young Admiral*, Herbert inscribed the following unctuous license:

The comedy called *The Young Admiral*, being free from oaths, prophaness, or obsceness, hath given me much delight

---

[1] The manuscript is in the British Museum, Lansdowne 807; it has been reproduced in The Malone Society's Reprints. For another manuscript censored by Buc see *Sir John van Olden Barnavelt*, British Museum Addit. MS. 18653, reprinted by A. H. Bullen, *Old English Plays*, vol. ii.

and satisfaction in the reading, and may serve for a pattern to other poets, not only for the bettring of manners and language, but for the improvement of the quality, which hath received some brushings of late.

When Mr. Shirley hath read this approbation, I know it will encourage him to pursue this beneficial and cleanly way of poetry; and when other poets hear and see his good success, I am confident they will imitate the original for their own credit, and make such copies in this harmless way as shall speak them masters in their art at the first sight to all judicious spectators. It may be acted, this 3 July, 1633.

But Herbert was not always so well-pleased with what he read, and at other times we find him writing in quite a different tone:

I took it ill, and would have forbidden the play, but that Beeston [the manager of the company] promised many things which I found fault withal should be left out, and that he would not suffer it to be done by the poet any more, who deserves to be punished. And the first that offends in this kind, of poets or players, shall be sure of public punishment.

This day, being the 11 of January, 1630, I did refuse to allow a play of Massingers because it did contain dangerous matter, as the deposing of Sebastian, King of Portugal.

Received of Mr. Kirke, for a new play, which I burnt for the ribaldry and offense that was in it, £2.

On one occasion, however, Herbert's censoring hand was curbed by no less a person than the King, as he records in his note-book:

This morning, being the 9th of January, 1633, the King was pleased to call me into his withdrawing chamber to the window, where he went over all that I had crossed in Davenant's play-book, and, allowing of *faith* and *slight* to be asseverations only and no oaths, marked them to stand, and some other few things, but in the greater part allowed of my reformations. This was done upon a complaint of Mr. Endymion Porters in December.

The King is pleased to take *faith, death, slight* for asseverations and no oaths; to which I do humbly submit as my mas-

ter's judgment — but, under favour, conceive them to be
oaths, and enter them here to declare my opinion and submission.[1]

After the play had been thus censored, and the official
license duly placed at the end, the company could arrange
for its public representation. First the stage-manager
undertook to make it practicable for acting purposes.
He went through the manuscript grouping the scenes into
acts, usually indicating his divisions by the word "Musicke" written in large letters. The author commonly did
not specify the act-divisions,[2] for to him there was little
significance in such notation. The players, however,
found it desirable to rest the audience at intervals, and
to let them refresh themselves with nuts, apples, ginger-
cakes, beer, ale, wine, and tobacco. The pause was filled,
as in modern times, by an interlude from the playhouse
orchestra, and hence the manager's call at this point
for "Musicke."

Moreover, the manager commonly found it necessary
to cut certain passages, to omit some scenes entirely, or
to run two scenes together, in order to make the play
shorter or, in his judgment, more effective on the stage.
Virtually all the extant Elizabethan playhouse manuscripts show passages marked for omission; and the custom is frequently referred to in the printed form of the
plays. The publisher of Brome's *The Antipodes* declares:
"You shall find in this book more than was presented upon the stage, and left out of the presentation for superfluous length"; the title-page of *The Duchess of Malfi* promises the buyer "the perfect and exact copy, with divers

[1] For a fuller discussion of the censorship of plays see my *Dramatic Records of Sir Henry Herbert*.
[2] Scores of Elizabethan plays, including many of Shakespeare's, are
printed without act-divisions at all. The omission is to be expected except
when the publisher edited the manuscript for the readers. At a later date,
however, dramatists began to indicate these divisions themselves.

things printed that the length of the play would not bear in the presentment"; and Humphrey Moseley in issuing the 1647 Folio of Beaumont and Fletcher says to the reader: "One thing I must answer before it be objected; 'tis this: when these comedies and tragedies were presented on the stage, the actors omitted some scenes and passages (with the author's consent) as occasion led them ... but now you have both all that was acted and all that was not, even the perfect, full originals, without the least mutilation."

It is clear that in many of Shakespeare's plays the actors, no doubt "with the author's consent," marked passages for omission, and in some cases (*Othello*, for example) whole scenes. The resultant "mutilation," though it might not be specially observed in the stage-presentation, is only too apparent in a careful reading.

After these practical alterations, the manuscript was turned over to the playhouse copyist, who transcribed each actor's part with the cues from the preceding speaker, and these parts were handed to the players to be memorized.[1]

Finally, the original manuscript, as it came from the author,[2] with the cuts and alterations by the stage-manager, and with the official license of the Master of the Revels, was bound up into the prompt-copy for the use of the "book-holder." For this purpose it was roughly stitched with a bodkin and thread, and enclosed in suit-

---

[1] An example is found among the manuscripts at Dulwich College in the actor's part for the rôle of Orlando, in Robert Greene's *Orlando Furioso*, prepared by the copyist of the theatre for Edward Alleyn. It contains only the speeches of Orlando, with the cues from the preceding actor. One may conveniently examine this interesting document in the first volume of J. C. Collins, *The Plays and Poems of Robert Greene*, 1905, or in *Henslowe Papers*, 1907, ed. by W. W. Greg.

[2] There is no reason to suppose that the players regularly employed a scrivener to make a fair copy. The prompt-copies of *John à Kent, Sir Thomas More, Believe as Ye List, The Captives, The Launching of the May*, and *The Two Noble Ladies*, are all in the hands of the authors.

able covers; the two prompt-books we have from the storeroom of Shakespeare's company are bound in vellum wrappers taken from an old Latin manuscript of the thirteenth century (apparently kept for that purpose), and on the outside of the covers is written in large heavy characters "The Booke of," followed by the title.

In the course of the rehearsals that followed, the bookholder inserted stage-directions to serve as a guide to him in engineering the play from behind the scenes, often employing the imperative form (as "Whistle, boy"), and often using the name of the actor instead of the character impersonated. A few examples from the extant prompt-copy of Massinger's *Believe as Ye List* will serve to illustrate.

"Enter Demetrius — Wm. Pattrick."
"Table ready: and 6 chairs to set out."
"Mr. Hobs called."
"The great book of accompte ready."
"Gascoine and Hubert below ready to open the trap-door for Mr. Taylor."
"Antiochus ready: under the stage."
"Harry Wilson: and boy ready for the song at the arras." [1]

This prompt-copy, called "The Book," was carefully preserved in the storeroom of the playhouse, doubtless under lock and key.[2] Bearing the signed license of the Master of the Revels, it constituted an official document which would protect the actors in case of trouble. How necessary its preservation was is shown by the records of Sir Henry Herbert. When late in the year 1623 the King's Men desired to present *The Winter's Tale*, they found that the original licensed manuscript was missing. Pos-

---

[1] The manuscript itself is in the autograph of Massinger; the stage-directions are added in a different hand.

[2] One should examine a few of the stage-copies that have been preserved. *Believe as Ye List, Sir Thomas More, John à Kent and John à Cumber* have been reproduced by J. S. Farmer in photographic facsimile. *The Captives* and *The Launching of the May*, both with the license of the Master of the Revels at the end, are to be found in the British Museum.

sibly it had been mislaid by the printers of the First Folio. The actors, however, regarded it as so imperative to have in their hands a properly allowed copy of the play that they sent Heminges to the Master of the Revels with a text (doubtless as printed in the Folio) to secure his re-license and official signature. Herbert made the following entry in his office-book: "For the King's Players, an old play called *Winter's Tale*, formerly allowed of by Sir George Buc, and now likewise by me, on Mr. Heminges' word that there was nothing profane added, or reformed, though the allowed book was missing."

Obviously "the allowed book" of each play had to be preserved as a matter of safety to the company. Moreover, from it at any time new actor-parts could be made, if the old ones were lost or worn out; but except in special and unusual cases no other complete copy of the play would be made,[1] or allowed to be made. There was, indeed, no occasion for a second copy, and the ever-present danger of theft by pirates of the publishing trade, or by rival companies, had to be guarded against.

From the foregoing, it will be seen that the printed text of many, if not most, of Shakespeare's plays would necessarily be derived immediately or ultimately from the prompt-books; furthermore, that in some cases, possibly in the majority of cases, these prompt-books were in the autograph of the poet. Normally, therefore, we should expect to have a Shakespearean play set up from the author's original draft (modified by the cuts and

---

[1] Sometimes the author might retain a copy for his own purposes, as Jonson seems to have done; Heywood declares that he did not thus preserve his own plays. And sometimes a special shortened version might be prepared for the use of the troupe while traveling in the country. It is true that the publisher of the Folio of Beaumont and Fletcher, 1647, speaks of transcripts, for private reading made by friends of the actors; but these transcripts, I suspect, were permitted after the closing of the theatres in 1642. In the case of Shakespeare, *Troilus and Cressida*, and possibly *Hamlet*, represent the exception; see pp. 347–49, and 521.

alterations inevitable in a prompt-book), or from a transcript therefrom made for the use of the type-compositors. There are, of course, a few exceptions, to be discussed hereafter.[1]

[1] For a more detailed discussion of the topics handled in this chapter the reader is referred to the following works: A. W. Pollard, *Shakespeare Folios and Quartos*, 1909, *A New Shakespeare Quarto*, 1916, and *Shakespeare's Fight with the Pirates, and the Problems of the Transmission of His Text*, 1920; Percy Simpson, "The Play of *Sir Thomas More* and Shakespeare's Hand in It," *The Library*, 1917, viii, 79.

CHAPTER XXVIII

THE PRINTING OF THE QUARTOS

THE question frequently is asked, Why did not Shakespeare himself publish his plays, freed from the cuts of the actors and the scars of the tiring-house, "absolute in their numbers as he conceived them"? One reason, doubtless, may be found in the prevailing opinion that plays were not lasting contributions to literature, and would confer little honor on the poet. But a more potent reason is to be found in the fact that when Shakespeare sold his manuscripts to the company he parted with all right in them, and the company, regarding them as its own property upon which its income depended, was unwilling to let them be printed. As Heywood tells us, the actors "think it against their peculiar profit [i.e., personal gain] to have them come into print." Years after Shakespeare's death, Leonard Digges wrote:

> But oh! what praise more powerful can we give
> The dead than that by him the King's Men live.[1]

Naturally, as long as his plays were among their important sources of income the King's Men would be anxious to prevent their sale to the public. And how deeply concerned actors in general were to forestall the publication of their manuscripts is shown in the Articles of Agreement signed by the members of the Company of the Revels at Whitefriars in 1608. One clause of the agreement reads: "That no man of the said company shall at any time put into print, or cause to be put into print, any

[1] Lines prefixed to the 1640 edition of Shakespeare's *Poems*, but doubtless written earlier, for they seem to have been designed for the First Folio of 1623.

manner of play-book now in use, or that hereafter shall be sold unto them, upon the penalty and forfeiture of forty pounds sterling, or the loss of his place and share of all things amongst them." [1]

The reason for a company's great anxiety to prevent the printing of its manuscripts is obvious. Representing a substantial outlay of money, they constituted the company's stock-in-trade; and so long as they could be enjoyed only in the theatre, enabled the actors to draw thither the London public. When the King's Men in 1637 complained to Philip Herbert, Earl of Pembroke, then the Lord Chamberlain, that divers of their plays, which they had for "their own use bought and provided at very dear and high rates," had been "lately stolen, or gotten from them by indirect means," and "are now attempted to be printed," he promptly ordered the Master and Wardens of the Stationers' Company to prevent it, on the ground that the publication of the actors' property, "if it should be suffered, would directly tend to their apparent detriment and great prejudice." [2]

Yet theatrical manuscripts, of course, were often printed. During Shakespeare's lifetime no fewer than sixteen of his plays — not counting *Pericles* — came to the press; and hundreds of plays by other authors were offered for sale on the stalls of the bookshops. Between 1590 and 1600, for example, over one hundred and fifty plays were entered in the Stationers' Registers. Clearly so large a number would be possible only through the consent of the actors, who for one reason or another released their manuscripts for publication. The main occasions for these authorized editions may be noted as follows.

---

[1] The New Shakspere Society *Transactions*, 1887-90, p. 276.
[2] This interesting letter, bearing the date June 10, 1637, is printed by George Chalmers, *Apology*, p. 513, and by J. P. Collier, *The History of Eng*

First, when a company disbanded, its manuscripts, along with its costumes and properties, were divided among the sharers, and so came upon the market. Some of the more successful manuscripts might be disposed of at good rates to rival companies; some would be sold to publishers. This was the case when the Earl of Pembroke's Men went into bankruptcy in 1593. The Lord Strange's Men seized the opportunity to purchase from them certain plays, notably *Hamlet*. At the same time other plays were secured by publishers, notably *Titus Andronicus*, which was issued in February, 1593–94. This was the first of Shakespeare's plays to come into print, and, so far as we know, the only one to reach the reading public in this manner.

Secondly, when hard times or other misfortune reduced a troupe to a state of poverty, the actors might sell a few of their manuscripts in order to supply their pressing needs. This is why during and immediately after the visitations of the plague we find an unusual number of plays entered in the Stationers' Registers. Since, however, the prosperous Chamberlain-King's Company never was in dire pecuniary straits, none of Shakespeare's manuscripts was disposed of by them for this reason.

Thirdly, some unusual circumstance might render the publication of a play desirable. When *Sejanus* was hopelessly damned on its initial performance, Jonson naturally wished to offer it to the reading public in order to demonstrate its merits as literature, as well as to clear himself of the charge of its treasonable nature, which had led to his being summoned "before the Council." Daniel likewise published his *Philotas* after "the wrong application and misconceiving" of its plot had involved him in serious difficulty with the authorities. A somewhat sim-

lish Dramatic Poetry, 1879, ii, 17, note 1. See also a similar letter of 1641, in The Malone Society's *Collections*, i, 367.

ilar reason, I think, explains the printing of *I Henry IV* only a few months after its composition, and while it was still the chief sensation of London, crowding the pit and galleries of the theatre. The dramatist, it will be recalled, had unwittingly given offense to Lord Cobham, and, after that nobleman made complaint, had altered the name of the fat Knight from "Sir John Oldcastle" to "Sir John Falstaff." This change of name proving inadequate, however, Shakespeare and his company sent the play to the press in order further to rectify the injury they had done to the Cobham family. The text was set up from authentic copy, possibly supplied by Shakespeare,[1] and was so accurate that it was used by the editors of the First Folio.

Fourthly, the actors out of courtesy might give the author permission to print a play. Heywood tells us that he was able to issue his *Rape of Lucrece* "by consent" of the players; and Ben Jonson no doubt received similar permission when he put forth his collected *Works* in 1616. But as a rule such consent would not be asked, nor granted, until the plays had almost served their usefulness on the stage. It must have been largely on grounds of courtesy that in 1623 the Globe actors (possibly with a cash payment to reimburse them somewhat for losses) consented to the publication of all of Shakespeare's "Comedies, Histories, and Tragedies" in the monumental First Folio.

In a great many cases, however, plays were printed contrary to the wishes and best interests of the actors, who were constantly engaged in an attempt to suppress piratical issues. The more important ways in which these unauthorized editions were made possible are noted below.

[1] That it was printed from the original draft is indicated by the survival of a word-play on the name Oldcastle; and that it was edited for the press is

First, an author might betray the company by disposing of a transcript to the printers. Heywood writes with pride: "Though some have used a double sale of their labor, first to the stage, and after to the press, for my own part I here proclaim myself ever faithful in the first, and never guilty in the last." [1] But the danger from this source was small, and we cannot for a moment believe that any of Shakespeare's plays were printed in so dishonorable a fashion.

Secondly, an unprincipled stenographer might conceal himself in the gallery of the playhouse and take down the speeches of the actors in shorthand notes, from which he could manufacture a crude copy for the press. Heywood twice complains of the theft of his plays in this manner, with the resultant corruption of the text. In the Prologue to his revised edition of *If You Know Not Me* (first published in 1605), in which he "taxeth the most corrupted copy now imprinted," he tells us that the audiences —

> Did throng the seats, the boxes, and the stage
> So much, that some by stenography drew
> The plot, put it in print, scarce one word true.

And in his revised edition of *The Rape of Lucrece* (first published in 1608) he says: "Some of my plays have (unknown to me, and without my directions) accidentally come into the printers' hands, and therefore so corrupt and mangled, copied only by the ear, that I have been as unable to know them as ashamed to challenge them." Yet, as in the former case, the danger from this source could not have been great. The actors, after one

suggested by the descriptive stage-directions instead of the usually curt notations entered by the prompter.

[1] "To the Reader," prefixed to *The Rape of Lucrece*, 1608. Robert Greene was charged with dishonesty of a slightly different nature, namely, of selling the same play to two companies; see Cuthbert Conny-Catcher's *Defence of Conny-Catching*, 1592.

such experience, would exercise due watchfulness, and the money-takers and other playhouse employees would doubtless have orders to keep their eyes wide open for such thieves. As Webster, in *The Devil's Law Case*, says:

> You must take special care that you let in
> No brachygraphy men to take notes.

If discovered such an unwelcome visitor would be quickly ejected by the attendants. So far as we know, the Globe Company suffered from the "brachygraphy men" only once: in 1609 *Pericles* was filched by stenography, and published in a fearfully corrupt text. But since Shakespeare's work in *Pericles* was merely to retouch the manuscript of another author, we may properly say that none of his plays was stolen by means of shorthand.

Thirdly, the company might be betrayed by one of its own members. The sharers, of course, could be implicitly trusted, for they were chosen men, distinguished in their profession, and their interests were entirely merged in the interests of the company as a whole. But a hireling, especially one who had considerable ability, yet from lack of ambition or deficiency in character had never been advanced to the higher rank of sharer, might be tempted to steal the manuscript of a successful play in order to eke out his small salary. The theft, to be sure, would not be easy for him to effect, for the company, fully realizing the ever-present danger of piracy, was on the alert to prevent it, and the prompt-copy — usually the only complete copy of the play in existence — would be carefully guarded under lock and key. The dishonest hireling, however, would have in his possession the actor-parts he himself was required to speak, and possibly he might on occasion be able to steal the parts of one of his careless fellows. Using these actor-parts as a basis, and trusting to his ready memory, he could patch up a mangled text that would serve the ends of an unscrupulous stationer.

The Globe Company, it seems, was very unfortunate in having in its employ such a disloyal hireling,[1] who for several years stole Shakespeare's plays in this fashion, and sold them to the publishers. Apparently he began his pilferings in 1597, when he made a theft of *Romeo and Juliet*, and also, we have good reason to believe, of *Love's Labour's Lost*. Since, however, no copy of the pirated edition of the latter play has come down to us, we must confine our discussion to *Romeo and Juliet*, with the observation that probably the same facts apply also to *Love's Labour's Lost*.[2] The hireling disposed of his corrupt manuscript of *Romeo and Juliet* to John Danter, who, without licensing it, and without employing a publisher, printed it in 1597. That Danter had a bad reputation goes without saying. Soon after thus issuing *Romeo and Juliet* he became involved in grave difficulties with the authorities, and, as Mr. Plomer puts it, "disappears in a whirlwind of official indignation and Star-Chamber shrieks." The texts of *Love's Labour's Lost* and *Romeo and Juliet* as thus stolen and offered to the reading public were so corrupt that Shakespeare was much aggrieved. The Earl of Pembroke may have had this instance, as well as later ones, in mind when he wrote of plays stolen from Shakespeare's troupe, and printed with "much corruption, to the injury and disgrace of the authors."[3] Accordingly, in order to defend his reputation, Shakespeare, with the consent of

---

[1] Unless we adopt the unlikely supposition that there were two, or more, disloyal hirelings in its employ. The theory here advanced has been ably championed by A. W. Pollard, J. Dover Wilson, and W. W. Greg. Though it falls short of absolute proof, its accuracy can hardly be doubted.

[2] In 1598 Shakespeare issued an authorized edition with the statement on the title-page that it was "newly corrected and augmented." He put the same statement on the authorized edition of *Romeo and Juliet*. The second certainly, as the first probably, was designed to supplant a pirated issue. Neither play was entered in the Stationers' Registers, again indicating that *Love's Labour's Lost* had already been printed, since a license was required only for new books.

[3] See the letter printed in George Chalmers' *Apology*, p. 513.

the actors, issued in 1598 and 1599, respectively, authorized editions of the plays. Apparently he had reserved no
private transcripts, and was forced to borrow the actors'
prompt-books. That *Romeo and Juliet* was set up from
playhouse copy is obvious; for example, we find the
phrase "Enter Will Kempe," Kempe being the actor
who assumed the rôle of Peter; and the stage-directions
sometimes take the curt imperative form used by the
prompter, as "Whistle, boy," "Knock," "Play, Music."

These two piracies must not only have annoyed Shakespeare but also have alarmed the Chamberlain's Company, which naturally feared a similar fate for others of its
manuscripts. At once the actors set themselves to the
task of checkmating the thief, and, so far as possible,
safeguarding their property. For some reason they seem
to have been especially uneasy about *Richard II* and
Richard III; and, although the publication of these two
successful plays could hardly have been welcome to them,
apparently they sold the manuscripts to Andrew Wise,
an honest and reputable stationer, who issued them late
in 1597. Both plays were set up from authoritative copy,
the text of the former being reproduced by Heminges
and Condell (with some corrections and additions) in the
First Folio.[1]

As a further means of checking the thief, the actors
conceived the idea of having their printer-friend James
Roberts (who was closely associated with them in his
capacity as sole printer of playbills) take certain manuscripts, about which they might feel uneasy, to the Stationers' Hall and make a "blocking entry" so as to prevent any one else from securing a license. Of course

---

[1] Wise, perhaps on his own initiative, omitted the scene of the deposing of
King Richard, to which later Queen Elizabeth took exception; it was restored to the printed play in 1608, but in so corrupt a form as to warrant the
conclusion that it was taken down by shorthand from an actual performance.

Roberts, who was not a publisher, had no intention of issuing these plays; he merely acted in behalf of the company, and no doubt promptly returned each manuscript to the custody of the actors. On July 22, 1598, he entered a blocking license for *The Merchant of Venice*, "provided that it be not printed by the said James Roberts, or any other whatsoever, without license first had from the right honorable the Lord Chamberlain." Since the Lord Chamberlain was the patron of the troupe, his protection may have been thus especially invoked. Furthermore, the Wardens spread on the books of the Stationers' Company, June 1, 1599, an order "That no plays be printed except they be allowed by such as have authority." For a short time the hireling was either frightened or foiled.

In 1600 the company seems to have become particularly nervous. On May 27 they sent Roberts to the Stationers' Hall to license two plays for them: "My Lord Chamberlain's Men's plays, entered 27 May, 1600, to Master Roberts, viz., *A Moral of Cloth Breeches and Velvet Hose, A Larum to London*," with the express provision that he was not to put the plays "in print without further and better authority," indicating that the Stationers' Company understood Roberts' purpose, and was coöperating with the actors in their attempt to prevent the theft of their plays. On August 4 the players themselves entered *As You Like It*, *Henry V*, *Every Man in his Humor*, and *Much Ado*, and had the Stationers' Company specially mark them "to be stayed."

The anxiety of the actors was, as it soon appeared, justified; but their various efforts to checkmate the thief proved unsuccessful. The hireling was able to dispose of a stolen copy of *Henry V*, one of the plays which the Chamberlain's Company had just marked "to be stayed," and it was issued by Thomas Millington and John Busby, 1600, without any license at all. An examination of the text shows that the thief probably made use of the actor-parts of the Governor of Harfleur,[1] for the speeches of this personage are remarkably correct, even to small matters of punctuation.

The publication of *Henry V* seems to have caused the actors at once to unload certain plays. To Andrew Wise (to whom they had sold *Richard II* and *Richard III* in 1597, and also *I Henry IV* in 1598) and to William Aspley now associated with him, they disposed of *Much Ado About Nothing* and *II Henry IV*. Wise and Aspley secured formal license for both these plays on August 23, 1600, and printed them from the prompt-copies; in the former (Act IV, Scene ii) the names of the actors Kempe and Cowley are substituted in the stage-directions for Dogberry and Verges; and in the latter (Act V, Scene iv), the name of the actor Sinklo appears for that of the Offi-cer.[2] To Thomas Fisher they sold *A Midsummer Night's Dream*, and to Thomas Heyes *The Merchant of Venice*. Both plays were printed by James Roberts, the actors' friend, from authentic playhouse manuscripts, and were properly licensed by the Stationers' Company. Since the Chamberlain's Men had recently put themselves to no little trouble and expense in an effort to block the publi-cation of several of these plays, we may suspect that they gave them to the press reluctantly, and only in order to prevent further piracies.

If so, they were again to be defeated, for the following year the hireling stole *The Merry Wives of Windsor*, and sold it to the same publisher, John Busby, to whom he had disposed of the similarly stolen *Henry V*. Busby

[1] See J. Dover Wilson, in the *News Sheet* of the Bibliographical Society, January, 1919.

[2] It is interesting to note also that in one instance the catch-name "Old." (for Oldcastle) appears instead of "Fal.," indicating that the manuscript the printers used antedated the change in the name of the fat Knight — in other words, was probably the original draft.

entered the play in the Stationers' Registers on January 18, 1601–02, and immediately, at some expense, transferred it to another publisher, Arthur Johnson, his purpose being to diminish the danger attending piracy.[1] It was shortly after printed in an exceedingly corrupt text. From the fact that the scenes in which the Host appears are suspiciously correct, it may be inferred that the actorparts for this rôle had been used as a starting-point for the manufacture of the copy.[2]

In the case of neither *Henry V* nor *The Merry Wives* did Shakespeare take the trouble to issue correct and authorized editions; perhaps they were not plays of which he was especially proud. But this could not be said of the next piracy he was called upon to suffer. The following year, 1603, the hireling made his most important theft, that of the popular new play *Hamlet*. This time, however, he seems to have had less success in covering up his tracks. Since he assumed in succession the rôles of Marcellus, Voltimand, one of the traveling players, one of the soldiers in Fortinbras' army, the Second Gravedigger, the churlish Priest, and one of the Ambassadors from England, and used his memory to reconstruct the scenes in which he appeared, superimposing these scenes on an earlier version, his trail was as plain as the way to parish church. The actors, apparently, succeeded in identifying him, and must promptly have expelled him from the company, for from now on they suffered no more from this sort of theft. Shakespeare, however, was so incensed at the mangling of a play which had won extraordinary applause from London audiences, and had received the very signal honor of presentation before

---

[1] Or, possibly, in order to block a revoking of the license.

[2] This conclusion, first suggested by Mr. W. W. Greg, is approved by Mr. A. W. Pollard; see the latter's *Shakespeare's Fight with the Pirates*, 1920, p. 40. The pirate seems also to have had access in some way to a manuscript copy of the play, in either an abbreviated or an unrevised state.

both the universities of Oxford and Cambridge, that he shortly issued an authorized and at the same time revised edition, making use, not of the actor's copy, but of a duplicate which during the course of the revision he transcribed for this special purpose. The First Folio reproduced the copy he delivered to the actors, with the various cuts and alterations to which a playhouse manuscript is inevitably subjected.

There remain only three other quartos for consideration. On November 26, 1607, John Busby (who had been associated with the piracies of *Henry V* and *The Merry Wives of Windsor*) and Nathaniel Butter (a book-seller of low repute) secured a license "under the hands of Sir George Buck," the Master of the Revels,[1] for *King Lear*, which they issued in 1608, printing directly from the original prompt-copy. The circumstances under which these not very reputable stationers came into possession of a successful play only two years old, the publication of which could hardly have been gratifying to the actors, and were able to license it with the formal sanction of the Master of the Revels, and to set it up from the playhouse prompt-book, are unknown to us. In the absence of definite evidence we may hazard a guess. Possibly they had earlier secured a corrupt copy of the play, and the actors, learning of the fact, had bargained with them to delay publication, on the payment of a sum of money, and the promise of ultimately furnishing them with the full and authentic text. We know that this procedure was sometimes followed. In 1600 Henslowe paid a publisher, Cuthbert Burby, the sum of £2 "to stay the printing" of a new play, *Patient Grissel*, then but two months old. Burby, accepting the money, deferred publication until 1603. There was no

---

[1] From 1607 on Buc insisted upon his right to license plays for the press as well as for the theatre.

reason why the King's Company should not in a similar predicament resort to the same device.

In 1609 Richard Bonian and Henry Walley published *Troilus and Cressida* under unusual circumstances. The play had apparently been written by Shakespeare in 1602, but the actors for some reason did not then see fit to put it on the stage. In view of the fact that it was not to be acted, the author probably allowed some of his friends to make transcripts for private circulation. The duplication of copies, however, involved the danger of a piracy, and hence on February 7, 1603, James Roberts made a blocking entry of the play in the Stationers' Registers to prevent its publication. Six years later, it would seem, one of the transcripts that Shakespeare had allowed to be made came into the possession of Bonian and Walley, who promptly entered the play in the Stationers' Registers,[1] and published it with the statement on the title-page: "as it was acted by the King's Majesty's Servants at the Globe." Soon learning, however, that it never had been acted, they excised the original title-page, printed a new title omitting the statement in question, and inserted a noisy letter to the readers announcing the strange "newes" that the play was "never stal'd with the stage, never clapper-claw'd with the palms of the vulgar." The transcript from which they set furnished an accurate text; but that it was not the actors' copy is shown by the fact that Heminges and Condell in the Folio used an entirely different manuscript taken from the archives of the playhouse.

These are all the plays of Shakespeare that were printed during his life. But in 1622 the actors allowed a publisher to issue *Othello*, their reason probably being that the play was immediately to appear in the Folio.

[1] Apparently its former license was overlooked.

The facts and inferences presented above may be summarized as follows:

1594. *Titus Andronicus.* Authentic text; sold by the Pembroke's Company when it disbanded in 1593.

1597. *Love's Labour's Lost* (?) and *Romeo and Juliet.* Corrupt texts; stolen by a hireling, and issued without license. Authentic texts published by Shakespeare in 1598 and 1599 respectively.

Richard II and *Richard III.* Authentic texts; probably sold by the company in order to prevent piracies.

1598. *I Henry IV.* Authentic text; probably issued by the actors in order to right an unintentional wrong done to Lord Cobham.

1600. *Henry V.* Corrupt text; stolen by a hireling, issued without license.

The Merchant of Venice, Much Ado About Nothing, II Henry IV, and *A Midsummer Night's Dream.* Authentic texts; probably sold by the company in order to prevent piracies.

1602. *The Merry Wives of Windsor.* Corrupt text; stolen by a hireling.

1603. *Hamlet.* Corrupt text; stolen by a hireling, issued without license. Authentic text published by Shakespeare in 1604.

1608. *Pericles.* Corrupt text; stolen by stenography, issued without license.

King Lear. Authentic text; possibly delivered to the publishers by the actors on an agreement to delay the issue of the play.

1609. *Troilus and Cressida.* Authentic text; probably from a transcript in private circulation.

1622. *Othello.* Authentic text; released by the actors in view of the immediately forthcoming Folio.

Thus it is clear that in no instance was a Shakespearean play voluntarily surrendered by the company. The fact corroborates Heywood's statement that the actors "think it against their peculiar profit to have them come into print," and fully explains why Shakespeare himself made no effort to collect and publish his dramatic works.[1]

[1] For a bibliography of this chapter see especially the works of A. W. Pollard cited at the end of Chapter XXVII; and also H. R. Plomer, "The Printers of Shakespeare's Plays and Poems," *The Library*, 1916, vii, 149; W. W. Greg, "'Bad' Quartos Outside Shakespeare," *ibid.*, 1919, x, 193; J. Dover Wilson, "The Copy for *Hamlet*, 1603," and "The *Hamlet* Transcript, 1593," *ibid.*, 1918, ix, 153, 217; J. Dover Wilson, in the *News Sheet* of The Bibliographical Society, January, 1919; A. W. Pollard, *A New Shakespeare Quarto*, 1916; A. W. Pollard and H. C. Bartlett, *A Census of Shakespeare's Plays in Quarto, 1594–1709*, 1916; H. C. Bartlett, *Mr. William Shakespeare*, 1922.

CHAPTER XXIX

THE ATTEMPTED COLLECTION OF 1619

In 1619, three years after the death of the poet, an unscrupulous bookseller named Thomas Pavier attempted to foist upon the public a small and for the most part fraudulent collected edition of Shakespeare's plays. As a beginning towards such an enterprise he had in his possession the copyright of five plays. (1) *A Yorkshire Tragedy*, which he himself had impudently put forth in 1608 as "by William Shakespeare"; the deception, he felt, could again be practised. (2) *Sir John Oldcastle*, by Drayton, Hathaway, Munday, and Wilson, printed in 1600 as acted by the Admiral's Men. Since Sir John Falstaff was still popularly known as Sir John Oldcastle, Pavier resolved to reprint this play as Shakespeare's, hoping that the unwary public would be deceived by its title into supposing that it was *Henry IV*, or at least that it was from the pen of the master. (3 and 4) *The Contention betwixt the Two Famous Houses of York and Lancaster*, and its sequel *The True Tragedy of Richard Duke of York*, two old Marlovian plays that had been refurbished by Shakespeare for the Pembroke's Men, and which, after the disbanding of that troupe, had been printed in 1594 and 1595. Later they had been further revised by Shakespeare for the Chamberlain's Company as *II Henry VI* and *III Henry VI*. The original texts of 1594 and 1595 Pavier resolved to reissue as "newly corrected and enlarged, written by William Shakespeare, Gent." (5) *Henry V*, in the corrupt and mangled edition of 1600.

Although these were all the plays that Pavier owned

in order to increase the size of his volume he was prepared, at some risk to himself, to lay hands on three others. *Pericles*, which had been issued ten years earlier without license from the Stationers' Company, he decided to appropriate for his own use. And *The Merchant of Venice* and *A Midsummer Night's Dream* he resolved to seize as derelicts in the trade; they had not been reprinted in nineteen years, their original publishers were dead, and the question of their ownership either was obscure or might at a pinch be treated by him as doubtful. Apparently he was investigating the ownership of the various Shakespearean quartos, and making an effort to secure other plays for his proposed volume. In this effort he was successful in two cases: from Nathaniel Butter and from Arthur Johnson he got permission to include *King Lear* and the pirated *Merry Wives of Windsor*.

Thus in all, rightly or wrongly, he could print ten plays, which, correctly or with more or less plausible effrontery, he could issue as "by William Shakespeare":

A Yorkshire Tragedy, not by Shakespeare.

Sir John Oldcastle, not by Shakespeare.

Pericles, not mainly by Shakespeare, and excluded by his actors from the First Folio.

The Contention and *The True Tragedy*, old chronicles refurbished by Shakespeare.

Henry V, in a corrupt text.

The Merry Wives of Windsor, in a corrupt text.

The Merchant of Venice.

A Midsummer Night's Dream.

King Lear.

Having assembled his material, he engaged William Jaggard to print the book.

Ten plays would, of course, hardly warrant the issue of a folio volume, but would make an attractive collection in large quarto.[1] We may suspect that Pavier had in his mind's eye some such general catch-penny title as: "Tragedies, Comedies, and Histories. By William Shakespeare, Gent. As They Have Been Often Acted with Great Applause by His Majesty's Servants at the Globe on the Bankside, and at the Private House in Blackfriars. Now Collected into One Volume. Printed by William Jaggard for Thomas Pavier, and are to be sold at his shop, The Cats and Parrot, near the Royal Exchange. London, 1619." Partial collections of this sort were not uncommon. Jonson had issued nine of his plays in 1616 as *The Works of Benjamin Jonson;* and six plays by Marston were published in 1633 under the title *Tragedies and Comedies, Collected into One Volume.*[2]

But after some or all of the work was in type, the arranging of the galleys into page-form had begun, and possibly the first three plays, namely *The Contention, The True Tragedy,* and *Pericles,* had been put through the press, the scheme was suddenly abandoned. What caused Pavier, who had already spent no little time and money on the volume, to change his plans? Though we can only conjecture, we may speak, I think, with reasonable assurance.

William Jaggard had secured from James Roberts the monopoly of printing all playbills, and this, as in the case of his predecessor, brought him into constant touch and into friendly relations with the Globe actors. It may be that as the printer of this interesting volume he dropped the news at the theatre that he was preparing a collection of Shakespeare's plays for Pavier; or it may be that

---

[1] Pavier's quartos can readily be identified by their unusual size; they are considerably larger than any of the other Shakespeare quartos.

[2] Other instances may be cited: *Six Court Comedies,* by Lyly, 1632; *Five New Plays,* by Brome, 1653; *Six New Plays,* by Shirley, 1653; *Three New Plays,* by Massinger, 1655; *Three Excellent Tragedies,* by Goffe, 1656; *Five New Plays,* by Brome, 1659.

Heminges, or some other member of the company, in taking copy to Jaggard's establishment saw the work in the press. However the information came to the actors, they would at once be on the alert for piracies, and would seek detailed knowledge of so threatening a project. When they learned that Pavier was issuing no hitherto unprinted plays, they might not feel disposed to interfere with him on their own account. But certain friends of Shakespeare who had his interests at heart — Heminges and Condell, we may suppose [1] — after discovering the nature of the proposed volume, made efforts to protect the reputation of the dead poet.[2] They could point out to Pavier that his collection contained only three plays furnishing anything like a fair representation of Shakespeare's work; that two of the plays, though by Shakespeare, were in a sadly corrupt and mangled shape; that one play was by Wilkins (?) only slightly touched by Shakespeare, and in a stenographic text of unusual debasement; that two plays were old chronicles by another author (Marlowe?), with only preliminary revision by Shakespeare; and that two other plays could not by any stretch of the imagination be attributed to Shakespeare. But it is doubtful whether these facts would influence a man like Pavier. It is probable that Shakespeare's friends had to take the matter to some one in authority who was also interested in the poet's reputation. In all likelihood they appealed to the Lord Chamberlain, an officer having special control of such affairs.[3] This person was no other than William Herbert, Earl of Pembroke, Shakespeare's patron and friend, to whom Heminges and Condell, in words that

[1] Burbage had died on March 13, 1619.

[2] That Heminges and Condell were deeply concerned in guarding Shakespeare's reputation as a poet is shown by the First Folio.

[3] The actors commonly appealed to the Lord Chamberlain in regard to the publication of their plays; see above, p. 511.

may be significant in this connection, dedicated the authentic collection known as the First Folio.[1] Whatever the source of the interference, an order was issued that immediately forced Pavier to abandon his scheme.

Since some if not all his plays had been put into type, the order left him in a dilemma. Not wishing to lose the money he had spent in the venture, he decided to issue the plays separately, with individual title-pages, and then quietly to dispose of them as single quartos resembling those already on the market. Yet in view of the peremptory order he had received he thought it necessary to remove all traces of his original intention of issuing a collected volume.

With so perilous a scheme to circumvent the order of the authorities Jaggard refused to have his name associated; and although, having set up the type, he completed the presswork according to Pavier's instructions, he was careful to keep his imprint off the title-pages.

The first three plays, namely *The Contention, The True Tragedy*, and *Pericles*, had already been printed,[2] or at least had been made up into final page-form, with continuous signatures. This section of the originally proposed volume was now divided into two units (*The Contention* and its sequel *The True Tragedy* making one unit), for which separate title-leaves were printed: *The Whole*

---

[1] Philip Herbert, who succeeded his brother in the office, wrote in 1637: "Whereas complaint was heretofore presented to my dear brother and predecessor by His Majesty's servants, the players, that some of the Company of Printers and Stationers had procured, published, and printed divers of their books . . . by means whereof not only they themselves had much prejudice, but the books much corruption to the injury and disgrace of the authors; and thereupon the Master and Wardens of the Company of Printers and Stationers were advised by my brother to take notice thereof, and to take order for the stay of any further impression." George Chalmers, *Apology*, p. 513.

[2] This is indicated by the fact that the title-page of *Pericles* is a single sheet pasted in.

Contention betweene the two Famous Houses, Lancaster and Yorke . . . Divided into two Parts: [1] *And newly corrected and enlarged. Written by William Shakespeare, Gent.;* and *The Late And much admired Play, called Pericles, Prince of Tyre . . . Written by W. Shakespeare.* They were, of course, bound and sold as two separate quartos. The printers, however, failed to remove the tell-tale signatures, which, running continuously through all three plays, clearly show the original purpose of combining them in a single volume. The other seven plays were then struck off with separate title-pages, and bound up to be sold as miscellaneous quartos.

But Pavier did not stop with merely splitting his proposed collection into individual units. He prudently sought to conceal his tracks by using false dates, and false imprints. To *The Whole Contention* he gave no date at all; to *Henry V* he gave the purely fictitious date 1608; to *Sir John Oldcastle, The Merchant of Venice,* and *A Midsummer Night's Dream,* he gave the date of their first issue, 1600; to *King Lear* he gave the date of its original issue, 1608. *A Yorkshire Tragedy* (the copyright of which he owned), *The Merry Wives of Windsor* (which he had authority to print), and *Pericles* (treated as no man's property) he correctly dated 1619. Two plays, *The Merchant of Venice* and *A Midsummer Night's Dream,* he issued as from the press of James Roberts, who was then dead. *King Lear* he issued with the imprint of Nathaniel Butter, and *The Merry Wives of Windsor* with the imprint of Arthur Johnson. On the rest of the plays he put merely the brief statement "Printed for T. P.," without giving his name in full, or specifying, as was

---

[1] It is possibly significant that Pavier did not give these two plays the title *The First and Second Parts of Henry VI,* the title under which he had shrewdly entered the transfer of copyright from Millington in 1602; see W. W. Greg's article in *The Library,* 1903, New Series, iv, p. 258.

customary, the location of his shop where the volumes might be purchased.[1]

By these miscellaneous devices he so successfully concealed his original purpose of issuing a collected edition that the fact was not discovered until 1906, and then only through a fortuitous combination of circumstances.

But though he succeeded in obeying the strict order of the authorities forbidding him to issue a collected volume of plays by Shakespeare, he paid no attention to the real purpose of that order, which was to protect the dead poet's reputation. On each of the quartos, with the exception of *Henry V*, he had conspicuously displayed the name of William Shakespeare as the sole author. Thus he did almost as much damage to the posthumous fame of the dramatist as if he had carried out his original project of including all ten plays in a single volume.

The ten plays thus bound as nine individual quartos, with various dates and various imprints, were put on the stalls of Pavier's bookshop and disposed of to an unsuspecting public. Doubtless there was a ready sale for them; years before, the publishers of *Troilus and Cressida* had predicted that the time would soon come when booklovers would "scramble" for Shakespeare's plays. In a few cases eager buyers seem to have seized the opportunity to secure all ten plays at once. Since, as was then customary, the sheets were merely stitched in paper covers, some of the book-collectors who purchased all the plays had them at once substantially bound in a single volume. Several such volumes are known to have been

---

[1] Since title-leaves were commonly displayed on posts throughout the city for advertising purposes, the omission of the place of sale suggests that Pavier made no effort to give wide publicity to his latest venture. The early dates would also preclude the possibility of his advertising some of them as new.

formerly in existence; but in later times, with the great increase in the pecuniary value of Shakespeareana, these volumes were split up, and the individual units offered to buyers separately. Only one collection of all ten plays remains in its original form as bound at the time for its purchaser. In 1919, exactly three centuries after Pavier first set the quartos on sale at his shop, this volume was sold to an American collector for the sum of $150,000.[1]

[1] The volume is now in the library of Mr. Henry Folger, of New York City. For the best discussions of Pavier's quartos see A. W. Pollard, *Shakespeare Folios and Quartos*, 1909, and W. J. Neidig, "The Shakespeare Quartos of 1619," *Modern Philology*, 1910, viii, 145.

CHAPTER XXX

THE FIRST FOLIO

THE injury done to Shakespeare's reputation by Pavier, and the constant danger of a repetition of the offense, were probably among the causes that led the poet's actor-friends, at some date before October, 1621,[1] to plan a complete and authentic edition of his dramatic works. At this time all the original venturers in the Globe enterprise were dead except John Heminges and Henry Condell. For nearly a quarter of a century they had enjoyed the poet's closest and warmest friendship (they were among the three persons in London to whom he left memorial rings), and now they were old men,[2] ready to retire from active life. As a final tribute to their comrade, who had been so loyal to their interests, they resolved to collect and publish his plays. "We have but collected them," they write, "and done an office to the dead ... without ambition either of self-profit or fame, only to keep the memory of so worthy a friend and fellow alive as was our Shakespeare."[3]

In the scheme they interested two men, William Jaggard, who by virtue of his monopoly of printing the

[1] The date on which *Othello* was entered in the Stationers' Register. The play, it is clear, was released for publication because arrangements were under way to issue the First Folio, as shown by the manner in which the copyright was treated.

[2] In 1613 Heminges had been described as "old Heminges"; see p. 438. Both were parishioners of St. Mary Aldermanbury, Cripplegate, and both served there as churchwardens.

[3] That they initiated the enterprise is clearly indicated by their statement: "We pray you, do not envy his friends the office of their care and pain to have collected *and published* them"; by Digges's line: "Shakespeare, at length thy pious fellows give the world thy works"; and by the poems from the Salisbury Papers cited on p. 342.

players' bills was well-known to them,[1] and Edward Blount, a publisher likewise on friendly terms with the King's Men,[2] and one whose literary tastes and discrimination as a critic [3] qualified him to edit the volume for the reading public. Jaggard, it seems fair to suppose, took main care of the business arrangements, and Blount assumed the responsibility, with the aid of Heminges and Condell, of selecting the copy and preparing it for the press. He classified the plays, determined their sequence, and made an effort, imperfectly carried out, to divide them into acts and scenes, and to change the curt stage-directions of the theatre into literary forms more descriptive in character. The editors, after completing their work, properly observe that "it had been a thing worthy to have been wished that the author himself had liv'd to have set forth and overseen his own writings"; yet in fairness it must be said that Heminges and Condell did all they could to furnish the best texts then available, and that Blount, though at times he grew weary and slighted his task, did not a little towards producing a really creditable volume.

Sixteen of Shakespeare's plays having already appeared in print, the question of copyright presented at the outset a serious obstacle to a complete collection of the poet's work. Since these copyrights were distributed among various publishers, each of whom had to be reckoned with, much dickering was necessary. Some of the owners were disposed to make trouble, and the resultant negotiations, it seems, considerably delayed the appearance of the volume. John Smithwick, who held the

---

[1] And who may have earned their good will in connection with Pavier's volume.

[2] In 1608 he secured for them blocking entries of *Pericles* and *Antony and Cleopatra*, thus taking the place of James Roberts, who "in or about 1608" sold his business and retired.

[3] See Sir Sidney Lee, "An Elizabethan Bookseller," in *Bibliographica*, ii, 474.

copyright of no fewer than four plays,[1] had to be admitted to partnership with Jaggard and Blount; and so, likewise, William Aspley, who held the copyright of two plays,[2] and possibly was able to control certain others. These four men, however, Jaggard, Blount, Smithwick, and Aspley, either themselves, or through their business allies, were able to control all the copyrights except that of *Troilus and Cressida*, which belonged to Henry Walley. For a long time Walley refused to allow the inclusion of this play, and only after the volume had been printed off and was ready to be issued did he surrender. This explains why the play was awkwardly inserted, without pagination, between the "Histories" and "Tragedies," and why its name was omitted from the printed Table of Contents.[3] The inclusion of *Troilus and Cressida* was a final triumph for the editors, who at last were able to announce to the public that their volume contained "all" of Shakespeare's "Comedies, Histories, and Tragedies."

The statement was true; but Heminges and Condell thought fit to omit those plays which were largely by other hands, or in which Shakespeare's task was merely that of a reviser. On these grounds they excluded *Pericles*, although the copyright belonged to Blount; and possibly they intended to exclude *Timon of Athens*, which was set up and printed to fill the gap originally held open for *Troilus and Cressida*.[4] By the same standard they excluded also, we may suppose, *The Two Noble Kinsmen*, possibly *The History of Cardennio*, and other plays, prompt-copies of which were doubtless at their disposal. And it goes without saying that they rejected those plays

---

[1] *Hamlet, Romeo and Juliet, Love's Labour's Lost*, and *The Taming of the Shrew.*

[2] *Much Ado* and *II Henry IV.*

[3] See the writer's article, "*Timon of Athens* and the Irregularities in the First Folio," *The Journal of English and Germanic Philology*, 1908, vii, 53.

[4] See above, p. 403.

which had been falsely attributed to the master, for example, *A Yorkshire Tragedy* and *Sir John Oldcastle*, which Pavier had recently issued under Shakespeare's name, and *Locrine, Thomas Lord Cromwell, The London Prodigal, The Puritan Widow*, and *The Troublesome Reign of King John*, which crafty publishers had issued as by "William Shakespeare," or "W. S.," or "W. Sh.," and which, with still other plays, constitute what we call the Shakespeare Apocrypha.[1]

Besides making the collection complete within the strict limits of this standard, Heminges and Condell devoted their best energies to the task of seeing that the texts of the plays were, as they expressed it, "set forth according to their first original." In their efforts to do this they spared neither pains nor expense. Fortunately they were able to make use of the prompt-books in the storeroom of the Globe Theatre.[2] Since, as we know, the actors' prompt-books were in many cases — at this time probably in most cases — made by binding up the author's original manuscript, not a few of those available to Heminges and Condell may have been in Shakespeare's autograph;[3] and even those that were not in his autograph accurately represented the plays as they were acted by his company.

But the use of the actors' prompt-books for such a volume as the editors had in mind carried with it certain difficulties. The company might not be willing to have

[1] All these plays have been admirably edited by C. F. Tucker Brooke, *The Shakespeare Apocrypha*, 1908.

[2] For the manuscripts of those plays which never had been printed they may have been required to pay the actors a suitable sum. The publishers of the First Folio of Beaumont and Fletcher, 1647, say: "'Twere vain to mention the *Chargeableness* of this Work; for those who own'd the *Manuscripts* too well knew their value to make a cheap estimate of any of these Pieces." But on this point speculation is vain.

[3] It will be observed that in addressing the readers of the Folio they say: "We have scarce received from him a blot in his papers," and they assert that the plays were printed from "their first original."

its licensed manuscripts taken from the playhouse and put into the hands of careless typesetters.[1] The stage-manuscripts, too, were often patched up, with additions, alterations, interlineations, scored-out passages, and marginal scribblings by the prompter, so that they would constitute poor copy for the printers, and would need to be carefully edited for readers.[2] Still they represented the most authentic, and in many instances the only, texts available.

The plays that had already been printed in quarto form, sixteen in number, had also to be considered as possible copy. Since Shakespeare himself had put forth authorized editions of *Romeo and Juliet, Love's Labour's Lost,* and *Hamlet,* all but two of the quartos (*Henry V* and *The Merry Wives of Windsor*) existed in more or less authoritative form, having been set up from properly supplied manuscripts. The natural temptation, therefore, would be for the editors to make use of those quartos which gave a reasonably accurate text; for these quartos could be cheaply purchased, were far more easily edited, and were better to print from.

Yet in only three cases did the editors resort to this convenient expedient, and then, it seems, for good and sufficient reasons. They rightly made the quartos of *Love's Labour's Lost* and of *Romeo and Juliet* the basis of the Folio text, because both plays had originally been set from the prompt-books, apparently under Shakespeare's supervision; and they similarly used the quarto of *The Merchant of Venice,* which had been printed by their friend James Roberts from an authentic playhouse manu-

---

[1] Yet that they may have permitted this is indicated by the loss of the "allowed book" of *Winter's Tale,* see pp. 507-08.

[2] In some cases, it seems, Heminges and Condell were forced to resort to the actors' parts, which had to be assembled in order to reconstruct the text. Further light on this hypothesis may be expected from Dover Wilson in the new Cambridge edition of Shakespeare.

script, possibly also under the author's supervision. In the case of these three plays no better text could be supplied, or perhaps desired.

In the case of the two corrupt quartos, *Henry V* and *The Merry Wives of Windsor*, which Shakespeare had not seen fit to supplant with authorized editions, the original prompt-books, preserved in the actors' storeroom, were placed at the disposal of the editors. Heminges and Condell must have had these two plays especially in mind when they declared to the readers: "Where before you were abus'd with diverse stolen and surreptitious copies, maimed and deformed by the frauds and stealths of injurious impostors that expos'd them, even those are now offer'd to your view cur'd and perfect of their limbs."

All the other quartos, eleven in number, though originally printed from authentic manuscripts, were rejected in favor of more accurate copy. In the case of six plays (*Richard III*, *II Henry IV*, *Hamlet*, *King Lear*, *Troilus and Cressida*, and *Othello*), though the quartos had been set either from the actors' prompt-books, or from careful transcripts of the author's text, the editors preferred to make use of the playhouse manuscripts. This painstaking selection of copy bears eloquent testimony to their effort to get as near as possible to the exact language of Shakespeare, or, as they put it, to have the texts "truly set forth according to their *first* original." And in the case of five other plays (*Richard II*, *A Midsummer Night's Dream*, *I Henry IV*, *Titus Andronicus*, and *Much Ado About Nothing*), though the quartos were based upon authentic copy, the editors made use not indeed of playhouse manuscripts but of the actors' special copies of these quartos which had been converted at the theatre into prompt-books. The reason we may readily guess. Since the prompt-books made from the author's manuscript were unwieldy, and often hard to read, the book-holder had probably discarded them in favor of the much more convenient and legible printed copies. These printed prompt-copies would receive corrections (from the author, or from the actors), alterations, and additions, and such stage-directions as were found necessary. The old manuscript prompt-books may have been kept, as in the case of the six plays just discussed, or they may have perished in the printer's office, or through accident.[1] Perhaps when Heminges and Condell instituted a search for Shakespeare's own manuscripts of these plays it was discovered that they had been destroyed or mislaid. Hence in the absence of the "first" originals they resorted to the actors' quarto prompt-books in order to utilize the corrections made by the author or the players, and occasionally important additions. In preparing their copy they seem to have purchased from the stationers' shops the most available editions of these quartos,[2] and after comparing them with the actors' prompt-books, to have introduced such corrections, alterations, and additions as they saw fit; and these collated quartos they placed in the hands of the compositors.

Twenty of Shakespeare's plays, however, had never been issued in printed form. For these Heminges and Condell turned to the manuscripts in the archives of the Globe. Whether the typesetters worked directly from the actors' prompt-books, or from transcripts specially prepared therefrom we cannot say; in either case the Folio text represents the plays as they were then acted, with many of the notations by the stage-manager.

Thus, to sum up, the editors of the Folio printed

[1] For example, through the burning of the Globe in 1613. Unless the Master of the Revels had transferred his license to the printed copies, the manuscripts would hardly be treated carelessly.

[2] The fourth, and last, edition of *Richard II*, 1615; the fifth edition of *I Henry IV*, 1613; the only edition of *Much Ado*, 1600; the second, and last, edition of *A Midsummer Night's Dream*, 1619; the third, and last, edition of *Titus Andronicus*, 1611.

twenty-eight plays from prompt-copies, or what they called the "first original." Three plays they printed from authorized quartos which in the first instance had been set up from prompt-copies, possibly under the poet's supervision. And five plays they printed from the actors' quarto prompt-copies, the original manuscripts probably having been lost, or perhaps being regarded as less authoritative.

In view of all the labor involved in this conscientious attempt to issue the plays "according to the true original copies," we can understand Heminges and Condell when they say to the readers: "We pray you, do not envy his friends the office of their care and pain to have collected and publish'd them," and when they declare to the Earls of Pembroke and Montgomery that to make the text perfect hath been "the height of our care." [1] Moreover, this should give us confidence that in the Folio, barring printers' errors, we have as near an approach to the "comedies, histories, and tragedies" as Shakespeare wrote them as it was possible for the editors to supply, working solely from playhouse copy. We cannot, however, believe that here we have the plays "absolute in their numbers as he conceived them." It is ever to be regretted that Shakespeare himself could not have prepared his plays for the press, so as to rectify the damage done in cutting their text and often mangling them to meet the necessities of stage-presentation; or more happily still, to take advantage of the occasion, as did Ben Jonson, to rewrite and improve many scenes with a view to their being examined by critical readers. Yet this being denied us, we should not forget our debt of gratitude to the Folio editors for their arduous labor of love.

[1] The language they use is very significant: "Wherein, as we have justly observed, no man to come near your Lordships but with a kind of religious address, it hath been the height of our care, who are the presenters, to make the present worthy of your Highnesses by the perfection."

As a final tribute to their friend and fellow, Heminges and Condell employed Martin Droeshout to engrave a portrait of the author to accompany the volume. The choice of Droeshout cannot be called happy, and his effort is far from satisfactory. It is said that when Gainsborough accepted a commission to paint a portrait of Shakespeare he refused to bother with the engraving: "Damn the original picture," he exclaimed; "I think a stupider face I never beheld." His judgment, however, is too severe, and from other critics Droeshout has received a modicum of praise. On the page facing the portrait were set the following verses by Ben Jonson:

To the Reader

This figure that thou here see'st put,
It was for gentle Shakespeare cut;
Wherein the graver had a strife
With nature to out do the life.
O, could he but have drawn his wit
As well in brass, as he hath hit
His face, the print would then surpass
All that was ever writ in brass
But since he cannot, reader, look
Not on his picture, but his book.

A volume so notable as this would naturally call for a dedication. For this honor Heminges and Condell chose two of Shakespeare's Court friends, that "most noble and incomparable pair of brethren," William Herbert, Earl of Pembroke, and Philip Herbert, Earl of Montgomery. The choice, we are told, was made because both Earls had thought these plays "something heretofore," and had "prosecuted both them and their author" with "much favour." The favor with which the Earl of Pembroke held Shakespeare may be inferred from his deep affection for Burbage. More than two months after the death of the latter, the Earl wrote to the English Ambassador in Germany giving the news of the Court: "My Lord of Lennox made a great supper to the French Ambassador this night here, and even now all the company are at a play; which I, being tender-hearted, could not endure to see so soon after the loss of my old acquaintance Burbage." And perhaps Pembroke, who died in 1630, is "that English Earl" referred to by Richard Brome in *The Antipodes* (1638), I, iii, in connection with Shakespeare's plays; Letoy, assuming the part of a nobleman fond of the drama, says:

> I tell thee,
> These lads can act the Emperor's lives all over,
> And Shakespeare's chronicled histories to boot;
> And were that Cæsar, or that English Earl
> That loved a play and player so well, now living. . . .

We may thus believe that Pembroke deserved the honor awarded him, and probably the same was true of the Earl of Montgomery. "There is a great difference," write Heminges and Condell, "whether any book choose his patrons, or find them. This hath done both. For so much were your Lordships' likings of the several parts when they were acted, as, before they were published, the volume ask'd to be yours. . . . In that name, therefore, we most humbly consecrate to your Highnesses these remains of your servant Shakespeare."

Apparently the volume was being rushed through the press in great haste, and no effort was made to solicit commendatory poems from the author's friends. A few such poems, however, came in, one after another, and were inserted, not without awkwardness to the volume. The first, and by far the most significant, eulogy was by Ben Jonson; others were by Hugh Holland, Leonard Digges, and a man who signs merely his initials "I. M." Jonson's tribute of affection can hardly be omitted here, though it is too long to be quoted in full.

To the Memory of My Beloved,
The Author,
Mr. William Shakespeare,
And
What He Hath Left Us.

To draw no envy, Shakespeare, on thy name,
Am I thus ample to thy book, and fame:
While I confess thy writings to be such
As neither Man nor Muse can praise too much.
'Tis true, and all men's suffrage. But these ways
Were not the paths I meant unto thy praise. . . .
I therefore will begin. Soul of the age!
The applause! delight! the wonder of our stage!
My Shakespeare, rise! I will not lodge thee by
Chaucer, or Spenser, or bid Beaumont lie
A little further to make thee a room.
Thou art a monument without a tomb,
And art alive still while thy book doth live,
And we have wits to read, and praise to give. . . .
And though thou hadst small Latin and less Greek,
From thence to honour thee I would not seek
For names, but call forth thund'ring Æschylus,
Euripides, and Sophocles to us,
Pacuvius, Accius, him of Cordova dead,
To life again to hear thy buskin tread
And shake a stage: or, when thy socks were on,
Leave thee alone for the comparison
Of all that insolent Greece or haughty Rome
Sent forth, or since did from their ashes come.
Triumph, my Britain! Thou hast one to show
To whom all scenes of Europe homage owe.
He was not of an age, but for all time! . . .
Sweet Swan of Avon, what a sight it were
To see thee in our waters yet appear
And make those flights upon the banks of Thames
That so did take Eliza and our James!
But stay! I see thee in the hemisphere
Advanced and made a constellation there!
Shine forth, thou Star of Poets!

The finished volume made a folio of portly size, consisting of 908 pages, and measuring, in the largest extant copy, $13\frac{3}{8}$ inches in height by $8\frac{1}{2}$ inches in breadth. The paper employed was of excellent quality, much to the disgust of the Puritan William Prynne, who complained that it was "printed on the best crown paper, better than most Bibles." On November 8, 1623, it was registered at Stationers' Hall, and shortly after it was offered to the public at the goodly price of £1.[1]

With the appearance of this complete and authoritative volume from the hands of Shakespeare's actor-friends, the biography of the poet naturally closes.

[1] The Burdett-Coutts copy sold in London in 1922 for £8,600. For a fuller discussion of the Folio and its editors see W. W. Greg, "The Bibliographical History of the First Folio," *The Library*, 1903, *N. S.*, iv, 258; A. W. Pollard, *Shakespeare Folios and Quartos*, 1909; Sir Sidney Lee's Introduction to his facsimile of the First Folio; A. W. Pollard, *Shakespeare's Fight with the Pirates*, 1920; and various recent articles in *The Library*.

THE END

INDEX

INDEX

INDEX

INDEX

INDEX

INDEX

INDEX

INDEX

INDEX

INDEX